FAMILY DYSFUNCTIONALISM
AND THE ORIGIN OF CODEPENDENCY ADDICTION
EMOTIONAL VIOLENCE, REPRESSION, MANIPULATION, DECEPTION, ALIENATION, SELF-DEGENERATION,
AND SEPARATION-LEARNED IN CHILDHOOD AND WEAVED-IN ADULTHOOD

FAMILY DYSFUNCTIONALISM
AND THE ORIGIN OF CODEPENDENCY ADDICTION
EMOTIONAL VIOLENCE, REPRESSION, MANIPULATION, DECEPTION, ALIENATION, SELF-DEGENERATION, AND SEPARATION-LEARNED IN CHILDHOOD AND WEAVED-IN ADULTHOOD

MARTEAUX X, PH.D.

FAMILY DYSFUNCTIONALISM AND THE ORIGIN OF CODEPENDENCY
ADDICTION EMOTIONAL VIOLENCE, REPRESSION, MANIPULATION,
DECEPTION, ALIENATION, SELF-DEGENERATION, AND SEPARATION-
LEARNED IN CHILDHOOD AND WEAVED-IN ADULTHOOD

iUniverse books may be ordered through booksellers or by contacting:

iUniverse
1663 Liberty Drive
Bloomington, IN 47403
www.iuniverse.com
1-800-Authors (1-800-288-4677)

Because of the dynamic nature of the Internet, any web addresses or links contained in
this book may have changed since publication and may no longer be valid. The views
expressed in this work are solely those of the author and do not necessarily reflect the
views of the publisher, and the publisher hereby disclaims any responsibility for them.

Any people depicted in stock imagery provided by Getty Images are models,
and such images are being used for illustrative purposes only.
Certain stock imagery © Getty Images.

ISBN: 978-1-5320-9870-3 (sc)
ISBN: 978-1-5320-9871-0 (e)

Print information available on the last page.

iUniverse rev. date: 04/22/2020

Contents

List of Figures

List of Tables

Dedications

E very human being, from the beginning of human history during the Savagery Period, roughly one million years ago, to the new Millennium that started in 2000, was born into a *dependency* state. Throughout a majority of this long tenure of man and woman's journey on Earth, mother, father, or mother-surrogate love played a vital life sustaining part in evolving family relations, by paving the way for their babies to evolve into a higher conscious awareness state known as *interdependency*. Naturally, love is the single most important ingredient, or elixir, which on one hand, help an infant to become aware of his or her Self as "being love," and on the other, it is none other than this self-same love that aids children to give the love awakened in them, during the first six years of their lives, by their mother, father, or mother-surrogate, to another human being.

Therefore, this book is dedicated to the millions of American Men and Women, and to people worldwide, regardless of race, color, and religion, who were not nurtured through their dependency state into interdependent adults; and, in one way or another, became ensnared in a CoDependency Addiction Web, when, unbeknownst to them, they, in accordance with the irresistible call of nature, could not *selflessly* give their unawakened love to another person, although being unable to shutdown their need to receive love, they could not give any authentic love to another human being, regardless of their age, due to the fact their mother, father, or mother-surrogate failed to love them through the critical, natural dependency state. Although unable to give their early onset of Codependency Addiction its true name at such a young and tender age, each affected baby, with the passage of time, realized something was wrong in their lives based on one's *feelings*.

In addition, this book is dedicated to those Americans, and those people worldwide, who served as an *unwitting enabler* of their codependent partner's CoDependency Addiction. In either case, both the codependent person and the enabler deserve a life free of this dreadful psychological condition of the former, along with its clandestine influences on the latter. After reading this book, I sincerely hope this generation of codependent people liberate themselves from their mental prison, namely CoDependency Addiction. The greatest Reggae Singer-Bob Marley, sung this lyric in one of his songs: "You think you're living in heaven but you're living in hell" captures the essence of the CoDependency Addiction Prison. Hopefully, future generations of Americans will be able to bypass the CoDependency Addiction Mental Prison, which, currently, has so many thousands on lockdown. Freedom is our birthright.

Lastly, I also dedicate this book to M, a woman I married early in my life, and because of my sincere ignorance, namely, a lack of awareness of the CoDependency Addiction Trap I *unconsciously* walked into unknowingly, I, without any *apriori* knowledge of the CoDepedency Addiction Disease, proceeded to divorce her and my two year old son, L II, for a woman, whose persona seemed to be 100% in *synchronicity* with my feelings and needs. In short, M suffered from the collateral damage of the CoDependency Addiction that I was *blindly* caught up in at the time of our divorce. I dedicate this book to M because when we divorced, I left her in Baltimore, MD with my two year old son at the tender age of 29 years old. My inconsiderate action, conscientious stupidity, and poor decision placed her squarely in the category of being a single-parent.

After living 36 years in a relationship with my codependent partner, and by 2015, I became aware, for the first time, that I lived-all of these years-in a relationship with a codependent person, whose subconscious Codependency Addiction, or distorted emotional attachment to me, was, on a conscious level, intentionally repressed by her within her Self during this time. Because E kept her psychological challenge a secret from me, I *enabled* a relationship in which she admittedly sacrificed 36 years of her life! Because of her years of sacrifices were both-carefully and strategically-kept pushed down inside of herSelf, I believed, simultaneously and wholeheartedly, and without a single strand of hair of a doubt, that our relationship was one nearest to being as perfect as it could be, and if this does not completely astonish you, everyone of our "friends," and so-called "friends," family members, and workplace associates, excluding none, likewise thought and felt, as I had for 36 years, that E and I had discovered a *formula* for creating endless love and perfection in our relationship!?!?...

Sadly, much later on, I discovered E's repeated sacrifice refrain throughout the 36 years we were in a relationship, like a broken record frozen in a time warp, was a self-attack attempted projection: SACRAFICE IS ATTACK, IT IS NON-LOVE; FEAR DEMANDS THE DESTRUCTION OF LOVE. (Paraphrase is mine). In short, no thought can mysteriously disconnect itself from the mind of its owner, and, therefore, the consequences of it rest primarily in the mind and body of the person who selected the thought. This indestructible law of nature is what makes denial such a powerful obstacle to overcome.

Acknowledgement

This book took me six months to write, from December 28, 2018 to May 28, 2019. I could not have completed it without the use of valuable information contained in the books written by Darlene Lancer, <u>Codependency For Dummies</u>, 2015, M. F. Ashley Montagu, <u>The Direction of Human Development: Biological and Social Bases,</u> 1955, and John Bowlby <u>Maternal Care & Mental Health,</u> 1995. Melodie Beattie's Book <u>CoDependent No More</u>, was a very valuable resource as well. Before 2015, I was unfamiliar with the CoDependency Addiction Disease, although I lived 36 years in a relationship where it was *actively and consciously* repressed by E through her use of denial, guilt, judgment, resentment, anger, and projection.

Moreover, I consulted the classic works of Charles Dickens and Victor Hugo, namely <u>A Tale of Two Cities </u>and <u>Les Miserables</u>. These literary giants, including Frederick Engels and Karl Marx played a significant role, which enabled me to work through many of the finer subtleties normally overlooked by conventional thinking.

Unlike many of the books already written on the subject of CoDependency Addiction, this research, in an attempt to be as thorough and inclusive as possible, includes 415 footnotes for readers to consult, which, hopefully, will assist them in their own search toward discovering new ways to deepen their own, and other peoples,' understanding of this debilitating and self-destructive disease.

Preface

The idea for this book originated out of my need to examine CoDependency Addiction, which is classified as a mental illness. It has been active in my relationship with E, who claims to be codependent, which I was unaware of for more than 36 years of its *undisclosed and active* existence in it. I consider myself to be a logical, sensitive, feeling, self-reflective, kind, loving, giving, and aware; yet, during this time, I failed to detect its existence while living with E on a daily basis during this time; until one day, without any forewarning, in early 2017 she walked through the front door of our home and declared she is *codependent*. As anyone might imagine, I did not know what to think, feel, or say, given the fact I was a 100 percent cooperative member in my family relationship, which I thought would continue to grow even stronger as more of our *Golden Years* went by. Actually, as a partner in our relationship, everything one would think Golden Years should be such as taking exotic vacations to various beach locations around the world, traveling to various countries to experience different cultures, spontaneously taking domestic road trips to places of interests, going to New York City to experience a Broadway Play, going to a jazz club to listen to some of the best jazz musicians of the day, or, simply sitting in silence and absorbing the beauty of nature under a tree on our farm among others-All-evaporated, and melted like snow in the sunshine, without any prior warning when E's CoDependency Addiction was openly acknowledged by her for the first time in 36 years. What was equally unbelievable to me is I participated in the building of a *bill-free vegetable farm* with a partner, who, somehow kept *her Codependency Addiction a complete secret from me*, while everything I thought we both were working for, was constructed on a *leaning foundation*. You might be wondering how I felt when E hit me with this CoDependency Addiction news? I was absolutely devastated...

For example, during my childhood, I never heard this term used in my household to describe one of my immediate family members, or likewise, I never heard it used to describe another person outside of it. Actually, I never heard this term used in the house I grew up in L.A. Throughout my K-12 years of public school training, CoDependency did not cross my awareness radar. Even after my high school graduation, and during my four years of undergraduate college education at the University in LA, none of my college friends ever used the CoDependency term during the many conversations I remember having with them. I earned my Doctoral Degree from the University of Colorado, in1977, and having taken several courses in psychology at the time, nothing ever surfaced about CoDependency. There might have been a chance for me to encounter information related to CoDependency since the latter initially began to be used in professional circles during the 1970s. According to Darlene Lancer, "the term *codependency* has been used since the 1970s."[1] That being so, I set out on my life journey, and there was nothing that told me to be aware that one day CoDependency Addiction would spill out onto the fabric of my life, and like a 7.5 Earthquake, shake the relationship I was in, for 36 years, to its foundation.

---

[1] Lancer, Darlene, <u>Codependency For Dummies</u>, 2nd Edition, For Dummies, A Wiley Brand, 2015, p. 1.

Malcolm X once accurately said "history is best qualified to reward all research." Therefore, after getting over the initial shock of learning from E that she claims herself to be a codependent, and after realizing it is nearly impossible to have a discussion with E about her CoDependency Addiction to me, I immediately resorted to a two prong strategy of becoming a keener listener when E shared anything about being a codependent, and I simultaneously submerged myself deep into the CoDependency Literature in a hopeful search for any clues-anything-that might shed some needed enlightenment on what was happening to E and myself, which, unbeknownst to me, had been subtly threatening the survivability of our relationship for more than 36 years.

By the time I was twenty years old, a junior in college at Southern University, LA, I married the woman who I thought would be the one who would have our children; and, I thought I would be with her for the rest of my life. Everything was going so well between M (I will only use the first initial of her name to protect her privacy) and I. M was tall, beautiful, and smart. She gave me love unconditionally. M graduated from Southern University in the Fall 1971, and she was hired as an accountant by Company in New Orleans, LA. During the second semester 1972, I met a seemingly free spirited and unfettered woman, who seemed to have a worldly outlook and an outgoing personality that always seemed like it placed her at the center of everybody's attention. I thought this was a special talent being able to attract the attention of some of her peers at such a young age. We were a mere 20 years old. And, like her peers, I was also attracted to E (I use the first initial of her name to protect her privacy); we began talking to each other initially; we later became friends, and at some point, we became intimate. At the time, E was medium height, beautiful personality, very talkative most of the time, an also very out-going, and seemingly unafraid to take risks. These attributes were-All-CoDependency indicators, but I did not know they were the external signs of a person, who was in a *desperate search for the mother and father love* she missed during her childhood. Later, I would discover something about E, which would shake me to my core.

After graduation from Southern University in May 1972, I was awarded an academic Fellowship to attend graduate school at the

University of Colorado, beginning in the Fall 1972. M resigned her job with the company in New Orleans, LA, and we moved to Boulder, Colorado. I was very happy with my life and M. I was enrolled at Colorado's flagship university, and the latter liked my potential to contribute to it through my chosen discipline of study-Geography. M was great. She helped me in every way she could to complete my Masters Degree in Geography, which I did in 1974. Just two years after graduating from Southern University, I had earned my Masters by 24 years old. M earned her MBA Degree also. Things were going great in every way-at home and at school. I made a lot of friends, including formation of strong bonds with many geography faculty members-both with those who I studied directly under and those who I did not. They all enjoyed my work ethic, and my ability to shift gears and add to a festive evening at a party hosted by this or that faculty member. After completing my Masters Degree in Geography, I re-applied to the Doctoral Program, and I was accepted. M provided me with unconditional love at a time when I needed it most. By the time I defended my doctoral dissertation, M gave birth to our son in May 1977, and, two months later, I walked across the graduation stage and received my Doctoral Degree in Geography at 27 years old! I was the Mozart of Geography. Many of my fellow peers were in their late thirties when they graduated with me. M and I moved to Longmont, Colorado where we stayed while I worked as an Assistant Professor of Geography at the University of Northern Colorado. By 1978, M and I moved to Baltimore, MD, where I took an administrative position in the Planning Department at Morgan State University, namely, Director of University Evaluation. M and I were doing well; however, after being married seven years, E resurfaced. I was married to M and I had a two year old son; yet, strangely, whatever the attraction I had to E at Southern University reemerged in my mind, and strangely, though I had a 2 year old son, I decided to divorce M and my son, feeling E's seeming *willingness to take risks* was what I needed in my life at that time. When I met E at Southern University, she had a very *outgoing personality*, and it appeared on the surface she was unafraid of taking risks, and she behaved in an *uninhibited promiscuous manner*. That is, it appeared to me E was very clear about her femininity and *inner Self.* Again, this was E's public persona that she used to attach her Self to my feelings and needs while hers' were repressed 24/7. These were all CoDependency Addiction Signs that I merely overlooked without giving any careful analysis or deliberation to them! I knew absolutely nothing about CoDependency Addiction, although I had recently been awarded a doctoral degree!

Though the decision to divorce M and my son was one of the most difficult decisions I ever made in my life then, and since then (!), I truly, and genuinely, thought everything would somehow be better. If this seems difficult to understand, it still amazes me how I did that. The only thing I can think of that might even make a single grain of salt of sense is I was determined to write a revolutionary book; become a revolutionary myself in both theory and practice; and this would mean taking some risks such as jeopardizing my career, or limiting my ability to earn income necessary to support my family and so forth. So, I equated E's willingness to take risks as someone who had her own strong independent beliefs and feelings about revolution and social development. Whenever we spoke about a revolutionary vision, E spoke of her independent feelings and needs to embrace a revolutionary philosophy. There was nothing in 1979 that warned me otherwise; and, I had nothing to warn me that her spoken words about revolution were just a mirror reflection of my own feelings that she attached herself to for survival.

I genuinely felt both E and I were prepared to embark on a life journey of mutual revolutionary change. Because I was so determined to study revolution and become one in the process, I simply overlooked all of the "red flags" along the way, and there were many you will discover I missed as you read this book. There was one thing; however, that did surface early in our relationship in 1979. That is, I did not give any serious attention to, regarding E's staunch position related to her expressed *unwillingness to examine objectively her belief in the significance of individualism in her life, or have an open discussion about it.* As a trained social scientist, and research practitioner, I was trained by some of the brightest professors of my day, who taught me to place emphasis on aggregate samples of socio-economic data among others, for the purpose of making generalizations about human behavior. Rather than challenge E on the individualism topic, which is highly subjective and indefensible at any serious level of social research, I naively, along with an abundance of innocence, thought when the social research I would engage in got underway, it alone would be best qualified to demonstrate the limitations of her individualism thinking (Later, I will give some sustained attention to the individualism question). At the time, E did not have any interest in revolutionary philosophy and practice; she needed to survive; and, therefore, she locked her Self onto my feelings and needs, like a hungry baby nursing at its mother's breast, to make me feel she-too-had a strong and independent interest in revolutionary philosophy and change as well. As you will discover later, E's dogmatic, or Pit Bull hold on the idea of individualism springs from the lack of love she received from her mother and father during her childhood. Its absence caused her Ego to blossom out of control, and predominate over her Super Ego, or moral conscience.

For the next 36 years of the relationship E and I were in until 2019, there was never a dissenting view offered by E, which consciously served to mask any internal disillusionment I had about how we decided to mutually live our lives, from the time we got together in 1979 right up to this time. Everything was always alright with E. Not once do I recall in 36 years she ever mentioned, during the countless conversations we had over the years, that there was something we were doing that she disagreed with. To demonstrate what I have abruptly come to realize about E and my relationship during this time, I have developed several purposes to guide this discussion.

Therefore, this book has three purposes. First, it provides a detailed discussion of the *historical development of man and woman's conscious awareness*, alongside their engagement in social production, which made the former possible, from the Lower Savagery Period to the Civilization Period. During this discussion, we shall witness the overthrow of mother right in the family, which was replaced by father right, or the Patriarchal System and the rise of alienation in the Monogamy Family. Second, a detailed and thorough discussion of CoDependency Addiction is provided, which places sustained emphasis on the connection between the mother's relationship to her infant child; and, equally important attention is given to the affects a mother, father, or mother- surrogate's lack of nurturing of their infant child, has on the latter's mental health characterized by a development of sustained codependent behavior. In effect, in the absence of a sustained, generational unavailability of economic resources in a family, the caregiver-mother, father, or mother-surrogate, cannot successfully nurture her infant. Third, to provide a case study of the impacts CoDependency Addiction has had on E, and how they affected E and L's relationship during the past 36 years, from 1979 to 2019. For example, on December 28, 2018, two days before I started writing this book, E went to the Meritus Credit Union in Lafayette, LA and unilaterally, without any mutual discussion, and took $3,000 out of our joint savings account. The death of one of E's sisters coincides with the time she secretly removed this money from the mentioned financial institution. She removed to help cover the cost of the burial of her sister (L would have gladly agreed to help cover such a cost. This money was earned by L while he was employed at Southern University in LA. Because E was so connected to L's feelings and needs, she thought the mentioned money belonged to her rather than, realizing more accurately, it was money she could use for a cooperative purpose.

Worse, suffering with CoDepedency Addiction, E erroneously pursued a lifelong attachment course to L emotionally, which completely blinded her to the fact that by the end of her years of work in the workforce, she would need to have accumulated a life-sustaining Retirement Income for herself, after her years of work came to an end. Because of Codependency Addiction, she was unable to see any need to create a retirement income of her own; but, as a codependent person, and under the influence of her addiction, she rationalized that L's Retirement Income was her own similar to her belief that the $3,000 she took out of the Meritus Credit Union solely belonged to her.

CoDependency Addiction Disease, under the best of circumstances, has a devastating effect on its host. This book offers hope. Through a journey of close-up, personal observations, it uses them to systematically peel away, layer by layer, the repressive scab surrounding the inner

Self, which forbids any rehabilitative light to disturb its oppressive, emotionally violent, and life-threatening darkness. Upon engaging in some critical reflection, it now makes all of the sense to L why E became so "emotionally moved" by a PBS Television Program we both watched together called the "Ice Truckers." These are Eighteen Wheeler Trucks that haul heavy loads over frozen ice in some parts of Alaska during the winter.

The life and death risk a drivers takes is at any moment, his or her truck could break through the ice, resulting in the lost of the cargo and death of the driver. While the latter steers his or her truck across a frozen water body, the energy of the truck creates a "wake of water," which moves, beneath the surface of the ice, in the same direction the truck is headed. The great challenge for the drives is to know exactly how to steer the wheels of his or her truck so they do not cause the "wake of water" beneath them to break the frozen ice over which the truck is moving.

After E finished watching this amazing and suspenseful TV Show, she wrote and recorded a CD, symbolically applying the dangers and risks taken by the Ice Truckers to everyday human life. The Ice Truckers CD is an excellent work, and it was well-received by E's peers, whom some remarked the CD helped them to understand something better about their personal life. However, what everybody missed, or failed to realize, including myself, is the Ice Truckers CD was really about E's life and not their own. As we shall clarify throughout this discourse, one of the main goals of a codependent person is to, generally speaking, shift the main focus and attention away from one's issue(s), while, all the time, bringing others into an energetic individual or group discussion about their own shortcomings, failures, and mistakes. The codependent person's personal life story usually goes unexamined by oneself or others.

In reflection, it is now clear to L that E's strong attraction to the Ice truckers Adventure related directly, at the time, to the CoDependency Addiction she repressed, beneath the surface of her conscious mind within her inner SELF; and, similar to the Ice Truckers, she-too-was self-tasked to keep the mentioned life threatening "dark night of the soul" from surfacing into the full view of the LIGHT. E was able to keep it repressed for 36 years until one day, similar to the fate of an unfortunate Ice Trucker, when his or her vehicle broke through the frozen ice; and, in E's case, the "wake of repression of CoDependency Addiction," flooded onto the conscious surface of her relationship with L. Exactly how this occurred, and its consequences, is explained in great detail in the Chapters of this book.

Before proceeding, it is necessary to point-out here that the alphabet "L" noted throughout this book refers to a person name Lamar, and "E" refers to Evelyn. Lamar and Evelyn lived in a codependent relationship for more than three decades. This true account of the CoDependency Addiction in their relationship is narrated by Lamar based on his firsthand account. Whenever the pronoun I appears anywhere in this book, either before or after this point, it refers to Lamar.

Marteaux X, Ph.D.

LA

December 30, 2018

CHAPTER ONE

Introduction

This book is a carefully thought through true story, based on L's direct observations, which were derived from living 36 years of his life in a relationship with a codependent partner-E. The most puzzling thing I (I refers to Lamar) repeatedly ask myself is "How did I live this long in a relationship with a codependent partner without ever becoming suspicious about what was happening to me?" Everything E and I did seemed so honest and altruistic, from the intimacy we shared to the mutual work we engaged in toward helping people in our community live better lives. In fact, the thought of being in a relationship with E for 36 years was beginning to feel like E and I had discovered some formula that would allow us to continue in our relationship down the path of life for another quarter century. When I reflect on my relationship with E, there was nothing I could identify as a potential fetter capable of overthrowing our relationship. Nothing told me to be aware. In spite of what seemed like "smooth-sailing," an unexpected event occurred on July 25, 2015, which was L's birthday, and it sent a shockwave through our relationship like none before. This significant emotional shock touched off an outpouring of repressed energies that shook me awake like a Five Alarm Fire Siren on a Sunday morning. What L felt can also be described "as bullets coming at him from all directions" (Paraphrase is mine).

After finishing our Yoga Class on that fateful day, E, our daughter, and I shared a birthday lunch at Jolie's Restaurant in Lafayette, LA. Everything was festive; the food was good as usual; and we had a usual good conversation. However, that night, an incident occurred unexpectedly and without any prior warning; and, the harmonious relationship I shared with E for 36 years, changed instantly, drastically, and forever. The event that ruptured our relationship was a stroke. Of course, people have various health challenges every day, but E's stroke was different because something had been boiling at a subconscious level, for several decades? What triggered E's stroke was 65 years in the making(!), which stretched all the way back to her childhood.

It is this fact that made E's stroke different because she hid her childhood traumas from L for 36 years, which essentially sabotaged any assistance he could provide her years before the conditions in E's mind-body metastasized in a stroke. When E and L became partners in a relationship in 1979 in Baltimore, MD, L changed his diet to vegetarian; after L exposed E to a new way of thinking and eating, she became a vegetarian too. However, since E was secretly harboring a mountain of childhood pains and emotional traumas, the diet change, exercise, foreign travels, frequent visits to the oceans, meditation and more were, collectively, not powerful enough to break the grip E's childhood traumas had on her. For many years, these activities held them at bay; however, as the years went by, and similar to two massive Tectonic Plates faced-off against each other deep inside the Earth's Crust, and at a given moment, one of the affected Tectonic Plates break, resulting in an outpouring of stored energy. In most cases, volcanoes and earthquakes occur, causing landmasses to change. What changed in E was the onset of a stroke, which released her repressed CoDepedency Addiction into the forefront of her consciousness and daily life. As much as E tried to avoid this inevitability, everything we did for 36 years was consistent with "Taking One Step Forward And Two Steps Backward."

As I mentioned earlier, I was clueless about how E's stroke was created by her; that is, E and I were 29 years old when we got in a relationship in 1979, and whatever she experienced in her early life, from birth to 29 years old, she kept that part of her life a tightly guarded secret from me, for the next 36 years we were in a relationship. On July 25, 2015, E's stroke unlocked the door to her repressed Self, and everything that she kept a secret came rushing out into the open. What was taking place before my very eyes was quite surreal because many buried emotions, feelings, and needs exploded openly in our relationship. To me, it felt like our house was on fire and I did not have any water to put it out! No one should ever have to experience this feelings!

The explosion was repressed energy built-up in E's subconscious mind since birth. When E and I, and all other human beings, were born, and on that birthday, Montagu wrote "there burns a pure flame within us; that flame is love. It is the source from which we draw and convey our warmth to others. It is the light which guides us in relation to our fellow men [and women]; it is the flame before which we warm the hands of life, and without which we remain cold all our lives. It is the light of the world. The light which it casts enables us clearly and unambiguously, unfalteringly, to see our relation to our fellow men [and women]."[2] The pure flame we are all born with inside of us is entrusted by nature to the caring and powerful hands of mother, father, or mother-surrogate love that nurtures this pure flame so that it does not go out but continues to burn continuously and ever more brightly. If mother, father, or mother-surrogate love do not keep our pure flame burning brighter until we, the bearer of it, recognize the pure flame as our Self, or Who We Are, then it will wane like the light of an approaching dust, and the hands of life and ours' will progressively cool, and our hearts will remain cold for the rest of our lives. When early man and woman discovered fire, they had to carefully blow oxygen on a tiny spark to make it burn brighter. To keep our pure flame burning brighter so it can be a light to the world, Montagu added "…an infant… must be loved for the greater part of the day-all the day-until he [or she] has had those inner securities built up within him [or her] which will later render it unnecessary for him [or her] to be in any way anxious about

---

[2] Montagu, M.F. Ashley, The Direction of Human Development: Biological and Social Bases, Harper & Brothers Publishers, New York, 1955, p. 306.

those stimulations which at the outset of his [or her] postnatal career are so indispensably necessary for his[or her] development…namely, *maternal love*."[3]

The key to the satisfaction of the basic needs of the infant at the outset of his or her postnatal career is the guiding and loving hands of the mother, father, or mother-surrogate. Without this act of non-negotiable truth, an affected infant will wither tragically away similar to a raisin that dries up in the sun. The mother, father, and or mother-surrogate must nurture the infant into knowing his or her pure flame is love, and it is the torchlight that one must give to another person in order to successfully fulfill one's purpose on this Earth. This is priceless and cannot be bought or sold! It is the soul! Montagu wrote "the tragedy is that so many of us have failed to learn, because we had not been properly taught, how to satisfy others. To be rejected at any age because those who have been responsible for us have failed to teach us how to love others is, perhaps, the most unkind of all the inhumanities which human beings commit against human beings…The child that is unloved does not develop properly…principally as a consequence of insufficient love."[4]

Such a tragedy releases a child into his or her adulthood with a *nearly extinguished pure inner flame*. In the absence of a pure inner flame burning brightly for others to receive and give love "in kind," the lifelong preoccupation of an affected child/adult is on one hand, to keep a secret the "cold hands of life" and on the other, maintain a false, public smile beneath which resides a "cold heart." Thus, throughout one's life, the shivering hands and coldness that rise and fall within the mind-body of an unloved child, who as an adult, never learns "one cannot secure love by seeking it, but only by giving it."[5]

Thus, on that fateful day of L's awakening on July 25, 2015, E could no longer hold within her Self the repression of her childhood feelings and needs, and due to the pressure of engaging in this behavior for 36 years, which had steadily increased for 29 years before her stroke in

---

[3] Ibid., pp. 290, 291 and 310.
[4] Ibid., pp. 292 and 293.
[5] Ibid., p. 298.

2015, finally reached a breaking point. The primary catalyst that drove E to have a stroke was revealed by 2018, when she told me she was not loved by her mother or father during her childhood years. This was devastating news to me, and I felt very empathetic toward E's plight of having been abandoned and rejected by her parents. When the cork of the champagne bottle was suddenly removed, similar to what the stroke did for her subconscious mind, a lot of built up pain began to come out of it. I tried to help but I did not know how exactly because by the end of 2016, E declared she was codependent, and I did not know what that meant? The person E was when L first met her at Southern University, throughout the 36 years we were together until she had a stroke on July 25, 2015, disappeared *energetically and spiritually* immediately after this event. That being's energy, which was repressed deep-down within her Self for more than 36 years, suddenly broke free into E's conscious mind, and because it was a personality characterized by pain, anger, mental injuries and wounds suffered during childhood, fear, suspiciousness, anxiety, and narcissisism and more, L could no longer connect with E due to her need for *revenge*. At this point, now that the parental source of E's personal suffering were no longer available for her to direct her malcontent, and for survival purposes and maintenance of her public persona among her friends and community, she redirected her anger toward L, who did not know E existed on the Earth until the 1970s. In short, L did not know anything about E's *Pre-Existing Condition* when he initially met her.

However, after finding out from E that she has been challenged with a CoDependency Addiction since her birth, I became curious to discover how, as I mentioned earlier, this condition was kept a secret by E for 36 years. I am also very curious to discover what mental and physical effects her CoDependency Addiction has had on her personal well-being and my own.

From the beginning of my search for answers, I quickly discovered that E's biological parents failed to provide her with the critical love and attention she needed from birth as a necessary and indispensable pre-requisite to keep her pure inner flame burning inside of her. If any gasoline or electrically driven engine is denied gasoline, fuel, or electricity, the vehicle will not have the power to run or perform the task for which it was initially designed. The human being needs mother, father, or mother-surrogate love to function harmoniously. Of additional importance is the fact such love is required to help the infant to evolve from a dependency state to an interdependent state, where one is capable of understanding the importance of giving love to another person and receiving love in return. After reading more than 600 pages of <u>A course In Miracles</u>, everything I read came down to one simple but profound point, and that is, the only social goal, or purpose for which any baby is born on Earth, is to discover he or she only has to succeed with the *social work of loving one other person only*. If this social goal is achieved, then one has realized how to love oneself, another person, and all the rest of the people on Earth because, doing so, is no different than one human being giving and receiving love from one human being, or 8 billion.

With a coldness of life and a cold heart, an adult, who has lived through the emotional trauma, wounds, and injustices of a childhood growing up in a dysfunctional family, he or she leaves home *seeking love*, and in the process of his or her external search, connects oneself to the feelings and needs of another person; while, at the self-same time, the seeker of love simultaneously engage in the repression of his or her own feelings and needs. Thus, "codependency is characterized by a person belonging to a dysfunctional, one-sided relationship where one person relies on the other for meeting nearly all of their emotional and self-esteem needs…"[6] When I wrapped my mind around this definition, and pondered it for some time, I finally grasped how I lived 36 years in a relationship with E without ever knowing she was codependent; that is to say, she was completely locked into my feelings and needs, and no matter what the situation was such as buying land, buying a house,

---

[6]   https://www.google.com/search?rlz=1C2BLWB_enUS568US568&source=hp&ei=e6LZXPDVEImT0PEPmOOVgAg&q=how+many+known+codependents+are+in+the+United+States%3F&oq=how+many+known+codependents+are+in+the+United+States%3F&gs_l=psy-ab.12..33i160.4397.49311..52833...21.0..0.212.8305.23j53j1......0....1..gws-wiz.....0..0j0i131j0i10j0i22i30j33i22i29i30j0i13j0i13i10j33i10j33i299.Cz04BnYeqN8

decorating the house, buying a car, where to travel and when, what to eat and more, I seldom, if ever, received *any resistance* from E about a decision that needed to be made. E always came off as if she was in total agreement with what I thought should be done! Yet, in private, she resented herself and me for not speaking up for her own Self.

This behavior went on in our relationship for 36 years until the pressure of resentment and self- sacrifice became so great that by July 2015, the dam broke in the form of E's stroke. And, then, 36 years of Es feelings and needs rushed into her conscious mind. Below are a few statements E made to L, since she had a stroke that I recall exactly as she shared them. They are included so the reader can see what feelings were *repressed* by E for 36 years.

- "Trying to exert power or influence where I have none is the story of my life. From childhood so much fear of uncertainty and lack of nurturing made me feel crazy, fearful, alone, and unloved. Always fearful. Control became my way of dealing with that fear. All of my relationships I tried to set up some kind of need for my services in the scenario. Unhealthy need of services. A dependency of sorts-so I would be indispensible. Constantly trying harder and harder. I had to be needed to feel safe."

- The who is making me feel crazy and victimized right now in my life is my partner. He is the external expression of my internal view of myself. My need to look to him for understanding, kindness, and validation is my own inability to give these to myself. Situations, feelings, realities have been running from, denying, or avoiding."

- "...thinking someone outside of myself holds the "key"-the answers that will take the anxiety away. Will say something, understand something, do something that will make my life feel strong and complete. Running from taking full responsibility for my joy!"

- "I would have to face my own powerlessness if I tried or if I stopped controlling other people, other situations. I would have to look and see all I do not know about myself. Where is my creative expression? All I have known is work to please others. What might happen if I could see myself for the first time without the external focus?"

- "...lots of anxiety which is fear of the future. Difficulty in feeling joy of any kind, under any circumstances. Will smile and make kind comments but not true "joy.""

- "...lots of fear around lack. Not having set myself up to be independent even though I have worked all of my life. Viewing L's separation of finances as a personal attack."

- "...doubting and questioning how my devotion to a spiritual practice, which was so complete; I thought how could it lead me to this difficult time? Wondering why so much fear when I intellectually know a lot of information. Obviously, it is not in my heart? Questioning my heart."

- Regarding my family, "...don't want to speak honestly about myself and my situation. Same detached, coldness I felt as a child."

- Regarding friends, "I do feel alone and isolated...I am remembering that my mother was depressed. My father was absent. When does that no longer sit in my front row?"

- "My 2015 stroke is what caused me to start CODA Meetings... So much of my identity was based on this relationship" [with my partner].

- "Growing up in my household was a very lonely affair. I have very little memory of it and most things I remember were painful. Not really having anyone to talk with...The house I lived in was simple and basic. My first recollection was no indoor plumbing. We took baths and brushed our teeth but no real bathroom...Everyone it seems was struggling for attention, mostly from my mom and dad. Both parents were emotionally unavailable."

- "...I did not feel people really cared for me. I became a people pleaser because I was so unnurtured and felt so isolated. This followed me all my life in my adult courtship years. All the men in my life I had a tendency to overdo. Always giving more than my 50%. Trying to make myself important to them with my doing, with my smarts. The three most important men in my life were all motherless. None of them were raised with a mother. So I tried to be the mother. I thought if they needed me-they would love me."

- "The absence of guidance from my family was incredible. My only guidance was myself...My thoughts of non-worthiness were very intense."

- "Communicating with the male energy in the presence of any distress was frightening because I immediately went to abandonment fears. Having never felt the love of my father, I seem to live in "Free fall" around intimate relations with me... The people pleaser in me continue to create situations in which I had to please someone even if it was just in my mind. My fear of being alone caused me to enter lots of unholy relationships-both male and female."

- "...had moments when I did get out of the workplace which were timely and beneficial; these times were not spent focusing on my dysfunction. I started studying <u>A Course In Miracles</u> which could have been an excellent opportunity but I went into it with the thought of "How do I teach this information? And for many years, I did that and helped many people. But, the person in greatest need was not healed "me"!

- "I started seeing my deficit in my daughter when she started to show a lack of confidence in herself socially...She was a physically very attractive girl but her lack of self-confidence socially attracted males who lacked confidence. I saw my life all over again playing out before my very eyes."[7]

The above thoughts and feelings of E indisputably demonstrates that the vast majority of the emotional trauma, wounds, and pain,

---

[7] These are reflections I remember from many conversations E and I had since July 2015. Before this date, we never spoke about CoDependency Addiction in our house. It was being repressed in E's subconscious, while we spoke about the typical daily world maters of politics, people issues, and others.

subtle sarcastic dagger statements embedded in humor, which played out in our relationship for 36 years, are primarily residual repressions carried-over from E's childhood into our adult relationship. No human being is without some shortcomings, and I am not professing sainthood in our relationship. The central question that flows through the above repressions of E's Self is this: How could E sit down at the table in our house and openly discuss any problem, whether it pertained to our daughter or my professional relationships in the workplace, if she harbored the above, hidden feelings inside of her Self? Every situation E and I faced was secretly influenced by hidden emotional trauma and family dysfunctionalism, which occurred several decades earlier before I ever met her. Surely, my responses to issues in our relationship, over the 36 years we were together, no doubt, were subtly conditioned by E's hidden emotional trauma, which I subtly felt at ground zero in our relationship, which angered me because instead of E's pure inner flame burning with more light, no matter what L tried to do, there was an air of coldness and joylessness always seated at the table amongst us. It constantly poured coldwater on every positive idea or plan of action aimed at making our lives better and brighter. Had I known about the above repressed feelings and needs in E's Self, we could have resolved them within a year after we got together in Baltimore, MD in 1979. I was engaged in a major research related to the socio-economic and political impact the American Capitalist System has had on the American Working Class Family, both past and present. This was a prime time for E to disclose her childhood wounds so we could research and resolve them (The next to the last Bullet Information outlined above proves in E's own words that she opted not to research and study an intervention that could have resolved the CoDependency Addiction she *learned* during her childhood). L disclosed many of his unresolved childhood issues; most notably, he wrote an extensive letter to his family requesting answers, but, to the contrary, his requests were met with 100% resistance. This opened L eyes and woke him up. On the other hand, E impassively watched this action play out, stubbornly claiming, in a dogmatic fashion, that her childhood was a near perfect one. For example, E told me in 1979 that her father was always home at night, but L found out after E's stroke in July 2015, that her *father never touched her; never spoke to her; never took her anywhere; and never told her once that he loved her during her childhood!* Today, it's too late to resolve these difficult and painful issues, given the fact too many years of repression and denials have metastasized into a hypnotic rhythm, causing them, and others, to acquire a deep-rooted and nearly irresolvable status. As a result of years of neglect, the end of the relationship was inevitable. At the outset of our relationship in 1979, some type of intervention could be applied to heal E's CoDependency Addiction.

The above thoughts expressed by E were not ever expressed in my presence during the 36 years we were in a relationship, from 1979 to 2019. To prove how I was manipulated and deceived by these repressed thoughts, E gave me a gift, around 1979 or shortly thereafter, with a Lion Image on one side of the 81/2 sheet of paper, and a handwritten message on the other. The Lion Image is shown on the next page.

Figure 1.0
Lion

Having observed the power depicted by the Lion Image in the picture E gave me as a gift, it is a perfect example of how L was being manipulated on a conscious level to believe that this is how E felt about me; however, at a subconscious level, E harbored the above hidden emotional traumas she had experienced during her childhood, which were still active inside of her Self by 1979, when she gave me the Lion Image with the following words written on the other side of it.

"This is what I see when I look at you. All of the courage, strength and integrity of one of the greatest creations of nature. Thanks for the six happiest years of my life. Nothing can take from me the feelings and memories we have shared. You are in my eyes the most wonderful person that has ever walked this earth. I see everything that is good and strong reflected in your eyes. You are my lion and as history will have its say you will be a lion for the cause of justice. I never doubt this for one second. Millions of people will come to recognize the courage, strength and integrity of their own souls as well as the souls of their fellow man because of your work."

How does a person write a glowing review of another person's meaning to him or her, and beneath the pomp and circumstance, hideaway their fears and pain? In our case, the former was strategically used in an attempt to survive the horrors of her childhood past. For decades, the picture frame did not matter to E; what mattered more than anything else was the ever-changing content in it, which was designed, by her, to keep me believing our relationship was one to be envied by many. Never one to believe in superiority over another human being, L did believe if he worked daily to be a moral human being embodying the highest levels of integrity and dignity possible in his life, my happiness would be guaranteed. However, after 36 long years of partnership, L learned that a mother, father, or mother-surrogate love is what determines, to a large extent, how far down the path of life anyone can go. For E, the Sisyphus Stone Metaphor plagued her life during the 36 years we were in a relationship.

Every time E an L bought an acre of land; bought a house and had it moved onto our five acres of land in LA; added a new room to our house; bought and paid for two automobiles; traveled to another continent; or bought a new tractor to farm the land with, our Sisyphus Stone, and having been pushed to the top of the hill, by us, in our relationship, would roll back down to the bottom of the same hill we had just finished rolling it up to the top. What caused this "take one step forward and two steps back" is the emotional traumas buried and repressed inside of E's Self since her childhood.

After 36 years of toiling under the weight of what I now know is Codependency Addiction, which is a carryover from E's childhood as shown above, our ability to sustain a relationship finally succumbed to severe *communication failure* four years after the above repressions collectively manifested a stroke in her. Interestingly, the ten most common reasons given by a Your Tango article titled "The 10 most Common Reasons People Get Divorced" are, to a large extent, related to CoDependency Addiction, which is the primary subject matter addressed in this book. Before we give an overview of what each Chapter will address in it, take a few minutes and re-read the common reasons people divorce. They are:

- "Getting in for the wrong reasons.
- Lack of individual identity.
- Becoming lost in the roles.
- Not having a shared vision of success.
- The intimacy disappears.
- Unmet expectations.
- Finances.
- Being out of touch…literally.
- Different priorities and interests.
- Inability to resolve conflicts."[8]

Each one of the above 10 most common reasons Americans get divorced fit neatly within the CoDependency Addiction Framework. E got into a relationship with me out of her desperate need to survive, which was due to the fact she had not been loved through the dependency state by her biological parents. Being totally reliant on my feelings and needs stifled E's ability to learn Who she Really is; she became lost in

---

[8] Payne, Lisa L., Olver, Kim, and Deborah Roth, "The 10 most Common Reasons People Get Divorce," By YourTango Contributors, September 16, 2016, pp. 1 and 2. Based on a poll taken of over 100 YourTango experts, "…communication problems came out on top as the **number** one **reason** marriages fail," www. Google.com.

self-sacrifice, always doing more than her share to get me or someone to give her the love that her mother and father failed to give her. Our vision was never based on our mutual feelings but, unfortunately, E's internal reality was a direct copy of my feelings and needs. Intimacy was always artificial, given the fact some type of stimulant was usually used in place of sharing authentic love. Because E's feelings and needs were repressed by her in her subconscious Self, none of her expectations, desires, and needs were ever put forward and acted upon. Because E's life revolved around my feelings and needs for 36 years, she did not see a need to develop a financial portfolio that would yield her a significant retirement when her work days came to an end. All of her financial needs would be taken care of by me consistent with CoDeopendency Addiction Thinking and Behavior. And, throughout the 36 years of our relationship, it was constantly sabotaged by one argument after the next. This was done due to the fact my codependent partner lived each day in constant fear of abandonment and rejection, and by engaging in meaningless arguments, it was reasoned that I would feel guilty for expressing my own feelings and needs. Since E's were repressed inside of her Self, each argument was designed to control me in hopes that I would not leave the relationship. I stayed in it for 36 long years! Before moving forward with a brief overview of what is covered in each Chapter in this book, I need to point-out here that before E and I engaged in intimacy, we would get bogged down in some long argument(s) about some inconsequential and irrelevant thing, and the purpose of this or that argument, was to avoid sharing feelings with each other so E's feelings could remain clandestinely hidden. One year passed and another New Year began, and it passed and gave away to another one and so forth for 36 years.

Therefore, when I became aware it is learned CoDependency Addiction that tore down E and L's relationship while we built up an impressive material reality on top of its hidden darkness, L was convinced he had to write this book because it would be next to impossible to get E to admit the former was the destructive force that brought down our relationship. After many attempts ended in failure over a three year period, from 2015 to 2018, L decided to proceed with this book so that the millions of Americans, who are currently suffering with a Codependency Addiction, may find some part of L's experience helpful to them in either avoiding becoming entangled in a relationship with a codependent person, or, if like myself, those who have been in one for several years can discover there is a way out of the snares of CoDependency Addiction before it is too late.

Chapter II opens with a discussion of the role family dysfunctionalism plays in the formation of Codependency Addiction in the very early life of an infant. Some emphasis is given to Who We Are. That is, are we an individual, or are we social creatures? This discussion demonstrates that the task of mother, father, or mother-surrogate love is to create social creatures, who must fulfill their purpose on this Earth by first learning we are love, and second, that we must give love to our fellow human beings, or social creatures, which, ultimately, validates mother, father, and mother-surrogate love is as essential to the harmonic development of an infant and adult as the oxygen one breathes. Chapter III demonstrates that mother love is not a new phenomenon, but it has been a primary pre-requisite for the development of infants into human beings since the beginning of the Savagery Period more than a million years ago.

Special attention is focused on the fact that the position of the mother, during this historical stage of human development, was primary in the Gens or family. The mother was in charge of the workings of the tribe, or commune. CoDependency Addiction was unheard of because all of the basic needs of the infant are met, and the males in the tribe insured that no child would be neglected, or left behind, especially when it came to the availability of foodstuffs. However, as time passed, it is shown that the conscious awareness of women and men in the tribe increased as their development of new instruments of production evolved. As such, more wealth in the form of cattle and tools made significant advancements in the Gens or family commune. Sometime toward the end of the Savagery Period and the beginning of the Barbarism Epoch, a significant accumulation of wealth had occurred, and hitherto for thousands of years, the children in the Gens were identified through their mother lineage *only*.

With the introduction of pastoralism and the discovery of fire, and with a surplus of foodstuff, the male in the Gens, and we do not know exactly when, decided he wanted to change the way his children were identified through their mother lineage, and change this identification to the male lineage so his wealth could be inherited by his children. This act led directly to the overthrow of mother right, and it marked the first revolution carried-out on Earth. Shortly after the overthrow of mother right, the Patriarchy System came into existence in the Monogamy Family, along with various forms of alienation. We provide a discussion of the various ways in which alienation manifest itself during social production. Moreover, some attention is given to the methodology used by the Slave Master, which is embodied in the Willie Lynch Letter, to transform his African People, from their natural state of interdependent human beings into African Slaves with a Codependency Addiction. How this change is brought about is elaborated on, regarding how the minds of the African Slaves were impacted.

In Chapter IV, we introduce CoDependency Addiction and provide a definition for it. One of the interesting concepts brought out in this Chapter is the duality of the personality of the person who suffers with CoDependency Addiction. On one hand, the Self of the codependent person is repressed, and on the other, a carefully arranged public persona is overlaid on top of it to fool the public that everything in one's life is going well. By doing so, the codependent person often feels like a fraud inasmuch as he or she presents a false picture of themselves while their authentic feelings and needs are enclosed within the Self. In short, the core Self of the codependent person is where one's CoDependency Addiction is locked away as a secret for years, or for a lifetime. Moreover, the codependent person is shown to be alienated from his or her Self, given the fact it is repressed and nearly forgotten as a part of their mental reality. Although, repression of the Self cannot extinguish one's CoDependency Addiction, and the negative feelings associated with it such as those E kept hidden from me and the public for 36 years. Chapter V explains the inevitability of a CoDependency Adiction by offering a thorough discussion of the importance of the relationship that must exist between a mother or mother-surrogate and her infant.

Infants are born in a normal dependency state, and there is only one way to the next level, which is the interdependency state. This Chapter reiterates the critical importance of mother love and mother-surrogate love in particular. It is a fact that from the moment an infant is born through his or her first six years, the latter's basic need for love cannot be taken for granted of withheld. It is during this stage of early childhood development that an infant grows into conscious awareness that he or she is love, and by giving it to another person, only then can one be loved in return. Therein lies the seed cause of cooperation. If this exchange of love between mother or mother-surrogate is missed completely, or significantly interrupted, regarding the transmission of love to an infant by the parents, then, sadly, the affected infant is set upon a course of CoDependency Addiction for the rest of his or her adult life.

The affects of this void of love and invalidation of the infant inevitably has tremendous negative consequences on the psychological well-being of the infant, child, and adult over the entire course of his or her life. Chapter VI highlights just how serious a problem maternal deprivation is on the normal development of the child during the childhood years and continuing into one's adult life. Chapter VII provides a thorough examination of the characteristics of a codependent person. Everyone one of them presented originates out of the invalidation of an infant by his or mother, father, or mother-surrogate. Some attention is given to psychopathology and its contribution to the production of the Codependency Addiction Disease. In order to keep the latter undercover from public scrutiny, many codependent person's resort to the use of psychopathic manipulation to deceive self and others that they do not have a problem with Codependency Addiction. This behavior is learned by children in dysfunctional families because from the outside looking in, everything seems balanced, but on the inside, emotional trauma is going strong.

Chapters VIII, IX, and X shows how codependent people maintain their CoDependency Addiction secret. Denial, shame, guilt, and projection are all used interchangeably in an attempt to make the non-codependent person responsible for the codependent's problem. One of the biggest projection tactic used by codependent people is they seriously try to get the non-codependent person to believe the relationship they are in with a codependent person failed because of something they did not do. This Chapter provides information that makes this projection tactic transparent and disempowers its negative influence on other people who are not codependent. In Chapter XI, emphasis is placed on the codependent person's repression of the Self. It is possible for someone to remain in a relationship for several decades, or a lifetime, and never become aware of their Codependency Addiction. Usually, a **significant emotional shock** abruptly thrusts the hidden Self into their conscious view such as a catastrophic health problem i. e., stroke, etc., financial crisis, or a problem with a close family member. Chapter XI provides more information that demonstrates just how determined a codependent person is toward keeping their CoDependency Addiction a secret. Additional information is shared related to blame, control, and conflict. Many codependent people would prefer to die than allow their CoDependency Addiction to be exposed to their partner, or other people.

The ego and super-ego are two very necessary and important components of an infant, child, and adult's personality. Chapter XII highlights the fact that narcissism replaces the normal functioning of an infant's and child's ego, if mother, father, or mother-surrogate love is not provided to him or her during the first six years of life. When narcissism takes precedent over the ego, and exert its negative influences on it, the infant, child, and adult experience an arrested development of their **conscience.** Without the latter, Codependency Addiction Disease becomes nearly uncontrollable because the super-ego, which is a natural regulator of the ego, is no longer able to do so similar to the way the pancreas in people with diabetes is unable to secrete sufficient insulin in the bloodstream necessary to regulate glucose in it. Without active use of one's conscience, knowing right from wrong becomes severely blurred and distorted. In the absence of the development of conscience, the codependent person, and many who are not, get diagnosed as being **bi-polar.**

Chapter XIII, is included to direct attention to the scientific connection that exist between loneliness and the human brain. Some time is taken to demonstrate that loneliness is a powerful negative force within the human body inasmuch as it triggers the human brain to secret enzymes, which produce inflammation, and, ultimately, an array of catastrophic diseases. More information is provided that establishes the fact that an internal dialogue goes between the human brain and inflammation, which its host makes use of to create a toxic reality.

Chapter XIV includes a discussion of the extent to which codependent people have a tendency to self-sacrifice for others, which is a manifestation of one's loneliness and alienation from their feelings and needs. There is an overdoing and over-compensation. Underlying the latter is the codependent person's desperate need to gain the goodwill of others hoping they will give them the love that they never received while growing up in their dysfunctional families. Caretaking and care-giving are explained because the former is done to "get" something in return, while care-giving is engaged in from a place of abundance and security. In Chapter XV fear of abandonment and fear of rejection are examined in detail. Once this type of fear is imprinted in an infant's mind, it is nearly impossible to reverse the damage. Every action taken by a codependent person, during much of their lifetime, is influenced by the thought of "Go Along to Get Along."

The CoDependency Addiction Disease progressively breakdown communication in every phase of a codependent person's life, especially in their intimate relationship. Boundaries are crossed where the codependent person tries to control their partner by thinking for them, or by finishing their sentences or thoughts. In Chapter XVI we address this problem as well as show why codependent people have a hard time taking responsibility for their own thoughts, actions, and behavior.

Throughout every Chapter of this book, and in one form or another, we deal with a codependent people's repression of their feelings and needs. In Chapter XVII, a thorough, and chronological accounting of my codependent partner's health-related problems, are dealt with in detail, including my own. Many, if not all, of E's illnesses were created by her due to her fierce loneliness she repressed inside of her Self.

Stress creates negative cortisol enzymes in the human bloodstream, which changes into Free Radicals, which begins the development of inflammation somewhere in a codependent person's mind and body, which, ultimately, create a disease, oftentimes, ones that are catastrophic in nature such as a stroke, heart attack, cancers of varying types, diabetes, and kidney disease among many others. Why codependent people are easily startled and make poor decisions are also addressed.

Lastly, Chapter XVIII, deals with the CoDependency Addiction Disease inspired Christmas Massacre-2018, which occurred in the living room of my home two days after Christmas Day. I was ambushed by my own family members, all of whom had already been conditioned and prejudiced by E that I am the primary cause of her health problems, both mentally and physically, including her CoDependency Addiction. I was shocked by the extent to which everyone expressed a low importance of history as a tool to use to travel back in time to consider what E's experience was like as a child growing up in a dysfunctional family in a very rural and isolated area. I learned a lot from that fateful evening because every family member gathered, I played a direct and positive role in their early life, both financially and as a mentor. Most striking is the fact E's son-T-unilaterally declared E and L's relationship "over," and H, our daughter, who L helped to become the person she is today with a doctoral degree and much more, ALL-turned their backs on me, and left me on the streets like a common stranger. No one would treat another human being this way, who is in touch with their feelings and needs. The final Chapter XIX, is the conclusion. The book must be read to fully grasp what is in it.

In sum, this book is not a theoretical discourse about CoDependency Addiction Disease; it is about E and L's real life experience living with it, both knowingly, and unknowingly, for 36 years. The information shared earlier are my recollections of E's hidden CoDependency Addiction Disease. Every Chapter included in this book demonstrates the extent to which she went to keep the latter hidden from L.

Before proceeding, it is timely to mention here that during the beginning of our relationship, Johnny Nash had a very popular hit song called "I Can See Clearly Now." It was released in 1972, and reached number one on the Billboard 100 Chart. This song, more than any other at the time, struck a very deep chord inside E. Although beneath the surface, E was challenged by some very deep emotional traumas, wounds, and pain experienced during her childhood, she diverted my attention away from her inner pain by closely identifying with the powerful lyrics in Johnny Nash's mentioned hit song. For example, L was led to believe E was emotionally healthy when she, for a long time in my presence, would sing these quoted lyrics from Johnny Nash's song: "I can see clearly now the rain is gone, I can see all obstacles in my way, Gone are the dark clouds that had me blind, It's going to be a bright, bright sunny day…I can make it now the pain is gone, All of the bad feelings have disappeared, Here is that rainbow I've been praying for… Look all around, there's nothing but blue skies…" (See genius.com/Johnny-nash-i-can-see-clearly-now-lyrics). There was nothing to warn me to be aware, and to paraphrase the great Afro-American songwriter-Smokey Robinson-"be careful what you ask for, some dreams should never come true." Nevertheless, there L was, several decades before Smokey Robinson wrote the song track for the Temptations Movie, getting myself involved in a relationship that was nearly flat lined from the outset. How it amazingly lasted more than three decades is answered by the real life experiences documented by L in this book.

Finally, Malcolm X once remarked "History is best qualified to reward all research." This is the history of L's firsthand observations of the CoDependency Addiction Disease he lived with for 36 years!!

CHAPTER TWO

Origin And Development Of Codependency And The Part Played By Family Disfunctionalism

By nature, human beings are genetically wired, by their DNA, to be social creatures. There are no exceptions, although many Americans have been led astray to believe they are not social creatures within and part of the *grand plan of nature*. In our prevailing capitalist society, and going back to the earliest days of its establishment as a Republic, Americans have been conditioned to believe otherwise. For example, M. F. Ashley Montagu was one of the most respected researchers in the field of human development during the Twentieth Century. His book titled The Direction of Human Development: *Biological and Social Bases*, 1955, added tremendous value to our understanding of the fact that human beings are not *individuals* but are born to function as social beings, who are part of a social group within *nature*. Montagu, and his colleagues, concluded, after years of research, that "…as the child matures and the socializing process continues…the child becomes more and more firmly bound to the socializing agent…and this social binding continues throughout life."[9] Montagu's research goes on to overthrow the misconception that we are merely disconnected individuals.

---

[9] Montagu, M.F. Ashley, The Direction of Human Development: Biological and Social Bases, Harper & Brothers Publishers, new York, 1955, p. 171.

A. Individualism Is A Myth

The view that we are social beings cannot be too strongly emphasized according to Montagu. He wrote "this view of the development of the person cannot be too strongly emphasized. Its implications are of the first order of importance. The conventional view of the person in the socializing process as developing to greater individuality is a seriously misleading one. Of course every person has a personality that is quite distinct and different from every other person's personality on the planet; however, no one cannot step out of their nature as a social being. Without the balancing compass of the socialization process, any structural personality differences "…which characterize each person [on Earth] would not exist."[10] For instance, a fox cannot become an elephant, and vis-à-vis, and, therefore, neither one of these animals can arbitrarily leaves its natural group. Nor can an individual ever stop being a social phenomenon! As such, Montagu added "every person is socially bound to the group he has been socialized. In this sense the "individual" is a myth. From the point of view of the social situation there are no individuals, except as abstracted biological entities or for the quantitative purposes of a census."[11] Given the fact we are now aware that we are social creatures, any talk about individualism implies the existence of *separateness, which in nature does not exist.* Imagine one day you wake up to suddenly find out that your arms and legs are disconnected to your physical self? This, no doubt would be traumatic and puzzling because whatever your arms and legs decided to do, at any given time, would suggest each of your body parts could do whatever they desire to do independent of your whole self. Moreover, Montagu wrote "it makes no sense," writes Sullivan, "to think of ourselves as 'individual,' 'separate,' capable of anything like definitive description in isolation…the notion is beside the point."[12] There are other well-known scholars, who like Montagu, have also discovered the mythology of individual thought.

---

[10] Ibid., p. 171.

[11] Ibid., pp. 171 and 172.

[12] Ibid., p. 172.

Maurice Cornforth's book titled <u>Historical Materialism,</u> 1954 sheds a shining light on individualism. He wrote "Social science abstracts from the individuals and deals with the social relations. It is not concerned with individual but with aggregate humanity."[13] It is for this very reason that in our contemporary American society, obsessive emphasis is placed on such disciplines as Sciences, Technology, Engineering, and Mathematics (STEM) to subtly suggest to the American Public that the STEM area is more prestigious than the Social Sciences or Humanities. The latter does not deal with individuals but social relations and social class. STEM emphasizes individual excellence only. Individuals do not make history; quite to the contrary, movement of classes do. Cornforth clarifies this point saying, "if it is a matter of the personalities and motives of individuals accounting for what happens, then the historian is faced with the practical impossibility of finding sufficient evidence to know their personalities and their motives with any degree of certainty...The historian has to fill in his lack of knowledge from his own bias and imagination..."[14] It is obvious such history, and the literature is filled with the exploits of singular individual leaders, who are considered, by many historians and others, to be the embodiment of the history of an entire nation, excluding the masses of people. By standing the individual myth on its feet, it follows human beings are, in fact, social creatures.

B. Human Beings Are Social Creatures

The most important realization anyone can experience has nothing to do with material possessions, but, to the contrary, everything to do with the simple, profound fact, that human beings are an inseparable part of nature. To survive, human beings must work together to produce their subsistence, in an organized fashion, and in accordance with the prevailing conditions of a certain time period such as primitive Hunter Gatherer, Stone Age, Pastoral, and home production among many other

---

[13] Cornforth, Maurice, <u>Historical Materialism</u>, International Publishers, New York, 1954, P. 16.
[14] Ibid., p. 69.

stages of development. If each person attempted to produce his or her subsistence alone, without a doubt, human beings would have long ago become extinct like the Dinosaurs. Karl Marx, one of the greatest philosophers of the 19th Century, researched and developed the theory of Historical Materialism, which, generally speaking, demonstrates man and woman cooperate to produce their livelihood at each stage of the development of society, and as new forms and technology are discovered and entered into their process of production, there is a forward advancement made, or change in how man and woman-workers-reproduce themselves, and as such, they enter into new social relations of production, thereby continuously revolutionizing society as a whole. This world, as we know it, would not be possible if human beings did not behave as social creatures.

In his early work titled <u>Economic and Philosophic Manuscripts of 1844</u>, Karl Marx wrote "the worker can create nothing without *nature*... It is the material on which his labour is realized, in which it is active, from which and by means of which it produces."[15] Moreover, "nature is man's *inorganic body*...Man *lives* on nature-means that nature is his body, with which he [or she] must remain in continuous interchange if he is not to die. That man's physical and spiritual life is linked to nature... for man [and woman are] a part of nature."[16] Since the beginning of recorded human history, nature has served as the means against which human beings have socially interacted together to create their mutual subsistence, and reproduction of self. Animals, unlike human beings, produce only what they immediately need at a given moment.

For instance, Marx wrote "admittedly animals also produce. They build themselves nests, dwellings, like the bees, beavers, ants, etc. But an animal only produces what it immediately needs for itself or its young... It produces only under the dominion of immediate physical need, whilst man [and woman] produces even when he is free from physical need..."[17] On the other hand, because human beings gain increasing

---

[15] Marx, Karl, <u>Economic and Philosophic Manuscripts of 1844</u>, Progress Publishers, Moscow, 1959, p. 64.

[16] Ibid., pp.67 and 68.

[17] Ibid., pp. 68 and 69.

conscious awareness when they work together during production, they are able to change nature such as altering the flow of a river, or building a bridge over it where, formerly, one did not exist. Through self-reflection as social creatures, human beings become conscious of self development through their labor pursuits. In their book titled <u>German Ideology</u>, Marx and Engels wrote "men can be distinguished from animals by consciousness, by religion or anything else you like. They themselves begin to distinguish themselves from animals as soon as they begin to *produce* their means of subsistence…"[18]

C. Consciousness Development Is A Function of Social Existence

We already know human beings' survival is directly dependent on their continuous connection to nature. The latter is a means of production, and in due course of the creation of labor products, man and woman engage in dialogue with each other to learn how to overcome obstacles in the production process. In this way, they also gain increased consciousness of self. Contrary to what we have already seen, individualism is a myth, and without individuals engaging in social production, many have come to falsely believe that their consciousness determines Who They Are, rather than their social existence, namely, being social creatures engaged collectively, and cooperatively, in social production. Zeitlin wrote "it is not the consciousness of men [and women] that determines their existence, but, on the contrary, their social existence determines their consciousness."[19] In addition, Marx and Engels added "the production of ideas, of conceptions, of consciousness, is at first directly interwoven with the material activity and the material [social production] of men–the language of real life."[20]

Human beings, who, as we have already seen, are social creatures by their inherent, biological nature; and, if the human species continues

---

[18] Marx Engels, <u>German Ideology</u>, Progress Publishers, Moscow, 1964, p. 37.
[19] Zeitlin, Irving M., <u>Marxism: A Re-Examination</u>, D. Van Nostrand Company, New York, 1967, p. 63.
[20] Marx Engels, Op. Cit., p. 42.

to survive during the coming millenniums similar to those already passed into recorded human history, they must continue to increase their conscious awareness through their willing and free participation in social production. When, and at anytime during their social evolution, social creatures, or human beings, are no longer able to produce their subsistence socially and freely, and recreate themselves, their conscious development will stagnate. To the contrary, man and woman experienced a continuous increase in their conscious awareness during the first million years of their human journey on Earth. Much of this Great Human Development occurred during an epoch in which the woman's position in the tribe, namely, *Mother Rights,* reigned supreme.

CHAPTER THREE

Mother Right

A. Mother Right: From Savagery To The Lower Stage Of Barbarism

I n his book titled <u>The Origin Of The Family, Private property And The State</u>, 1972, Frederick Engels wrote it was during the Savagery Epoch, and its Lower Stage in particular, that the "Infancy of the human race"[21] began, and evolved subsequently. Evelyn Reed, who wrote the introduction to this book, added "Savagery began with the emergence of the first humans (or hominids) from our ancestral branch of the anthropoids about a million years ago."[22] During the early centuries of the Lower Stage of the Savagery Epoch, man and woman lived partially in trees, offering them safe haven from various large beasts. Moreover, early man and woman worked closely together to overcome various challenges to their survival, and as Engels points-out, "fruits, nuts and roots served him as food; the formation of articulate speech was the main achievement of this period."[23] Although no recorded

---

[21] Engels, Frederick, <u>Origin Of The Family, Private Property And The State,</u> Pathfinder Press, New York, 1972, p. 39.

[22] Reed, Evelyn, Introduction, Ibid., p. 9.

[23] Ibid., p. 39.

records are available from this period, it is estimated that "…this period may have lasted for many thousands of years [;however,] once we admit the descent of man from the animal kingdom, the acceptance of this transitional stage is inevitable, "[24] wrote Engels. One fact is certain, and that is, humankind exist today across all expanses of the Earth in numbers exceeding 8 billion, and given this fact, early man and woman most certainly laid the social foundation upon which all subsequent human development took place during each successive Millennium to the present. Working together in accordance with their nature as social creatures, there was a noticeable increase in human consciousness by the Middle Stage of the Savagery Epoch.

In particular, unlike during its Lower Stage, man and woman's food supply consisted mostly of a vegetarian diet-fruits, roots, nuts, leaves, and so forth. However, by the Middle Stage of the Savagery Epoch, man and woman learned, through simple social production, how to use fire. Having discovered this life-sustaining element, Engels wrote the Middle Stage of Savagery "begins with the utilization of fish (under which head we also include crabs, shellfish, and other aquatic animals) for food and with the employment of fire. This new food… made man [and woman] independent of climate and locality."[25] With the knowledge of the use of fire, man and woman successfully moved through the Middle Stage of the Savagery Period, bringing with them crude stone implements. The club and spear were invented during the period, which allowed man and woman to introduce larger game into their diet. By the Upper Stage of the Savagery Period, the bow and arrow were invented, adding wild game as a regular part of their diet. Engels wrote the Upper Stage of this period "begins with the invention of the bow and arrow, whereby wild game became a regular item of food, and hunting one of the normal occupations. Bow, string and arrow constitute a very composite instrument, the invention of which presupposes long accumulated experience and sharpened mental powers…"[26] By the end of the Savagery Period, Engels emphasized "the

---

[24] Ibid., pp. 39 and 40.
[25] Ibid., p. 40.
[26] Ibid., p. 40.

bow and arrow was for savagery what the iron sword was for barbarism and the firearms for civilization, namely, the decisive weapon."[27] It should not be forgotten that none of these inventions would have been possible, during the Savagery Period, were it not for man and woman engaging continuously in social production aimed at changing nature, which resulted in a simultaneous increase in their conscious awareness.

Following the Savagery Period, Barbarism was the next major time period through which the social development of man and woman passed. Evelyn Reed stated ""Barbarism came in about eight thousand years ago..."[28] When man and woman entered on the Lower Stage of Barbarism, the latter "dates from the introduction of pottery... [; however, according to Engels,]...The characteristic feature of the period of barbarism is the domestication and breeding of animals and the cultivation of plants."[29] This change in social production, which appeared on the stage of human history, would prove to be a centerpiece of the Barbarism Period because it would eventually allow man and woman to discover that they could reduce their need to engage in migrations from place to place. They could remain in one area due to the domestication of animals and the cultivation of maize and other edible plants and fruits. In fact, Engels wrote "...the middle stage of barbarism commenced with the domestication of milk and meat-yielding animals...[and] formation of herds led to pastoral life..."[30] Unlike any other previous moment in world history since the beginning of the Savagery Period, domestication of animals and cultivation of plants were new discoveries made during the Barbarism Period. What is more, these inventions, or life activities of man and woman, for the first time in human history, made it possible for them to begin to produce more products than they actually needed to satisfy their basic needs. In the collected work titled The Woman Question, 1951, Engels wrote "the increase of production in all branches-cattle-raising, agriculture, domestic handicrafts-gave human labor-power the capacity

---

[27] Ibid., p. 41.

[28] Reed, Evelyn, Introduction, Op. Cit., p. 9.

[29] Ibid., p. 41.

[30] Ibid., p. 42.

to produce a larger product than was necessary for its maintenance."[31] In addition, by the Upper Stage of the Barbarism Period, all previous means of procuring food now sank into the background. Hunting, once a necessity, now became a luxury"[32] This is significant and the surplus products eventually led to the very first known *revolution* on the Earth insofar as early human development is concerned. We will say more about this revolution later; presently, it is worthwhile mentioning the following.

That is, one effect of the accumulation of a surplus product due to the domestication of animals, was it contributed directly to man and woman's passage into the Upper Stage of Barbarism, namely, civilization. The Middle Stage of Barbarism was one in which man and woman acquired knowledge of cattle breeding and land cultivation. More ways to increase productivity were discovered. According to Engels, the Upper Stage of Barbarism "begins with the smelting of iron ore and passes into civilization through the invention of a alphabetic writing and its utilization for literary records."[33]

The following diagram-Figure 1.1-shows the historical changes in the mode of production, from the Savagery Period to Civilization and to the return to Communism practiced more than a million years ago.

---

[31] Engels, Frederick, Lenin, V. I., Marx, Karl, and Stalin, Joseph, The Woman Question, International Publishers, New York, 1951, P. 9.
[32] Engels. Op. Cit., p. 65.
[33] Ibid., p. 43.

Historical Changes In The Mode Of Production: From The Savagery Period To Civilization To Return To Communism

A Theoretical Framework

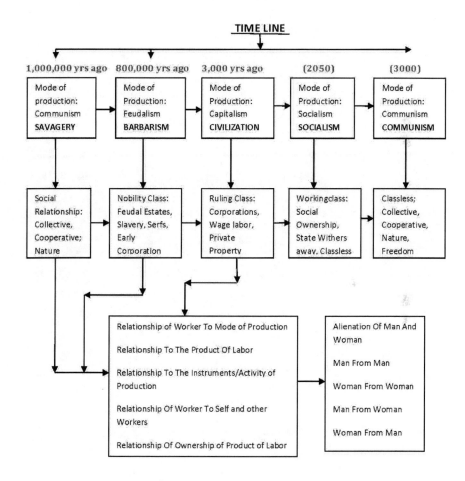

B. Overthrow of Mother Right During The Barbarism Period In Human History

Earlier, we mentioned the first revolution known to humans occurred during this period, and could only be accomplished as a result of an accumulation of surplus products obtained from the domestication of animals. From the Savagery Period to the Barbarism Period, social relations among men and women underwent progressive changes in accordance with their social production and inventions, both of which influenced the development of the family. It is not our intention here to trace the evolution of the family as an evolving feature of human activity; however, it is useful to mention what Engels wrote in this regard. He stated "the family," says Morgan, "represents an active principle. It is never stationary, but advances from a lower to a higher form as society advances from a lower to a higher condition."[34] The main point during man and woman's evolution up from the Savagery Period through the Barbarism Period is women held the highest decision-making position in the tribe, and later the family. Echoing this fact, Engels wrote "...the communistic household implies the supremacy of women in the house, just as the exclusive recognition of a natural mother, because of the impossibility of determining the natural father with certainty, signifies high esteem for the women, that is, for the mothers."[35]

The idea, originating during the so-called period of Enlightenment of the Eighteenth Century, that a woman was a slave of a man is ludicrous, absurd, and without any foundation upon which a provable argument could be reasonably made and supported. Actually, Engels wrote "that woman was the slave of man at the commencement of society is one of the most absurd notions that have come down to us... woman occupied not only a free but a highly respected position among all savages and all barbarians of the lower and middle stages and partly even of the upper stage."[36] As we shall see shortly, the first revolution known to human beings during this time, is, in fact, what eventually

[34] Ibid., p. 45. See Lewis Morgan, <u>Ancient Society</u>, 1877.
[35] Ibid., pp. 60 and 61.
[36] Ibid., p. 61.

casted the woman down, which many enlightened professors, upon narrowly seeing woman in a casted down place, rapidly concluded that she was *the slave of man*. Nothing could be farther from the truth!

By the end of the Upper Stage of Barbarism, the woman held, as she had from the beginning of the lower Stage of Savagery, a supreme position in the gens, or family. Engels wrote "the women were the great power among the clans {gentes], as everywhere else. They did not hesitate, when occasion required, to knock off the horns, as it was technically called, from the head of the chief and send him back to the ranks of the warriors."[37]

a. Ownership Of Wealth

At the beginning of the Middle Stage of Barbarism, the woman was in complete charge of the household, and all children born in a gen, or family, were only known through the female lineage. According to Engels, "until the lower stage of barbarism, fixed wealth consisted almost entirely of the house, clothing, crude ornaments and implements for procuring and preparing food: boats, weapons, and household utensils of the simplest kind."[38] From the time man and woman still lived partially in trees, as a protection from large beasts, up to the Middle Stage of Barbarism, the majority of these assets were owned by the woman head of the household. Moreover, Engels wrote "communistic housekeeping...means the supremacy of woman in the house; just as the exclusive recognition of the female parent, owing to the impossibility of recognizing the male parent with certainty, means that the women-the mothers-are held in high respect...the position of women is not only free, but honorable."[39]

In view of increased productivity, and according to the division of labor prevailing then in the family, Engels wrote "...the procuring of food and the implements necessary thereto, and...also. The ownership of the latter, fell to the man; he took them with him in case of separation,

---

[37] Ibid., p. 61.
[38] Ibid., p. 65.
[39] Engels, <u>The Woman Question</u>, Op. Cit., p. 12.

just as the woman retained the household goods…the man was also the owner of the new sources of food stuffs-the cattle."[40] As it was, given the newly accumulated surplus, and the means of production, man's children could not, according to the customs of the gens at the time, inherit his property, or wealth, from him.

b. Inheritance Of Man's Wealth Set Stage For
The First Revolution in Human History

Right before the beginning of Civilization, especially during the Upper Stage of Barbarism, any wealth or property owned by man wrote Engels "…had to remain in the gens…The children of the deceased [man], however, belonged not to his gens, but to that of their mother. In the beginning, they inherited from their mother…but they could not inherit from their father, because they did not belong to his gens, and his property had to remain…"[41] with the mother's gen. As was the practice, "his own children …were disinherited."[42] That being the case, man, as his wealth and property continued to increase in value, felt compelled to discover a way for his children to inherit his property after his death. And, he did!

c. Overthrow Of Mother Right

With an increase in his wealth, this gave man a more important status in the family. Engels wrote "…as wealth increased, it, on one hand, gave the man a more important status in the family than the woman, and on the other hand, created a stimulus to utilize this strengthened position in order to overthrow the traditional order of inheritance in favour of his children. But this was impossible as long as descent according to mother right prevailed."[43] With his attention being less on survival, as it was for the first million years of more of man and woman existence on Earth, the idea of inheritance upset the traditional

---

[40] Engels, Op. Cit., p. 66.

[41] Ibid., p. 66.

[42] Ibid., p. 67.

[43] Ibid., p. 67.

order of appropriation of wealth and property through the mother, and this historical act set off the first social revolution on Earth, when the former was, for the first time, now inherited by the man's children by the end of the Upper Stage of Barbarism. Wealth and property descent, through the mother, had to be overthrown!

According to Engels, "this had…to be overthrown, and it was overthrown; and it was not so difficult to do this…For this revolution-one of the most decisive ever experienced by mankind-need not have disturbed one single living member of a gens. All the members could remain what they were previously. The simple decision sufficed that in future the descendents of the male members should remain in the gens, but that those of the females were to be excluded from the gens and transferred to that of their father."[44] As it was during several millenniums, everything, from children to ownership of wealth in all of its forms during that time, had a common descent through the mother in the gens, or family. But, that practice abruptly was reversed, and Engels wrote "the reckoning of descent through the female line and the right of inheritance through the mother were hereby overthrown and the male lineage and right of inheritance from the father instituted."[45] Moreover, Engels added "the overthrow of mother-right was the *world historical defeat of the female sex*. The man took command in the house also; the woman was degraded and reduced to servitude, she became the slave if his lust and a mere instrument for the production of children."[46] Later, we shall see how this overthrow of the female sex, i. e., mother-would come to play a very important role, regarding the origin of Codependency Addiction. Presently, it is necessary to say a few words about the coming into existence of *Patriarchy, which had been hitherto non-existent throughout all human history prior to the beginning of civilization, at the close of the Barbarism Stage of human evolution.*

---

[44] Ibid., p. 67.

[45] Ibid., p. 67.

[46] Engels, The Woman Question, Op. Cit., p. 16.

d. Patriarchy: A Cornerstone Of Civilization

Leading up to civilization, property advanced through several forms. Marx and Engels wrote in <u>The German Ideology</u> "the first form of property is tribal property…It corresponds to the undeveloped stage of production, at which a people lives by hunting and fishing, by cattle-raising or, at most by agriculture."[47] As we have already seen, it was this elementary division of labor that called into existence the first revolution, namely, the overthrow of mother right, and the establishment of the man as the owner of property and head of the family household. As the division of labor continued to change over time, the former linked to tribal property transformed into feudal or estate property, and later, into factory production underpinned by capital. With the defeat of mother right, patriarchy got its start, and it has continued to prevail unabated right up to the present time.

As Engels wrote, "the man now being actually supreme in the house, the last barrier to his absolute supremacy had fallen. This autocracy was confirmed and perpetuated by the overthrow of mother-right, the introduction of father-right, and the gradual transition of the pairing marriage into monogamy."[48] The sole rule of the men, and we must be very clear here and state that the *sole rule of men in the family, which originated on the world social stage with the defeat of the female sex caused by the overthrow of mother right, primarily rest with men who own property, and later, unheard-of sums of capital right up to the present Twentieth-first Century in the Millennium 2,000.* There is mass confusion today, especially among women, who falsely believe that all males are part of the Patriarchy System, or Autocracy. Actually, the vast majority of working class men

---

[47] Marx, Karl and Engels, Frederick, <u>The German Ideology</u>, Progress Publishers, Moscow, 1964, p. 38.

[48] Engels, <u>The Woman Question</u>, Op. Cit., p. 11. "At this stage one man lives with one woman, yet in such manner that polygamy and occasional infidelity remain men's privileges, even though the former is seldom practiced for economic reasons; at the same time, the strictest fidelity is demanded of the woman during the period of cohabitation, adultery on her part being cruelly punished. The marriage tie can, however, be easily dissolved by either side, and the children belong solely to the mother, as previously."

today do not own large sums of capital, but, as a result of brainwashing through the various social media platforms, many aspire to become wealthy capitalists, a dream that has for, millions, actually been a nightmare. Now that we have this perspective cleared up, a few more comments are appropriate related to the Patriarchy System.

Frederick Engels wrote "the first effect of the sole rule of the men that was now established is shown in the intermediate form of the family which now emerges, the patriarchal family. Its chief attribute is...the organization of a number of persons, bond and free, into a family, under the paternal power of the head of the family."[49] During the previous Millenniums before civilization entered upon the world stage, nothing was known, as we have already seen, about patriarchy, nor was it practiced. However, with the end of mother right, the Pairing Family, in which the natural mother and attested father co-existed, gave away with the fall of mother right. Out of the Pairing Family arose Monogamy, and according to Engels "...this arises out of the pairing family in the transition period from the middle to the upper stage of barbarism, its final victory being one of the signs of the beginning of civilization. It is based on the supremacy of the man; its express aim is the begetting of children of undisputed paternity, this paternity being required in order that these children may inherit their father's wealth as his natural heirs."[50] In order to protect father right, the Monogamy Family, which now consists of one female and one male, at its inception, instituted "...greater rigidity of the marriage tie, which can now no longer be dissolved at the pleasure of either party. Now, as a rule, only the man can dissolve it and cast off his wife....The wedded wife is expected to tolerate all this, but to maintain strict chastity and conjugal fidelity herself."[51]

Over the years, I have been privileged to listen to, and take part in conversations during which the great question of Where did Slavery come from? was discussed in detail, and at times painful, without ever arriving at a satisfactory conclusion. After hours of discussion, usually

---

[49] Engels, Op. Cit., p. 68.
[50] Ibid., pp. 71 and 72.
[51] Ibid., p. 72.

the former question was given the too often worn-out answer; and that is, "slavery has always been with us." When I looked deeper into the question, I now find the provided conclusion has merit. Slavery has always been with us since the end of Mother Right and the beginning of civilization to the Present Day. During Mother Right, and going back to the beginning of the Lower Stage of Savagery, there was no such thing as slavery known to human beings anywhere on Earth. Utilizing available and relevant literature, I can now see how slavery entered upon the world stage since the inception of civilization. Slavery made its appearance *side-by-side with the world defeat of Mother Right, and the rise of Patriarchy in the Monogamy Family.* Oddly, one surely would not look for its roots here because how could such a low conscious, inhuman endeavor exist in the same civilization bedroom alongside apparently free men and women? Engels focused light on what had been hidden in plain sight for centuries! He wrote "...for the husband, however, she is, in reality merely the mother of his legitimate heirs, his chief housekeeper, and the superintendent of the female slaves, whom he may make, and does make, his concubines at will. It is the existence of slavery side by side with monogamy, the existence of beautiful young slaves who belong to the *man* with all they have, that from the very beginning stamped on monogamy its specific character as monogamy *only for the woman*, but not for the man. And it retains this character to this day."[52]

As we see, by the time the monogamy family appeared in world history, the woman, who once ruled over all tribal affairs in the gens, or family, including production, became the first casualty of slavery. Engels wrote "...the woman was degraded, enthralled, the slave of the man's lust, a mere instrument for breeding children."[53] For example, isn't this what the African Slave woman was used for during the infamous American Slavery Institution? She was all of these things an unimaginable more! During the reign of Father Right and patriarchy since the beginning of civilization, the man, over many years thereafter, realized that the woman captured during wars could be put to the same

---

[52] Ibid, p. 72.
[53] Ibid., p. 68.

use as he had put his own, after he casted her down from her highly respected position during mother right. Therefore, it can be said that the father of slavery was the redirection of production, its products, and surplus to the man's heirs, and the defeat of mother right, which, in essence, was the defeat of socialist property owned by all members of the gens, or family.

During the present stage of human development commonly known as *capitalism*, there has been a stagnation in human consciousness development, owing to the workers separation from nature, their instruments of production, and also from themselves as social creatures. During his lifetime of closely examining the way workers socially interact during the course of social production, Karl Marx is credited with being the first social scientist to discover the cause of the stagnation in human consciousness development, which he called *alienation*.

C. Alienation

Let us begin this part of our discussion based upon a premise that we are all in agreement with; and that is, man and woman are inseparably connected to nature; they are social creatures; they are not individuals having a personality only; they possess labor; and they must engage in social production in order to survive and recreate men and women and satisfy their other basic needs and so on. As long as man and woman, who are known as workers, are able to freely produce their life subsistence in relationship to other workers, they will remain indefinitely whole inclusive of a balanced mind, body, and spirit, and consciously aware of their inner selves. Not only is this state of existence true for man and woman, but it will also be *forwarded through the generations to their offsprings, or stated in another way, in the form of recreation of themselves embodied in their children.* As we have already seen, the overthrow of mother right, which was supplanted by father right and the entrance of the Patriarchal System, did not end with the defeat of the female sex, but, to the contrary, the *memory of this experience has continued through the generations, owing to the fact it has been scientifically proven that* **memory outlives the cell.**

a. Alienation And Memory Outlives The Cell

From the moment the first revolution known as the overthrow of mother right quietly occurred more than a million years ago during the Savagery Period of human existence, the emotional and psychological impacts of this event on the man and woman were embedded in their cells, and also transmitted through the cells of their descendents, and so forth, throughout all the succeeding generations, right up to the present time during the Civilization Period. Figure 1.2 below provides insight related to how thoughts move through the generations, and it also shows when artificial thoughts began to *infiltrate, or artificially invade our minds during the last 3,000 years, which marks the beginning of the civilization epoch.*

Stream Of Thought And The Production And Reproduction Of Human Behavior From One Generation To The Next: A Theoretical Framework With Emphasis On The Civilization Epoch

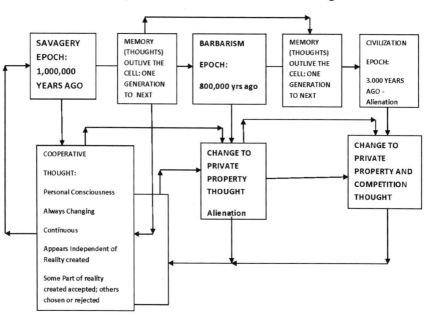

In Dr. Chopra's book titled <u>Quantum Healing: Exploring the Frontier of Mind/Body Medicine</u>, the latter gives considerable attention to the way *memory* function in the mind/body relationship in human beings. Before we elaborate further, refer to the Stream of Thought Theoretical Framework shown above. As we see, during each epoch shown, information was transmitted from one generation to the next via thoughts passed on as memory(s), from biological parents to their offsprings. This was true during the savagery epoch a million years ago, and it is still going-on during the civilization epoch today. According to Dr. Chopra, *memory outlives the cell.* This is the connective linkage that locks together the generations similar to freight and tank cars of a passing railroad train. Everything that exists in the memory of one generation is transferred to the next generation's memory and so on.

Biologically speaking, our physical bodies consists of millions of cells of various types. Each cell type carries-out its function within our genetic blueprint. However, when our human bodies die, everything, cells, tissues, etc., return to dust. However, our thoughts, including those attached to skills, etc., do not die, but, to the contrary, they are transmitted to the next generation in the form of *personality.* As such, during the sex act, which is the first act of labor, the personality of the biological parents, and all of the thoughts included therein, are passed on to the next generation of offsprings. This is done without any fanfare or major effort; the process of *memory outlives the cell takes place, effortlessly, constantly and seamlessly.* According to Ra Un Nefer Amen, "there are two important facts concerning memory that must be understood. One is the fact that nothing that has been experienced is ever forgotten, no matter how out of view, or difficult to recall it may be. The other is that, many of our stored memories, especially, those that are difficult to recall, because of psychological suppression, exert powerful influences in shaping our beliefs and behavior."[54]

Interestingly, we see today's generation is directly influenced by yesterday's; nothing is lost; and every thought passed through the Stream

---

[54] Amen Nefer Un Ra, <u>Metu Neter: The Great Oracle of Tehuti And The Egyptian System of Spiritual Cultivation</u>., vol. 1, Khamit Media Trans Visions, Inc, Brooklyn, New York, 1990, p. 94.

of thought *must be eventually addressed, although it may have been placed in the mind of human beings during the slavery period in America or before.* In short, there is no interruption because this process is a part of the life process itself. Dr. Chopra stated "A personality has no molecules [cells] in it, being composed only of memories and psychological tendencies; yet these are more permanent than cells being affected"[55] when our biological bodies make their transition. However, if any external influence impinges upon what makes man and woman a human being, namely, their labor, then, it is safe to say the worker, or producer, will henceforth experience alienation from oneself until such time the inertia of the latter is finally and permanently removed from themselves and the community, including a nation and so forth.

For the first million years of human existence on Earth, man and woman lived harmoniously during the Savagery Period, and for the better part of the Barbarism Stage of Human Development. There was an external circumstance that impinged upon man and woman's emotional beings in the form of the First Revolution known here as the overthrow of mother right. The memory of this traumatic event on the woman and man eventually made it more and more difficult to remain mentally and emotionally balanced. The result was the onset of a condition discovered by Karl Marx, which he named *alienation*. It is necessary to remind you that, by the time Large-Scale Manufacturing evolved during the Civilization Period, there were more Working Class male workers living at or below the poverty level than ever before during all previous periods of human history hitherto discussed. Even the very small percent of males and females, who owned the vast majority of wealth in American Society as much as 90 percent, were also significantly impacted by the First Revolution, or overthrow of Mother Right. Later, we shall see how the typical Working Class Household was impacted when we begin our discussion of the *origin of codependency Addiction.*

---

[55] Ibid., p. 125.

Presently, a brief discussion of alienation is provided, which will lay the groundwork for how young children have been, and continue to be impacted by a breakdown in parental nurturing during the *critical years of their childhood*.

b. Alienation From Labor's Product

Since the beginning of the reign of father right, or the Patriarchal System, and before this time, man and woman both owned the products of their labor, although before mother right was pronounced dead in human history, the woman commanded and decided how all products in the gens, or family, would be distributed; however, when the former arose on the scene, the products now remained with the man, and all other producers of them, moving forward in time and space, became separated from their labor's product. And, man and woman, that is to say, the large majority, especially as production during civilization progressed, actually owned few of their labor's product, if any at all. According to Karl Marx, who wrote in his book titled <u>Economic and Philosophic Manuscripts of 1844</u>, "the worker becomes all the poorer the more wealth he produces, the more his production increases in power and size...This fact expresses merely that the object which labour's produces-labor's product-confronts it as *something alien, as a power independent* of the *producer*...Under these economic conditions this realization of labour appears as *loss of realisation for the workers;* objectification as *loss of the object and bondage to it*; appropriation as *estrangement,* as *alienation."* [56] There is no reason to unnecessarily ponder what is meant by "loss of the object" inasmuch as we have repeatedly mentioned on several occasions before that when mother right was laid to rest by father right, all of the objects thenceforth produced by man and woman were owned by the few men in the gens, and later during civilization, who owned the means of production while the vast majority of men and women now toiled as wage- earners. Marx added "for on this premise it is clear that the more the worker spends

---

[56] Marx, Karl, <u>Economic and Philosophic Manuscripts of 1844</u>, Progress Publishers, Moscow, 1959, p. 63.

himself [and herself], the more powerful becomes the alien world of objects which he [or she] creates over and against himself [herself], the poorer he himself [herself]-becomes, the less belongs to him as his [her] own."[57] Plainly speaking, the workers', gender inclusive, labor's product ends up as an external existence to them, but equally his or her labor, the substance which make human beings social creatures, at the self-same time, exists outside of the producers in their loss labor's product.

Given the workers are alienated from their labor's product, it follows also that they are equally alienated from the production process in which they work.

c. Alienation From The Production Process And The Instruments Of Production

It is possible for a wage-worker to be alienated from his or her labor's product, and, on the other hand, with this being so, it is impossible for them to not be alienated from the act of production. The workers experience estrangement from his labor's product and the act of production itself. Marx wrote "...the estrangement is manifested not only in the result but in the *act of production,* within the *producing activity,* itself...The product is after all but the summary of the activity, of production. If then the product of labour is alienation, production itself must be active alienation, the alienation of activity, the activity of alienation."[58] When man and woman produce during the act of production, this is considered their life activity. Stated in the most simple way, all beings, including humans, engage in productive activities as a means of their survival. The life activity of man and woman is a means toward this end. Accordingly, Marx wrote "for labour, *life activity, productive life* itself, appears to man in the first place merely as a *means* to satisfying a need-the need to maintain physical existence."[59]

As we have already seen, from the Lower Stage of Savagery to the upper Stage of Barbarism, man and woman's consciousness awareness of

---

[57] Ibid., p. 64.
[58] Ibid., pp. 65 and 66.
[59] Ibid., p. 68.

self, including their labor power, progressively increased as they made new discoveries and inventions such as the stone axe, discovery of fire, and the bow and arrow among others. However, after the overthrow of mother right, and the rise of father right, or the Patriarchal System within the Monogamy Family during Civilization, the worker has become progressively alienated from his or her life activity; that is, production, causing them to become increasing alienated from it. For example, animals are one with their life activity and they do not distinguish themselves from it. On the other hand, the opposite is true for man and woman. The latter distinguishes themselves from animals because, during their life activity, or production, man and woman creates their character, which answers the most critical question among all others, namely, Who Am I? Thus, Marx wrote "conscious life activity distinguishes man immediately from animal life activity…he [or she] is a conscious being… Estranged labour reverses this relationship…"[60] Later, we shall see if this applies throughout a human beings' life, from birth into adulthood; if so, the affected person becomes *an estranged, codependent person.*

Meantime, once some men gained control over the production process, this rendered the vast majority of other workers increasing dependent as a result of their alienation from their production, or life activity. As such, the workers do not feel themselves at home when they are working; they do not feel at home at work due to their alienation from the means of production. This brings us to the final way the workers manifest their alienation, which is via an alienation from *self.*

d. Alienation From Self

The ultimate driver of this type of alienation is forced labor. For more than a million years before civilization, man and woman owned their labor, and employed it freely in the changing forms of life activities. However, by the onset of civilization, and especially during its middle and upper stage, a smaller and smaller number of people, with similar class interests, gained increasing control over the means of production, the production process, instruments of production, and

---

[60] Ibid., p. 68.

over the workers' labor through their class ownership of these life sustaining components of production. Because the workers' labor was externally owned by this Ruling Class, Marx wrote "external labour, labour in which man [and woman] alienates himself [and herself], is a labour of self-sacrifice, of mortification. Lastly, the external character of labour for the worker appears in the fact that it is not his own, but someone else's, that it does not belong to him, that in it belongs, not to himself [or herself], but to another."[61]

The separation of the man and woman from their labor brings, in its aftermath, a whole host of debilitating internal psychological conditions characterized by, namely, poverty of mind, body, and spirit, social dependence, powerlessness, creation of an alien power standing outside and over the workers' in the form of his or her labor's product, devaluation of self-esteem, valuelessness, mental deformity and cretinism of narrowness, stupidity, unworthy and undeservedness, among many others. In fact, Marx wrote "the worker becomes all the poorer the more wealth he [or she] produces, the more his [or her] production increases in power and size."[62] Based on this premise, the more labor the workers expend during production, "…the more powerful becomes the alien world of objects which he creates over against himself [and herself], the poorer…his [or her] inner world-becomes, the less belongs to him as his own."[63] Moreover, the more technological and civilized the workers' labor product becomes, the more barbaric he or she becomes manifested by mass layoffs, police brutality, White Nationalism, public school mass murder, predatory wars, and mass murders by lone gunmen.

All-in-all, as alienation of the self intensifies, and as changes in technology continuously intensify and steadily improves the formed world of commodities, the workers become, at the same time, more deformed. Marx predicted as early as 1844 that the human beings' consciousness awareness would sink to its animal function. As it has come to pass today, roughly 175 years after Marx first saw this development in its early coming into existence, human beings' consciousness have fallen

---

[61] Ibid., p. 66.

[62] Ibid., p. 63.

[63] Ibid., p. 64.

to a very low level, although their labor's product is highly advanced technologically. He wrote "as a result...therefore, man (the worker) only feels himself freely active in his animal functions-eating, drinking, procreating, or at most in his [or her] dwelling and in dressing-up, etc.; and in his [or her] human functions he [or she] no longer feels himself [or herself] to be anything but an animal...what is human becomes animal."[64] Such a social condition was unheard a million years ago during the Savagery Period. As shown in Figure 1.1, sometime between the middle and upper stage of the Barbarism Epoch, the idea, or thought of high self-esteem, was weakened, and reduced to an hitherto low level, by the beginning of the Civilization Epoch. The CoDependency Addiction Thought likely emerged during this time also.

D. Emergence of CoDependency Addiction As An Effect of the Overthrow of Mother Right

During the transition from Feudalism, which was associated with the upper stage of the Barbarism Epoch to Capitalism, at the beginning of the Civilization Epoch (See Figure 1.1), there arose a more formal and more intense method of exploitation of the labor of a human being, particularly those known as working-class people. Man's inhumanity to man/woman was problematic during the Barbarism Epoch 800,000 years ago. However, in order to more effectively and systematically extract the value and surplus value out of man and woman's labor product on a continuous an uninterrupted basis, during the rise of the Capitalist System shortly after the downfall of Feudalism, an Institution of European Style Slavery was introduced in the so-called New World known as the Americas.

As we have already witnessed, the position of the mother was greatly undermined, and significantly so, when her position, as the central and dominate figure in the Gens, or family, was torn apart and replaced by Father Right due to major changes in the organization of social production at the time. For a million years during the Savagery

---

[64] Ibid., p. 66.

Period, All-foodstuffs and instruments of production, simplistic in form as they might have been at the time, were controlled by the mother. The downfall of the mother was equivalent to a right jab to her head by a World Heavyweight Champion Boxer. This concussion sent a shockwave through existing society at that time, and it has continually had a rippling effect, from one generation to the next-through time and space-right up to the present time-2020.

That being so, and without going any deeper into this compelling history here, our intent is to briefly establish the existing linkage between the American Slavery Institution and Codependency Addiction Behavior. Because Memory Outlives the Cell (See Figure 1.2), a purposeful intention of the slave owning class, during the 18th and 19th Centuries, was to strategically impact the mind of the African Slave in such a way that the male and female's connection to each other would be severed and to Nature itself. The effects of this method are still subconsciously at work in the minds of African-Americans, Whites, and other ethnic groups. The basis for the information to follow comes from the Willie Lynch Letter, which was published in the August 23, 2005 issue of The Final Call, the national newspaper of the Nation of Islam, United States of America.

a. CoDependency Addiction And The Infamous Willie Lynch Letter

According to this source, Willie Lynch "...was a British slave owner in the West Indies [who] was invited to the colony of Virginia in 1712 to teach his methods [of mind control] to slave owners there."[65] Before we consider the fundamental premises of the Willie Lynch Speech, and its influence on the origin of CoDependency Addiction, it is necessary to challenge Professor Keith Heingburg's assertion that the "... "Willie Lynch Speech" and its assumed influence...authenticity and widespread adoption during the slavery era is nothing more than a modern myth."[66] The primary reason Professor Heningburg gives for

---

[65] _____"Willie Lynch letter: The Making of a Slave," Final Call, August 23, 2005, p. 22.

[66] Heningburg, Keith, Professor, "THE DEATH OF THE WILLIE LYNCH SPEECH," https://www.scc.losrios.edu/ethnicstudies/willie-lynch/, Sacramento

the non-existence of the Willie Lynch Speech is "the "Willie Lynch Speech" is not mentioned by any 18th and 19th century slavemasters or anti-slavery activists. There is a large body of written material from the slavery era, yet there is not one reference to a William Lynch Speech given in 1712…Frederick Douglas, Nat Turner, Olaudah Equino, David Walker…Richard Allen…were African Americans who initiated various efforts to rise up against the slave system, yet none cited the alleged Lynch speech."[67]

This claim of the non-existence of the Willie Lynch Speech is baseless and void of truth because it grossly overlooked the fact it was definitely not in the interest of the slave masters to publicly reveal the existence of the Willie Lynch Letter inasmuch as it was a *political tactic aimed at destroying the minds of thousands of African Slaves in order to keep them docile and productive without any claims related to a violation of their human rights.* The Willie Lynch Letter was classified information before so-called intelligence-intell-information became a household word used by American Government Officials to keep secret all information the modern day wage-slave-owners need to keep secret from working class people. In short, Professor Heningburg, and his colleagues got it wrong. Now that we know why the Willie Lynch Speech was kept secretive for several centuries during the American Slavery Institution, and thereafter, we shall proceed and provide a brief breakdown of its major components, which indicates how they laid the critical foundation for the development of CoDependency Addiction, and many others related psychological maladies.

b. Methodology Used To Transform the African Slaves
From An Inter- dependent Human being to One With
A CoDependency Addiction To The Slave Master

Of utmost importance toward the psychological production of African Slaves, who are totally dependent on the slave master, is the employment of a number of differences among them. Willie Lynch

City College.
[67] Ibid.

encouraged the use of this divide and conquer tactic. He stated "I guarantee every one of you that if installed correctly it will control the slaves for at least 300 years."[68] Actually, his method continues to control the modern day African-American today. One might think Willie Lynch's Method is highly complex. It is neither complex nor complicated, but it is simple, profound, powerful, and it lays at the core of all human emotions, namely, Fear, Distrust, and Envy (FDE). To implement his insidious method of mind control, Willie Lynch encouraged the slave master to divide his African Slaves along the lines of the following: (1) Age (2) Color or shade (3) intelligence (4) size (5) sex (6) sizes of plantations (7) status on plantations (8) Attitude of slave owners, where the slaves live–hill, valley, East, west, North, or South (9) Hair, fine or course, and tall or short. These demographic variables were used to sew division and suspicion among the African Slaves. The overriding purpose was to weaken them emotionally; create a rift between them; separate male from female; female from male; establish measures of self-worth that can never be achieved by either, and sever each one from their source of existence–Nature. Willie Lynch assured the slave masters that his mentioned method would create the desired CoDependency Addiction in the mind of every African Slave based on the fact "…distrust is stronger than trust and envy stronger than adulation, respect or admiration. The Black slaves after receiving this indoctrination shall carry on and will become self-refueling and self-generating for hundreds of years, maybe thousands."[69]

CoDependency Addiction is an observed manifested behavior in the African Slaves notably when they no longer trust one another; but, to the contrary, "…your slaves trust and depend on us. They must love, respect and trust only us."[70] The CoDependency Addiction induced in the African Slaves caused them to love their slave masters and hate themselves and their children. *They loved their slave masters out of their*

---

[68] _____"Full text of "willie lynch letter 1712, "https://archive.org/stream/ WillieLynchLetter1712/the_willie_lynch_letter_the_making_of_a_slave_1712_ djvu.txt, p. 1.

[69] Ibid., p. 1.

[70] Ibid., p. 1.

desperate need to survive! This is a classic trait of a person in our American society today, who is suffering with a CoDependency Addiction.

In order bring this unnatural change about, where African Slaves were made codependent on their slave masters only, the Willie Lynch Method required the latter to use some of the most inhumane techniques to destroy the self-esteem and self-worth of his slaves. The terrorism employed to produce CoDependency Addiction in African Slaves was planned and approved for implementation by the slave masters. Willie Lynch warned them they would not be able to escape the horrors, and he further told the slave masters they would be "conscious of the injustice and wrong they were every hour perpetuating..."[71]

Since the CoDependency Addiction Disease could not be developed in every African Slave all at once and simultaneously, Willie Lynch Method called for an example to be made of a few to condition the behavior of the many.

c. Making Of The CoDependency Addiction Disease
(CAD) In The Minds Of The African Slaves

To make the CAD, Willie Lynch asked the slave masters listening to his speech this question: "What do we need? First of all we need a black nigger man, a pregnant nigger woman and her baby nigger boy. Second, we will use the same basic principle that we use in breaking a horse...What we do with horses is that we break them from one form of life to another that is we reduce them from their natural state in nature."[72] An attempt to sever-cut-off-any living being's connection to nature is the same as cutting the tap root of an Oak tree; strong as it is, the Oak Tree will die in a matter of days! In addition, Willie Lynch added "whereas nature provides... [horses, etc.] with the natural capacity to take care of their offspring, we break that natural string of independence from them and thereby create a dependency status, so that we may be able to get from them useful production for our business and

---

[71] Ibid., p. 1.
[72] Ibid., p. 1.

pleasure."[73] Once the mental processing, or brainwashing–is completed, the African Slaves remain dependent on the slave master for his or her survival, and he or she spends the rest of their waking hours, until their deaths, sacrificing for him.

Willie Lynch warned the slave masters that "…both a wild horse and a wild or nature nigger is dangerous even if captured, for they will have the tendency to seek their customary freedom…Hence both the horse and the nigger must be broken; that is breaking them from one form of mental life to another. Keep the body take the mind! In other words break the will to resist."[74]

At this point, Willie Lynch told his attentive listening audience of slave masters that "…the breaking process is the same for the horse and the nigger, only slightly varying in degrees."[75] We are not going to go into any of the horrible details of the Willie Lynch breaking process used on a sample of African Slaves as an example to all others, which demonstrated they must give up their *independent minds for a codependent one* on the slave masters, if he or she intended to survive. This is where the modern day thought of "GO ALONG TO GET ALONG" first originated! We highly recommend you read the Willie Lynch Letter of 1712 for yourself. The initial breaking process of the African Slaves' minds involved all of them on a plantation be assembled in a chosen location by the slave master to watch the "meanest and most restless nigger"[76] be literally tied to two horses; set afire; and then be ripped apart when the horses moved in opposite directions. All the other male African Slaves were then beaten with a whip to the point of death in front of their female African Slave Women. This was done to show her that she could no longer depend on her African Slave Males for protection and security but now only on the slave master himself.

In sum, given the fact we already know that memory outlives the cell, the Willie Lynch Breaking Process was consistently used by the slave masters for more than 500 years, and the imprinting of Codependency

---

[73] Ibid., p. 1.

[74] Ibid., p. 2.

[75] Ibid., p. 2.

[76] Ibid., p. 2.

Addiction in the African Slaves' mind has continued to ripple down through the generation to the present day. It should also be pointed-out here that the general White population that benefited from the Southern Slavery Economy also were conditioned to be codependent on the slave master for their survival. The same was true in the Northern Factory Economy, where thousands of American wage-earners depended on the capitalist factory owners for their survival. Thusly, their minds were also contaminated with the CAD.

Moreover, we clearly see that the CAD originated out of the historical economic condition that prevailed at a given moment in American History. Yet, many intellectuals today still have not taken the time to research this connection so they can expand their research and beliefs beyond their myopic thinking that postulates that the CAD's origin lies inside of a relationship in which a codependent partner and an enabler exist in a perpetual antagonistic struggle for many years, inclusive of lying, denying, and blaming, among many other self-destructive and passive aggressive actions aimed at tearing down the self-esteem of the person who is not codependent in the relationship.

Lastly, my relationship with E ended in separation because the CAD's was examined by her through a very narrow lens, or straw, which inhibited her from understanding that the CAD did not originate in our relationship, nor in her biological family. Instead, because the Willie Lynch Breaking Process had reduced her childhood to one in which she received no love and attention from her biological parents, E could not see beyond her wounds and emotional injuries to consider the possibility that something else was the cause of her CAD, although to survive, she lied to herself that the socialist philosophy we studied together could help her see beyond her immediate pain, but those were mere empty words. E was unable to sustain an historical study of where her biological family came from, and others, and the impact American Social and Economic History had on them.

What this narrow-minded thinking did to our 36 years relationship is outlined in more detail in the following Chapters of this book.

CHAPTER FOUR

Codependency, Alienation, And The Lost Self: Perfectionism, Public Persona, And Fraud

T he foregoing information traces the historical evolution of man and woman's life activity, from the Lower Stage of the Savagery Period to the Civilization Period. Conscious development increased right alongside the various inventions and discoveries made by man and woman during this long period of social and economic class development. The overthrow of Mother Right opened the door for the re-direction of power away from the woman to the man. When Mother Right exited the stage of world history, the Pairing Family disappeared and the Monogamy Family replaced it.

As we have already seen, alienation became a psychological problem, given the fact, for more than a million years before the overthrow of Mother Right, *women nurtured their infants throughout their childhood, or early years.* CoDependency was unknown during this time! It was unheard-of due to the fact women were the matriarchs of the tribal family, and all of the life-supporting resources necessary for survival were disseminated by her. *This means all of the children given birth to by mothers in the tribe automatically had enough food, clothing, water, medicine, and shelter among others to survive.* Therefore, nurturing of the children by the mothers in the tribe was a priority! Interdependency was the intended result. That is to say, each newborn grew up into adulthood knowing "who Am I; and, this meant each child was taught by his or her parents how to *love the Self.*

Having instilled this crucial knowledge in their newborns, the latter were, then, able to share his or her love with another human being in the tribe and so on through the next generations, or insofar as long as their nurturing the newborns was a high priority and sustainable. In short, by the time the child reached adulthood, he or she was keenly aware of Self and of the need to take responsibility for the satisfaction of one's own feelings and needs. In other words, it was unheard-of, before the Monogamy Family, that a time had come afterwards during which the mother and father, or mother-surrogate, stopped consistently "nurturing" their own children, thereby placing them at-risk. In many Monogamy Families children do not learn, at an early age, "Who They Are" as human beings, nor do they learn the importance of taking responsibility for their own feelings and needs.

Of all the manifestations emotional trauma can cause regarding a mental health breakdown, for the parents or mother surrogate, which are transmitted, by the latter to their newborns within the Monogamy Family-some are listed here-but not limited to them, such as obsessive compulsive behavior, anxiety, fear, anger, control, denial, delusions, and depression among many others. All of these disorders come under the umbrella term commonly known as CoDependency, which is the primary subject of this Chapter and those that follow it. What does CoDependency mean?

A. CoDependency Defined

According to Lancer, "addicts obsess about their "drug" of choice, whether it's alcohol, food, or sex…Codependents do that in relationships. Their lives revolve around someone else-especially those they love. Their loved ones preoccupy their thoughts, feelings, and conversations… they react to everything, put aside what they need and feel, and try to control what they can't." [77] Melody Beattie wrote "a codependent

---

[77] Lancer, Op. Cit., p. 7.

person is one who has let another person's behavior affect him or her, and who is obsessed with controlling that person's behavior."[78] The common denominator in any definition of Codependency Addiction is an affected person sacrifices his or her own feelings and needs, and places an undue amount of sustained attention on another person's or group. On the surface this behavior may not appear to be harmful, but below the surface, the codependent person commits a serious, and sometimes, irreversible injury to his or her personal well-being. That being so, what aspect of the being of a codependent person is seriously injured?

B. The Core Self Is The Core of CoDependency Addiction

The Self is the heart and soul of a human being. The Self is the engine that drives one's life towards ever higher creative outcomes at every age during the life journey. For example, M.F. Ashley Montagu, in his landmark book titled, The Direction of Human Development: Biological and Social Bases, 1955, wrote "a human being should be a work of art. He [or she] can be turned into a work of art by other human beings who are artists, and thus learn to become an artist himself [or herself], an artist who, in turn, works continually to improve himself [or herself] and help others to improve themselves."[79] As long as the person is in contact with his or her Self, and so long as it is unfettered by any form of deprivation during early childhood save an unavoidable genetic defect, he or she would be expected to grow into an increasingly conscious aware person based on one's creative life activities. In short, if there are limitations, or deprivations that interrupt the development of the Self during the early months of childhood and thereafter, it follows that the Self of an affected person will experience pain and suffering, and the latter will diminish one's prospect of fulfilling his or her mission

---

[78] Beattie, Melody, Codependent No More: How to stop Controlling Others and Start Caring for Yourself, Hazelden Publishing, 1986, p. 34.

[79] Montagu, M.F. Ashley, The Direction of Human Development: Biological and Social Bases, Harper & Brothers Publishers, New York, 1955, p. 305.

on Earth, and simultaneously inhibit self-actualizing as a human being who is, from birth, a work of art in the making.

Metaphorically, the Self is synonymous to our sun in the Milky Way Galaxy. Every planetary object, including the Earth, revolves around the sun; it plays a central, leading role toward maintaining life on Earth, for example, through the never-ceasing Law of Attraction and Repulsion. The Earth is attracted to the sun to receive its life-giving energy, and it is repulsed by the sun to prevent life on Earth from being destroyed by keeping it from getting too close and overheated by the sun. Similarly, a person's Self is his or her *core*, and if the latter is not actualized by an infant during the first year of life, the affected infant will inevitably become emotionally unstable, and increasingly emotionally dysfunctional; and, without the unconditional love of his or her parents, or mother surrogate, the former will *regress inward and consciously repress one's Self behind a sealed-off wall of mounting denial, setting into motion unintended consequences in the future.* More will be mentioned about denial later.

For now, it is crucial that we establish, without any doubt or uncertainty, that the infant's Self is even more important to his or her personal well-being than its heart or lungs, which pump life-blood throughout the body while simultaneously transporting oxygen to billions of cells, and, in the process, removing toxic waste from it such as deadly carbon dioxide. Plainly speaking, someone with a perfectly good heart and lungs will place both of these vital organs at-risk over time, if their inner Self is repressed during a majority of their lifetime.

D. Fraud And The Alienated Hidden Core Self

In the end, when a person's core Self is buried on the inside, the inevitable outcome of this self-destructive behavior is he or she becomes codependent. A person with a healthy Self is in constant communication with their feelings and needs in their *gut, namely, he or she is in communication with their primordial past incarnations.* One is able to give this love with another human being. On the other hand, if the Self is being repressed, this connection is not being actively utilized to create one's life. Rather, Lancer wrote *"a codependent is a person who can't function from his or her innate self and instead organizes thinking and behavior around a substance, process, or other person(s)"*[80] When I did some self-reflection, I realized there were a number of "red flags" that popped up over the years that pointed to E's disconnect with her inner Self. One was every time we planned to spend some intimate time together, E would make sure we had some type of substance to use that would shift her attention away from her feelings and needs. This was a persistent pattern during the 36 years we were in a relationship together. We always, being under the influence of this or that substance, talked about non-reality such as other dimensions, or anything that did not deal with our personal feelings, needs, and reality at that moment. There are others which will be shared later in this book. It is timely to mention here that "nothing written in it" is aimed at attaching E's, or anyone else's integrity; every word is designed to demonstrate how CoDependency Addiction took a destructive toll on E and L's relationship. Due to E's closely held secret about her CoDependency Addiction over the years, many of her family members and friends are probably surprised to learn she has been challenged by this problem since her childhood.

Returning to the repressed Self of a codependent, Lancer explained the role of this substance diversion away from reality when she wrote "codependents have adapted and reacted to others' behavior in order to cope, instead of referring back to the internal impulses of the Self. Over time, these impulses became obscured and veiled by a proxy personality and the ability to access them weakened."[81] The less Self-Referral E did related to her feelings and needs, the more the world of her Self shrunk. Imagine being in a room with the four walls constantly closing in on you? At best, this narrowing of the Self inevitably generates feelings of anger, anxiety, and terror. E, regardless if it was a sunny day at 12 Noon, she would always gasp for breath when I walked into an area of the house where she was unannounced.

---

[80] Lancer, Op. Cit., p. 31.
[81] Ibid., p. 32.

L recently learned that E's startled reaction to me has nothing to do about her being potentially harmed by an external stranger. The stranger is her alienation and estrangement from her concealed, repressed, an abandoned Self. Without knowing her genuine, authentic Self, E is consumed with fear; and, therefore, the slightest change in her immediate environment was enough to scare her. Being alienated from her inner Self, E, on one hand, has shutdown her feelings and needs-her true Self; and, on the other, being alienated from her authentic Self, E attached herself to L's feelings and needs, or those of other friends and persons in the empowerment group she spent 20 years of her life facilitating. E's feelings and needs have confronted her as something alien because the latter do not belong to her but other people she participated in *survival codependent behavior to survive throughout her childhood and adult life especially.*

As it has been for E for the past 36 years, she has lived her life clandestinely alienated from her own genuine, authentic Self, within which everything that makes human beings social and loving creatures, such as self-esteem, deservedness, enough, validation, and worthiness among many others, were summarily repressed deep on her inside. As we have formerly mentioned, in order to cope, E attached herself to L's feelings and needs and others in her community. In order to successfully engage people, and get them to believe E was expressing her own feeling and needs when she was not, E developed a public personality for the community. Lancer wrote "to be acceptable to others and to themselves [codependents], you hide who you are and become who you aren't...Even though you may not relate to this, it still operates beneath your conscious awareness."[82] E created a public persona among her circle of friends in her community that is second to none.

She spoke of herself having the *greatest compassion* for someone else no matter how difficult the predicament someone else was in; she always spoke glowingly of her love for everybody; she always told people no matter what the outcome of a situation was they were in, detach from it *for the greatest good*; she always explained everything

---

[82] Lancer, p. 8.

within the context of the *Law of Attraction*, and seldom, if ever, did I ever hear her say to a person in my presence that it could be possible that something is going-on deep inside of the recesses of one's Self that could be causing their pain and suffering. Any abstraction of reality was fair play, and E carefully walked the tightrope always steering away from personal self-disclosure.

E facilitated a Women Empowerment Group (WEG) for more than 20 years, and during this time, not once (!) when I ask her what did she say about her own Self during this or that session, E consistently told me that "time ran out and she did not get a chance to talk about her own shortcomings, injuries, wounds, and feelings she experienced during her childhood, and how they may have caused her to bury her Self within her core. E was so *perfect, that is, her public persona*, that our daughter, H grew up and majored in psychology because there was always an external conversation going-on in our household dealing with what this or that individual need to do to correct their behavior. E did not have a grasp of Psychology when we got in a relationship in 1979; by mimicking L's knowledge of Socialist Philosophy, and due to the fact she had a CoDependency Addiction, E was able to memorize intellectually how to explain this or that social problem.

Although these things were all a part of the window dressing of an abstract reality, L failed to act on any of them because E was so passionate about her external focus that I kept waiting to see what the outcome might be. Clearly, this was a mistake on my part. On those occasions when I did challenge E about her external focus on other people (Sometimes she would get on the telephone before mobile telephones became vogue/popular and talk with a caller for 2 to 3 hours at a time), she and I would end up in an argument again and again. Over the years, I simply gave up on trying to get her to explain herself about why she was spending so much time talking to other people about their personal problems.

L became exhausted and stopped making more attempts, which I knew were going to deteriorate into another argument, if pursued. L stayed in the relationship as long as he did to help H grow up; get a good education; and get her doctoral degree. All the while, in some fantasy somewhere in my mind, L thought the fog would lift and one day E would come home from a facilitated group meeting and say she discovered something about her inner self that had her locked into the external feeling and needs of other people. That never happened though!

As L pondered what this external focus was about, recently, after E had a stroke in July 2015, a close friend of E's suggested it was all about *fraud*. At first, I laughed replying "you've got be kidding me, right? Then, as time passed, and after E told me two years after her stroke, for the very first time in her life and mine, that she is codependent, and after I started to seriously study and learn more about what Codependency Addiction means, L was able to see two years after E's stroke that her projected public persona could be defined as a fraud. Webster's Ninth New Collegiate Dictionary, 1984 defines fraud as follows: "An act of deceiving or misrepresenting: Trick…One who is not what he pretends to be: IMPOSTOR…One that is not what it seems or is represented to be."[83] Lancer added "some codependents complain that they feel like "a fraud." Or that they experience a gap between their public and inner selves. When you can't connect to your Self, you find it hard to identify feelings, make decisions, and set boundaries. You react to people and situations and look to others for answers, validation, and approval. Sometimes you may feel resentful, lost, and confused, which leads to depression."[84]

Moreover, over the years, E would often ask L if he felt abandoned because my biological mother did not raise me during my childhood. On the surface her inquiry seem to be an appropriate one, but now L know E's question about abandonment came from her fear of being abandoned by me, given the fact that her own mother and father did not provide her with any nurturing during her childhood. At best, E received the same attention from her mother and father that a child

---

[83] Mish, Frederich C., Webster's Ninth New Collegiate Dictionary, Merriam-Webster Inc., Publishers, Springfield, Massachusetts, U>S.A., 1984, p. 490.
[84] Lancer, Op. Cit., p. 32.

in foster care might receive. Lancer wrote "codependents remain in unhappy relationships because of the pain of rejection and loneliness."[85]

Because of their lost Self(s), and E's in particular, or the gap that exists between their "public persona and repressed inner Selves," and, as we have seen above, E, from the time she was born, progressively became alienated from her authentic Self, and in its place, she created a perfectionist personality primarily centered around *overdoing for me and other people hoping one day the gap between the latter and her authentic Self would disappear, and miraculously, she would be free of every mental and physical imbalance caused by her failure to express her genuine feelings and needs.*

At this point, everything we have discussed so far has prepared us to now address the grand question we are all wondering about, namely, where does Codependency Addiction originate?

---

[85] Ibid., p. 32.

CHAPTER FIVE

Mother, Infant, And Codependency: Origins And Development From Birth Through Adulthood

As we proceed with our discussion of Codependency Addiction, with an emphasis on the part played by the mother during the childhood of her infant children, we shall take a close look at what happens to a mother's infant after her *umbilical cord is severed*, at once releasing her infant into the world, and each moment afterwards, regarding what a mother does for her infant, will, no doubt, play a deciding role toward determining the life-potential of her infant. This vital connection cannot be overstated in its overwhelming importance! What the mother does for her newborn infant ranks just below her baby's inhalation of oxygen and exhalation of carbon dioxide in importance. As we have already seen in Chapter One, for more than a million years, Mother Right was the traditional mode of rearing children in the gens, or communistic family. This was decreed by nature itself because literally, *no child was left behind during the Savagery Period through the Lower Stage of Civilization.* However, when the latter came into existence on the world stage of human history, mother right had already been overthrown by father right and replaced by the Patriarchal System in the Monogamy Family.

Although these historical events took place, we are, nevertheless, compelled to examine the role of mothering of her infant children in today's Monogamy Family to see if we can discover exactly "...where codependency comes in,"[86] or how Codependency Addiction originates within the new invisible, *nurturing,* umbilical cord that exist between mother and infant, or between the latter and a mother surrogate. This invisible, nurturing, umbilical cord, if interrupted due to a breakage in the mother-infant relationship, the infant is placed at high risk of not learning anything about the Self. That is, he or she is placed at-risk of not learning what love is due to the absence of a Mother's Hand.

A. Mother, Infant, And Dependency

Earlier, we made the case that all human beings are social creatures. This fact has been true since the beginning of human life on Earth. The deciding factor whether an infant becomes a healthy, balanced social creature rests with his or her mother. The greatest work a mother will do on this Earth is nurture her baby from a dependent state of existence at birth to an interdependent one by the time he or she moves out childhood into their adulthood. Montagu wrote "the fundamentally social nature of all living things has its origin in the physiological relationship between parent and offspring which is embraced in the reproductive relationship...The dependency of the newborn is a continuation of the dependency of the fetus, a dependency which has its origin in the once inseparable connection between the organism and that other organism out of which it grew."[87] In essence, an infant, both in utero and at birth, is according to Montagu, "...entirely *dependent* upon the maternal organism for its sustenance, for the satisfaction of its needs...At birth the dependent relationship simply becomes a more externally active process on the part both of the newborn and the maternal organism or its substitute."[88] Montagu goes further, and drills down farther beneath the surface, so even the greatest skeptic will agree that every infant, barring any significant birth defect(s), is

---

[86] Ibid., p. 33.
[87] Montagu, Op. Cit., p. 161.
[88] Ibid., p. 161.

given birth into the world by his or her mother in a completely 100% dependent state of being. This is completely normal. Montagu wrote "to be dependent means to rely upon some other person or persons for the satisfaction of one's needs...The child is born in dependency, and it also learns that it is dependent...Interdependency is the social state. Nondependent individuality is the non-social state."[89]

Foremost, the mother is the socializing agent to which her infant child is bound. Montagu wrote "the process of caring for the infant consists principally in satisfying its needs. The process represents the commencement of the socialization of the person, the preparation of the person for participation in the social group...This view of the development of the person cannot be too strongly emphasized."[90] No matter what else is said from now on about the mother, she is the world to her dependent infant. The same is true of a newborn calf; its mother cow must, without fail, prepare her calf to standup and walk within a few short hours after its birth. As a young boy growing up on a large farm in LA, I witnessed mother cows repeat this nurturing skill after giving birth to their calves. If she fails, no doubt, predators will consume her calf, if the mother and calf cannot move a distance safely beyond the birth site. The elixir is a dependency of the infant on its mother's love.

B. Mother Love For Her Infant

It is within the orbit of love that a mother's infant revolves around her ever connected to his or her source of love similar to the way gravity holds the Earth, and other planetary objects connected to the sun. As we mentioned earlier, this linkage between mother and infant cannot be too strongly emphasized. If an asteroid, for example, frees itself from its gravitational linkage with the sun, it will plunge toward Earth, and in a matter of a few seconds, it will burn up in a brief ball of streaking fire somewhere across the Earth's Atmosphere. The mother love, or a mother

---

[89] Ibid., p. 162.
[90] Ibid., p. 170.

surrogate love, for her infant must remain intact, avoid disruptions as much as it is humanly possible, and be unconditionally given to him or her, consistently and appropriately, from birth of an infant through the latter's childhood. Montagu wrote "the greatest treason that one human being can commit against another is to fail him [or her] when he [or she] most needs…[their mother]"[91] The withholding of mother love, or that of a mother surrogate, is not only the greatest treason the former can commit, but what is equally detrimental to a mother's infant is the creation of a feeling of betrayal inside of the latter, which, oftentimes, influences the behavior of the affected infant well into his or her adult life. When all is said that can be, and there is more we will say on this subject, the opportunity cannot be passed up here to further add evidence to the power a mother love has on the development of her infant. Montagu wrote "normally…the infant receives its love from the person best qualified to give it, the mother."[92] Central to a mother being able to give love to her infant is, first and foremost, her own basic needs must be met.

In his book Historical Materialism, 1954, Maurice Cornforth wrote "before people can do anything else, they must obtain the means of life-food, clothing and shelter…Only on the basis of associating to produce and exchange the means of life can they develop and pursue any other of their social interests…[politics, science, art, religion, spirituality, and most important of all-reproduction of themselves in the form of children]."[93] *It is a prerequisite that in order for a mother to love her infant, she must, prior to the birth of her infant, have had her basic needs met during her own childhood, and the former must continue to be met during the moment when mothers give birth to a new generation of children and so forth.* This abundance frees the mother up from the harshness and grind of trying to piece together basic needs from little or nothing. Having to do so seriously affect the mothers' personal emotional stability as well as her emotional connection to her infant. Montagu wrote "to love, one must

---

[91] Ibid., p. 176.
[92] Ibid., p. 201.
[93] Cornforth, Maurice, Historical Materialism, International Publishers, New York, 1954, p. 35.

be emotionally involved with the loved one–unemotional love is *not love*...and this emotional involvement must be conveyed to the loved one. To love is to confer developmental and survival benefits upon... [her infant]."[94] For clarification, this does not mean if a mother has had her basic needs met over time, and has sufficient basic needs available for her newborn infant at birth, that she will be able to give her infant love that offers developmental and survival benefits. We already have seen due to the downfall of mother right in world history, and the rise of the Patriarchal System at the outset of the Monogamy Family, the mother has been relegated, since then, to a greatly diminished position in her family. No doubt, her emotional capacity to nurture her infant, regardless of socio–economic status, has been impaired as we shall see later. Therefore, it is unmistakably crucial and necessary that a mother give emotional love to her infant because, by doing so, this is how the infant learn to love his or her Self.

C. Mother Love Of Infant Creates Self-Love And It Empowers Infant To Learn To Love Another Person

There is no other way for a human being to love his fellow human beings, if, in the very first place, his or her mother did not teach the former to love one Self during the early years of childhood. Montagu wrote "the infant can suffer no greater loss than the privation of its mother's love, for...the satisfaction of the generalized feeling of dependency, in itself a basic need, is best accomplished through mother-love. An old Egyptian proverb says that since God could not be everywhere He created mothers."[95] Love is not something that can be talked into existence; purchased with a diamond ring or fancy car; even granted with the reception of a Nobel Prize! Montagu added "the importance of love in the early social development of the infant cannot be overemphasized...The emotional need for love is as definite and compelling as the need for food. The basic needs of man [and woman]

---

[94] Montagu, Op. cit., p. 176.
[95] Ibid., p. 201.

must be satisfied in order that he [or she] may function on the organic level."[96] That is to say, if an infant is to self-actualize as a human being, who clearly recognizes Self-Love, and has been made consciously aware of this non-negotiable fact, the former must receive sustained and adequate love from his or her mother first! And, not infrequently but daily during childhood! Montagu wrote "the infant obtains satisfaction for its physiological needs, the need for oxygen, the need to feel, the need to move, the need to suck-all needs quite as strong as the need for food-from the mere act of contact and being held, carried about, and fondled by the mother. Such acts are indispensably necessary if a well-equilibrated child is to develop."[97]

Thus, in one of his most popular and deeply resonating songs, namely, One Love, the King of Reggae, Bob Marley sung "Could you be love and be loved?" The answer to this critical question hangs in the balance of the Scale of Justice demonstrating on one side of it an affirmative answer, and on the other side, a negative one, if the mother did not love her infant during the dependency state of existence. Montagu wrote "by being loved the child learns to love...by being loved the child in its turn learns to love."[98] This outcome, which set the compass for the infant the rest of its life on Earth, is set in motion under the nurturing direction of mother love. Montagu wrote "the inner requirements of the infant are such as to cause him [or her] to want to be loved and to want to love others, and the basic needs of the infant are structured to function in this manner. The infant expects to have its needs satisfied, and when the infant's needs are satisfied it develops as a loving, cooperative, harmonic human being-that is, as a healthy human being."[99]

No matter which way a coin is flipped, whether it lands on heads or tails, and in either case, a mother's infant must be given unconditional love by his or her caregiver in order for her infant to realize that all of his or her satisfactions are derived from mother, which stimulates her

---

[96] Ibid., pp. 200 and 245.

[97] Ibid., p. 257.

[98] Ibid., pp. 249 and 260.

[99] Ibid., p. 290.

infant to take pleasure in reciprocating her love. Anything short of this development of a mother's infant will cause one to be unable to love others. The infant's super-ego is, therefore, paralyzed in the absence of the development of the love relationship with his or her mother, and this allows the infant's ego to takeover, which makes it nearly impossible to form loving relationships with others, either as *friends or intimate partners*. Montagu wrote "in short, unless the infant has an opportunity to develop object-love, that is, to recognize and value the mother or mother-substitute as a person from whom love and all its satisfactions are derived, and comes to take pleasure in reciprocating her love, he [or she] will never learn to love others."[100] For the mother's infant to learn how to love Self and others, he or she must remain in close contact with the mother during the first hours, days, weeks, months, and years of its early life. The point here is important and must not be overlooked: Without mother's love, CoDependency Addiction is in the making inside of the affected and unloved infant during childhood.

D. Mother And Infant Connection During The First Few Days Following Birth

Having spent his or her first nine months of life in utero connected to the mother by the umbilical cord life-line, during the birthing process, the infant is thrust out of the womb by the mother. For several months, the fetus enjoyed the warmth and security of the mother's womb. However, once the mother frees her infant from the warmth and security of her womb, the attending doctor, or mid-wife, severs the umbilical cord, and now the newborn infant must begin his or her life journey in a totally "dependent state." While in utero, the mother supplied all of the fetus' basic needs. She must continue to supply all of the newborn infant's basic needs, from the first moment after birth throughout its childhood years, of course, in ever-changing forms. Montagu wrote "the dependency of the newborn is a continuation of the dependency of the fetus, a dependency which has its origin in

---

[100] Ibid. p. 231.

the once inseparable connection between the organism and that other organism out of which it grew."[101] After birth, the mother's infant "… needs the presence of a loving, solicitous voice, the warmth and softness of touch of its mother's body. Bevan-Brown considers the infant's experiences at the breast of fundamental importance for its subsequent healthy mental development."[102]

That being so, the mother must be in close contact with her infant, similar to the close contact shared between fetus and mother before birth. In fact, Montagu wrote "the infant must be in close association with the mother for the first hours, days, weeks of life, so that whenever he wakes he has the feeling of security."[103] The single most important desire a newborn infant has is a *feeling and need, which cannot be spoken or written, yet it is as real as the sunshine at 12 Noon on a clear blue sky day,* namely, the satisfaction of all of its basic needs by its mother. Montagu wrote "the satisfaction of its basic needs becomes indissolubly associated in the infant's mind with persons who have become linked with those satisfactions. The mother is…normally the principal producer of satisfactions and she becomes the first love-object of the child."[104]

During the first hours and weeks after a mother's infant is born, the latter "…is born in dependency, and it also learns that it is dependent… [and,] To have one's needs satisfied is to be loved and at one and the same time to learn to love."[105] Much of the discussion about a mother and her infant and the former's satisfaction of all of her newborn's needs reduce itself down to one indispensable fact, and that is, *security.* Moreover, when a mother supplies all of her infant's basic needs all of the time, regardless of age during his or her childhood, this creates an inner feeling within the infant that his or her mother is one's caregiver of the most important substance known, which is love. Lancer wrote "mothers

---

[101] Ibid., p. 161.
[102] Ibid., p. 168.
[103] Ibid., p. 168.
[104] Ibid., p. 182.
[105] Ibid., pp. 162 and 163.

are wired to care for their children…This is because caregiving comes from abundance…"[106]

Abundance is a mother's realization that she has the personal power to satisfy all of her children's basic needs, regardless of how many she has to provide for. Montagu wrote "the biological basis of love consists in the organism's drive to satisfy its basic needs in a manner which causes it to feel secure. Love *is* security-but security alone is not love. Mere satisfaction of basic needs is not enough. Needs must be satisfied …in a manner which is emotionally as well as physically satisfying."[107] It is a gross simplification, for example, for anyone to say that during my childhood, as E shared with me many times during the past, "I always had food to eat" and "clothes to wear" although there was an absence of emotional and physical touching of her by her mother and father during her childhood. This view glosses over social reality similar to the way a thrown rock skids across a frozen ice pond. Holding this viewpoint, the fundamental basis of social life is violated which is, according to Montagu, "the basis of all social life has its roots in this integral of all the basic needs which is expressed as the need for security, and the only way in which this need can be satisfied is by love."[108]

In the absence of emotional and physical touch, an infant is denied the feeling of being a positive part of his or her family, and, what is more devastating is the lost of "…dependent security, the feeling that one is part of a group, accepted, wanted, loved, and loving; the positive freedom which makes…self-actualization…and finally, the opportunity to develop interdependently, not as an "individual" but as a person."[109] When E and L got together in Baltimore, Maryland in 1979, L was heavily engaged in a study and practice of socialist philosophy, which was a carryover from my years of graduate study in Colorado a few years earlier. Once E and L had a conversation during the many late night ones we had on the subject, and during one of them, L mentioned human beings are social creatures, and their collective history is made by

---

[106] Lancer, Op. Cit., p. 35.
[107] Montagu, Op. Cit., p. 244.
[108] Ibid., p. 244.
[109] Ibid., p. 182.

their cooperative interaction with each other during social production. Based on this premise, L added it is compelling that we freely take a deeper look into it; however, surprisingly, L was met with E's strong resistance; and, being at an early stage in my own personal social growth as a person at the time, who was searching for the social threads that inseparably tie human beings together in commune-community, L failed to clearly understand what E was telling him about her own view of herself.

What threw L off balance is E did not share with him her experience as a neglected infant, which L found out about more than 36 years later after she had a stroke, who was not *emotional and physically touched by her biological parents during her childhood.* E told L in 1979 that she had a "wonderful" childhood, and there was nothing she could point to that was vaguely injurious to her self-actualization as an interdependent person. However, cutoff and hidden behind a repressed wall of pain and wounds, underneath this repression of the Self, or behind E's veil and smoke and mirrors, was an opposite emotionally traumatic childhood, which did not nurture her into any realization of her inner Self as a loving being, and this distorted her ability to see her Self as *being love*, which she could give to another person, for the purpose of *being loved.* Therefore, when we had the earlier conversation L mentioned related to social philosophy; E insisted she was an *individual and that she would not ever give up her belief that this is who she perceived her Self as being.* Because L was still socially and, and in many ways, politically naïve, L did not grasped the deeper meaning of E's belief in individualism, which, as we have already seen, is a *myth.* Being young and excited to push forward with the study of social revolution and change, L made a decision in 1979 that, far from my awareness then, would come back to haunt him in a devastating way. This was the red flag waving in L's face that he needed to act on to end the relationship with E, from the beginning. Individualism and social revolution do not mix like oil and water. L failed to act erroneously feeling E would wake up from her individualism dream. L made a big mistake because individualism is the same as independent, and the latter stands counter-opposed to social revolution and change. Moreover, the individual does not understand he or she is a social creature whose destiny on Earth is revolutionary change. E resisted letting go of individualism because it is synonymous with CoDependency Addiction. E told L in 1979, when they got together in Baltimore, MD, that she did not have any residual childhood issues; more accurately at the time, E had many hidden childhood carryovers in her life. L did not know this is what E's motivation for clinging to individualism was driven clandestinely by. More on this topic will be presented later.

Presently, it is timely to provide more information that emphasizes the infants' development, from the first weeks of life through the sixth year and beyond.

E. Early Childhood Development During The Formative Years: First Weeks To Sixth Year And Beyond

The compounding of mother love, during the early years of development of her infant, cannot be overstated nor over-emphasized. For example, tomatoes are a spring and summer vegetable crop, and the latter cannot be planted in the field during the winter where the temperature averages 40 degrees. The point is once the normal outdoor growing season has passed, the tomato plant will not grow. Similarly, once the early critical weeks, months, and years when a mother nurturing of her infant has to be done, and if those times during which such nurturing are missed, then, like the tomato plants, the infant will grow abnormally-both emotionally and physically. Bowlby wrote "... it is in the first few years of life that the pattern of later parent-child relationships is laid down. The troubles of adolescents are no more than the reverberations of conflicts which began in these early years. Difficulties which are unsolvable at 13 may be handled quickly and effectively at three."[110] Montagu added "...within the first two years or so of the child's life determines the primary pattern of his subsequent social development. It is within this period that he learns to love others;

---

[110] Bowlby, John, <u>Maternal Care &Mental Health</u>, Jason Aronson Inc., Northvale, New Jersey, 1995, p. 89.

the mother…has consistently, intimately and lovingly attended to his [or her] needs…the father…has participated in the process of satisfying his [or her] needs."[111] The father is a part of the working class. We saw earlier that when mother right was overthrown and replaced by father right or Patriarchy, those fathers, who own vastly more of the surplus value of the labor product, participated less in the nurturing of his infants, given more of his attention was placed consistently on getting more money, and controlling the growing sums under his control. Table 1.0 below shows the critical early developmental stages that an infant grows through, which succeed one another, from a low to high order of development.

Table 1.0
Critical Developmental Stages

STAGES	BEHAVIORAL DEVELOPMENT
Five to six months	Infant in process of establishing a cooperative relationship with mother
Six months to the end of the Third Year	Child needs mother's ever-present support and companion
Fourth and Fifth Years	Child maintain a relationship with Mother in Absentia
Sixth to Eight years	Development of social competence and ability to make friends

Source: Montagu, M.F. Ashley, The Direction of Human Development: Biological and Social Bases, Harper & Brothers Publishers, New York, 1955, p. 211 and 243.

As we see, if all goes well for the infant, by the end of the fifth year of his or her life, the latter is moving visibly through the dependent state in which he or she was born into toward becoming an *interdependent being*. In order for an infant to successfully reach the latter social status, everything depends on the mother or mother surrogate (The role of the father is also important, and it becomes even more so as the child grows

---

[111] Montagu, op. cit., pp. 181 and 182.

older). The only way to achieve this human status is the mother, or mother-surrogate, must play a supreme role in the early life of her infant similar to the United States Supreme Court, where all other courts seeks its guidance, if a legal dispute cannot be resolved at a lower level.

F. Importance Of Mother Or Mother-Surrogate

At birth, the infant receives irreplaceable nourishment and stimulation from the mother's body. Placing a bottle filled with artificial milk in a baby's mouth is simply not the same as a baby feeding at its mother's breast. Montagu wrote "...the mother's body activate every sustaining system of the body: the alimentary, the endocrine, nervous, the genitourinary, and particularly the respiratory system."[112] Thus far, I have referred to myself in this book as L, and I will continue to do to the conclusion.

My biological father passed away when L was 8 months old; my biological mother was 25 years old when he made his untimely transition. Being present of mind, my mother brought L to live with his grandmother in LA. L was born in Oakland, CA. L's parent surrogate, his grandmother and aunts took turns holding him; playing with him; touching him constantly; feeding him; and L's grandmother, at the appropriate time, introduced him to farm life on her 50 acres farm. L's grandmother taught him how to love himself, and love others by teaching L how to nurture other animals on the farm and plant life. L was able to transfer his feelings of love of Self to other people as he moved toward becoming a young adult. Montagu wrote "the best place for the infant is with its mother, and if its own mother is not available, with a warm foster mother [or parent surrogate], for what the infant must have is love."[113] After being in our relationship over 36 years, E shared with me that her mother and father did not touch or speak to her during her entire childhood.

---

[112] Ibid., p. 168.
[113] Ibid., p. 200.

What happens to an infant who goes through this experience, and as we just observed, Montagu informed us that an infant must be loved by the mother. As we already have seen, the privation of maternal, or mother surrogate, love is the greatest loss an infant can ever experience in a lifetime! If the loss of maternal or mother-surrogate love, in particular, and if this loss is internalized and repressed by its host, one day, whether it is five years or thirty-six years after the loss of love initially occurred, the memory of the loss of the mentioned love will contaminate every *present experience* of an affected adult later in life. *Usually, this situation cause irreparable communication failure in a relationship.*

Many infants, who do not receive their mother's love during their childhood, will suffer an inability to make *friends*. Without having the glue, that is, love that cements friendships together, the affected child becomes either manic-depressed or withdrawn. In either case, the affected infant, especially those who develop an engaging personality, often attract a lot of people to themselves in search of their mother's love; friendship is not a priority although, superficially speaking, it is the conduit through which an external search for love takes place. Montagu wrote "it cannot be too often repeated that in the dependency relationship of the child to its mother, and later to the father and older persons, is to be seen the primary socializing pattern, a pattern which is variously elaborated throughout one's life…This at the same time lays the basis for later attitudes of friendliness, affection, and trust."[114] Regarding the importance of the mother's love, especially during the earliest weeks and months of her infant's life, Bowlby wrote "…what is believed to be essential for mental health is that the infant and young child should experience a warm, intimate, and continuous relationship with his [or her] mother (or permanent mother-substitute) in which both find satisfaction and enjoyment."[115]

The absence of mother love, or that of a permanent parent surrogate, may not seem to have much, if any, long-lasting affect on the infant's mental health. Later, we will address how privation of

[114] Ibid., p. 262.
[115] Bowlby, op.cit., p. 11.

mother love, or permanent parent surrogate love, during the earliest stages of child development actually mushroom into serious behavioral problems later in adult life. According to Lancer, "experts agree that codependent [mental illness] patterns are passed on from one generation to another..."[116] For the moment, our intention is to provide more evidence of the importance of mother love by addressing how it is the source in which an infant first discovers he or she must cooperate.

G. Fundamental Cooperative Act

One of the great cornerstones of the American Capitalist System is competition. Many Americans falsely believe that competition is a part of their human nature; however, nothing could be farther from the truth. Competition is an acquired behavior, and it is closely connected to individualism, a myth, which we discussed earlier. Montagu wrote "competition is an acquired, not an inborn, drive...Competition is... certainly not a basic need of any kind."[117] It is plainly inhuman behavior carried-out between individuals, who believe, erroneously, that by out-competing his or her fellow human being, somehow "getting more and winning" will bestow greater social status on one over the other based on the former acquiring more inorganic material things than the latter. The root of competition and individualism is a by-product of a mother's, or parent surrogate's, failure to satisfy the basic need an infant has for love. Such a gross failure then predisposes the affected infant to a pattern of life in which he or she is unable to establish lasting friendships and, most importantly, give love to other human beings. Montagu wrote "men [and women] who do not love one another are sick-sick not from any disease arising within themselves, but from a disease which has been enculturated within them by the false values of their societies. Belief in false values, in competition instead of cooperation, in narrow selfish interests instead of altruism, in atomism (especially atom-and hydrogen-bombism) instead of universalism, in the value of things and money

---

[116] Lancer, op. cit., p. 7.
[117] Montagu, op. cit., p. 148.

instead of the value of life and of man [and woman], represents man [and woman] turning upon all that is innately good in him [or her]."[118] So, we do not have to search too far now to recognize that the mother and parent surrogate play a central role in the creation of cooperation in their children, and therefore, this mother-infant relationship directly determines whether a healthy or sick society is created over time.

For instance, Montagu wrote "social, cooperative behavior is the continuation and development of the maternal-offspring relationship; it is therefore as old as life itself..."[119] which, as we have already seen, extends back more than a million years to the beginning of the Lower Stage of the Savagery Period. It was during this period in world human history when Mother Right prevailed! Cooperation has its biological basis in the mother-infant connection as was the case with every newborn during the Savagery Period while mother right was in effect. As we see, cooperation is not something that can be taught; it is produced inside of the Self of an infant with active, sustained mother love. Montagu wrote "the biological basis of cooperation, in short, has its origins in the same sources as social behavior, namely, in the process of reproduction."[120]

The first act of labor of humankind on Earth is the recreation of a new generation of offsprings. Montagu added cooperation is a "... part of [human beings'] protoplasm."[121] This simply means, though the point is very profound, namely, cooperation is an inseparable part of the DNA of human beings, and as a matter of fact, human nature is designed by nature as a safeguard against human beings becoming extinct, although, as it seems today, we are well down the path headed toward self-destruction. Many Americans have a built-in cooperation trait in their DNA, but, *to date, the vast majority still have not learned they are social creatures wired to cooperate to insure the continuation of human life on Earth.* Moreover, Montagu wrote "without the state of infant dependency human love would not be what it is, and without those

---

[118] Ibid., p. 247.
[119] Ibid., p. 247.
[120] Ibid., p. 247.
[121] Ibid., p. 247.

affective bonds which tie one human being to another it is more than doubtful whether there could ever have been any future for the human species."[122]

The key is inside the kernel of the seed of the reproductive act itself, along with the mother love given to her infant, from the second it is born throughout its childhood. Montagu wrote "the infant soon learns that in order to be satisfied, in order to be loved, he [or she] too must love, he [or she] must satisfy the requirements of others, he [or she] must cooperate."[123] *Without mother or mother-surrogate love, the socialization of her infant cannot be achieved,* and this adds one more person to a growing number who still think they are individuals, whose purpose on the Earth is to argue, fuss, and fight with anyone about everything. As a cooperative human being, namely, one who has been loved and cooperate, peace and harmony fills his or her life. Montagu wrote "the first fulfillment of the infant's drive to receive love from the mother constitutes a fundamental cooperative act...The organism is born with an innate need for love, with a need to respond to love, to be good and cooperative."[124] L did not learn until recently, i.e., 2017, that E, his partner in relationship *was not touched or spoken to by her mother or father during her childhood!* L was devastated to learn E went through such an emotionally traumatic experience! Yet, for more than 30 years, L could not understand why he and E argued all of the time; *we argued so much that our daughter H told us she did not want to be around us, at the same time, because we argued all of the time.*

L does not know how he went through this antagonism and conflict for so long? For example, now I understand that due to a lack of mother love and father love, it has been nearly impossible for L to get E to help him produce vegetable crops through the years. The more I encouraged her to give it a try, the more resistant she became. So, I ended up buying the seeds; planting the seeds; cultivating the plants; doing pest management chores; harvesting the fruits and vegetables; cleaning them for either food preparation or storage in the freezer. L

---

[122] Ibid., p. 184

[123] Ibid., p. 199.

[124] Ibid., pp. 169 and 243.

could not get minimal cooperation from E. But, I man-hauled forward anyway erroneously thinking and feeling E would one day see the value in this farming activity, and miraculously take an active interest in it. That day never came; in fact, that day, similar to the headless horseman charging, with his long sword drawn, toward the turning windmill, which receded farther and farther into the distance like a mirage on a blacktop highway on a sunny day. Similar to the Sisyphus Stone, everyday Sisyphus would roll his huge stone nearly all the way uphill, for it to roll down the hill again-over and over. L believe he has been successful, to a large degree, with his farming activities because L aligned himself with an active farming community, which provided him motivation and courage to get up and return to the field to work the next day. L dearly see how great cooperation is, and how it was turned into an on-going antagonism for more than 36 years E and L have been together in a relationship. The arguments were a projection tactic used by E to make it seem as if L is unkind, insensitive, a bully, and dominant. All of these denials were used by E to hide her CoDependency Addiction to L!

In a nutshell, L's struggle to get E interested in the natural environment proved futile although Karl Marx discovered more than a century ago that human beings are social creatures because they must socially interact to produce their subsistence, and in the process of social production, their interactions alter the natural environment significantly. Little did L know that E had experienced some serious emotional trauma during her childhood, which significantly influenced her ability to self-actualize the cooperation trait in her DNA. Montagu wrote "the dominant principle which informs all behavior which is biologically healthy is love. Love, social behavior, cooperation, and security mean very much the same thing. Without love the other three cannot exist."[125]

Therefore, the vast majority of the time E an L spent together usually ended up in this or that conflict because only mother and father love, or that of a mother-surrogate, could serve as a moderating and

---

[125] Ibid., p. 247.

socializing agent. What else could E do through the years, if her *reference point* is perpetually one of *insecurity*? Unlike E's relationship was with her mother, Montagu wrote "what the developing child apparently needs is a stable and continuous development in relation to its mother or mother-surrogate. The stability and continuity must be prolonged, and not…interrupted."[126] Unfortunately, E kept her earl and *impaired relationship* with her mother and father a secret from L; he has concluded, after studying Codependency Addiction, that E's fear of abandonment overrode her ability to share her pain and suffering with him because she likely felt L would discontinue his participation in the relationship. The tragedy in both of our lives should be very clear by now, namely, E's failure to receive love from her mother and father short-circuited her ability to love herself, and this led to her inability to love L. Everything else was what L call theoretical and fantasy love.

What, then, may we ask is essential for mental health?

Bowlby wrote a thoughtful response to this important question. He wrote "it is now demonstrated that maternal care in infancy and early childhood is essential for mental health…Deprivation in infancy and early childhood is an experience which deranges it to a severe degree…"[127] The earliest years of infancy are critical to the development of mental health in families, which to the degree mother love and mother-surrogate love exist, the society at-large will manifest harmony and peace or disharmony and disease. Bowlby added "…what is believed to be essential for mental health is that the infant and young child should experience a warm, intimate, and continuous relationship with his [or her] mother [or mother-surrogate), in which both find satisfaction and enjoyment."[128] Underlying this nurturing environment, which we can easily call the infant's external household womb after birth, is the production within the latter of feelings and needs one comes to recognize as his or her own, owing wholly to mother or mother-surrogate love. As we have repeatedly shown, the infant grows into becoming aware of Self as love, which, in due time, he or she makes

---

[126] Ibid., p. 212.
[127] Bowlby, op. cit., p. 59.
[128] Ibid., p. 67.

use of it to form friendly, co-operative, secure, and loving relations with other human beings. Bowlby wrote "the outstanding disability of persons suffering from mental illness, it is now realized, is their inability to make and sustain confident, friendly, and co-operative relations with others."[129] On the other hand, the opposite pole of CoDependency Addiction is cooperation.

Because a codependent person is unable to sustain confident, friendly, and co-operative relations with others, the *inner world* of the latter is shutdown, regarding knowing and being in constant touch with one's own feelings and needs. These are the social prerequisites necessary to sustain one's life; however, without the use of them, for example, E was only able to survive by attaching herself to L's feelings and needs, and, in order to give the impression she was contributing to decision-making on a daily basis, she developed a controlling personality aimed at micro-managing L's feelings and needs through a process of deception that involved conflict and antagonism.

By engaging in continuous antagonistic behavior during more than 36 years, L tried to reconcile the long line of conflicts in our relationship by thinking *something was wrong with his feelings and needs, if E constantly presented an antagonistic viewpoint about them.* In short, L was constantly making adjustments to his feelings and needs in order to resolve an argument with E. Stated another way, E used L's feelings and needs, and by thinking they were her own, which is a cornerstone of Codependency Addiction, she used them and turned whatever situation was being discussed into an argument in order to overshadow the fact that E was not expressing her own shutdown feelings and needs. *The end result inevitably was always an argument to control L, for the purpose of getting through another day.* Over the years, E would often repeat this phrase: "Oh, what a beautiful web we weave, when first we choose to deceive" (I am only paraphrasing here). But, looking back through the years, L has come to understand E's use of this phrase was as a way for her to gauge if I was still asleep, regarding whether he had become aware that she was not expressing her repressed feelings and needs that are,

---

[129] Ibid.p. 91.

to a large extent, still shutdown and locked-up inside of her wounded Self today. L has also learned that all of the arguments were merely repeated attacks on L's self-esteem inasmuch as one of the cornerstones of Codependency Addiction is low-self-esteem and low self-worth.

Tragically speaking, a gross miscarriage of creativity and opportunities lost went on throughout the more than 36 years we were in a relationship. A few major opportunities lost are discussed below.

H. Opportunities Lost: An Effect Of CoDependency Addiction

It was approximately 1986 when E an L returned from Oakland, CA to establish a residence in St. Martin Parish in Louisiana. Before we left Oakland, CA, and while L worked for the City of Oakland, CA, some money was saved for the purpose of purchasing several acres of land when we returned to Louisiana. After securing public school teaching employment, a search for land was undertaken. When we examined the Teche News Newspaper, which was a popular outlet for the circulation of land for sale opportunities in St. Morgan Parish, we came across a land for sale advertisement in the newspaper posted by MK and G M. At the time, they were farming 110 acres of land in LA. However, by 1986, the prices of commodities such as corn and soybeans fell to a very low level, and MK and G M were forced to begin selling some of their land to try to make up the difference in the low prices of corn and soybeans they produced. E an L called MK and G M, and we took an instant liking to each other, and they sold us five acres of land, which we still live on by January 2019. The sell of a small number of acres of their land did not get MK and G M out of the red. As the price of commodities continued to decrease throughout the mid-to-late 1980s, and by 1993, they were forced to sell all of their 110 acres of land, or risk losing everything as a result of bank foreclosure.

That being the case, and because E an L had become close friends of MK and G M, the latter gave *us first option to buy all of the 110 acres of their land*. Sometime in 1993, while L was working for the Department of Public Safety and Corrections in Baton Rouge, LA, G M called E, and informed her that she and MK had decided to sell their 110 acres of land to us, thereby keeping their word that they would give us first option to buy at least 100 acres of land. At the time, an unbeknownst to L, E did not share the fact that G M called her about offering us first option to buy 110 acres of their land for $60,000, which is all G and MK M owed on the 110 acres of land when the bank placed it in foreclosure proceedings. Since E did not share this opportunity to buy the 110 acres of land with L, another person bought it, who I will refer to here only as Mr. N. The latter and L became good neighbors and maintained good neighborly relations throughout the 30 years we have been next door neighbors. Once L found out that Mr. N bought G and MK M's 110 acres of land for $60,000, L told Mr. N he had made a great deal! However, toward the end of 2018, L had and unplanned encounter with G M in the Wal-Mart Supercenter located in Brentwood Crossing, LA.

G M spoke about the old days when they farmed their land before selling it to Mr. N. Out of curiosity, L ask G how did the land sale unfold. And, *she shocked me into speechlessness when she told me that she called E and asked her if we wanted to buy the 110 acres of land?* L did not know what to say other than to ask G M if she is certain she called E and gave us first option to buy the 110 acres of land. G M told me she is certain she called E; gave us first option to buy the 110 acres of land; and E told her we were not interested in buying the land. L turned this new revelation over in his mind for at least two weeks before he gathered enough courage to call G M and ask her again if she was positive she gave E an L first option to buy the 110 acres of land for $60,000. When L called, G M told him the exact same story, only adding that when we turned down the purchase of the land, she offered it to other residents, who live in the neighborhood where E an L resided. And, G M told me no one wanted to buy it.

Having this knowledge G M shared with L about the opportunity to purchase their 110 acres of land for $60,000, one evening L calmly asked E about whether G M actually called her and gave us the first option to buy the land. E told me she did receive a call from G M related to us being the first option to purchase the land. However, when L asked E why she did not share G M's message about the first option land sale with him, nothing could have prepared him for E's response. E told me that *"she felt I was too busy working for the Department of Public Safety and Corrections to buy the land and care for it; and furthermore, what would we do with all that land anyway because we did not need it."* This is a manifestation of the codependent behavior that was going-on in E and L's relationship from the beginning! Clearly, E, being codependent, did not express her own feelings and needs about the potential land sale, but she expressed to G M what E thought were L's feelings and needs and not her own. E's Codependency Addiction led to the lost of an opportunity for us to purchase 110 acres of land for $60,000, a sum that is miniscule relative to what the 110 acres of land are worth on the 2019 real estate market. *For example, if an acre of land is sold for $20,000 today, and if we sold 110 acres, the sale price would be $2,000,000! This is by any measure, a great opportunity lost!* What is at the root of this opportunity lost is the failure of E's mother and father to love her during her earliest years as an infant and throughout her childhood. This is how Codependency Addiction destroys a relationship and people-both directly and indirectly. As we shall discuss in detail later, one of the biggest characteristics of a codependent person is an inability to respect the boundaries of another person. Rather than E give L an opportunity to consider the purchase of MK and G's 110 acres of land, she inserted herself, once again, in L's mind, and in some ungodly manner, unilaterally decided for L that he did not need to buy MK and G's land.

E's CoDependency Addiction to L was fully at work beneath her conscious mind. Although E claims she did not know she was suffering with a CoDependency Addiction problem to L, in truth, she knew, from moment to moment, during the 36 years she and L were in a relationship, exactly how she felt deep-down on the inside of her Self, and, at all cost, she was determined to maintain her clandestine hold on L's feelings and needs to survive- "By Any Means Necessary."

Another key opportunity that was lost is a failure to establish a friendship with Oprah Winfrey in 1979, while she was employed by a local Baltimore Television Station as an anchor for the 5 PM evening news. When L first saw Oprah Winfrey in this role, L and E were living together in Baltimore, MD in its Golden Ring Community located in the county. L told E he was certain Oprah Winfrey was going to become a huge Television Star. It was just a matter of time because L recognized Oprah Winfrey's calm and very easy command with the use of the spoken language to penetrate inside of a problem; dissect it; and then present a clear analysis and conclusion. L expressed Oprah Winfrey is someone we need to befriend. Being a woman, L deferred to E as the one who would reach out to Oprah Winfrey to determine if we could sit down and talk about our social philosophy, get to know each other, and, hopefully, become friends. At the time, L was heavily involved in researching and writing a book about the history of capitalism in the United States, and he was employed by a certain University full-time.

The opportunity to make friends with Oprah Winfrey went nowhere. What L did not know in 1979 that he understand clearly in 2019, is it is nearly impossible for a codependent person to make friends because of the mother love he or she did not receive during the dependency stage of infant development and thereafter. It should be pointed-out here, however, that codependents can either be withdrawn or highly gregarious, oftentimes presenting themselves as happy, loving, compassionate, and helpful to others. L now knows this attitude does not foster true friendship development, but it is an endless, external search on the part of the codependent person, to find the love his or her biological parents, or mother-surrogate did not give to their infant at a critical stage in their early childhood development. In short, Oprah Winfrey, as L anticipated, left her Baltimore, MD Anchor Position, and relocated to Chicago, IL, where, in a short time thereafter, she became the hostess of the Oprah Winfrey Show, which became commonly known as Oprah, and the rest is history. L did research on the relationship between diet and health as part of the history of capitalism book he researched, wrote, and published.

As early as 1980, L had discovered the linkages between diet and various catastrophic diseases such as heart disease, cancers of various types, and many others. It would be easy for E alone, or as a duo with L, to create themselves as national presenters of health information that people could use to cure an existing array of illnesses, or take preventive action to guard against becoming challenged with this or that disease. But again, no action steps were taken by E to weigh in on the coming wave of the American Public's interest in its health condition, which we were on the cutting edge of by 1980. This is not bragging; we were truly trailblazing! Rather than demand we take some creative action to position ourselves to become leaders in the coming proliferation of diet debates, this opportunity, like the others hitherto mentioned, went unaddressed. E, and as codependents often think, do not feel they deserve to be listened to, or that they have something good to share, which grows out of their mother-infant disfunctionalism learned in their family of origin.

By 2000, L published a book titled <u>Triumph of The Spirit</u>. It was written to excavate any issues that affected his life during childhood and thereafter. When the book came out, E and L made plans to work together as a spiritual team aimed at assisting couples and groups with challenges in heir relationships, or with problems they experienced in their families. Again, here we were, both E and L planning to help others when, unbeknownst to L, there was a serious, long-standing problem brewing in E an L's relationship, which was carried over into it from E's childhood. We produced flyers, posters, took pictures together-All-designed to *inform the public that we were ready to help anyone with their most difficult life challenges.*

Again, nothing ever became of this idea. Nothing at all! By 2000, L worked for a local university; doing research; writing more books; traveling to Africa and other countries making presentations; and this gave L little, if any time, to build a spiritual team with E. Because L did not throw his feelings and needs into the effort, and because E's feelings and needs were repressed deep inside of her wounded Self, that idea died before it got off of the ground. Other opportunities to do book signing were also forfeited.

Another opportunity that nearly got lost, like all of the others, was the national Black Farmers Class Action Lawsuit, namely, Pigford vs. USDA. In short, this was a lawsuit filed against the federal government's USDA, claiming that Black Farmers, for decades, were overlooked for loan assistance by the USDA due to racist practices, the most devious of which was the destruction of loan applications, by local Agricultural Extension Services Offices nationwide, which were filled out by Black Farmers for assistance to improve their farming practices and crop production. Starting around 2003, L filled out an application to become a part of the mentioned class action lawsuit. When L did so, E repeatedly told him *"I do not see why you are spending your time on this lawsuit because nothing is going to ever come out of it regarding financial compensation."* L became angry with E's negativity!, but he proceeded to fill out any forms the federal government, or its lawyers, required him to complete through the years. L did this all by himself with no help from E. Absolutely none!

After five or six years, and by the beginning of the Obama Administration's second term, the U.S. Congress passed the legislation, which provided financial compensation to Black Farmers involved in the class action lawsuit. *And, in September 2009, the federal government sent a check to E and L's house written for $50,000. E could not believe L's years of work preparing the paperwork the federal government required resulted in a positive outcome!!*

As usual, there was no celebration of L's accomplishment; E did not share L's joy and happy feelings; E hardly put a smile on her face!! L was now really confused about what was happening in our relationship. L did not know E could not express any feelings and needs of her own because her own Self, in which her feelings and needs reside, was completely repressed by E. L needed to address E's cold response to the $50,000 check because that check paid off all of our bills!! But, L did not address the problem. Today, however, it must be addressed because E's codependent illness blew up like a dormant volcano in July 2015, and similar to lava flows out of it, the origin of E's codependent childhood has, since 2015, taken center stage.

And, unfortunately, all of the opportunities lost discussed thus far are explained by the privation of love E experienced in her childhood, and particularly, the lack of love E received from her mother and father. L know *E's childhood history now* but has too much damage been done to E's personal well-being and L's to put the pieces of a broken glass back together? This reminds me of the nursery rhyme "Humpty Dumpty." It says Humpty Dumpty sat on a wall; Humpty Dumpty had a great fall; and all of Humpty Dumpty men could not put Humpty Dumpty back together again." The pieces of E's and L's relationship have been scattered all over the place through the years, and my intention is to continue to dig deeper and deeper into CoDependency Addiction, and continue to investigate how E's codependent behavior has impacted her, myself, and our relationship.

The list of opportunities lost is long, but I will share one more because of the fact this one consumed more than twenty years of E's time, namely, Women's Empowerment Group (WEG) Sessions.

Roughly 20 years ago, E, and one of her girlfriends, attended a workshop organized by Iylanya Vanzant, who is a well-known Family Therapist. Currently Iylanya Vanzant has a show on the Oprah Channel that deals with "fixing" people lives. E returned from the Vanzant Workshop motivated to replicate something similar to the workshop she participated in facilitated by Iyanla Vanzant. After feeling out who would be interested in participating in a women's only workshop to help them fix their life challenges, a core group of about 10 women became involved and E became its facilitator. No compensation was exchanged for the work E provided to the Women Empowerment Group (WEG). E called upon the social philosophy-study and research-we did in Baltimore, MD in 1979, which E cleverly intermixed, like a gumbo, by adding in religious metaphysical idealism. E used the socialist philosophy L introduced her to as the well from which she drew "high sounding words, which were deformed because of the absence of any practical application to life. It should be pointed-out here that E was adamant that no males could regularly participate in the WEG sessions. Initially, L resisted this decree because he felt males needed to share their ideas along with their companions and friends. But, E was not hearing any of the male participation idea! L has come to realize that the reason E was against male participation is her childhood secrets would no longer be safe. As her partner, L would ask questions that could unravel her CoDependency Addiction to L.

As the years passed by, and during the early years of the Women Empowerment Group (WEG), it was not uncommon for the latter to meet 4 or 5 times per year. The meetings did not last 2 hours, but usually, they lasted from 5 to 8 hours per session; and eventually, the Women Empowerment Group started holding their meeting at a local hotel in Lafayette, LA, which allowed its members to meet well into the night and during the better part of the next day. After each meeting of the Women Empowerment Group, when E returned home, L consistently asked her what did she share with the group related to her life challenges stemming from E's childhood and into adulthood. Invariably, E gave me one consistent answer, which was–nothing! When L inquired about E's lack of sharing of her *feelings and needs with the members of the WEG, she always told me the time ran out, and she did not get a chance to disclose anything about her own Self.* Rather than challenge E on her non-disclosure of her feeling and needs, L, as part of his historical pattern of omissions and silence, gave E another pass. Although L was disallowed to participate, in any meaningful way, in the WEG, E invariably responded to any questions any of the WEG Members ask her, by nearly always prefacing any response to it with "L said this or that and so forth." As we see, this was her CoDependency Addiction to L playing out in real time.

After E's stroke in July 2015, she revealed to me a shocking revelation related to why she did not disclose anything about herself. E told me *she used the Women Empowerment Group to serve her own selfish needs in an attempt to obtain the love she so desperately missed receiving from her mother and father during her childhood.* L was dumbfounded when E shared with him what her underlying intention was, namely, to facilitate the Women Empowerment Group so its participants could tell her how wonderful, loving, and giving a person she is. What was even more striking to him is when L asked E did she realize what she told me about her intentions related to the Women Empowerment Group, she calmly replied–yes. Che Guevara summed up the error perfectly when he wrote the following: Here we are. We come to give you the charity of our presence, to teach you with our science, to demonstrate your errors, your lack of refinement, your lack of elementary knowledge… that the first thing we will have to do is not go offering our wisdom, but showing that we are ready to learn with the people…We should go with an investigative zeal and with a humble spirit, to learn from the great source of wisdom that is the people."[130]

All-in-all, rather than facilitating the Women Empowerment Group, and taking her group leadership to another level, the whole process repeated itself over and over for 20 years. After E's stroke, the group gradually met less and less. Nothing was off limit to E when it came to her desperate external search for love like a needle in a haystack.

One other situation worth mentioning related to opportunity lost, namely, household interior decorating. Throughout the 36 years or more E and L were in a relationship, L cannot remember E taking any initiative to decorate the interior of the home we lived in. Although the house we lived in had great potential be a warn, loving one, L ended up making at least 98 percent of the decisions related to what should be purchased and placed on the inside of the house. For many years, L thought this was wonderful that E would allow him to choose how the interior of our house would be decorated. However, as time passed, and one year blended into the next, the same non-creative energy prevailed. L needed to insist E take a greater role in interior decorating but he did not. He thought, "Why make a fuss about it because it is not a big deal?" By 2015, and thereafter, L realized it is a great big deal because E's interior decorating absence is but one more manifested branch on E's codependent tree.

"There are none who are so blind than those who refuse to see". And L *enabled E's hidden codependent life.* Many signs were flashing in my face like a yellow caution light; but, because L wanted E and his relationship to work, he ignored all of the codependent indicators, which sunk their relationship like the Titanic. When I learned for the first time about E claiming to be codependent, the news struck me like the Titanic when it crashed into a giant iceberg! L felt devastated, but not a victim (!) because L allowed himself to be deceived and manipulated. L take responsibility for that; hopefully, there is someone going down the road

---

[130] Guevara, Che, <u>CHE GUEVARA READER: writings on politics &revolution</u>, Duetschmann, David and Ariet, Maria del Carmen, Second, Expanded Edition (Editors), Ocean 2003, p. 117.

I walked for 36 years or more, who might be able to turn their situation around before it is too late ro do so. L shared this warning because once a person represses their Codependency Addiction for many years, it becomes like solid cement, and it is awfully difficult to breakthrough it. According to Nathaniel Hill's book titled <u>Outwitting the Devil: The Secret to Freedom and Success,</u> a hypnotic rhythm sets up inside the affected person's mind, and as a result of daily repetition during one's childhood in particular, fears, abandonment, insecurity, scarcity, low self-esteem, denial, and others become fixed in the infant's mind, which, unfortunately, makes change, for example, nearly impossible during a codependent person's lifetime.

Because E an L could not establish authentic co-operative relations with each other, she faked such relations, for example, with women in the empowerment group she facilitated for 20 years, and this condition contributed directly to the opportunities lost mentioned above and others not disclosed. Bowlby wrote "the potential ability to do this is as basic to man's nature as are the abilities to see and digest, and, just as we regard failing vision or indigestion as signs of ill-health and the results of trauma, so have we now come to regard the inability to make reasonably co-operative human relations. The growth of this ability, as has been seen, is determined in very high degree by the quality of the child's relation to his parents in his [or her] early years."[131]

The failure in E an L's relationship to establish authentic, co-operative relations with other people and groups, is directly due to the dominant presence of Codependency Addiction in it because the principal producer of satisfaction and love, who is the mother, failed to satisfy E's early feelings and needs for her mother's love. Not only did this failure predispose E to becoming codependent, it also was a major prescription for the later turmoil, lost opportunities, and emotional trauma, which diffused like a dark cloud that spread over every corner of our relationship. Montagu wrote "the relationships of his [or her] family life condition his [or her] personal relationships throughout his life."[132]

---

[131] Ibid., p. 91.
[132] Montagu, op. cit., p. 199.

The one thing human beings seek all of their lives is security-love. In short, if an infant was given love, he or she has it to give to another human being. The search for love all of one's life will become an external and nightmarish one, if his or her key-love-given by mother, father, or mother-surrogate-does not open the lock-love-of another person and vis-à-vis. If the key is not given to an infant at birth by his or her mother, or mother-surrogate, and if one's mother does not teach her infant how to use the love key, the latter's search for love will, as it must, inevitably end in one becoming codependent, and living the rest of his or her life never feeling what authentic love truly is. The love key is similar to the needle one searches for in a haystack (!) but never finds.

It has been known since the first Homo Sapiens learned to walk on the Earth with an upright gait that it is a vain, empty, fruitless, ridiculous, and hopeless attempt to seek love; it can only be experienced and realized through giving love to another human being first. For example, to drive your car anywhere, you must first shift its transmission into "D," and, then and only then, can you drive to your destination. For those with a standard transmission, one must first shift the transmission through a number of gears, beginning with the first one and so on.

CHAPTER SIX

Affects Of Maternal Deprivation On The Normal Development Of The Child During The Childhood Years And Into Adulthood

Thus far, we have spent some time stating, and restating, the importance of mother and father love and mother-surrogate love in an infant's life, literally beginning seconds after he or she is born. Before this discussion, time was allotted to the equally and extremely important role played by the mother in the tribe-gens during the Savagery Period of human existence more than 1 million years ago. We made it clear that during this time well into the Barbarism Period, mother continued to hold the supreme position in the tribe, gens, or clan. This meant all of the newborns for centuries were nurtured and loved by their mothers. Children were located in the tribe according to maternity. Not paternity. In recent times, the African Proverb, namely, "It takes a village To Raise A Child" has its origins in the million year old experience of the tribe, in which the women held the supreme position; and, the whole tribe contributed to the raising of the child/ren.

Those times have long passed. By the time of the Lower Stage of Civilization, the male in the tribe, given he owned the instruments of production and its products, and in view of the surplus product now under his control, along with a new desire to keep his products under his sole ownership, the male engaged in the First Known Revolution, during which he overthrew mother right, and replaced it with father right. From that time to the present day, the Monogamy Family came into being, along with the appearance in it of a *hitherto unknown inequality between man and woman called the Patriarchal System*. For the better part of the past 3,000 years, during which time, Civilization has been in existence, women have been casted down into a diminished almost slave-like condition in the Monogamy Family. It is within the context of this family type that CoDependency Addiction gained its initial and emotionally destructive foothold.

It should be clearly pointed-out here in order to prevent any distortions of the real facts, and that is to say, because of the rise of the Patriarchal System in the Monogamy Family, this change can serve as a justification for some females to choose to cease giving their infants love at birth and thereafter. Recall, we mentioned earlier that only a small percent of males in the United States own the vast majority of all financial resources, roughly 90 percent. This means the vast majority of working class people, who live in Monogamy Families, practice patriarchy in them, which allows its demeaning and harsh realities to adversely affect a mother's ability to nurture their offsprings. Before we consider the trail of social and emotional traumas caused by the production of codependent infants in this family type, Table 1.1 below demonstrates the movement of an infant from a dependency state to either one of interdependency being based on mother love and mother-surrogate love, or to a CoDependent state of being characterized by an absence of such love.

Table 1.1
Mother Love and Mother-Surrogate Love:
Determinants Of Whether Infant Develops Into
Interdependent Being or CoDependent Being

DEPENDENT STATE	INTERDEPENDENT STATE	CODEPENDENT STATE
Infant's basic needs satisfied by mother and mother-surrogate, and by whoever else participating in the process of satisfying needs.	Infant develops not as an individual but as a person belonging to a family.	Basic needs not satisfied by mother love or mother-surrogate love.
Humans most desire to have their basic needs satisfied.	Independence is a form of social poverty.	First two years of a child's life produces interactive behavior that determines primary pattern of one's subsequent development in life.
Infant desires to feel dependent, secure, safe, and feeling accepted as part of family; also, feeling wanted, loved, and helpful.	Dependent infant grows into self-realization one is love and capable of loving others.	Love not given by mother or mother-surrogate insures love transference to another human being is aborted, and the condition becomes nearly permanent due to hypnotic rhythm.
The first love-object of the infant is the mother or mother-surrogate.	Infant grows into co-operative adult, and forms friendly, warm, and social relations with others.	"…psychoanalysis can make so little headway with the person who has been unloved is that such a person is often incapable of transference…"★ of love to another person.
A dependent infant who is loved is enabled to self-actualize, and become aware of Self.	Co-operative human beings recognize they need each other to create their livelihoods, rather than one becoming dependent on the other to survive.	Co-dependent individual negates cooperation with another person.
Infant does not become aware of its needs unless it is not loved by its mother or mother-surrogate.	Interdependent person is able to express his or her feelings and needs in order to make good decisions.	Codependent person represses the feelings and needs inside of the Self, and attach to the feelings of another person, falsely believing the other person's feelings and needs are his or her own.

Source: ★Montagu, p. 183.

The summarization does not need much more explanation other than two types of children are produced in Monogamy Families, namely, those who have been loved and grow into interdependency, or those who become codependent. It is latter that is our focus. Particularly, the average American does not have an understanding of just how emotionally devastating Codependency Addiction is on the long-term mental health of an affected person. I was one of those average Americans, who, for more than 36 years, did not realize he was living everyday with a codependent person. Yet, after E's stroke in July 2015, L began a serious process of self-reflection, and to my surprise, I recognized many of the lasting effects of the psychological impacts of the absence of mother love, or mother-surrogate love have on the well-being of a person, and in particular on E, who claims she is codependent; although, since July 2015, L has been unable to get E to admit how the former condition has emotionally impacted her life. Worse, L has not been able to get E to take responsibility for holding her Codependency Addiction a secret within herself, for more than 36 years; and, also what is more emotionally unsettling, L has not been able to get E to take responsibility for how her Codependency has destroyed the social fabric of our relationship. Whenever the subject of responsibility is brought up by L, and time after time, E would become emotional, most evident by speaking an elevated voice tone, and saying to L, "Oh, I see where this conversation is going, and I am not having it." E would then abruptly walk out of the room. This is a classic case of denial, and a refusal totake responsibility for her CoDependency Addiction.

Many of the factors discussed below played a big part in the downturn in E and L's relationship.

A. Psychological Impact Of The Absence of Mother Love and Mother-Surrogate Love On The Development Of A Distortion In The Psychic Structure Of The Codependent Infant's Ability To Love and Be Loved

The primary path, along which a mother-love and mother-surrogate love must flow to their offsprings is, during the parenting process, *an infant must not be allowed to become aware of its basic needs.* However, if an infant becomes aware of its needs, unfortunately, the former will experience increasing trouble getting through the dependency state. Montagu wrote "the evidence indicates that from birth onward the direction of the human being's drives is toward cooperation...If... we interfere with the development of those drives by opposing to them requirements that are antagonistic toward the development of cooperativeness, these drives tend to become deformed and weakened, while at the same time conflicts, are engendered within the psyche which produce great personal and social disoperativeness."[133] The infant only become aware of its basic needs, if it is unloved.

It is within this earliest moment of an infant's childhood in which the die is cast, which will determine whether the infant develops into an awareness that he or she is a social creature; one's entire life is predestined to be social; and the infant matures into an awareness his or hers' core Self is love, which serves as an immunity to competition and individualism. Instead, by giving love to other social creatures, he or she shares their authentic Self with them in the form of cooperation and interdependency. Montagu wrote "social, cooperative behavior is the continuation and development of the maternal-offspring relationship..."[134] In short, an absence of love, during the critical early days and months of an infant's life, and although such a lost may not be obvious at the outset, usually creates the mental soil in which the roots of serious deficits in the psychological structure of the infant are formed. E repeatedly claims she did not know she is codependent. CoDependency Addiction behaves like oxygen, one knows its there, but it cannot be seen.

Accordingly, Montagu wrote "children who have been deprived of the most important factor essential for normal development-that is, continuous and satisfactory contact with a person who can offer the opportunity for satisfactory identification-suffer a distortion of psychic structure."[135] Love is the engine of the socialization process, and

---

[133] Ibid., p. 297.
[134] Ibid., p. 247.
[135] Ibid., p. 188.

otherwise, "…that process often has the effect…of rendering the person functionally asocial."[136] Earlier, we mentioned those infants, who were not mirrored with love by their mother or mother-surrogate, become adults who have difficulty making friends. Bowlby added "in this way develops the unstable neurotic personality, unable to come to terms with himself [or herself] or the world, unable especially to make loving and loyal relationships with other people."[137]

In 1979, L left his wife and 2 year old son to establish a *loyal relationship* with E. At the time, L thought this was possible to do. However, ironically, *L did not know he was making a mistake because E withheld from him the fact that her mother did not give her any love when she was an infant, nor during her childhood.* E told L that she did not know her parents did not give her any love. This is the same as what Malcolm X said in a speech about Black People sitting at the Dining Room Table, but they are unaware that they are not being served any food while others at the table are enjoying a delicious meal.

On the surface, it appeared everything was orderly, but beneath it a gathering codependent storm was going-on of which L knew absolutely nothing about. Unfortunately, every decision L ever made in his relationship with E was made without any prior knowledge of the fact that whatever L and E decided to do, one day E's repressed Codependency Addiction would burst out of her repressed Self into their relationship like the water did from Lake Ponchatrain when the levees broke during Hurricane Katrina, which sent floodwaters all over a good part of New Orleans East destroying everything in its destructive path! The neurotic personality referred to by Bowlby earlier manifested itself in L and E's relationship through E and L's constantly reminding each other of our love for the other. We engaged in this behavior almost daily for more than 36 years even though, while doing so, E knew underneath the words of consciously reminding one another of our shared love, a negative codependent vibe lurked just

---

[136] Ibid., p. 189.
[137] Bowlby, op.cit., p. 26.

beneath E's repressed awareness of the trauma she experienced during her childhood.

Although E and L spoke about loving each other almost daily through the 36 years we were together, and because *E was not loved by her mother or father, she failed to learn from them she is love; and, therefore, it was impossible for her to genuinely love another person*, regardless of what her public persona led others to believe to the contrary. While this is very difficult for L to share, he would not do so, if keeping this information a secret would make it untrue. L is as astonished as you are, and actually, he is more astonished with E's codependent revelations because L lived in a relationship with her at ground zero! Those standing on the outside of our relationship do not know anything about what went on it over the past 36 years; how could they know because L was in the relationship itself everyday, and he did not know what was going-on beneath its surface.

Bowlby wrote "...parent-child relationships have many dimensions...arising from separation or outright rejection, in which they may become pathogenic...The commonest [one is] an unconsciously rejecting attitude underlying a loving one."[138] When L discovered this passage in Bowlby's research, it explained nearly everything that he had experienced in my relationship with E for the past 36 years or more. That is, although E told L repeatedly that she loved L, and she also told other people the same thing; the truth is she rejected her Self and L, and everything he stands for and accomplished. It did not matter if I published books; successfully got grants funded; paid off all of the bills with a lump sum payment; bought E a new car; made it possible for E to travel all over the world, from Africa to Western Europe and the Far East back to the Caribbean as well as Alaska, and the Grand Canyon among many others, L was, nevertheless, unconsciously rejected by E as a human being an unappreciated.

Moreover, for 36 years, E engaged in a pattern of self-rejection, which is caused by her Codependency Addiction. Although to anyone who will listen, she is quick to say she sis not know she was codependent

---

[138] Ibid., p. 13.

during this time. No human being can claim "ignorance of a disease, or dis-ease," as long as a feeling is connected to it. My mother, for instance, was sexually abused by her father, and when this emotionally traumatic event occurred in her young life, L is sure his mother did not know the scientific term associated with this particular abuse; yet, she, without a doubt, was constantly reminded of it occurrence, regardless of her age, as a result of her memory of it.

The greatest loss an infant can suffer is his or her mother, father, or mother-surrogate failure to love the former. As such, many effects borne out of a privation of love challenge the well-being of an infant. Before we discuss some of them, it is timely to document here that Codependency Addiction is a direct product of an absence of mother and father's love, or a mother surrogate's.

B. Origin Of CoDependency As A Byproduct Of An Absence Of Mother And Father Love, Or Mother-Surrogate's

The preponderance of the evidence leaves no doubt that love is the key ingredient necessary for an infant to progress from the dependency state he or she is born in to the interdependent state one achieves later in life. To the contrary, in any case where mother love or mother-surrogate love is absent, an infant experiences significant trauma to his or her Self. Bowlby added "it is submitted that the evidence is now such that it leaves no room for doubt regarding the general proposition- that prolonged deprivation of the young child of maternal care may have grave and far-reaching effects on his [or her] character and so on the whole of his [or her] future life...there is a curious resistance to accepting [the proposition]...But when all the evidence is fitted together [there] is no doubt that the main proposition is true."[139] One of the most damaging effects on an infant, who is deprived of mother and father love, or mother-surrogate's at the outset of life, is an absence of the development of *love circuits* in the brain.

---

[139] Ibid., p. 46.

That is, love must be given continuously to an infant where the frequency does not fall below a certain minimum. Consistency is critical. Montagu wrote "electrical circuits of certain kinds are not established in the neuronal net of deprived children because the necessary charges of energy have not been received. Such a child develops a neuronal net which is wanting in certain patterns of electrical circuits. If a child has not been loved it does not have any developed "love" circuits."[140] This is amazing information to L, given the fact for more than 36 years, L frequently wondered what made it so difficult for E to share her feelings of love for L from a deep place within herself. There was always a strain insomuch as L and E talked about love superficially, but when it came to expressing love from the place of E's authentic Self, seldom, if ever, did this happen.

One of the tactics E used in an attempt to cover up her superficial talk about love, was her constant reminding L of the differences between "How men and women think." Frequently, E would ask L "How many couples do you know that Love each other?" L was not concerned about an answer to her question, but, more importantly, L was feeling a need for E's love, which came from a place of unfettered giving. These tactics were defaulted to because E was not taught how to love by her mother and father; there was no love circuit developed at a critical stage in her development after she was born. Montagu added "…when the critical developmental period for their development has passed, incoming changes resonate or reverberate at most against the inadequately developed "love" circuits, and the responses to them are inadequately made. The "know-how" just is not there because it was never developed."[141]

This truth became evident to L when he reflected on the fact that L divorced his wife and son in 1979; L did not have a relationship with his ex-wife or son for more than 36 years after the divorce. However, after L retired in 2012, he actively reached out to his son, who L will refer to as D, in 2013. Since that time to the present, L has visited with

---

[140] Montagu, op. cit., p. 238.
[141] Ibid., p. 238.

D on several occasions, for the purpose of opening up a dialogue with D in order to establish a father-son relationship, if possible. L admitted to D that he did not participate in his life, from 1979 to 2013. L did not send D a birthday card; he did not call D; he did not come to any of D's graduations; and he did not attend any of D's musical performances. L admitted to D that not participating in his life was a major mistake! That is, L took responsibility for the mistake he made.

Because L was open, genuine, sincere, honest, and disclosing with D, L and D began to talk on the telephone, which turned into face-to-face visits. What struck L as being very interesting is the fact D did not hold inside of himself any hostility or anger against his father, although L was not involved in his life during crucial periods in D's development as a child and young adult. In fact, the most interesting thing of all is the fact D, *after many years of L's absence in his life, is now able to share with L that he loves his father!* If you are wondering what is responsible for this welcomed turnaround in D and L's relationship, it has everything to do with the fact that D's mother-M-gave D love, from the first moment she gave birth to him continuing throughout his childhood into his young adult life. By doing so, M taught D how to love himself; in turn, D is able to give that love to others. M laid the ground work that established the "love" circuit in D's brain during the first several months of his life. The complete opposite is the case related to L and his daughter-H.

H was born in Oakland, CA in 1985; E and L's midwife-B-ask L to catch H with his two hands when she was being delivered by E. From the moment L assisted B with the cutting of H's umbilical cord to the day H defended her Doctoral Dissertation, L has been a constant presence in H's life. *L taught H everything he knew about education, life, and love. Throughout H's childhood, L took H to the beach so she could have a spiritual connection with the ocean and the sun during sunset time. L made it possible for H to travel to Cairo, Egypt as a milestone recognition, for her Senior High School Trip. This was a Rite of Passage Experience during which H was provided an opportunity to touch the Great Pyramid of Giza and lay her eyes on the one-of-a-kind Sphinx. H was given the privilege to travel with L to Fayoum, Egypt, and stay in the same hotel in which General Pattin resided, for a time, during World War II.* All of the pages in this book would not be enough to write down on them all of the activities and experiences L provided for H during her childhood and afterwards.

Yet, today, L and H are strangers! After finding out H's mother-E-is codependent, and by E's own admission she was not given love as an infant, nor during her childhood, E's mother and father did not establish the "love" circuit in her brain when she was an infant; and therefore, E was unable to give authentic and genuine love to her daughter H during the crucial months after her birth, although if you ask E if she established a "love" circuit in H's brain, she would definitely tell anyone who ask yes! In short, this is why L believes H shows no love for L-her father-while D, his son, easily and freely tells L he loves him without being ask to do so. Regardless of what anyone feels about this information, and whatever commentary anyone has to offer, the fact of the matter nothing can change this truth. From January 2019 to May 31, 2019, L received zero telephone calls from H with the sole purpose of checking to see if her father is doing alright! For the sole purpose of simply being humane.

Thus, when the love circuits are absent in the brain, other circuits are built up in their place such as anxiety, insecurity, rage, aggression, not enough, conflict, low self-esteem, shame, and denial among others. Moreover, Montagu wrote "the responses...which such children or persons will frequently make to expressions of love are often in terms of the circuits which have been built up in their brains in terms of aggressiveness, rage, and insecurity."[142] In the absence of the formation of the "love" circuits, these attributes-instead- become a part of the nervous system of the affected infant throughout his or her adult life. Montagu wrote "when in such persons some part at least of the neurologic structure associated with the patterns of mental functioning of the person is destroyed, that pattern of functioning more or less disappears...the experiences of the infant become a part of its nervous system and to a very large extent determine the pattern of functioning of that nervous system."[143]

---

[142] Ibid., p. 238.
[143] Ibid., p. 256.

L is 68 years old and so is E; we began our relationship when we were 29 years old, and L was 65 years old when he first learned of E's claims that she is codependent, a condition that was implanted in her at birth! Codependency Addiction becomes imprinted then in the brain circuitry, if the "love" circuit does not develop. Bowlby stated "... the evidence is fairly clear that if the first phase of development-that of establishing a relation with a clearly differentiated person-[mother or mother-surrogate] is not satisfactorily completed during the first 12 months or so, there is the greatest difficulty in making it good: the character of the psychic tissues has become fixed."[144] Of course, a codependent person, an alcoholic and so forth can attend therapy meetings, but the meetings themselves, and the best therapists available, cannot re-grow a client's nervous system or replace anxiety, aggression, and anger circuits, for example, with the "love" circuit one missed during the earliest weeks and months of his or her childhood.

That being so, one of the most debilitating afflictions, caused by an absence of the "love" circuit in the developing infant, is one called *Codependency.*

As evidence of this truth, an extended quotation from Montagu's Research follows: "The child who has been inadequately mothered, who fails to receive a sufficient amount of love, generally fails to learn to love, and such children generally fail to become satisfactorily socialized. Such a child's personality development frequently follows a definite and predictable course. Both as a child and as an adult he continues to exhibit a marked dependency upon others, he is insecure, he is extremely jealous of his siblings, he is excessively dependent upon others for affection, he has an inordinate desire to be loved, and while he is himself *anxious* to return love, to love others, he finds himself quite incapable of doing so. An additional trait generally present in such persons is a state of anxiety which is dominating and constant motive underlying much of their behavior. Observations which have been made on persons exhibiting many of these forms of behavior strongly

---

[144] Bowlby, op. cit., p. 54.

point to the same causes: inadequate mothering during childhood."[145] Of everything this statement accurately explains about CoDependency, the one sentence that reveals who the codependent person is follows: "both as a child and as an adult he [or she] continues to exhibit a marked dependency upon others..."

Lancer added "when you're enmeshed, you feel responsible for and react to your partner's feelings, needs, actions, and problems, but don't think clearly about your own needs and feelings, nor take responsibility for them. You feel, "I'm glad when you're glad," and I'm sad when you're sad."[146] Enmeshed is an understatement of this mental disease; the codependent partner in a relationship actually identifies so closely with one's partner that the former actually believes their partner's feelings and needs are his or her own. L recently found out that his partner-E-thought L's feelings and needs were her own! During more than 36 years of struggle to build a life; raise a family and give support to our children's families; and create an estate, including a home and land, L went through the toils and strife life put him through sincerely, genuinely, and dedicated only to find-out, after more than 36 years, that everything he worked for did not include E's feelings and needs. As a codependent, she went along repressing her feelings and needs until she could no longer do so. By then, it was too late for L to undo all of the buildings of life and start over.

Lancer also explains "the reality is that so much of yourself is invested in others that [the codependent] lose who you are-your feelings, needs, hobbies, and goals. Your thinking and actions revolve around getting, changing, worrying about, and reacting to someone else. In advanced stages of the disease, codependents have become shells-their entire life having been squandered on someone else in the way that a compulsive gambler or debtor squanders his or her life savings."[147] When I discovered this tragedy going-on around me in the most intimate ways, all I felt was a feeling anyone gets when they experience a major earthquake, where the very ground upon which

---

[145] Montagu, op. cit., pp. 258 and 259.
[146] Lancer, op. cit. p. 50.
[147] Ibid., p. 51.

they once felt was permanent begins to shake, buckle, break, fall down, snap, fold in grotesque ways, and sometimes turn to sand due to the rapid and intense energy vibrations flowing through hit. I felt this way and more. I felt the ground moving from under my feet; I always felt nothing could bring down E and L's relationship, but nothing prepared me for CoDependency's shattering jolt!

Shortly after E told me she is codependent, L thought there might be a chance to work through the minefield of her CoDependency Addiction, but, as we shall see later, denial entered into E an L's relationship, sealing off any areas where some change and reconstruction might be possible to turnaround the problem and defeat it. The greatest barrier quickly became blame (This term will be discussed at length later also) inasmuch as E continually tried to get L to feel responsible for her giving up on he life-potential, creativity, and herself, namely she wanted L to take responsibility for her unhappiness, pain, woundedness, fear, and self-hatred. The wall was just too high for L to throw a *rope of hope* over so we could come up with a strategy to climb out of Dante Inferno's lowest level-Hell.

For example, Lancer wrote "[a codependent is] usually looking for someone to make you [him or her] happy if …single, and when…in a relationship, you focus on making that someone happy. In neither case do you take the time to make yourself happy. You're rarely content with yourself and become overly invested in pleasing or helping someone else…Soon you're reacting to and controlled by that person's feelings, needs, and behavior, and you try to control the other person to feel better, rather than honor your needs and feelings."[148] Interestingly, when E and L got together in a relationship in 1979 when we were 29 years old, *E emphatically told L that it was his responsibility to make himself happy, and her's to make herself happy.* I believed E's statement was true so I lived by it, but, ironically, E was not being honest with L because she actually depended on him to make her happy and figure-out her life for her.

---

[148] Ibid., p. 52.

As we have already seen, this statement was a bold lie!! On top of that fact, it is filled with insincerity because if E could get L to make himself happy, and if E is covertly attached to L's feelings and needs, she figured correctly that whatever L created; wherever he traveled in the world; and whomever he befriended-these things would be available for her to enjoy without having to expend any of her own energy to figure-out what her feelings, needs, and goals are. About five years into our relationship, E enrolled in graduate school at San Francisco State University to get her Masters Degree. L was very happy for E to express her feelings and needs and achieve her goals. However, within two months, E returned to our Hillcastle Apartment, and arbitrarily declared she was dropping out of graduate school. E dropped-out and, uncharacteristically, gave little or no real explanation for doing so, other than she felt she was "too old to go to graduate school at 34 years old!!" L was somewhat confused by her decision to quit graduate school, but I reasoned that was what she felt she needed to do. How wrong L was looking back at that experience. *E was frightened by her own thought that she might actually be good enough to obtain her Masters Degree, and, because of her hidden and latent Codependency Addiction, L was clueless about, E defaulted to the unworthiness that she grew up in in her household as an infant, and during her childhood.* If I had followed my first instincts and pushed for a deeper explanation from E related to why she dropped-out of graduate school, E and L's relationship probably would have ended during the early 1980s, which would have been the best thing to happen, given what L now know about CoDependency Addiction today. We were building a castle higher in the sky erected upon a sandy foundation. The passage of time has proven this realization true.

At this point, it is time to transition to a consideration of some of the debilitating impacts CoDependency Addiction have on the person who claims to be codependent, and also on the other person in a relationship to which the codependent person is attached. If the codependent person is single, then, regardless of what the situation is, everyone will feel the debilitating impacts of CoDependency Addiction, and they are especially heartfelt by the person a codependent is attached to in a relationship such as the one E an L have been in for more than 36 years. In either case, the codependent person is the carrier of the CoDependency Addiction Disease, and he or she is by far, more impacted. Montagu wrote "unless the child has been firmly grounded in the discipline of love and dependency, it is injured in its capacity to develop clear and definite judgments concerning people and things, and its ability to form such judgments as an adult is seriously handicapped. As adults the judgments of such persons tend to remain blurred and vague...characterized by doubt, suspicion, uncertainty, misgiving, and unsureness. They vacillate...They are characterized by an inability to enter into the feelings of others because, when they were young, no one adequately entered into theirs."[149]

One very poor judgment E made during the early 1990s, was her failure to proactively respond to G and MK M's offer for us to purchase 110 acres of their land for $60,000! No matter which way L looks at E's decision to not inform him of the land sale offer, which she kept a secret from L for nearly 25 years, no doubt, E's CoDependency Addiction handicapped her ability to see the value in this potential land purchase opportunity.

Another example of E's challenged judgment and decision-making unfolded before me, but being unaware what CoDependency Addiction is, L gave little thought, if any, to E's persistent need to always have someone accompany her to the shopping mall, or other locations, when she had to make a purchase. Whether she had to buy a dress, paint for a room, or purchase a table or sofa, someone had to go with her to select the item, and recommend this or that one is what E should buy. Nearly everything inside of our home was selected by L, from the curtains that cover every window; kitchen appliances; artwork placed on the walls; Jacuzzi Tub and face bowls in the bathrooms; and televisions among many other items. L did not know beneath the surface, and due to E's childhood trauma, her decision-making and judgment abilities were handicapped and crippled.

In addition, when E and L lived in Oakland, CA during the early 1980s, we lived with L's mother for a brief period-approximately one

---

[149] Montagu, op.cit., p. 213.

month. During this time, every evening L's siblings would come by our mother's home. Since E had prepared dinner for us and my mother, my other siblings joined us for dinner as well without being invited to do so. E and L had no jobs at the time, and we were primarily living off of $5,000 we brought with us to Oakland, CA when we moved in L's mother's house. Day-after-day, some of my siblings joined us for dinner, but E was hesitant to inform them that we did not have enough food prepared for everyone. After everyone left to go to their homes, E would mention the dinner situation to me, but strangely she did not tell anyone that there was just enough dinner prepared for us and my mother. As a codependent, E most likely felt she could not tell my siblings what the dinner situation was because she was repressing her own feelings and needs buried deep down on the inside of herself. This was another red flag that L did not see because he thought E was expressing her feelings and needs; to the contrary, E was not doing so, but *going along with the situation to get along!* Also, E was a people pleaser maxima! She wanted to gain my siblings attention and love, but, as we already know by now, anyone who seeks love will *never* find it!

In addition, throughout E's career as a schoolteacher, especially during the 36 years we were in a relationship, she developed a pattern of persistently asking other colleagues to provide her with assistance with anything to do with computer technology. L thought this pattern was due to E's lack of familiarity with new developments in the computer technology field; however, L has now realized this outreach to get someone else to figure out a technology issue is related to E's repression of her Self, which had a direct impact on her feelings, imagination, decision-making, and creative ability. This situation also severely limited E's ability to recognize L's creative expression as a writer, researcher, farmer, woodcarver, and public speaker. Whenever, L produced anything, it was very painful for E to feel joy, and, in turn, express her joy to L for finishing a book publication or woodcarving and so forth.

Moreover, as a reminder, the human race would likely be extinct today, if during the Savagery Period we discussed earlier, mother right did not create the necessary "love" circuits in the brains of their infants, from one generation to another. Unfortunately, as it was by the latter stage of Barbarism and the beginning of the Civilization Period, mother right was overthrown and replaced by father right, and the Patriarchy System became a household practice in the Monogamy Family thereafter. It is within this household context that all of the psychological impacts of CoDependency Addiction have surfaced, and during the reproduction of more and more people on the Earth, the number of codependents in American society has skyrocketed since the beginning of the Monogamy Family!

CHAPTER SEVEN

Codependency, Characteristics Of A Codependent Person, And Psychopathology Behavior

For 36 years or more, L lived in a relationship with a codependent person-E. The first time E's codependent claim was made known to L is when she showed him a list of the characteristics of a codependent person. When L finished reading them, he asked E how many of the fourteen characteristics applied to her, and she told me all of them! I was, to say the least, shocked and nearly speechless, especially since L knew nothing about CoDependency. The list of codependent characteristics is shown below:

A. Characteristics Of A Codependent Person

- "Typically, he/she comes from a dysfunctional home in which his/her emotional needs were not met.
- Having received little real nurturing himself, he/she tries to fill his/her unmet need vicariously through others, events and /or substances.
- Because he/she couldn't change his/her parents into warm, loving caretakers he/she longed for, he/she responds deeply to the familiar emotionally unavailable person whom he/she can again try to change through his/her love.

- Terrified of abandonment, he/she will do anything to keep a relationship from dissolving.

- Almost nothing is too much trouble, takes too much time, or is too expensive if it will "help" the person with whom he/she is involved.

- Accustomed to lack of love in personal relationships, he/she is willing to wait, hope and try harder to please. They see that the other person has the POTENTIAL to meet their needs, and they keep hoping and believing the other person will fulfill their unmet needs.

- He/she is willing to take far more than 50 percent of the responsibility, guilt and blame in any relationship for anything.

- His/her self-esteem is critically low, and deep inside he/she does not believe he/she deserves to be happy. Rather, he/she believes he/she must earn the right to enjoy life.

- Having experienced little security in childhood, he/she has a desperate need to control and exercise power over his/her partner and the relationships. He/she masks his/her efforts to control people and situations with "being helpful."

- In a relationship, he/she is much more in touch with the ***dream of how it could be***, than with the reality of how the situation is presently.

- He/she is addicted to people and emotional pain.

- He/she may be predisposed emotionally and often biochemically to becoming addicted to drugs, alcohol, and/or certain foods, particularly sugary ones.

- By being drawn to people with problems that need fixing, or by becoming enmeshed in situations that are chaotic, uncertain, and emotionally painful, he/she avoids focusing on his/her responsibility to him/herself.

- He/she may have a tendency toward depression, which he/she tries to forestall through the excitement provided by an unstable relationship." [150]

---

[150] _____RealistictRecovery, 27 Codependency Characteristics (Person Addiction), realisticrecovery.wordpress.com/2009/05/20/27-characteristics

Another common list of characteristics of a codependent person is shown below:

Characteristics of Codependency: "Following is a commonly used list of characteristics of codependency.

1. My good feelings about who I am stem from being liked by you
2. My good feelings about who I am stem from receiving approval from you
3. Your struggle affects my serenity. My mental attention focuses on solving your problems/relieving your pain
4. My mental attention is focused on you
5. My mental attention is focused on protecting you
6. My mental attention is focused on manipulating you to do it my way
7. My self-esteem is bolstered by solving your problems
8. My self-esteem is bolstered by relieving your pain
9. My own hobbies/interests are put to one side. My time is spent sharing your hobbies/interests
10. Your clothing and personal appearance are dictated by my desires and I feel you are a reflection of me
11. Your behavior is dictated by my desires and I feel you are a reflection of me
12. I am not aware of how I feel. I am aware of how you feel
13. I am not aware of what I want - I ask what you want. I am not aware - I assume
14. The dreams I have for my future are linked to you
15. My fear of rejection determines what I say or do
16. My fear of your anger determines what I say or do
17. I use giving as a way of feeling safe in our relationship
18. My social circle diminishes as I involve myself with you
19. I put my values aside in order to connect with you
20. I value your opinion and way of doing things more than my own
21. The quality of my life is in relation to the quality of yours"[151]

---

[151] _____http://fullspectrumrecovery.com/wp-content/uploads/2013/06/Characteristics-of-Codependency.pdf

The above list of 34 characteristics of a codependent person are consistent with one another. After carefully reviewing each item, each one has been active in my relationship with E during the 36 years or more we have been together. Like L, there are millions of other codependent people in our society today, who are in a relationship with another person with whom their codependent partner has repressed their core Selves, and because they cannot express their own feelings and needs as a result, the codependent person in the relationship identifies so closely with their partner's feelings and needs they actually think the latter's are their own. Herein lies the mental disease's affect on the psychic structure of the codependent person. Some of the most debilitating symptoms are discussed below.

B. Psychopathic Character Of A Codependent Person

After L learned his partner-E-after 36 years or more being a codependent, the single question L tried to answer unsuccessfully for four years following E's stroke in July 2015, is: "How did L remain unaware of E's CoDependency Addiction Disease, for this long, without ever becoming aware, years earlier, that she is codependent?" The more L tried to piece this puzzle together, the absence of an answer persisted. Being a formally trained researcher, L did not give up but continued to delve deeper into the CoDependency Addiction waters, and to my surprise, an answer to the mentioned question surfaced one day.

The main clue that solved the problem is, after studying some of the CoDependency Literature, a common thread emerged, namely, codependent persons are unable to express their feelings and needs, and similar to a vampire, their feelings and needs are transfused into themselves through their strong attachment to another person in a shared relationship. Feelings are repressed inside the Self of a codependent person. Codependents do not manifest any libidinal ties, that is, emotional love ties and psychic energy with other children or adults. Bowlby wrote "they fail to develop libidinal ties with other children or with adults and consequently have no friendships worth the name...they are sometimes sociable in a superficial sense but if this is scrutinized we find that there are no feelings, no roots in these relationships."[152] Bowlby added Bender "…gives a full clinical description of the syndrome, which she terms 'psychopathic behavior disorder of childhood.' "There is an inability to love or feel guilty. There is no conscience. The unconscious fantasy material is shallow and shows only a tendency to react to immediate impulses or experiences… Their inability to enter into any relationship makes therapy or even education impossible. There is an inability to conceptualize, particularly significant in regard to time. They have no concept of time, so they cannot recall past experience and cannot benefit from past experience or be motivated to future goals."[153]

For further clarification, the definition of conscience is "the sense or consciousness of the moral goodness or blameworthiness of one's own conduct, intentions, or character together with a feeling of obligation to do right or be good."[154] Everyone who drives a car has had the experience, at one time or another, of finding the battery in their vehicle being "dead,' namely the car etc, would not start. Similarly, a codependent person is, likewise, depleted of feelings due to the fact the latter is sealed-off inside of the Self. Thus, without functioning on a moment-by-moment basis utilizing one's feelings, the codependent person is alienated from his or her conscience, or from their feeling of obligation to do right or be good. Moreover, the absence of the use of one's conscience shuts down the codependent's ability to take responsibility for his or her conduct such is the case in E and L's relationship. Of course, E blames L for every wrong because, as we now see, it cannot be otherwise due to the fact E's conscience is shutdown like the dead battery metaphor, and she thinks, literally speaking, that what she is feeling in real time is her own self-generated feelings but, in reality, they are L's. Therefore, L must be in E's conscienceless mind the blame, scapegoat, and villain for her codependent life experience. *Nothing could be farther from the truth-however.*

---

[152] Bowlby, op. cit., p. 31.

[153] Ibid., p. 33.

[154] Mish, Frederick C., et al, <u>Webster's Ninth New Collegiate Dictionary</u>, Merriam-Webster Inc., Publishers, Springfield, Massachusetts, U. S. A., 1984, p. 278.

In short, L could not discern the Codependency Addiction going-on in his relationship with E because the only feelings and needs ever expressed were L's only. So, how can anyone discern a difference in the same feelings? That is impossible to do! Yet, E really thinks two different sets of feelings were expressed in our relationship during its existence. The truth is only one person's feelings and needs was expressed in E and L's relationship, namely, L's. This is how the codependent game lasted so long without L's detection of it! It was hidden within the confines of *psychopathic behavior disorder of childhood.*

In his article titled "This Charming Psychopath," Robert Hare stated "everybody has met these people [once they grow into adulthood]... been deceived and manipulated by them...These often charming... individuals have a clinical name: psychopaths. Their hallmark is a stunning lack of conscience; their game is self-gratification at the other person's expense...All take far more than they give."[155] Similar to Hare's research findings, E could turn-on an amusing and entertaining personality and storyteller; she could usually present herself as very likable and charming. Moreover, Hare further clarifies the codependent character of a psychopath stating "psychopaths show a stunning lack of concern for the effects their actions have on others, no matter how devastating these might be...Their lack of remorse or guilt is associated with a remarkable ability to rationalize their behavior, to shrug off personal responsibility for actions that cause family...to reel with shock and disappointment. They usually have handy excuses for their behavior, and in some cases deny that it happened at all...Many [have] a profound lack of empathy and inability to construct a mental and emotional "facsimile" of another person. They seem completely unable to "get into the skin" of others, except in a purely intellectual sense. They are completely indifferent to the rights and suffering of family..."[156]

While writing this information about psychopaths, and like an old Polaroid Camera Picture gradually unfolding, L could answer

---

[155] Hare, Robert, "This Charming Psychopath," http://www.psychologyToday.com/US/articles/199401/charmingpsychopath, January 1, 1994, p. 2.
[156] Ibid., p. 4.

affirmatively that E definitely fits some of Hare's traits of psychopathic behavior, which, no doubt, originated out of the psychopathic behavior disorder of childhood mentioned earlier. Everything we discuss, from now on, is definitely linked to a codependent's failure to develop a conscience during his or her childhood, and also a necessary "love" circuit in the brain of an infant, which is required for the socialization of the person in the family and community.

C. The Interchanging Worlds Of CoDependency And Psychopathology

Although this may sound harsh what L is about to share, codependents' main goal in life is to use another person to survive; figure-out their lives for them; and enjoy the creations of their unwitting partners, friends, and others. Nothing else matters to them because they live a life set on the dial of constant desperation! This is part of their world that is intensely emotionally traumatic; it is kept repressed from public disclosure by any means necessary. In my case, L remained a committed partner in his relationship with E. Throughout this time, nothing happened in our relationship that would have awaken me to the Codependency Addiction flowing just beneath its surface. E seemed very confident that her Codependency Addiction would never be discovered by L in this lifetime. The development of a smooth public persona made it very difficult for L to discern what was going-on inside E's Self. Her use of psychopathic tendencies mixed in a soup of a perfectionist, public persona kept L from pursuing what was happening inside of E. For example, over a 36 year period, every time we relaxed before engaging in intimacy, we usually began the latter with some kind of stimulant. For L, this diverted his attention away from concrete questions and discussions about E and L's childhood histories, or other important matters going-on in our lives at the time. Hare wrote "with their powers of imagination in gear and beamed on themselves, psychopaths appear amazingly unfazed by the possibility-or even by the certainty-of being found out. When caught in a lie or challenged with the truth, they seldom appear perplexed or embarrassed-they simply change their stories or attempt to rework the facts so they appear consistent with the lie."[157] As L became more aware of CoDependency Addiction, every time he put forth any subject that made E uncomfortable to the extent that it might lead to a discovery about her past behavior, E would abruptly raise her voice tone, which his abuse, and quickly remove herself from the room. After E's stroke in July 2015, in a moment of clarity, *L was amazed to hear E tell him that he was never suppose to find out that she is a codependent.* For 36 or more years, E's public persona worked for her, but when she had a stroke, it caused her to focus on her childhood and the fact she grew up in a dysfunctional family. Sadly, though, after E admitted keeping a secret her CoDependency Addiction, an hour later she changed her story *saying "she did not remember ever telling me that I was not suppose to ever find out about her CoDependency Addiction."*

Being caught living between two worlds, on one hand, CoDependency and all of the emotional trauma of childhood sealed-off in a repressed Self, and on the other, constantly having to keep everybody from discovering their hidden inner world in which their Self is repressed, codependents, as we have repeatedly mentioned, do not express any of their own authentic and genuine feelings and needs. To cope, or steer L away from realizing this serious flaw in E's personal reality, she resorted to hyperactive mood swings.

Hare stated "…psychopaths seem to suffer a kind of emotional poverty that limits the range and depth of their feelings. At times they appear to be cold and unemotional while nevertheless being prone to dramatic, shallow, and short-lived displays of feelings. Careful observers are left with the impression they are playacting and little is going on below the surface."[158] For years, before E and L would go to a social gathering, E would invariably use a stimulant before we left home. When L ask E what was the need for using a stimulant, she would only answer "I am using it because I want to." Knowing today what I did not know back then, E used the stimulant in an attempt to relax, to some degree, which would allow her to show some feelings and emotions,

---

[157] Ibid., p. 4.
[158] Ibid., p. 4.

however shallow they might be. Besides being unable to express their true feelings and needs, Psychopaths are impulsive.

Recall, earlier I mentioned G and MK M gave E an L first option to purchase 110 acres of their farmland. Although G told me she called E and gave us first option to buy their 110 acres of land, E never shared that telephone call and its message with me! Hare explained E's behavior as follows: "psychopaths are unlikely to spend much time weighing the pros and cons of a course of action or considering the possible consequences. "I did it because I felt like it," is a common response. These impulsive acts often result from an aim that plays a central role in most of the psychopath's behavior: to achieve immediate satisfaction, pleasure, or relief."[159] The possible purchase of 110 acres of land was sabotaged by E's impulsive desire to keep L from owning the land, which would bring into play uncertainty and fear of the future related to whether he would find out about her hidden CoDependency Addiction within. Being a large landowner would, no doubt, increase L's confidence in himself, and, at the same time, significantly threaten E's unspoken dependence on him for her survival. By not sharing the first option to buy the land, E was satisfied and relieved to maintain her Codependency Addiction status quo. She never a gave a second thought to the fact L never knew about G and MK M's first option land sale telephone call, or the fact he was secretly forbidden an opportunity to make a choice. Bowlby's Research, in a few short sentences, captures the essence of the making of a codependent person, who manifests, later in his or her adult life, psychopathic behavioral tendencies, which are thought by them, to be necessary to survive from day-to-day.

He wrote, "here, in brief, are many of the typical features: superficial relationships; no real feeling-no capacity to care for people or to make true friends; an inaccessibility, exasperating to those trying to help; no emotional response to situations where it is normal-a curious lack of concern; deceit and evasion, often pointless..."[160] What Bowlby has outlined in brief is a precise profile of a codependent person, which

---

[159] Hare, Ibid., p. 4.
[160] Bowlby, op. cit., p. 31.

are the self-same attributes of a person who manifests psychopathic behavioral tendencies, and the latter originates as psychopathic behavior disorder of childhood. What is the cause of the psychopathic character manifested by a codependent person?

Bowlby answered "both Bender and Bowlby...independently advance the hypothesis that there is a specific connexion between prolonged deprivation in the early years and the development of an affectionless psychopathic character...love deprivation is the cause of the psychiatric condition..."[161] One thing L noticed about E and L's intimate life through the years is on the many occasions when we had intimate contact, there was not a follow through, or carryover of any feelings of love. That is, once the stimulant wore off, which was used during intimate times, it was back to the non-expression of feelings and needs. We were definitely on a roller coaster of highs and lows.

The impact of love deprivation during the early years of childhood cannot be overstated, regarding a codependent's development of a cold, rigid, affectionless, and psychopathic character. Bowlby wrote "many affectionless characters crave affection, but nonetheless have a complete inability either to accept or reciprocate it...it is known that very many people who are psychiatrically disturbed are able to make a tolerable external adjustment for long periods."[162] Through the 36 years or more L was in a relationship with E, she often would say to him "I am so glad I found someone like you who can love me as deeply and strong as I love you." L genuinely thought E was sincere about her feeling, but L did not know what was going-on on the inside of E, namely, she is codependent; she is alienated from her "Self;" and the appearance of E's sharing her feeling about how much she loves L was not a genuine expression of her feeling but her use of a deceptive tactic to keep L believing E loves him. As we mentioned earlier, a codependent person can neither "accept" or "reciprocate" love. Even though within 24 hours after L and E were intimate, and although E kept telling L she

---

[161] Ibid., pp. 34 and 35.
[162] Ibid., pp. 38 and 39.

loves him deeply and strongly, the fact is during the 36 years of our relationship, E was codependent, and still is today.

In sum, a codependent person, who is essentially alienated from his or her feelings and needs due to the deprivation of mother and father love or mother-surrogate's, is unable to accept or reciprocate love. Therefore, since love is not an option which social creatures-human beings-can arbitrarily do without, paradoxically, it is typical for codependents to engage in a fruitless, external pursuit of life, happiness, and, ultimately, love, which leaves a vast majority of them emotionally bankrupt internally. As a reminder, Montagu has proven whenever a mother, father or mother-surrogate's love is absent in an infant's life over a prolonged period during his or her childhood, the love circuits, which would have developed in the brain of the host if such love was not absent, do not develop, which, unfortunately, manifests a later condition in which an affected adult is unable to genuinely love another person. This is the reason many codependent people search for love in external places most, if not all, of their lives!

Armed with a better understanding of CoDependency and codependent personality characteristics, along with its psychopathic behavioral tendencies, in addition to the fact many households within the Monogamy Family are the incubators of increasingly larger numbers of codependent tragic stories, we are prepared, at this point, to proceed with a discussion of some of the primary psychological flaws in the psychic structure of the codependent person, *which they employ, both consciously and unconsciously, in their vain attempt to survive their oppressor within-CoDependency Addiction.*

CHAPTER EIGHT

Psychological Impacts Of Codependency On The Psychic Structure Of Infants During Their Early Childhood Development And Into Adulthood

O nce the chains of CoDependency are set in motion in an infant, and usually its generational, during which each sibling-one after the next-is submerged in a CoDependency web of emotional trauma, the chains that bind them to this mental disease is nearly unbreakable due to *denial*. Because of family dysfunctionalism, it "...prolongs denial and perpetuates self-destructive behavior."[163] According to Lancer, "when infant parenting is inadequate, it...reflects dysfunction in the whole family, which further damages the growing child's emerging self."[164] We have emphasized this mother and mother-surrogate role, thus far, for this very reason.

---

[163] Lancer, op. cit., p. 204.
[164] Ibid., p. 99.

A. CoDependent Mother, Father, or Mother-Surrogate

The likelihood an infant becomes codependent, if his or her mother, father, or mother-surrogate is not, is, statistically speaking, nearly impossible. Adequate parenting means, according to Lancer, "starting at four to six months [, and as early as day of birth itself,] and continuing onward, babies must confidently achieve separation from their mothers and establish their own boundaries. They must individuate, which is a psychological process whereby a child and later a young adult... develops a whole self...who is separate psychologically, cognitively, and emotionally, and owns and trust his or her perceptions, thoughts, feelings, and memories."[165] Without the guided development of a "love" circuit we mentioned earlier, the likelihood of this psychological process becoming a reality for an infant, during his or her lifetime, is as far from the child's reality as it is a remote impossibility of growing collard Greens on the Moon. Lancer added "CoDependent mothers may unconsciously fail to support their children's emerging drive for independence. Instead, mothers' needs and automatic responses cripple their children by keeping them dependent, and consequently, codependent as adults."[166] As a reminder, such inadequate parenting was unheard-of during the more than1 million years of mother right where women in the tribe nurtured and gave their offsprings the love they needed to become interdependent and forward a new mentally healthy generation and so forth. If the problems mothers have today, struggling to function in this advanced technological age of Civilization to find the time to love their children was the case during mother right during the Savagery Period, we could easily see, based on what is going-on today related to CoDependency, there would be a better than average chance that human beings would not have managed to reach the new Millennium. Extinction would not be out of the question. Therefore, since all of the codependent siblings are given birth by a codependent mother, the households in which CoDependency prevails are inclusive of dysfunctional families.

---

[165] Ibid., p. 100.
[166] Ibid., p. 101.

B. Dysfunctional Families And CoDependency: Appearances Are Deceiving

When I visited E's family home in a little village south of Brentwood Crossing, LA during the early 1980s, at which time L and E were in their early 30s, there were a lot of CoDependency Red Flags flying, but I was still too naïve and inexperienced to understand what I was encountering inside of E's mother's house. Having been raised on a large agricultural farm in LA, and having grown up in a large home consisting of 10 rooms, L's attention was drawn to how small the family house E grew up in was. It had only six small rooms and one bathroom. At one time, E's eight siblings and two parents occupied the small house. When I was introduced to E's siblings, who lived in the family house at the time, one of them asked me a question that was definitely a CoDependency Red Flag, but I did not know it at the time.

L was asked by one of E's older sisters this question: "What are you going to do with your life?" L thought this was an appropriate question. So, he eagerly answered replying, "I intend to write a book and get it published." To my surprise, E's older sister told me emphatically these few words: "You Can't do that!" This comment came straight out of the intellect of a person whose inner feelings and needs were being repressed. Thus, when I expressed my inner feelings and needs about writing and publishing a book, E's older sister's anger and resentment about her own limitations were projected on L, which, fortunately, L did not accept or own! L was caught off guard to say the least. At that time, L was 30 years old; he earned his Doctoral Degree from the University of Colorado, when he was 27 years old; and E's older sister did not know me; I had made her acquaintance only an hour before *she pronounced my feelings and needs were of no significance, regarding my literary aspirations.* What I needed to do then was drill-down deeper into the latter's doomsday prediction because it is possible L might have been able to peel back a layer of CoDependency in existence in E's family during the early 1980s, especially if it was expressed to me by her older sister, who grew up in the same dysfunctional family a generation before E. The other thing that made it difficult for me to pick up on the CoDependency

Addiction he encountered in E's family is, there were no obvious overt signs of it being a dysfunctional one.

According to Lancer, "many dysfunctional families look healthy on the outside, but the internal dynamic revolve around a family member's...trauma...families are dysfunctional due to rigid control or lack of empathy and acceptance that...cause children to become codependent. The strongest predictor of Codependency Addiction is having codependent parents."[167]

E's mother got married when she was 15 years old, and for the rest of her life, she depended on her husband for nearly everything, regarding her survival. Being the catalyst, Lancer wrote "CoDependency usually starts when you feel emotionally abandoned. In response, you repress feelings, needs, observations, and thoughts. You learn to numb your hurt, distrust your parents, and become self-sufficient."[168] Rather than the mother, father, or mother-surrogate guiding the infant through his or her childhood, the latter, out of a desperate necessity to survive, loves one's own self and crafts a fraudulent public personality to trick others into believing he or she is a lovable person. Underneath this artificial veneer is a "rejecting attitude" of being not good enough and undeserving.

Because of CoDependency mixed-up with prolonged poverty, dysfunctional families, in their attempt to hide the former, they practice what is known as clannishness. That is, contact with the larger community is monitored by the codependent parents, and when there is any contact, special efforts are made to avoid any family or self-disclosures. Lancer added "dysfunctional families are closed to varying degrees. Some won't allow differing or new ideas to be discussed among members or with outsiders. They may not welcome guests or friendships...Some families are isolated and don't interact with the community. Others do, but appearances are everything. The family may be respected in the community, but hides the truth. Talking about

[167] Ibid, p.106.
[168] Ibid., p. 106.

the family to others is considered disloyal."[169] This description fits E's dysfunctional family perfectly.

When E and L came together in a relationship in Baltimore, MD in 1979, E did not disclose any of these characteristics befitting the family she grew up in during her childhood. L often noticed through the years we were together, whenever E visited with any of her siblings, either in our home or theirs, and whenever L was sitting in circle with them, nothing was ever discussed related to anything that anyone had trouble with during their childhood. Talking about their past family challenges was highly forbidden; their conversations usually were highly superficial around non-family members. Hide the truth at all cost-even if it means death. The most amazing thing about CoDependency Addiction in E's dysfunctional family is E, presently speaking-2019-who is a self-proclaimed codependent, is willing to risk everything that she and L worked for during their 36 years together so long as her family loyalty and secrets are maintained at all cost, namely, separation, dissolution of the farm, living free of any bills, and much more!

In our relationship, and especially after E had a stroke in July 2015, she was impacted in such a way that any conversation between us is forbidden, if it has anything to do with making a connection between her dysfunctional family life during her childhood and her professed CoDependency Addiction. The quickest way for L to start an argument with E is to *inquire whether her codependent behavior is caused by the lack of love she received from her mother and father during her childhood;* and, with that being so, *could E take responsibility for the emotional trauma it has caused her in the first place, and secondly, for how her codependent behavior, an addiction to L, allowed an entire life of accumulation of material and non-material resources to be summarily sabotaged and destroyed?*

As we shall see momentarily, E's tactic to cover up her CoDependency Addiction to L relies on her quickly setting up an adversarial dialogue, which could lead to an argument. For example, after being away all day on February 6, 2019, E returned home and tried to start an argument with L related to why he did not reply to a one sentence informational

---

[169] Ibid., p. 106.

text message, regarding where she was going. Later that evening, E shared her brother called her and said he called his brother-in-law, although E did not disclose anything that would require a follow up question from L. Yet, E tried to once again start an argument, which L refused to participate in. The argument tactic is a major trait of a codependent person because his or her feelings and needs are repressed, and a desperate attempt is always made to try to control the feelings and needs of the person the codependent person is addicted to. This tactic was used by E for more than 36 years in our relationship. We will say more about this phenomenon later.

Presently, to hold the lid on her repressed Self within, E uses a heavy dose of denial to insure her authentic and genuine feelings and needs stay locked down and buried deep on the inside of her oppressed Self.

CHAPTER NINE

Denial: A Worthy Jailkeeper Of The Repressed Codependency Addiction Oppressor Of The Self Within

A. Denial

L has, on numerous occasions, encouraged E to come forth with the *truth* of why she did not share her feelings and needs with him for more than 36 years. Her response was consistently *"I do not want to have this conversation, and the reason I do not want to have it is L wants me to think I am the cause of the problem in our relationship, and he had nothing to do with it."* Inevitably, E would get up and leave the room. This is denial in practice. Lancer wrote "denial is an inability to acknowledge the truth of something. It's considered the hallmark of addiction, and that applies to codependents, too. Denial can prolong codependency for years or decades."[170] E is codependent and her addiction is to L.

Interestingly, E does not see the elephant sitting in the room; she will go to codependency meetings and acknowledge she is codependent. However, when she walks out of her CoDependency Meeting, and if she is asked "Are you addicted to L"? Her reply will be an emphatic no! Lancer added "you're…in denial concerning …your own addiction… to

---

[170] Ibid., p. 66.

others–your codependency."[171] E does not get it yet that what it means to be codependent is CoDependency is an addiction like alcohol, for example. No one can drink CoDependency; however, anyone who is codependent has an addiction to another person or group of people. E is addicted to L; and L is a person whom E is addicted to. Alcohol cannot be addicted to the alcoholic; CoDependency cannot be addicted to a person. It is the other way around. An alcoholic is addicted to alcohol, and a codependent person is addicted to L and others via E's CoDependency. Because of the denial of this fact, E and other codependents may take several decades to recover, or a lifetime!, if ever...

Denial is the warden of the imprisoned Self. And anger, violence, emotional abuse, sexual abuse, narcissism, deception, blame, shame, irresponsibility, conflict, control, repression, guilt, perfectionism, anxiety, resentment; not good enough, overdoing, reactionism, low-self-esteem, and self-hate among others are–All-prison guards, whose primary task is to keep the codependent person's inner Self *incarcerated within*, preferably for a lifetime. Consequently, Lancer added "codependents...are unaware of their needs, wants, and feelings...When ignoring your needs and feelings, you assess what others need and feel to guage your response."[172] That being so, the affected person becomes addicted to CoDependency, which manifests as an addiction to another person or group of people. When E and L began their relationship in 1979, L thought he was getting into a relationship with an *equal* partner; he did not know E was not getting into the relationship for the same reason. The sad tragedy is E got involved in the relationship with L because she was *addicted to him through a condition we now know as CoDependency, which she was born into and developed during her childhood, which she utilized during her adult life to survive.*

---

[171] Ibid., p. 66.
[172] Ibid., p. 66.

B. Denial Is Ungiven Love

At the heart of this denial, which makes it so difficult for a codependent person to heal, is they were denied love, during their childhood, by their biological parents, or mother-surrogate. Devastating does not come anywhere close to describing how an affected infant feels. In order to cope with the related stress of a loss of mother love, Montagu wrote "in his [or her] great need of loving care, comfort, and physical satisfaction, which he [or she] cannot provide himself [or herself], the little child…push out of his [or her] mind the picture of his [or her] mother who has (he feels) [she feels] so cruelly abandoned him [or her]. Because the child cannot tolerate such intensity of distress he makes the best of his [or her] situation by repressing his [or her] feeling for his [or her] mother."[173] The lasting question one has, who has repressed his or her feelings and needs, is one is not engaging in the latter because of making a C grade on a report card, but rather because of being abandoned by his or her mother or mother, father, or mother-surrogate! For a child under two years old, "…his [or her] mother is the entire world, she is omnipotent protector, and if the child loses her [love]…his [or her] whole world is shattered, and he [or she] experiences an overwhelming sense of loss and an overpowering anger when his [or her] imperative need for his [or her] mother is not met."[174] Will attending this or that therapy session reverse this familial abandonment that runs to the very core of a codependent person that started during infancy? L has been living with E for more than36 years, and instead of E taking the numerous opportunities to address being abandoned by her mother and father, E's denial has been so strong that she held on to the accumulated stress, which manifested into a stroke rather than *let go of denial.* E's stroke means she would rather die than cease being in denial.

E could not move beyond denial because as Lancer wrote "plain and simple, denial is a defense mechanism… [and] a characteristic of codependency."[175] Denial is a ball and chain. "This is why coming out

---

[173] Montagu, op. cit., p. 215.

[174] Ibid., p. 216.

[175] Lancer, op. cit., p. 71.

of denial is the crucial, first step in the healing process."[176] From 2015 to 2018, all E and L have done is argue about any issue related to the cause of her CoDependency Addiction, and, more importantly, although E is addicted to L, E thinks L is the cause of her CoDependency Addiction, and not her biological parents, and the dysfunctional household she grew up in during her childhood.

In order to keep the external world believing she is a Saint and L is a villain, E invariably resorted to the use of various forms of denial, depending on what the present situation calls for, namely, forgetting, self-deception, lying, minimizing, rationalizing, and repressing.[177] E has lied to L for 36 years, for the purpose of denying the negative abuse she received from her mother and father. No matter what L asked E, she usually responds by minimizing and justifying the situation. Her ace card is "everybody is codependent", or her *classic response* is "When my mother did not touch me, she saw nothing wrong with that because this is *how E thought everybody in the world was treated by their parents."* The denial is used by E to maintain this *secret* at all cost. As we witnessed earlier, an alcoholic does not love alcohol; and, a codependent does not love the person he or she is addicted to as a result of CoDependency Addiction. Thus, for 36 years or more, L thought E truly loved him; but, in reality, L was just a *usable object to demonstrate to the external public that she was loved by her mother and father because she has been in a relationship with a man for many years.* For two generations, E has repressed the pain and hurt she feels related to how her mother and father treated her during her childhood. This ball and chain can continue for another generation, and it, more than likely, has been passed on to our children?

If a dog, for example, is fed at a certain time everyday; in the same place; using the same feeding pan; and fed the same food, the dog will become conditioned by the repetitive behavior, and no matter where the dog is at feeding time, it will come running to be fed by its owner. Denial works the same way. E has denied her feelings and needs, due to the pain she suffered at the hands of her mother and father, that-today-she

---

[176] Ibid., p. 71.
[177] Ibid., p. 72.

has *nearly forgotten about her childhood experience because every day she denies it ever happen, and now she seldom, if ever, talk about anything with L other than superficialities and the mundane.* Lancer added "due to denial, many [codependents] don't realize that they've suffered abuse. Unhealed, they have difficulty experiencing intimacy."[178] Because of this blurred reality, and because E is unable to engage in critical thinking and analysis, she has placed her healing in great jeopardy inasmuch as the experiences she had as a child need to be linked to a family member(s) who perpetrated them in order for her to heal her SELF.

Accordingly, Lancer wrote "even if you know all about your abusive childhood, you must link childhood events and the behavior of family members to the effect they had on you and your feelings about it then and now. You must *feel to heal.*" [179] L has been extensively judged by E and other family members, whom E has spoken negatively about L, regarding his ability to analyze CoDependency Addiction and make real day-to-day practical applications to events and experiences that have occurred in our relationship, and further back to our childhoods. E does not ever engage in such a conversation, and If L brings one up, it invariably ends in an argument, which is a denial defense mechanism. What a waste of brain space (!), and a prolongation of CoDependency Addiction by the denial warden.

A final word about denial is many of its codependent practitioners develop a perfectionist type public personality to mislead those people they are addicted to. For instance, Bowlby stated "not infrequently people with these troubles deny their existence by an excessive show of cheerfulness and activity-hypomanic reaction...Naturally the hypomanic method meets with some success but, based as it is on denial, is in constant danger of cracking and leaving its owner in a state of despair."[180] L was drawn in by E, like a fisherperson reels in a fish, through her excessive show of cheerfulness, which, at the time L first met E, she came across to L as confident, purposeful, and self-aware. Of course, 36 years later, L found out differently when E's history of

[178] Ibid., p. 115.
[179] Ibid., p. 129.
[180] Bowlby, op. cit., pp. 49 and 50.

repression cracked, which resulted in her creation of a stroke in her body.

Therefore, while the denial warden, and its prison guards, work overtime daily to keep the secrets of CoDependency Addiction caused pains, suffering, and abuses neatly confined by this formidable oppressor within, their efforts, collectively, keep shame and guilt out of sight until a sudden catastrophe temporarily alters denial, allowing repressed shame and guilt, which overlays feelings and needs, to surface. It should be pointed-out here that although E had a stroke in July 2015, since that time, she has doggedly continued to deny her feelings and needs repressed beneath shame and guilt.

CHAPTER TEN

Shame And Guilt: Secrets Held On The Otherside Of The Veiled Curtain

Without missing the point, something "big" is at stake if a codependent person would prefer to be in denial even if he or she places themselves in a life or death situation, and preferring to choose death. If *the truth will set one free,* why would anybody deny it for one second? This sounds like a "no brainer, but it isn't! Many people deny the truth all of their lives, and some spend their last days in a Hospice Facility connected to a Morphine Intravenous Drip. As you may recall, the mother and father, and especially the former, is the entire universe for an infant. And, if he or she is abandoned by his or her caregiver at a crucial early stage of life when mother love is such a vital life support, it is inevitable that denial will, more often than not, find its way into the psychic structure of an affected codependent person. Shame is the by-product of fear of abandonment and fear of rejection by an infant's mother, father, or mother-surrogate.

A. Shame

In the world of many codependent people, Lancer wrote "childhood shame and trauma conceal their real, core self, which they can't access. Instead, codependents develop a persona in the world that reacts to others…To be acceptable to others and to themselves, you hide who you are and become who you aren't."[181] In order to hide who they are, codependents use shame and guilt laid over their core Self, in which reside their feelings and needs. The denial warden and the prison guards of the core Self are tasked with the job of keeping the *bones in the closet stuffed inside.* As the repressed Self within the codependent's core push against the closet door harder, from the inside out to get free, the denial warden and prison guards push back against the closet door, from the outside of it, in a repeated attempt to keep the feelings and needs of the codependent person stuffed inside the closet. Similar to two Tectonic Plates inside the core of the Earth's Crust, where both push harder against each other in opposite directions, and after enough pressure has been applied by both over time, one of the Tectonic Plates break, releasing stored up heat, energy, and lava among others.

Codependents oftentimes place themselves at risk of manifesting a catastrophic disease in their body because many cannot reconcile, in their own minds why their biological parents, or mother-surrogate, withheld their love from them. What could an innocent newborn infant have done to be rejected and abandoned by his or her parents? Codependent people are unable to find an adequate answer that would be acceptable to others so they repress their feelings and needs with shame and guilt. Lancer added "codependents repress their real Self and authentic feelings and develop deep, shame-based beliefs about who they are and their rights, needs, and lovability. This happens in reaction to dysfunctional parenting in childhood (such as critical, indifferent, rigid, invasive, inconsistent, or rejecting parents)."[182] After E shared with me she is codependent, and, given her declaration heightened my curiosity through the ceiling, the single most aggravating thing to L is not E's declaration that she is codependent, but, rather, her extreme resistance to talk about what she experienced as a child, who grew up in a dysfunctional household. To avoid any meaningful dialogue toward healing, and when I asked her some probing questions about her

---

[181] Lancer, op. cit., p. 8.
[182] Ibid., p. 11.

childhood, or offer his opinion about what he feels may have happened to her, E throws up *a wall of resistance and denial saying "this is my childhood experience but you think you know more about it than I do."* Obviously, such a remark will quickly end any dialogue so nothing get accomplished, and our understanding of CoDependency Addiction greatly suffers. Our relationship suffered too! Shame is another word for low-self-esteem, unworthiness, and not good enough.

Worthiness, high self-esteem, and feeling good enough are what make up a healthy, authentic Self. To the contrary, Lancer stated "shame is a painful feeling of unworthiness, inadequacy, and alienation...for codependents shame is internalized from experiences in childhood... You're ashamed of who you are."[183] When an apple is rotten at its core, the naked eye cannot see it's rotten; similarly, only a codependent person knows his or her core Self is deeply scared, injured, and wounded as a result of one's hurtful experiences encountered during his or her childhood while growing up in a dysfunctional family. E maintains she did not know she is codependent but no human being, regardless of how seriously abused they were during their childhood, the fact is, codependents may not know they have a CoDependency Addiction, but they do know they are ashamed of expressing their true feelings and needs. Nevertheless, their daily behavior has CoDependency traits, which they are not aware of, or take responsibility for.

Moreover, Lancer wrote "shame is an emotion that comes and goes, like anger or fear. But codependents have internalized shame so that it becomes who they think they are. They think they're bad, unlovable, guilty, selfish, weak, or responsible for abuse that they experienced."[184] Long-lasting, chronic shame changes ordinary shame into what Lancer calls shame anxiety. In fact, Lancer informed those seeking to gain a better understanding of CoDependency Addiction that "...prolonged shame...lead to hopelessness and despair or cause psychic numbing, being dead inside like a zombie. Internalized shame causes low self-esteem[185] and most codependent symptoms, such as pleasing, addiction,

---

[183] Ibid., p. 40.
[184] Ibid., p. 127.
[185] Ibid., p. 40.

control, caretaking, depression, lack of assertiveness, intimacy problems, and perfectionism."[186] All of these traits are of E's codependent life in our relationship. Although if you met E, your first impression of her is someone who is nearly perfect, using all of the right words and offering up an overwhelming amount of compassion. Her favorite phrase is *"I have compassion."*

This is only an abstraction of reality because beneath the veneer of perfectionism and caretaking is a deep void filled with pleasing, addiction, low self-esteem, hopelessness, lack of self-generation or creativity, control, and more. Whatever it takes to convince anyone she is a lovable person, E will "play a string" on the other person's heart. She has done this to L many times over the past 36 years in our relationship. In addition, Lancer wrote "the perfectionist has unreachable ideals concerning everything about you, your behavior, and the people in your life. It lives in a world of illusion…perfectionism is driven by shame. Although the perfectionist may focus on mistakes…or work, at its core is the belief that you're not adequate in some way-attractive enough, good enough, smart enough, strong enough, and so on."[187]

For example, in order to maintain control over L, while living with my mother in her home in Oakland, CA, E told my mother she was unhappy with the living arrangements my mother extended to us during our adjustment period to living in Oakland, CA." L's mother asked him about E's unhappiness, and, since L did not know at the time anything about E's CoDependency Addiction and need to control L, *he sided with E against his own mother!* Shame anxiety will make a codependent person do almost anything to maintain control over another person on whom the codependent person's survival depends. When L found out about what really took place during this exchange between E, L, and L's mother, L was completely flabbergasted and filled with no small amount of sadness, given the fact he has, since this experience, gone on, unknowingly to pour more than 36 years of his life-force into a relationship with E; and, only for L to find-out all that ever mattered

---

[186] Ibid., p. 40.
[187] Ibid., p. 159.

to her is her own selfish and narcissistic personal interest, of which the greatest was a continuous control of L's behavior. Because E sensed L's mother was a threat to her control of her son, E devised a clandestine plan to get L to leave his mother's house prematurely so the possibility of L waking up about E's control would not be jeopardized. After 30 days, L and E moved out of L's mother's house into an apartment in Hillcastle located near Lake Merritt in Oakland, CA. Psychopathology, or the use of other personality(s) was used by E to make up the false story that L's mother was dissatisfied with the living arrangements L's mother made available to us. Rather than challenge E further about the story she made up about L's mother telling him E was not happy with our living arrangements, *I went against my own mother in support of E's false story.* L's mother is deceased today, but, if my mother miraculously appeared reincarnated in her human body for only a second, I would apologize to her for being so naïve and ignorant of what was going-on in my relationship with E.

Had L taken a few more days to think deeply about this one incident, he could have unearthed E's CopDependency Addiction, and, given the deception, fraud, and moral bankruptcy involved, some hard decisions would have been made.

Psychic numbing allowed this to happen. And, today it is still entrenched inside E. Lancer added "the result is that, over time, you repress your inner life and turn off internal cues that give you data about reality and yourself. If you repress your feelings, observations, and reactions-not once, but on a regular basis-you become numb and depressed." [188] For example, L showed E a piece of Pecan Tree Branch shaped in the form of a snake. He asked E what does the shape look like? She could not come up with anything, but, when L told her what it is shaped like, and what I planned to do with the Pecan Tree Branch, E expressed no joy, amazement, or curiosity-no feelings! L does woodcarving, and he will woodcarve a snake out of the Pecan Tree Branch. This is the numbed psychic response L has received from E throughout the 36 years or more we have been in a relationship. There

[188] Ibid., p. 111.

is no particular reaction L feels E need to have about the Pecan Tree Branch; the issue is the absence of any genuine, deep-rooted feeling expressed about it that is the point.

Shame, therefore, is a codependent feeling. Thus, if a codependent person has low self-esteem, he or she feels unworthy, undeserving, and unimportant. Fears of abandonment and rejection are part of this codependent mixture. And, hardly anything a codependent person does, he or she often feel guilty about their own feelings, needs, and actions, and likewise about others' feelings, needs, and actions. This is why many codependents become addicted to other people because their estimation of who they are as a person is low. Once the absence of mother and father love transforms into shame, it is very nearly impossible to rebuild the inner, traumatized Self. The damage is widespread, and it would take enormous courage for E to go against the dysfunctional household she grew up in years before to begin making small steps toward a cure of her CoDependency Addiction to L.

Once E and L were at a House Warming Party given by one of E's friends. As we mingled among the attendees, one exchange between E and an artist, who paints on canvas stood out in my mind. I heard E say to the artist that she could "never be a painter." Before I knew it, I caught myself saying to E "why did you say you could never be a painter to the artist?' What E expressed, at the time, is what L now know, and that is, she was expressing a codependent feeling of shame! More accurately, E was expressing a codependent feeling that she cannot create anything that maybe classified as artwork. Usually, it has been my experience people admire and artist's creations, but normally they do not express diminished judgmental statements about oneself in the presence of the artist or another person. Another one of the Big Four Codependent Feelings is guilt.

B. Guilt

Being completely alienated from their core feelings and needs, which are hidden inside their repressed Self, and which are vigilantly guarded by the denial warden and prison guards discussed earlier, codependents live every day, every minute of every day, with a chip on their shoulders called guilt. Anything they recommend for their partner to do such as go to a movie, dance, play, dinner, or many others, the codependent person always has one thought in the back of his or her mind, namely, will their partner, friend, or others enjoy the activity he or she selected? If, by chance, someone says "I did not like the movie," then, the codependent person defaults to the guilt feelings he or she previously connected to their repressed Self. Everything, both feelings, needs, and actions are filtered through this codependent lens!

Since codependents repress their own feelings and needs, and, at the same time, attach themselves to another person's, and, moreover, whenever something turns out wrong or end up being a mistake, they wrongly take responsibility for the outcome. Under normal circumstances, when two people are in touch with their feelings and needs, and if an experience turn out sour, neither person feels guilty about the result, Both persons simply say to each other: We learned something from that experience, and we will not try that again. Finished and they both move on. However, this is not so, if one of the persons involved is codependent and the other person who is not says he or she did not enjoy the experience. The non-codependent person expresses his or her feelings about the experience, and the codependent person feels guilty the non-codependent person did not like the experience. Imagine being a codependent person, who lives daily taking responsibility for another person's dislikes! Lancer added "codependents feel guilty not only for their own feelings, but also about other people's feelings. They mistakenly feel responsible for them. You…feel guilty if your spouse didn't like the movie you chose, even though he or she agreed to see it. In relationships, you can't disagree without feeling guilty."[189]

The codependent in the relationship inevitably always ends up apologizing for his or her partner's behavior, and this must happen, over and over, because there is no way possible for one person to micro-manage another adult's feelings and needs. In many cases, codependents, nevertheless, try to do so, and some end up in verbal arguments with a

---

[189] Ibid., p. 45.

partner, while others suffer domestic violence. The codependent person cannot hear what his or her partner has to share about why he or she did not care for the movie because the former's feelings and needs are being repressed, and, therefore, the feelings and needs of the partner becomes the basis for an argument because they do not belong to the codependent person. *Understanding is the antidote for an argument*, but for the prescription to work successfully, two people must express how each feel about the movie, or any experience, which removes any ground for an argument to gain a foothold. Since this is not what happens in the world of a codependent person, and in E and L's relationship, a perpetual argument has been going-on for more than 36 years, and it is humanly impossible to reconstruct here the endless arguments we have had.

Of importance to remember about guilt is it is an extension of the repressed Self within a codependent person. On one side of the coin is an absence of expression of genuine feelings and needs by a codependent person; on the other, is his or her expression of guilt feelings such as "I apologize," "I am sorry," "I have compassion," "I should do more," and "I have done everything all my life for everyone else." Anytime one hears such statements made repetitively, be aware, for they are phrases-oftentimes-uttered by a codependent person to shift one's attention away from their lack of expression of their own repressed feelings and needs. In short, codependents work very hard at getting anyone who will listen to them to believe they are misunderstood, and the problem does not lie within their creation, but it has an external origin. Since the average American is completely unaware of what CoDependency Addiction is, it is no wonder the codependent person is able to easily get their audience to believe such is the case.

Thus far, we have laid-out the protectors of the codependent's great secret, namely denial, shame and guilt. As we have already seen, the Great Secret has its origin in a Monogamous, Dysfunctional Family in which the Patriarchal System prevails, and mothers give birth to their children in it in growing numbers, where the infant is not nurtured with love during his or her childhood. The codependent's Great Secret is exiting one's childhood into adult life with a grossly injured, wounded, and emotionally traumatized Self. Lancer stated "denial breeds secrets.

"[190]While many organizations have sprung up since the 1970s to help affected Americans with this problem, few of them, if any, have linked the mother's inability to love her infant to the devaluation of mother right, at a definite stage in the evolution of human history, as we have done in this book at its outset. We have pointed-out that a mother's lack of consistently providing love to her infant is an extremely hard piece of iron to break without the inclusion of knowledge of one of the landmark changes in the mother's role in human history.

Having anticipated the need for inclusion of such critical knowledge, and as we proceed with our consideration of CoDependency Addiction, we now pass to a discussion of the codependents' Great Secret, which is his or her *Repression of the Self.*

---

[190] Lancer, Ibid., p. 107.

CHAPTER ELEVEN

Codependents' Greatest Secret: Repression Of The Self By Their Learned Codependency Trauma(s) During Childhood

For hundreds of years, one common subject philosophers, social scientists, clergy people of all denominations, including New Age Spiritualists, and historians among many unnamed others have grappled with, and no doubt, pondered deep into the night in search of an answer to is this simple but profound question: "What is a human being?"[191] And, more specifically, what is the *nature of the Self?* This is more than a worthy question, but after so much has been written and spoken about the question through the years, the vast majority of Americans, and people worldwide, remain confused about the truth. Instead, most have been indoctrinated to believe that a *human being is born into sin and is, by nature, evil.*

A. What Is A Human Being? Good Or Evil?

Montagu threw much needed light on this heavy, dense, and crude darkness. He wrote "the age-old view that the human being is born "a natural barbarian," "an animal," not naturally 'good'…arises from the

---

[191] Montagu, op. cit., p. 288.

misinterpretations of "the Fall" or of "original sin."[192] Every infant born, during the 19th Century and the first half of the 20th Century, came into the world viewed as a *harden sinner without any hope of Earthly Redemption!* For example, one of my high school and college friends, who today is a Baptist Preacher, remarked to me several years ago that human beings, myself included, are *sinners*; and, our only hope of redemption, along with a chance to go to heaven, is based on whether God decides to offer someone *"Unmerited Grace."* Later, we shall document that every baby born is *"good."*

During this time in particular, Montagu added "the reinforcement which these views received...almost succeeded in hardening this view of the nature of human nature into something resembling an incontrovertible fact, a Law of Nature."[193] Research undertaken in the fields of biology and psychoanalytic theory has, to a large extent, laid to rest the view that men and women are born evil without any hope of redemption on Earth. Montagu wrote "...evidence has become available which indicates that the traditional view of human nature is unsound and, what is worse, capable of being profoundly damaging to human beings."[194] The vast majority of today's research-driven evidence points to the fact, since the beginning of human existence on Earth, beginning with the Savagery Period more than a million years ago, and that is, "...this evidence indicates that human beings are born good-"good" in the sense that there is no evil or hostility in them, but that at birth they are wholly prepared, equipped, to function as creatures who not only want and need to be loved by others but who also want and need to love others."[195] Everything we have included in this book thus far leads us to the singular fact that it is a mother and father love or mother-surrogate's that prepares an infant to know itself as love and use that same love to give others. Yet, for example, Louisiana leads the entire world today, regarding the incarceration of its residents with a rate of 1,605 per 100,000! The thousands of

---

[192] Ibid., p. 289.
[193] Ibid., p. 289.
[194] Ibid., p. 289.
[195] Ibid., p. 289.

incarcerated Louisiana Residents were not born destined to become violent and go to prison; many of these human beings were born into Monogamous Dysfunctional Families, which acted like a "border wall" between their mother and them, thereby preventing the former's love from flowing into infants at birth and thereafter. Later, we will address aggression and violence.

Presently, out attention is directed to the earlier question: What is a human being? Earlier, we mentioned Montagu said a human being is a work of art. That being so, it has been stated over and over that what makes a human being a work of art is mother and father love, or mother-surrogate's. All infants are born with an innate need for love, which his more compelling than the satisfaction of their basic needs. While both needs are crucial and life-saving, an infant, who has not been loved does not stop eating food, for example. The problem that arises is he or she will develop antisocial behaviors, which-oftentimes-lead to self-destructive behaviors, or destructive behavior aimed at others, or both. Enough cannot be said about the essential need for love all infants are born with. It is far too late to attempt to mentor love into a teenager or adult. For example, the cattle herds created naturally would greatly diminish, if the mother cow is unavailable to groom the external coat of a new born calf moments after it is born.

Therefore, the answer to the question "What is a human Being?: Love. Any defect that arises in an infant, save a genetic defect, has its roots in the breakdown of the mother's inability to transmit love to her babies. CoDependency Addiction is one such mental defect that originates this way, and due to denial, guilt, and others, it can persist in the life of an infant, from birth throughout the rest of his or her adult life. For 36 years or more, L did not know this was possible until after 2015, when he learned that E has been codependent during this time period, and still is today. The thing that holds such a tight grip on someone who is codependent is the latter's Self was not formed with mother and father's love at birth, but it is deformed by an absence of it. What makes a human being is mother, father, or mother-surrogate love; thus, a codependent person moves through life with an inactivated and invalidated Self, which is void of love, along with a simultaneous attachment to another person, whose Self is actively manifested by his or her expression of one's feelings and needs.

B. Codependent's Repression Of The Self

In our earlier discussion of the part played by shame, we indicated that codependents repress their real Self, and their authentic feelings and needs. By doing so, they are dehumanized due to an absence of mother, father, or mother-surrogate love. Yet, E, who did not receive mother love at crucial stages in her early childhood development, she, as a result of internalized shame and guilt, will say to anyone who will listen that she is a very lovable and compassionate person. Compassion is one of E's favorite words, which she uses-all the time- in an attempt to make the listener think she knows what love is, and capable of giving love to other people. What is actually repressed by a codependent person? Anyone who has some knowledge of what CoDependency Addiction is has realized, to some degree, that if a codependent's Self is repressed, it is not possible to love Self or other people even family members. Without the use of expressed feelings and needs, another person is seen by a codependent person *only* as an object for use.

The Self is our piece of inseparable connection to our primordial past, which is where life was first created and developed. It is where, nowhere, and everywhere and indefinable, timeless, and boundless reality. We carry our primordial beginnings inside of our Selves, and when our mothers deliver us to this world we know as Earth, which is a part of the Milky Way Galaxy, she anoint us with love that awakens us to our primordial past. As social creatures, A.K.A. human beings, it is our birthright to express our primordial love through our feelings and needs located inside our Selves, similar to the configuration of a nucleus in a cell, or atoms that exists inside of all of the chemical elements in the Periodic Table. Lancer boldly offers a definition of the Self. She says "the term *Self* is vague and difficult to identify and define. It's your unique, essential being. It's encoded in your DNA, waiting to be embodied, developed, and expressed. Famous psychoanalyst Carl Jung thought it's a coherent, unifying principle that integrates the totality of all that you are-both the center and whole of your psyche."[196] In addition, Lancer made note that the Self is a composite of our personality, unconscious, conscious, and ego (this helps you deal with reality, but makes up only a small part)[197]

After considering these indispensable parts of our Self, the trail winds back to our primordial beginning. What must not be overlooked, understated, underestimated, or minimized is our Self is our GPS, which guides us through all of the challenges we will ever encounter on Earth. More importantly, our Self shows us the way to the next life. That being so, can you imagine experiencing an emotional trauma during your childhood, which cause you to repress your primordial, essential being? Lancer adds "…codependents feel guilty and ashamed about…"[198] their feelings and needs, and, to their unfortunate detriment, they repress their primordial existence.

If you are codependent, then you have an addiction to another person called CoDependency. And, this addiction means the codependent person is attached to another person's feelings and needs, and his or her Self is repressed, namely, primordial beginnings, feelings and needs. Lancer wrote "my definition cuts to the core of codependency: a lost Self…*A codependent is a person who can't function from his or her innate self and instead organizes thinking and behavior around a substance, process, or other person(s).*"[199]

Therefore, it is clear CoDependency Addiction is equal to a codependent person's lost Self, which is one's repressed Self. E's CoDependency Addiction is equivalent to her lost Self. Not realizing the magnitude of this disease, she thought the answer to her lost Self is an attachment to L's Self. It is unnatural for one Self to navigate two people through this life-L with E attached to his feelings and needs; under the best of circumstances, this is impossible to do! This is similar to attaching a 100 pound weight on a person's back, and carry it every day like L did with E attached to his Self for 36 years or more. L carried

---

[196] Lancer, op. cit., p. 31.

[197] Ibid., p. 31.

[198] Ibid., p. 44.

[199] Ibid., p. 31.

the weight of E attached to his feelings and needs; however, when L discovered E's CoDependency Addiction to him, he could not carry the 100 pound weight any longer because, at best, by continuing to do so, this unnatural weight becomes increasingly life-threatening. It is worth repeating here what we mentioned earlier, and that is, E's sister's husband recognized E's CoDependency Addiction during a conversation E and L had with him during the early 1980s. E's brother-in-law, at some point during our conversation, remarked "somebody is not thinking." When L heard this remark, L downplayed it by laughing it off because L was 100% sure E's brother-in-law was wrong. E an L had spent several years in deep study of philosophy, and no subject was immune from our examination related to our own Selves, politics, education, and others. Whatever L's feelings about these topics were at the time, E bandwagon them

E's brother-in-law was right! Somebody was not thinking, and given the fact a codependent person lives with a repressed Self, E's thinking was not reflective of her own feelings and needs but of L's. L know this now, but it took me 36 or more years to figure it all out. No healing is possible until E accepts responsibility that she was addicted to L for 36 years, during which time, she never expressed what she felt or needed in our relationship. Once I found out E is codependent, I tried for three years to get her to accept responsibility for the emotional trauma she has endured, and for the trauma we all have experienced due to her CoDependency Addiction. No matter what I did to try to get past E's denial, nothing worked! Everything that requires four legs has three; the one leg missing is the codependent's repressed and lost Self. E and L live on several acres of beautiful land; we have a house that is paid for; no car notes; we have money to pay our bills; and more. Yet, the table has only three legs, which makes all material things and the people involved, stand on shaky ground, upon which everything has been falsely constructed. *Even as sacred as the reproductive act is, conception of new life takes place in an atmosphere of CoDependency Addiction!* The latter, according to Lancer, is a three-leg table because "growing up, [codependents] never learned to identify their feelings or felt safe expressing them, especially if they had no one to comfort them. Instead, they felt ashamed and buried and repressed their feelings."[200] Save the very bare necessities such as E told me on many occasions during our 36 year relationship, that she had some food to eat; yet, according to E, none of her needs and feelings were met on an emotional level.

E's key needs for love were ignored by her parents and other siblings, although her older siblings' key needs were ignored too. Lancer wrote "if key needs were shamed or ignored in your childhood, you grow up doing the same to yourself and shut down feelings associated with those needs...if you never received nurturing or had your feelings respected, you...attempt to fill this void with an addiction. Addictive relationships serve as a substitute for real connection."[201] L served as E's chosen addiction, but what E failed to realize, L could not fill the enormous void inside of her Self that was created by an absence of fulfillment of love by her parents. Put another way, the void inside of E's Self is proportional with the absence of her mother and father's love. As the amount of love ungiven to E by her parents, the void within her Self grew proportionally in size. As it was in E's case, who was not given mother and father love during her childhood, this meant, by the time E left home as an adult, the void in her Self was, more than unlikely, very, very large! Lancer adds "the result is that, over time, you repress your inner life and turn off internal cues that give you data about reality and yourself. If you repress your feelings, observations, and reactions-not once, but on a regular basis-you become numb and depressed."[202] The codependent person does not exit child- hood unscarred, wounded, injured, abused, and more...but the scars remain and account for problems in relationships and coping with reality."[203] Most of L's biggest challenges did not originate outside of his relationship with E in the workplace, but, rather, the majority was an *inside job*. L now understands he has been the target of E's codependent addiction for nearly 40 years; and, for example, no matter what L created, E showed no love, gratitude, or appreciation toward her Self or L's.

---

[200] Ibid., p. 77.

[201] Ibid., p. 79.

[202] Ibid., p. 111.

[203] Ibid., p. 122.

In 1979 E shared with L a profound red flag related to her *giving up custody of her five year old son to his father, who moved back to Tampa, FL after their divorce. I missed understanding the deep implications E's decision to give up custody of her son was having on E and L's less than one year old relationship.* E packaged her giving up custody of her son in an acceptable public box tied up neatly with an altruistic flower arrangement. At the time, L thought "how compassionate and wonderful a mother E is, one who is able to emotionally part with her son. When L divorced his ex-wife, M would have preferred to die than give up custody of our son-D. There never was a discussion about that being a remote possibility!

However, after more than 36 years after E told me she gave up custody of her five year old son, L finally grasped the darkness beneath E's decision. It grew out of her repressed Self in which E's feelings and needs were alien to her. E could not feel anything; she was suffering with CoDependency Addiction so the *gravity of giving up custody of her five year old son never had an impact on her as the years went by; and, L do not ever remember E crying one time about giving up custody of her son.* L did not give up custody of his son D; he divorced his mother-M, who maintained custody of our son. If L had only resisted the public box E placed giving up custody of her five year old son in, L would have come to this realization years earlier: How can E give up her mother love for her son, and simultaneously say she loves L? This is a grand impossibility (!!) and a contradiction. L accepts responsibility for not digging deeper into this problem, which, through the years, has grown into a castle in the sky built up on a foundation of sand. Had L challenged E about her decision to give up custody of her son, and if he had planned to stay in the relationship with E, L would need to insist E contact social services in 1979, and take back custody of her son, or leave the relationship. L needed to take this stand because no infant who grows up in a dysfunctional family, where mother love is absent, will have an opportunity to learn there is no difference between love and the Self, and the latter is a storage place for mother, father, or mother-surrogate love; and, that as an adult, the grown up gives it unconditionally to another person or group.

That being so, within the repressed and lost Self of the codependent person, nothing is right; every feeling and need is expressed negatively even when one tries to overcompensate with a polished public personality.

CHAPTER TWELVE

By-Products Of The Codependent Person's Lost And Repressed Self: Feelings And Needs And Creativity Aborted Replaced By-Self-Hate, Blame, Conflict, And Control

The compounding evidence, similar to gravity, brings everything we have discussed thus far down to one central theme: That an absence of mother, father, or mother-surrogate love produces codependent people. Because most codependent people suffers from a lack of a conscience, it is extremely difficult for them to own up to their past. E says "I do not want to talk about the past; I just want to talk about what we can do right now in the present." Nothing is incorrect with this viewpoint except there are experiences and behaviors that need to be examined so any decisions made in the present can be freed of the baggage of one's codependent past. Any good medical doctor will want to know about his or her patient's past lifestyle so a clear diagnosis can be made of a present condition. More importantly, this research is required so that any medical procedure recommended stands upright on the patient's history. Codependents, as we have already shown, and due to the fact they have an undeveloped conscience, many lose contact with time. This is why it is so difficult for them to remember their childhoods and many of the emotional injuries and injustices they have suffered. L spent his lifetime studying social and economic history; however, E, after her stroke, does not want the word mentioned, nor does she talk about her childhood history as a way to find out how to liberate her repressed Self from the years of emotional trauma she suffered in the dysfunctional household she grew up in.

A. Feelings And Needs

Generally speaking, codependents are not aware of their feelings and needs. They can express emotions such as arguing, screaming, rage, and engage in many forms of external disapproval about other people's behavior or situations; yet, when it comes to expressing their own feelings and needs, they do not because they are repressed. As L self-reflect about his relationship with E, he recalls a time when E would often ask him to express his feelings. L thought E was interested in helping him express his feelings, but, when the CoDependency Addiction to L came to light, he realized E wanted L to express his feelings because E thought L's feelings were her own as well. As long as L expressed his feelings and needs, E used them to help her know how to respond to anything L said. For example, if L said "I do not like to exercise on Sunday morning," E would use his feeling about exercise and counter saying "I do not like to exercise on Sunday either, or say I agree with you." It seems two feelings were expressed but, in reality, only one was, namely, L's feeling. Not knowing anything about CoDependency, or E's emotional trauma experienced during her childhood, L misinterpreted E's *zerox copying* of his feelings and needs as her way of expressing my feelings. How wrong I was for years!

Lancer wrote "some codependents complain that they feel like "a fraud," or that they experience a gap between their public and inner selves."[204] On the other hand, L does not feel like a "fraud;" rather, he feels it is a fraud that he gave so much of his life force to the relationship only to find out any decisions made did not reflects E's feelings and needs over the years. Lancer stated "codependents...are unaware of their

---

[204] Ibid., p. 32.

needs, wants, and feelings...When ignoring your needs and feelings, you assess what others need and feel to gauge your response."[205] This was E's pattern throughout the duration of our relationship! Just this Saturday morning-February 16, 2019-L asked E what is your feeling about Louise Hay's Book titled You Can Heal Your Life, 1999. No sooner than I asked E to express her feelings about the latter, she, in typical codependent fashion, asked me the same question. She needed to hear my response to my own question so she could gauge how to respond to my question about Louise Hay's book. This was classic CoDependency Addiction at work.

E, similar to most codependent people, usually know what other people feel and need; unfortunately, there is an exclusion of their own repressed feelings and needs. Lancer wrote "codependents are usually good at knowing what other people feel and spend a lot of time worrying about them, often with resentment, but they aren't much aware of their feelings...When people are obsessing about their addiction-whether it's to a person, food, sex, work, or a drug-it's usually a distraction from what they're really feeling."[206] E's addiction is L among others such as the Women Empowerment Group she belonged to for more than 20 years. For example, every time we spent intimate time together, E had to use some kind of stimulant. Every time without fail!! For many of the 36 years or more we were together, L thought E's interest in using a drug of choice during intimate times had to do with her interest in having a more heightened, relaxed experience. However, when her CoDependency Addiction came to light recently since 2015, L learned the real reason for E's use of a stimulant was to help her keep her true feelings and needs connected to her Self-repressed. Under the influence of a stimulant, all L remember he and E spoke about during intimate times was an obsession with fantasies of one kind or another. *Anything superficial was safe to talk about but E's CoDependency Addiction had to be kept a Great Secret at all cost.* There is always a cost to be paid for such behavior. Lancer added "an unintended consequence of denying painful feelings is that you become

---

[205] Ibid., p. 66.

[206] Ibid., p. 77.

depressed or numb to joy, gratitude, and love, too. Energy that can be used creatively and constructively gets channeled into holding down feelings, like trying to keep the lid on a pressure cooker."[207]

Throughout the 36 years or more of existence of our relationship, E rarely took an interest in any creative adventure that was *self-generated*. She participated in other creative activities some of her peers initiated; as Lancer noted, the energy that E could have used to be creative, she channeled it into keeping her CoDependency Addiction a Great Secret. Thus, anything L created such as publishing several books, traveling all over the world, and producing more than 15 woodcarvings among many others, E was "numb to joy, gratitude, and love, too." E could not tell L how joyous and filled with gratitude and love L's creations made her feel due to the fact she was cut-off from her Self, which is her *primordial well*, inclusive of joy, love, gratitude, compassion, trust, and so forth. As an artist, writer, woodcarver, and so on, L was confused, for many years, about E's cold response to his creative productions. E's creative needs and feelings were ignored during her childhood; and therefore, she shut down this aspect of her Self, and when she saw the woodcarvings that took L one year to complete, for example, to produce, *E could not see the creative spirit in L because she shut it down in her own Self years earlier before she ever knew L existed on Earth.* Lancer wrote "why feel a need if you don't expect it to be filled? It's less painful to deny it entirely."[208]

The trigger that sets the wheel of repression of feelings and needs in motion, for a codependent person, is unavailable and inadequate mother, father, or mother-surrogate love, beginning with the birth of an infant. Without the reassurance of mother love, an infant comes into the world feeling insecure and alone. The renowned British Group known as the Beatles asked this very important question in one of their hit songs, namely, Eleanor Rigby: "Where do all of the lonely people come from?" The answer is they are born and unloved at a critical stage in their early childhood development. This is where they come from!

---

[207] Ibid., p. 77.

[208] Ibid., p. 79.

Lancer wrote "they learn that their needs, feelings, and thoughts are unimportant, wrong, and shameful. They adapt to the environment and develop ideals of who they need to be for survival. A child's Self can become organized around…pleasing, and/or performing for others' approval in order to feel loved."[209] If the absence of mother, father, or mother-surrogate love is brief or short lived, the infant may be able to avoid the deep scarring and wounds his or her Self suffers; however, if there is a prolonged absence of this love, an infant's feelings and needs become repressed inside of the Self. Lancer added "repeated instances can teach children to repress their needs and feelings and tune in to the mother's expectations and emotions."[210]

And, by tuning into the mother's expectations and emotions without her first satisfying her child's need with mother love, this is the moment the affected child first becomes codependent. Although the mother's child does not know it, he or she is now codependent; that is to say, the latter develops an addiction to one's mother; and, by the time the child grow up to be an adult, he or she carries his or her addiction learned during infancy into one's adult life, and continues its existence by becoming addicted to another person. This is how E became addicted to L via the CoDependency Addiction she learned during her childhood.

All-in-all, we do not want to mislead anyone to think a codependent person does not express any feelings. They do express them but, unfortunately, for the codependent person and the person he or she is addicted to with one's Codependency, the feelings and needs expressed are, generally speaking, negative with a very low vibration. For example, Lancer research indicates that most of a codependent person's feelings are expressed within the following categories: Low Self-Esteem, Shame, Fear, and guilt.[211] For example, imagine being in a relationship with a codependent person as I was in one with E for 36 years or more, and it is possible that any conversation through the years, L is talking with E, who, beneath her public persona, lack self-confidence; feel unworthy; unlovable; and undeserving; fear of abandonment; and who feels guilt about her feelings. Where can E an L's relationship evolve to? Similar to

---

[209] Ibid., p. 101.
[210] Ibid., p. 101.
[211] Ibid., p. 40.

Sisyphus rolling his stone uphill every day, and when he nearly reaches the top, his stone rolls back down the hill to the bottom. Every day, the same result occurs year in-and-out. No change! If you have not guessed by now, L is Sisyphus, and what makes him lose concentration nearing the top of the hill with his stone (The stone is only symbolic) is the negative feelings E enters into the scenario, either verbally dressed up in a public persona or non-verbally.

For example, when L worked for Southern University, he and three other professor colleagues wrote a $6.2 million NASA Grant Proposal. Before L, and his colleagues, were notified by NASA that their grant proposal was awarded, L shared with E he was going to the Ford Dealership in Lafayette, LA and purchase a $30,000 brand new Ford F-250 Truck; E was totally against this purchase. She voiced scarcity, fear, undeservingness, anxiety, and lack of self-confidence. I was 100% certain my colleagues and I would get the $6.2 million. L spent two summers, living alone in an apartment, while he was being trained at John C. Stennis Space Center in Hancock, MS. L had put in his 10,000 hours of training, and he felt confident the NASA Grant would get awarded, and that he deserved the new Ford F-250 Truck. L persevered and bought this truck, and less than two weeks later, NASA awarded us the $6.2 million!

If L had listen to anymore of E's scarcity thinking, his Sisyphus Stone would have rolled back downhill, and it could have even sent an energetic message through the universe notifying NASA that one of the team member has serious doubts about executing the requirements of such a large grant. This is why L persisted and bought the truck; he sent a message of unwavering confidence to NASA's decision-makers, and they received it. Because I did not do the same thing related to the Land purchase opportunity mentioned earlier, and due to E's codependent feelings involved in the process, L and E lost out on the purchase of 110 acres of prime farmland at the low sale price of $60,000! I could add to this list.

However, at this time, our attention is directed to self-hate and blame, two behaviors that are commonly used by codependent people to keep their feelings and needs locked away inside of them Selves.

B. Self- Hate And Blame

It is not a stretch of the imagination to easily see how a codependent person would manifest the CoDependency feeling of self-hate. As we have already mentioned on numerous occasions thus far, an infant given birth by a codependent mother, who grow up in a monogamous, codependent family, is not provided any love by his or her mother, father, or mother-surrogate. Because an infant in this situation is completely vulnerable as a result, and worse, at the mercy of his or her rejecting mother; and, therefore, rather than focus its displeasure on his or her mother, the affected infant internalizes the emotionally traumatic pain of its mother's rejection of it Self, and due to this broken mother–infant relationship, the latter develops a growing dislike of Self, and as the infant grows older, *its rejection by its mother evolves into inner self-hate of the Self.* Codependent persons become overrun by anger within the Self; Lancer added "…they have turned [anger] against themselves because they couldn't direct it toward parents they looked up to and relied on for survival."[212] Although the codependent infant has turned its anger against its own Self, in reality, the latter really *hates his or her parents.*

This hate sets up a life-long duality within the infant, and it continues to smolder for decades, and oftentimes, the duality, namely, on one hand, the child desires to love his or her mother, and on the other, he or she hates the parents. By the time an infant reaches its second critical period of early childhood development, that is, between two-or three-year old stage, Montagu wrote "in the second critical period frustration arises from interference and punishment: the parent or parent-person is *present*, and the child wishes he were *absent*. The latter wish produces intolerable conflict in the child, who hates the parent whom he desires to love because he is punishing, and thus, confused and rendered anxious for fear of separation from the beloved figure, he [or she] tends to cling to his [or her] dependency more than ever."[213] This fact only reinforce our earlier contention, which is, in the absence of mother, father, or mother-surrogate love, the infant, during the normal dependency state, becomes

---

[212] Ibid., p. 11.
[213] Montague, op. cit., p. 225.

codependent, or addicted to the mother, and due to self-hate caused by the infant's hate of his or her parents whom they desire to love, the former, being terrified by the ever-present possibility of being abandoned by the mother, father, or mother-surrogate, *becomes conditioned by this possibility; and, therefore, he or she's self-hate is a manifestation of the child's CoDependency Addiction, which he or she clings to for the rest of one's life.* This self-hate, which is really *parental hate turned against the infant/child's Self,* is nearly, impossible to reverse because an affected child, and later as an adult, and hard as one may try, and as good as one's intention may be, *nearly nothing can fill the void inside of the child/adult with the love that was not given by a mother, father, or mother-surrogate during the earliest stages of an infant's life.*

It is a gross oversimplification of the self-hate of the parents turned against the Self that a codependent person, by adult age, is able to resolve this conflict, and proceed to live a normal life. E was asked to write a letter to her mother about her self-hate turned against her Self as hate of her mother and father. Nothing noticeable in the days and months that followed her writing the letter to her mother, in the way of practical changes, was observed by L in E's behavior. It is business as usual!

Rather than confront their parents at an appropriate time about their hate of their parents, codependents attempt to shift, or project their self-hate, and feelings of hate toward their parents, onto another person in the form of blame.

C. Codependent People Blame their Partners In A Relationship, Or Others, To Conceal Their Self-Hate And Parental Hate

Children usually "…blame themselves for not stopping abuse directed toward them…from an abusive parent…It's also natural to love and need love and affection from your parents despite abuse. Children will do anything to get it because they need love to grow."[214] One of the things codependents do is deny their self-hate pains, and seek, falsely, to ease it by saying to anyone who will listen that their

---

[214] Lancer, op. cit., p. 128.

codependent problem is caused by their partner or other external factor. Every since E had a stroke in July 2015, she has continuously asked me: "What did you do L to contribute to the cause of the breakdown in our relationship?" She asked me this question more times than I can remember since that time; yet, seldom, if ever, has E ever mentioned that concealing her self-hate, wounds, and pains she experienced during her childhood contributed significantly to our relationship's downfall. How many people do you know readily say "oh yes, by the way, I really hate my parents?." It is too painful to share this feeling openly with others; however, others are told, for example, L is the cause of all of the trouble in our relationship. Today, my daughter H and son H, for example, both have been spoken with at length, on many occasions, about how L is "so unkind, insensitive, and uncaring toward E. Neither one of these close family members ever had the courage to reach out to me and ask me if, in fact, L actually is guilty of behaving this way toward their mother. And, if I told them yes, then they would have to logically ask me "why am I behaving so uncharacteristically different now?" L believes they did not reach out to him about our relationship breakdown, is because both of them know what E–their mother–shared with them about L is a *lie*. Recall in the Introduction of this book, E mentioned that she experienced a significant lack of kindness during her childhood. Yet, she wants L to be *kind* to her, which is something she never gave to her own Self! Of all the females on Earth, L took E with him all over the world, to every continent except Antarctica and Asia. He even paid all of her bills so that by the time E retired, she did not have any bills save variable utility bills. This is not to mention the 10,000 hours L spent with E engaged in spiritual experience, either at the ocean; in the mountains; or, driving across country.

It is laughable for E to say to anyone L was not kind to her during the 36 years he was in a relationship with her; and, it is a tragedy for a family member or friend, who knows anything about L, to believe otherwise.

Lancer wrote "blaming others and external circumstances denies your power to effect change and achieve happiness."[215] On February

---

[215] Ibid., p. 20.

18, 2019, L came into the kitchen to prepare his lunch for work and breakfast. On the counter was a note with something scribbled on it. It caught L's attention, and when he read it, L was not surprised to see it had a lot to do with blame. The note stated the following: "He's a part of yourself you called forward for your healing"-2/16/19. Imagine a codependent person mentioning this statement to his or her partner.

When L read this statement, the first thing came into his mind is "selfishness," "narcissism," "egotism," and "arrogance." That is to say, if a codependent person, E for example, called L into her life to receive all of the low, negative, CoDependency vibrations she experienced during her childhood growing up in a dysfunctional family. The mentioned statement does not say if L knowingly agreed to serve E's purpose of purging her Self of the self-hate she holds inside toward her Self and parents? It merely says L was called forth arrogantly by E to experience all of her hurt and pain while she vainly tries to divest her Self of it at another human being's expense and life!

Is this what happened to Jesus in the Bible? He was sent into the world to heed the call of the people who were suffering damaged Selves, and in the end, Jesus was crucified for others pain and sins. L was not given a choice by E to see if he would agree to sacrifice his life so she could accomplish her goal of expulsion of her demons from her mind and Self. Have you ever heard of anything more arrogant than this tyranny? L falsely thought he was getting into a healthy relationship with E; being called forth to participate in E's healing of her childhood wounds and emotional trauma is not what L agreed to do then and not now! *If L was asked to make such a sacrifice when E and L got in a relationship together in 1979, L would not have agreed to do so!* But, to make it seem like L was getting into a healthy relationship at that time, E kept her CoDependency Addiction Problems a Great Secret, which was maintained through the years by her Denial Warden and Prison Guards of her injured and wounded Self.

In addition, the ultimate purpose E supposedly called L, unknowingly, to be part of her so-called healing is to have him available to, on one hand, figure out her survival needs in life, and on the other, to have him around to engage in emotional warfare daily in the form of arguments, attacks, and generalized abuse. E's healing has nothing to do with anything because she is too vested in denial and negativity. *Every time L asked E a question about why she repressed her feelings and needs, when she had ample opportunities to express them openly, she becomes very emotional; raises her voice; refuse to answer the question, changes the subject; and flees the room.* This is how her parents and siblings handled every situation that came up in their dysfunctional household.

L observed this dysfunctional behavior play out, for more than 25 years, of being in the presence of her mother and other siblings. L thought certainly this is not how E would ever react to any situation that might come up between us in our relationship. How wrong was L to think this fantasy because this is exactly how E has responded to every situation that has arisen in our relationship since 2015! According to Lancer, this is "another avoidance tactic…to focus on the other person [L] and blame him or her for something to avoid taking responsibility for your own actions. Low self-esteem makes it hard for codependents to admit anything."[216] *For 36 years, L has been continuously blamed for something so E could avoid taking responsibility for her repressed feelings and needs, and admit how much she hates her Self, and her Parents, and life in general.*

Moreover, the idea of E healing her wounded Self is, therefore, an illusion. Too much pain, hurt, and suffering have been repressed and internalized within her Self. E mentioned to L she could have used <u>A Course In </u>Miracles information to heal her Self; instead, she chose to *teach others*, hoping they would tell her she is a good person, and that they love her. E was merely another *"unhealed Healer."* Lancer added "when parents withhold love…and blame…their children, the shame and fear of abandonment become internalized."[217] This is a deeply broken spirit; it is the same if someone pours sugar in the gas tank of a car; the engine will not run again because the sugar destroys it similar to a mother, father, or mother-surrogate withholding love from her child.

Therefore, codependents blame has a purpose. First, it is engaged in to cover up "…shame and guilt, and self-blame…covers up anger

---

[216] Ibid., p. 218.
[217] Ibid., p. 111.

toward someone else…Attack and blame avoid self-examination."[218] E told me on numerous occasions that her ex-husband physically abused her. At the time she told me about this abuse, he thought oh how unfortunate! L really felt empathy and compassion for E. What I did not know at the time was E was repressing her feelings and needs, and she had been doing so while she was married to her first husband. The comments in the Introduction of this book proves this fact. Now that L knows codependents blame others to avoid taking responsibility for their own lives, it is likely that E's first husband felt the stinging attack of E's blaming him for something he did not do, and in a moment of anger, his physical attack of E came out of this vulnerable place by feeling his self-esteem was being attacked by her. Because of L's educational background, he was able to avoid engaging in any physical or mental abuse of E since he could see her blame coming from a mile away, giving him time to diffuse it.

E's blame of L for her CoDependency Addiction to him was on full display on the evening of February 19, 2019. L asked E to turn the Television off so he could take his bath in silence. E resisted L's request saying "you always get what you want" in an elevated voice. L calmly asked E to not speak to him in a loud voice. Although E did not know what her statement meant, L immediately discerned the CoDependency Addiction in it. That is, if E thinks L always gets what he wants, then this is clear evidence that she did not express her feelings and needs through the years. The origin of this wound occurred decades earlier when, as an infant and little girl, she never received what she wanted, which is her mother and father's love. For the unwitting observer, it would appear that E did express her feelings and needs but L overrode them, and dogmatically did whatever he wanted, regardless of how it affected E. Of course, that never happened; E made the statement about L always getting what he wanted because her feelings and needs were repressed. Another indicator of E's blame of L surfaced on the same day mentioned. E wrote the names of 21 people on a sheet of paper; the list represents those persons she has gratitude for. L accidentally saw the

---

[218] Ibid. pp. 200 and 202.

sheet of paper laying on the bed with the names visible. Most of the 21 names listed have not done anything for E in her life! The fact is, the reverse is true.

E has done everything for the 21 people on the list, mainly motivated by her insatiable thirst for their attention and love. Not surprisingly, L's name was not written on the list, although he has done everything for E humanly possible during the past 36 years. By not writing my name on the gratitude list signaled somewhere inside E's repressed Self that she is blaming L for her CoDependency Addiction troubles, although he is the one human being E attached her Self to; and lied to; for the past 36 years or more.

In sum, the only person E can blame is her Self, and no one else, for her CoDependency Addiction woes. Until E resolves her self-hate and hate of her parents, no healing will be possible! Another tactic codependents use to avoid dealing with this truth is the employment of the Big Cs: Conflict and Control.

D. Codependents Use A Conflict Tactic To Maintain An Argument To Avoid Exposing Their Repressed Feelings And Needs Buried In The Self

At the core of a codependent person's negative feeling of conflict, is his or hers' *internalized dichotomy of a desire to love one's parents and, at the self-same time, hate them. This is the Grand Conflict!* Existing in an internal state of conflict, nearly every exchange E an L have had during the past 36 years always began, or ended in a conflict, and before the exchange was over, it usually devolved into an argument. Even during those times before E and L spent some quality intimate time (?) together, there was, oftentimes, a conflict between us, which devolved into an argument. By the time H entered high school and later college, E and L engaged in so much conflict and arguments that H would ask us "Why are the two of you always arguing about everything?" At first, L thought the answer to H's question was E and L are not in conflict but having a debate about various ideas and situations. Again, L was wrong; we were not having a debate but conflict was inevitably introduced into every discussion due to E's internalized conflict related to her desire to love her parents and hate them at the same time. Lancer stated "as the disease progresses, anger and conflict are more common..."[219] During the late stage of CoDependency Addiction, increased conflict is predominant.

Moreover, because a codependent person is generally obsessive-compulsive, regarding helping others with a hope that someone will satisfy his or her need for love, and when the void inside of the Self remains empty, the codependent person feels guilty, and tries to do more; work harder; take the blame for other's mistakes; and apologizes for everything. Thus, Lancer wrote "guilt gets in the way of hearing the other person, perpetuating conflict."[220] In dysfunctional families parents blame children; children blame parents; and there are constant conflicts going-on all of the time. No one exercises his conscience geared toward "upholding what is right and wrong." Lancer added "... in dysfunctional families, children and parents are blamed repeatedly, and there are constant arguments or silent walls of resentment. Nothing gets resolved."[221] At the core of a codependent person's Self, is an on-going conflict between his or her hidden, inner, real world in which there exists a desire to love one's parents and hates them at the same time, and a manufactured, unreachable, world of illusion for public consumption. The gap between these two worlds cause a codependent person to *feel like a fraud*, given the fact that one's real world is repressed, and a *world of illusion is lived in everyday. Usually, the codependent person is the only one who knows his or her manufactured world of illusion is a lie.* Lancer wrote "paradoxically, until you accept yourself, it's difficult to change at all because you're in conflict with reality."[222] Guilt, therefore, inhibits a codependent person from listening to another person, which renders any possible communication impossible. Conflict is the product.

E says all the time that she "Does not know who L is anymore?" Her thinking process has been turned upside down by her stroke. After her stroke, E's Hippocampus, an area of the brain where her short-term

---

[219] Ibid., p. 22.
[220] Ibid., p. 45.
[221] Ibid., p. 114.
[222] Ibid., p. 159.

memory exists, was impacted adversely. Thus, E, independent of her desire to keep her CoDependency Addiction a secret, was forced to deal with her *contradiction inside of her Self.* That being so, and given the damage the stroke caused to her short-term memory, *today, she no longer remembers who L is before she had her stroke in July 2015.* Every day since that time, E tells everyone L has changed, but she is unable to grasp L did not change but she has, due to the fact she is being forced to, for the first time in her life, to deal with her own feelings and needs, and she does not remember L's feelings and needs that she has been addicted to as a codependent person beforehand for 36 years or more. *In short, E does not know who L is today because his feelings and needs are not hers' to use as her own anymore, nor can she remember them as she did before her stroke in July 2015.*

How, then, do codependent people keep their partners under their influence for many years without one's Codependency Addiction being detected? How do they walk the survival tightrope without falling into the waiting abyss? Just like codependent people use denial to keep their injured and wounded Self hidden from their intimate partners, they simultaneously use their partner and friend's feelings and needs to *control* them.

E. Codependent People Use Control To Hold Their Intimate Partners And Other People Under Their CoDependency Addiction Influence

The <u>Webster's Ninth New Collegiate Dictionary</u>, 1984 defines control as follows: "To exercise restraining or directing influence over…Having the capacity to affect behavior…with regard to possession and use…To have power over…"[223] The other person a codependent person is addicted to in a relationship is vitally important to his or her survival. Nothing can be left to chance as a result. Failure could result in the death of the codependent person. Thus, as the definition for control demonstrates, the person a codependent person is addicted to is perceived

---

[223] <u>Webster's Ninth New Collegiate Dictionary</u>, op. cit., p. 285.

by the latter as his or possession and use. The person the codependent is addicted to must be restrained and held under the direct influence of the latter. He or she exists in a relationship with a codependent person as a slave, for the latter's possession, use, and survival. A good metaphor of how insidious and destructive psychologically control is for the person the codependent is addicted to is found in a line of one of Malcolm X's famous speeches about the American Slavery Institution.

We paraphrase Malcolm X saying "How do you feel this morning massa," asked Uncle Tom? The massa responded Tom "I am not feeling well this morning." Then, Uncle Tom replied "We not feeling good this morning Massa; we sick." As we see, Uncle Tom identified completely with the feelings of the Massa, and this is how a codependent person maintains control over the person he or she is addicted to. That is, by using the latter's feelings and needs to exercise a restraining influence over him or her. At no time can the person, who the codependent person is addicted to, be allowed to freely choose this or that course of action without a negative challenge or judgment. Last night-February 20, 2019-L informed E again that Gayle and Mike Melancon offered us first option to buy their 110 acres of farmland, for $60,000, during the early 1990s. In an attempt to control L's thinking, E responded to L saying "Gayle Melancon and Mike Melancon told him a lie, and they did not talk to her about buying the land; and, worse, E told L he made this entire situation up, and L told her a lie!" We see, a codependent person, E in particular, will go to any length in their attempt to deny the truth, which is impossible to do. When L asked E how did she know Gayle and Mike Melancon told L a lie? An eerie silence came over her, as if E could not conceive the fact that she called Mike and Gayle Melancon a lie, and L would not ask her what is she basing her judgment on? Only upon E's desperate need to control L's thinking, feelings and needs!

Lancer wrote "codependents ignore their needs and depend upon others and frequently self-sacrifice to an unhealthy degree. They care for others in a way that leads to control..." [224] By being a superman

---

[224] Lancer, op. cit., p. 15.

or woman to another person, by satisfying the needs of the person, or group of people, the codependent person abnormally creates a false "you need me attitude in others," which eventually leads to the former's control of them. Codependent people control others, via manipulating their feelings and needs, is similar to driving a car.

The driver determines where the car is going; codependent people make vain attempts to determine where another person, or group, is going, which usually ends in failure such as a relationship crash or wreck. The aim of the codependent person is foremost and always to "...directly and indirectly try to control the other in order to get their needs met."[225] Recently, E, in a rare moment of self-disclosure, started sharing with me some of the pain and suffering she experienced during her childhood: (1) Her mother and father did not give her any love or attention (2) her feelings and needs were unimportant; (3) none of her older siblings ever spoke with her about anything that mattered; and she lived in very isolated surroundings, and no one ever took her anywhere among other revelations. After sharing these things with L, and as E was venturing further into her inner wounded Self, she abruptly stopped and turned her remarks into an attack directed toward L. This was done in attempt to blame L for the destruction of our relationship, rather than E making the connection related to how her CoDependency Addiction destroyed it. Ultimately, E tried to regain control of L's thinking by her attempt to make L feel responsible for the destruction of our relationship instead of her placing the cause where it belongs–on her long standing CoDependency Addiction.

Lancer wrote "codependents don't know how to meet their needs... but instead try to control and blame someone else in order to get your needs met."[226] One of the techniques E used through the years to get L to meet her needs is she would often say "That is L's interpretation but my interpretation is different." While there is some truth in this remark, it became suspect to L after many years of hearing E use it in his presence. The purpose of E's remark was to keep up an atmosphere

---

[225] Ibid., p. 37.
[226] Ibid., p. 61.

of *uncertainty about any facts so that L might go along with her interpretation, which, by his doing so, E would accomplish her hidden agenda of getting her needs met.* This CoDependency Tactic worked for many of the 36 years E and L were in a relationship. It does not work anymore, and now that E"s lies have been found out by L, now she want to get out of the relationship because her denial games do not work anymore. Codependents need total darkness to operate their schemes designed to get another person to figure out their lives for them. E's control of L through the years stems from her disharmonious relationship with her mother and father during her early childhood development. The Introduction in this book speaks volumes!

During her weekly-group therapy-CODA Meetings, E participates regularly in their roundtable talking sessions. The one thing that verified for me that these meetings could be leading codependents down a dead end street is L has never heard E mention anything about the impact the codependent person's addiction has on the person whom he or she is addicted to. L often hear E say the CoDependency Addiction matter is not about the other person, who the codependent person used to survive. Although the codependent person attached one Self to the addicted to person's feelings and needs, no mention is ever made related to the impact such a clandestine attachment has on the feeling and needs of the non-codependent person in the relationship. How can a codependent person recover from CoDependency Addiction without ever taking into serious consideration the exploitation of the non-codependent person's feelings and needs?

E always tell L "the CoDependency Addiction situation is not about him." Because of rampant denial, E believes it is not about her Self either! Who was it about when L was being manipulated, abused, used, bamboozled, deceived, controlled, and mislead by E? Every codependent person should be required to publicly stand before every man or woman he or she abused, and confess how the feelings and needs of the former were used and manipulated toward a psychologically distorted and narrow, self-destructive end, namely, *self-survival at all cost!* According to Lancer, "with enough faulty maternal interactions, instead of developing a harmonious and vital Self, these children's emotional functioning becomes distorted. As adults, they engage in futile and desperate attempts to control and/or please others in order to satisfy their own unidentified needs"[227]

The greatest mistake L made in his relationship with E is he overcompensated for her signs of CoDependency Addiction, and, regrettably, *enabled them.* He interpreted all of E's manipulations to cover up this emotional malfunction by believing E was a *revolutionary* who could resolve any problems she faced in her life. So, L did not dig deeper into various situations that came up through the years. One was meditation. E introduced me to meditating about two years after we came together in a relationship. She told L the meditation practice was designed to allow the practitioner-you or anyone else-an opportunity to observe any wounds, scars, or others that may surface in our minds during the meditation process. What this did essentially was to deceive L into believing E was excavating out of her Self any wounds and scars picked up during childhood and so forth. Little did L know, E was actually using the meditation process to continue to repress her childhood wounds. During the 30 or more years we engaged in meditation, not a single time after a session, did E ever mention anything that surfaced, from her childhood, in her conscious mind. L was given the erroneous impression that E's life was free of childhood damage and collateral damage. *How does anyone meditate for 36 years, and by the 36th year, have a stroke?;* then, when L asked E "How did she create her stroke?" She replied "I do not know." This was a vintage control tactic used by E to keep L under her direct control.

E successfully controlled L's behavior for a long time by framing his relationship with various female professor colleagues of mine in a distorted, twisted fashion. For example, during the early 1990s, L served as the Executive Director of a rehabilitation program for juveniles at the maximum security prison located in Baton Rouge, LA. He worked with a staff of eight persons, and one of them was EJ, who was a brilliant social worker, and she was very attractive physically, along with a winning personality. Anyone who has worked full-time in a prison

---

[227] Ibid., p. 102.

knows positive conversations are not common. So, L and EJ worked on various inmate cases together, and we shared moments of laughter; we sometimes had lunch together at work; and, occasionally, L had to call EJ from my home related to an incident that occurred in the prison, which involved one of the inmates in our rehabilitation program.

Suddenly, E accused L of having an affair with EJ; if L wanted to have one with her, then, why would he share with E everything EJ and L did at work? Furthermore. Knowing what L know today about E's CoDependency Addiction, it makes sense that she used my work relationship with EJ as a means to control L by attempting to make him feel guilty about sharing some of his work time with EJ. Nothing ever happened between EJ and L, although E used my work association with her to control L! There was one other case like this.

When I started working for Southern University during the late 1990s, I met a female professor, who I will refer to as R, in the department we both worked teaching courses and doing research. R is also a brilliant and knowledgeable person in her discipline. She is also physically attractive too with a warm and engaging personality. R an L talked a lot about teaching, our students, and research. We developed a friendship, and L called R regularly to talk about school and nothing more than being friendly. Again, E accused L of having an affair with R, which did not exist, but her unfounded accusation had control of L written all over it. On one occasion, E was included as a part of our traveling research team to the Bering Glacier, Alaska. One night in the females' living quarters, R informed me that E spoke to her crudely using some words of profanity. E did not tell me she had spoken to R in this way, or that she had a conversation with R related to some alleged, non-existent relationship he was supposed to be having with her.

After returning to Southern University, R and L met at Barnes & Noble to visit. R told me E spoke to her at the Bering Glacier in a manner befitting someone without any moral character. R also told me that she was done talking with me because of the way E spoke to her. Though L was unhappy about R's decision, he could clearly understand how she felt. R, L apologize to you for this unfortunate experience you went through with E at the Bering Glacier. Remember, L did not know

E was suffering with CoDependency Addiction at the time. Thus, L could not understand by 2008, what could be the motivation for E's reaction to any female friend he had, or might have in the future?

Besides control, including all of the rest of the prison guards that E uses to protect her repressed Self, L knows today what motivated him to reach out to various females through the years in the workplace. Every piece of the puzzle will fit perfectly in its place once it is sorted through and found, L felt "unloved emotionally" by E. E had trouble with genuine intimacy and validation of L as her male companion. It was very difficult for E to tell L she loves him; E could not give positive feedback to L for anything creative he did, which came from a deep place within her Self. L did not know it at the time, but now he realize this is the reason he attracted the females L mentioned earlier into my life due to my need to be around a female, who was aware of and connected to her inner Self.

The women L mentioned earlier fit this description; E does not because she has been codependent since birth; raised as a codependent; and practiced or lived by CoDependency Addictions, for the vast majority of her adult life, including the 36 years E and L were in a relationship. L is very sorry he did not share with the females what was going-on inside of him, which caused him to be attracted to them. Any confusion could have been dispelled before it got started if I had known beforehand that E-E-was unable to give L "authentic love."

L take this opportunity here to apologize to the females who he reached out to, and caused emotional harm. For behaving this way, L apologize to you. *You know who you are.* Some of the females may have felt they would like to have a serious relationship with L, but he still thought E was the woman for him, in spite of the fact L did not understand yet why he felt unloved by E. If I had known E was codependent, and if she had shared her problem with him when we first got together in 1979 (I do not mean E needed to know what the word CoDependency means, and all of its convoluted theories, but, instead, share with me some of her wounded feelings and needs), there is a better than 80 percent chance E would be healed today, and our relationship would not be in the intensive care ward with everybody realizing its heartbeat is nearly flat line. Tragic does not come close to describing the self-destructive power of CoDependency Addiction!

Lancer informed the concerned public that two sides makeup the CoDependency Addiction Coin; one side is the repressed Self and the other side, is *all beings are viewed as objects*. In fact, she added "without conscious awareness and empathy with their interior Selves, [codependents] treat themselves and others as objects, and being alone or too much intimacy threaten them with nonexistence or dissolution."[228] As we see, this is why L was attracted to some of his female co-workers because E viewed her Self as an object, and objects are inorganic and unable to supply any love to another person. Thus, L sought friendship and love from other women even though he never became intimate with any of them.

Moreover, E and another one of her friends started a Women Empowerment Group roughly 20 years ago. When this group was founded, L wanted to become an active participant as E's partner since the organization's purpose was to address some of the relationship challenges faced by many of the women in the group. When L made a request to participate in the group, E emphatically told him males were not allowed to participate in the Women Empowerment Group. The explanation E gave L was the women in the group would not open up and disclose their feelings and needs, if men were involved in the group meetings. Initially, L resisted this exclusion idea, but he quickly gave up on it. Again, L needed to be more assertive about his participation in the group because he now realize the real reason E did not want any male involvement is she inevitably would have to talk about issue going-on in her own life and relationship. During the 20 years or more the Women Empowerment group was in existence, E told me *"She never got a chance to express her feelings, needs, and concerns in the group setting because, invariably, time always ran out without her having a turn to do so."* This was no accident!

E used this exclusion of males from the Women Empowerment Group as a control tactic to insure that her repressed feelings and

---

[228] Ibid., p. 102.

needs, and her CoDependency Addiction to L, would not be ever be challenged by anyone in the group. And, they were not! Ironically, one of her friends, who helped E start the Women Empowerment Group, suggested to her that she need to attend CoDependency Association Meetings (CoDA) after E's stroke in July 2015. E's friend was aware of CODA because she attended meetings held by the latter to address some of her codependent issues before July 2015.

The main point here is, for 20 or more years, E was a member of the Women Empowerment Group (WEG), and one of the women participants could have helped E years earlier to deal with her repressed Self. This work did not get done because E did not start the WEG to engage in her own healing and Self-Care. *She participated in this group to help other women fix their personal and relationship problems so they could tell E how much they appreciated her as a person, and give her the love she sought that she did not receive from her mother and father during her childhood.* In the end, E continued to view her Self as an object and her partner-L. The only reason these facts came to light is E told me shortly after she had her stroke that she used the Women Empowerment Group for this purpose. L was shocked to hear this was E's ulterior motive!

While E's unspoken message is her desire to control L, many codependents overlook the fact while they are trying to control the person they are addicted to, they are controlled simultaneously by their own control schemes. Lancer put it simply when she stated "... whomever you're...trying to fix or control, controls you."[229] E has spent the vast majority of her lifetime, both as a child and an adult, being controlled by her own CoDependency Addiction to L. In the area of Law Enforcement, an accomplice to a crime committed is as guilty of the commission of the crime as the person who directly carried it out. In short, *the codependent person control thought is inseparably connected to one's mind, and it cannot be removed from its source.* In addition, a codependent person, regardless of his or her profuse, or repetitive denial of Self, and no matter how many times through the years he or she blames or attacks the other person who one is addicted to, Lancer concluded "when [a

---

[229] Ibid., p. 191.

codependent person] stifle…[their] feelings or ignore [one's] needs, the relationship suffers and you dishonor the Self you're trying to develop. If your motive is to control, manipulate, or fix someone, your words reflect these codependent attitudes…but when your motive is to express your Self…the focus is on you, not the other person…"[230]

Since E's stroke in July 2015, she has focused the vast majority of her attention on L, repeatedly asking him "What responsibility did you take for the development of her stroke?" L taught E everything she knows today about dieting and exercise, yet she want L to take responsibility for her stroke. This is understandable inasmuch as codependent people truly believe another person's feelings and needs are their own. The slave master-Uncle Tom Syndrome is a good example. How can L get into E's mind and body and create a stroke in her body that she is independently unaware of my doing so? This is insanity! No one can do that to another person no more than E can occupy my body and do the same destructive thing to me. L cannot make E feel like having a stroke; only E can create such an outcome in her own body, by using the codependent thoughts she learned from her mother and father during her childhood. This misplacement of E's focus on L only confirms that E is still at the starting line of healing. It is only when less, or no focus, is placed on anything outside of the Self that genuine healing begins to occur.

To the contrary, E is still blaming L for her CoDependency Addiction because she truly thinks, like the codependent person she claims to be, that L's feelings and needs are her own. Therefore, E mistakenly thinks L's feelings and needs caused her stroke, and the destruction of our relationship. Hopefully, one day E will come to recognize the bankruptcy of her codependent thinking, and, finally get it, namely, that any external focus on another person will continue to result in the arrested development of more CoDependency Addiction Behavior in her life. L hopes E moves beyond this place within her Self in this lifetime.

---

[230] Ibid., p. 211.

The likelihood of success is related to how much damage the Self endured during an infant's childhood. Because the Self is essentially everyone's essence, including codependent people's also, it is timely to devote some attention to an examination of what it is, given the fact the roots of CoDependency Addiction grows out of it.

CHAPTER THIRTEEN

Self-Esteem, Ego, Super-Ego, And Codependency Addiction

Mother, father, or mother-surrogate love exist as the single-most life-sustaining force and immunity to CoDependency Addiction. Nothing else known on Earth such as money, mansions, private jets, dynasties, or others, can take the place of *love* as an antidote for CoDependency Addiction. Although the mass media works 24/7 to build a *fantasy world* in which babies are being born into, and unfortunately, increasing numbers are being raised in dysfunctional families where love is absent. Fantasies dominate the household. Many Americans will quickly disclose how they feel about their job, foods, restaurants, movies, a novel, clothing, hairstyles, houses, animals, vacations, and automobiles among a list of endless others. However, those Americans who are codependent in particular, will seldom disclose anything real about themselves, or the Self especially. Thus far, we have delved deeply into the CoDependency Addiction World, which produces codependent people. Right now, we will share information about the Self.

A. Self And The Alien CoDependency Addiction Impostor

All anyone has of any lasting value is the Self. Everything in the material world will deteriorate, change forms, and disappear with time.

Even when a person makes his or her transition into the next life, or go to heaven as many Westerners believe, their body returns to the vast ocean of matter, which constitutes the Earth. However, the Self, which resided inside the person's body when he or she was alive, does not stay in the body of matter, but it transitions to the vast ocean of energy, which is omnipotent, boundless, formless, immeasurable, incomprehensible, and timeless. This is the seat of power inside of an infant when it is born, although the infant is not conscious of his or her feelings and needs beyond those related to *survival*. As the infant develops, they will be added to the infant's Self by mother, father, or mother surrogate love. It is necessary to note here that each infant embodies his or her own seat of power within the Self. While one car can jumpstart another's dead battery; the battery used to jumpstart the dead battery cannot operate the other car on the same battery system. From birth of an infant into adulthood, the job of the mother and father is to consistently nurture their baby(s) with love so that he or she gains an unfolding awareness of his or her own seat of power within its emerging Self. And, if this parental goal is met, the infant will emerge from childhood with an awareness of Self that is unscarred, uninjured, and free of any wounds, which is every human being's *birthright*.

Lancer wrote "your self-esteem reflects how you feel about yourself. It enhances or impairs your relationships, your professional success, your moods, and your sense of well-being."[231] Infants, whose mothers or mother-surrogates, did not give them love during the critical, early stages of their childhood development grow into adulthood psychologically challenged, which impairs their relationships. Because the absent of mother and father love shuts down the seat of power located inside the Self, unloved infants grow physically into adulthood unable to express their feelings and needs, and consequently, their ability to learn, plan, create art, and share love genuinely with other people is significantly impaired. Lancer wrote "you were born unique, with an innate capacity to feel and respond to both your internal awareness and external environment. That's how you learn, plan, create, and relate

---

[231] Ibid., p. 25.

to others from your authentic experience. Development of this natural process was interrupted or denied to codependents."[232] One of the lifelong and lasting effects of a malnourished infant, who experienced a prolonged absence of parental love during childhood, is loneliness.

B. Origin Of Loneliness And Its Negative Effects On The Self

It cannot be overstated what happens in the formation of an infant's psychic structure when he or she is not nurtured into becoming a social being. Instead of the affected infant growing steadily into a self-realization that one is love; unfortunately, his or her Super-Ego recedes into the background, and the Ego takes center stage. The product of this situation is loneliness. Several by-products are produced: (1) Inflammation increases in the circulatory system, and (2) Behavioral consequences produce a perceived threat that other social beings pose a direct threat to one's personal well-being.

a. Inflammation and Some Biological Effects

Thus far, we have repeatedly identified the absence of mother, father, or mother-surrogate love as the primary catalyst underlying the production of Codependency Addiction, and loneliness under consideration. Lynn Darling's article, which appears in the December 2019/January 2020 AARP Magazine, offers a deeper view of the consequences of the failure of parent's to love their offsprings during childhood. Regarding biological consequences on the human immune system, she wrote "...blood cells appeared to be in a state of high alert, responding the way they would to a bacterial infection. It was as though the subjects were under mortal assault by a disease-the disease of loneliness."[233] This finding supports Dr. Depak Chopra's assertion that molecules, or blood platelets, are *intelligent*; thus, the latter becomes excitable when parental love is denied an infant. "...being the social

---

[232] Ibid., p. 31.
[233] Darling, Lynn, "Is There A Cure For LONELINESS?, <u>AARP</u>, Volume 63, Number 18, December 2019/January 2020, p. 51.

animals that we are... 'Louise Hawkley, a senior research scientist at the University of Chicago' [stated]...there must be implications when those social connections are not satisfied." 'There is a human need to be embedded, connected, integrated in a social network, she notes. When that social network is missing,' "the consequences are very real in terms of mental and physical health."[234] Ultimately, the lack of parental love inevitably leads to Codependency Addiction, and social isolation. Although a codependent person may be living in what appears to be a social relationship, integration and connectivity with a partner is missing. In short, their words are void of action and observable deeds. The impact on human health is staggering!!

Lynn Darling wrote "according to a study by researchers at the AARP Public Policy Institute and at Stanford and Harvard universities, the impacts of people living in social isolation add almost $7 billion a year to the cost of Medicare..."[235] The production of loneliness during a child's childhood is deadly! Lynn Darling added "every day...scientists discover more ways in which loneliness can attack our bodies and shorten our lives. Loneliness is a killer..."[236] Numerous research studies "...have found that it leaves us more likely to die from heart disease and is a contributing factor in other fatal conditions. It makes us more vulnerable to Alzheimer's disease, high blood pressure, suicide...It's more dangerous to our health, researchers tell us, than obesity, and it's the equivalent of smoking 15 cigarettes a day."[237] Recently, some new research studies have appeared in the literature in which a radical examination is undertaken, which, for the first time, established a linkage between feeling and the loneliness disease mentioned earlier. Melissa Healy, Los Angeles Times Writer, wrote "the new research offers some new insights into a U.S. epidemic of so-called deaths of despair."[238]Before we provide information that further demonstrates the

---

[234] Ibid., p. 51.
[235] Ibid., p. 51.
[236] Ibid., p. 51.
[237] Ibid., pp. 51 and 52.
[238] Healy, Melissa, "US life expectancy declining," The Baltimore Sun, Thursday, December 26, 2019, p. 2.

alarming death toll the absence of mother, father, or mother-surrogate love is having on American Society nationwide, it is timely to briefly point-out how the new research shows the related feeling set-off a chain of negative forces within the biological processes, which, today, is causing life expectancy to sharply decline, along with an unprecedented upsurge in death.

b. Inflammation, Feeling, And US Life Expectancy Decline

Loneliness is a feeling. For many of the 36 years L was in a relationship with E, she invariably would ask him, given a choice, would he prefer to be struck with a baseball bat or suffer an emotional trauma at the hands of his spouse? Although L did not know it at the time, E gave him a deep insight into her pain. L responded he thought an emotional trauma was worse than being hit by a baseball bat; offering, once the initially blow caused by the baseball bat healed up, the transient pain would altogether disappear. An emotional trauma, on the other hand, could last a lifetime! Absence of mother, father, or mother-surrogate love generates a loneliness feeling, and its related pain, can create a fear powerful enough to produce an altered state of mind in which other human beings are perceived as a direct threat to an affected person's well-being. Worse, the loneliness feeling directly inhibits the formation of friendships with other people.

Lynn Darling stated "a growing number [of scientists] are focusing on the feeling itself, the intensely personal experience of rejection, disconnection and longing that some researchers believe produces a pain as real as any caused by a physical injury..."[239] A prolonged existence of a loneliness feeling in the blood "...can be deadly when it's ongoing. Inflammation amps up biological processes leading to tissue breakdown and impairment of the immune system, which, in turn, increases our susceptibility to conditions ranging from heart disease to Alheimer's."[240] The new research provides a glimpse into how the

---

[239] Darling, Lynn, Op. Cit., p. 53.
[240] Ibid., p. 53.

human brain processes the loneliness feeling caused by a sustained absence of love during a person's childhood.

c. Internal Dialogue Between Human Brain And Inflammation

Plainly speaking, inflammation and the human brain talk to each other because both are intelligent. That is, Lynn Darling quoted Steve Cole, a renown geneticist, saying "when you feel lonely, your brain activates inflammation in the white blood cells…Well, one of the weird things we've discovered is that inflammation talks back to the brain and changes the way it works…After loneliness stimulates that white blood cell inflammatory response, the response feed back to the brain and makes it irritable, suspicious, prone to negative emotions and fearful of meeting new people and making new friends."[241] This is the opposite of love; it is the unloved human being's ego in control of one's mind totally. It feeds off of a surplus of inflammation in the immune system! Under normal, evolutionary conditioning covering several millions of years, "the body…wants to be with other people, but the modern, lonely brain, under the influence of the inflammatory response and heightened levels of stress, senses a threat in its encounters with others and chooses to isolate [the affected person] further."[242] When L came across this research finding, he was amazed because, at a sub-cellular level in his relationship with E, L witnessed this internal dialogue played out within E's mind because there was always a manifestation of fear, irritation, suspicion, and a tendency to not make new friends, or make decisions about anything. Though E and L always had a lot of people around, none of them truly knew much about us. For more than 30 years, none of E's friends, including myself, did not know she was suffering with Codependency Addiction. In fact, L and E were not friends!! We tolerated each other; L enabling E's shortcomings, and E putting up with L's for survival reasons. Stephanie Cacioppo, director of the Brain dynamics Laboratory at the University of Chicago School of Medicine, explained the situation this way.

---

[241] Ibid., p. 54.

[242] Ibid., p. 54.

d. Body: Friend or Foe And The Emotional War

Being that we are social creatures, the human body, via millions of years of evolutionary conditioning, naturally trends toward long-term self-preservation mode. That is, human being are wired to approach others to survive. However, as previously mentioned, Stephanie Cacioppo stated "...the lonely brain has a short- term self-defense mode and sees, erroneously, more foes than friends. 'In the lonely state,' the brain is misreading social signals that it should read normally; suddenly it doesn't have the correct translation. You put someone who is lonely into a room alone and every person who comes there will be perceived as a threat."[243] When E got involved in the Women Empowerment Group roughly 20 years ago, initially and throughout this time, she spoke vociferously against my participation, claiming the group was made up primarily of women, and males would change the dynamics of the group's purpose? With this new research related to the lonely brain, L can see clearly now he was viewed by E as a threat to her well-being in the Women Empowerment Group. The women in the group were tolerated by E as long as they submitted to her facilitator/leadership role, namely, "I bring the answers to your problems and you do not know more than I so E's childhood wounds could remain safely locked up inside of her. One of E's weapons she used against L in her emotional war against her ownself, was L is not kind toward her.

Toward the end of our 36 year relationship, one of the ways E's lonely brain characterized L was she repeatedly misread the tone of my voice as aggression, and my curiosity was labeled by her as an intended attack on her self-esteem. Neither one of these was true! Stephanie Cacioppo helped me understand the true underlying situation that prompted E to come to these unfounded conclusions. She stated "lonely people...often misread a facial expression or tone of voice-characterizing curiosity as hostility, for the social world around them. That unconscious sense of threat can lead to an endless behavioral cycle in which a lonely person, in a mistaken attempt at self-protection, sends out signals of disinterest or even hostility, which then causes others to

---

[243] Ibid., p. 54.

withdraw."[244] E's "mistaken attempt at self-protection" was used against L as a weapon to fan the flames of projected antagonism, hoping she could get L to erroneously believe his "curiosity was hostility," or his "facial expression or tone of voice," was not nice but negative.

Moreover, before E had a stroke in July 2015, L was still asleep about her repressions and loneliness. Afterwards, E's lonely brain went into overdrive to try and make me feel like a villain, or the "bad cop," who is solely responsible for her self-deterioration. The longer E's emotional war raged on against herself, the farther her Codependency Addiction pushed me away from her. The situation got so bad that E told me she "did not know who I Am any longer" after living with her for 36 years. The truth is E never knew her authentic Self. E knew it was only matter of time before L would reject her so she tried to make L feel like he was a bully. E felt so convinced of these delusions that she placed three separate Temporary Restraining Orders (TROs) against L with the 16th Judicial District Court located in St. Martinville, LA (See Appendix A, B, and C). These TROs were placed against L even though he lived in another state, and never manifested any behavior in 36 years toward her that would lead any sensible person to conclude that E's physical or mental health were at risk during this time. Yet, E filed a baseless claim with the legal system, claiming L posed a threat to her personal well-being, and worse, he poses a present danger to her life. The TROs provide an objective insight into this mental imbalance. What is even more corroboration of the latter, is when E filed the mentioned TROs, L no longer lived in the same state as E does. How could he pose a present danger to E thousands of miles away?

The new research related to the impact the loneliness feeling has on its host's brain offers a credible explanation why E filed the TROs against L even though he never posed any threat to her personal well-being during the time they lived in a relationship. Stephanie Cacioppo stated "first, loneliness increases self-centeredness. And second, loneliness makes people more irritable and defensive."[245] As we will continue to

---

[244] Ibid., p. 54.
[245] Ibid., p. 55.

highlight throughout this discussion, when parental love is denied to an infant, and throughout its childhood, the former fails to socialize the child into a self-realization that love is who one IS, and one's love must be given to another human being to avoid becoming narcissistic and preoccupied with self-centered, narrow, egotistical behavior. Because of growing social isolation, other human beings withdraw, and the lonely person becomes simultaneously defensive and filled with fear. What lonely people desperately crave is the lost love they did not receive from their parents. Lynn Darling added "that's in part because the lonely can't get what they need simply from the mere presence of other people; what they crave is "core values and shared life experiences... Our survival and well-being depend on our collective well-being, not our individual might."[246] The affected child is starved for mother, father, or mother-surrogate love. Inoperably, many live out their lives in a dependent state characterized by constant alarm, sleep deprivation, fear, anger, and poor health.

As such, Lynn Darling added "those who are lonely live at such a heightened level of alarm that they lose sleep. Their brains also respond with greater alarm to words such as "reject" and "bully" than to other negative words, like "vomit."[247] Having been rejected by their parents and, in many instances spoken to aggressively by them, this hurt and pain becomes imprinted in the lonely brain, and its host *fears rejection for the rest of their lives.* Before we show more health consequences of the loneliness disease caused by a lack of parental love, which ultimately manifest in Codependency Addiction for millions of Americans, it is timely to bring to the forefront one of the Beatles songs titled Eleanor Rigby, which is one of the tracks on their Revolver Album released in August 1966. Eleanor Rigby is a symbolic character whose lonely brain was captured perfectly by the Beatles as follows:

> Eleanor Rigby pick up the rice in the church where a wedding has been
> Lives in a dream

---

[246] Ibid., p. 55.
[247] Ibid., p. 54.

Waits at the window
Wearing the face that she keeps in a jar by the door
Who is it for?

In short, Eleanor Rigby is anyone who is lonely and suffers with the loneliness disease. Interestingly, she wears her lonely face behind closed doors as she "waits at the window," but when she goes out in the public, she puts it in the "jar by the door" so no one can detect she is suffering with the loneliness disease, of which is a part of the CoDependency Addiction. "Who is it for?" Smokey Robinson sang in one of his classic songs titled Tracks of My Tears this lyric–"If you see a smile on my face, it there to fool the public. Take a closer look and you can see the tracks of my tears." (Paraphrased mine). Tracy Chapman, Revolutionary Singer, ask in one of her songs the following: "Why are there so many of us lonely, when there are so many of us?"

Senator Susan Collins, R–Maine, Chairwoman of the Senate Special Committee on Aging stated "…at a hearing in 2017…The consequences of isolation and loneliness are severe: negative health outcomes, higher health care costs and even death…"[248] Since 2011 to date, "…American's life-span stopped growing. By 2014, this vital sign of a nation's health tipped downward."[249] According to Healy, "beginning in the 1990s, Americans between the ages of 25 and 64…began dying at an increasing rate. And the causes of their deaths were not random."[250] As we pointed-out earlier, this upsurge in deaths is attributed to *deaths of despair, or the aforementioned loneliness disease.* During the 1990s, E an L were cohorts in the 25 to 64 years old age group. By July 2015, E had a stroke. Healy stated "midlife death rates also increased for illnesses that are strongly linked to drug use and alcoholism. Between 1999 and 2017, midlife deaths from alcoholic liver disease grew 40%…And alcohol poisoning deaths among those 25 to 64 rose almost fourfold."[251] Underlying this upsurge in deaths is psychological distress, and due to the conversation

---

[248] Ibid., p. 55.
[249] Healy, Op. Cit., p. 2.
[250] Ibid., p. 2.
[251] Ibid., p. 2.

between the lonely brain and inflammation, the latter produces in its affected hosts various "...diseases related to high blood pressure [strokes, dementia, and Alzheimer's], obesity and/or overeating and "organic mental disorders," a category that includes such ills as vascular dementia."[252] In 2015 a neurologist diagnosed E with dementia. From 2010 to 2017, 33,307 deaths occurred, and within this time frame, Healy wrote "between 1999 and 2017, the rate of drug overdose deaths among Americans between 25 and 64 increased close to fourfold, from 6.7 per 100,000 in this age group to 32.5 per 100,000."[253] It is going to take more than a TRO to reverse this trend!

Healy, in an attempt to sum up this avalanche of death, "these "excess deaths" don't nearly reflect the number of Americans who have succumbed in midlife to suicide, drug overdoses and chronic conditions during the period...It may seem like a modest number, said Dr. Woolf. But those "excess deaths" are the equivalent of almost three full Boeing 737s crashing every month for seven years. And they have made the U.S. the only high-income country in which life expectancy is moving in the wrong direction."[254] Suffering with CoDependency Addiction, in which loneliness disease is an active component, it is reasonable to expect the mentioned death trends among the American Population will continue to increase in the foreseeable future.

Moreover, in his book titled <u>Triumph Of The Spirit</u>, 2000, Marteaux X, Ph.D. wrote "if the power in us that create our reality is unnoticed, it is possible for us to create many realities without ever consciously knowing that what happened to us is our own doing."[255] E created a codependent reality throughout the majority of her life. She feared learning new technologies but covered up her fear, for example, by reading twenty volumes of St. Germain's collected works; she never engaged in any creative planning, although this was covered up by her facilitation of a women empowerment group. The curriculum

---

[252] Ibid., p. 2.

[253] Ibid., p. 2.

[254] Ibid., p. 2.

[255] Marteaux X, Ph.D. <u>Triumph Of The Spirit</u>, Writer's Showcase presented by Writer's Digest, New York, 2000, p. 33.

used to share information is nowhere to be found because it was not created. L enabled E's non-creativity by him feeling maybe tomorrow E will finally create a work of art reflective of her authentic Self. Moreover, while E was usually around people, and always dominating the conversation, the former thought she was really smart and offering practical solutions to many of the challenges they faced in their personal lives and relationships. For a long time, L thought E was genuinely trying to help other people understand their problems; however, *L has lately found out that E was seeking love from other people that was interrupted and denied her during her childhood years. The result of the latter is low self-esteem, or possessing in the mind a low opinion of the Self.* Whatever opinion a mother or father has of their infant, the latter will adapt its forming Self in the likeness of the caregivers.

Whoever claims to be a codependent person, that person's authentic Self is usually repressed, and an impostor self is used for public consumption. Its life expectancy is directly linked to how long the codependent person can live attached to another person's feelings and needs. *Whenever the person the codependent person is addicted to wakes up, the alien impostor self of CoDependency dies due to the disallowance of the codependent person to no longer be enabled to live a life of an impostor, namely clinging desperately to the feelings and needs of another person for survival.* At birth, an infant is not born with an alien impostor self of CoDependency Addiction; it is transferred to the newborn by the parents and other codependent siblings through their withholding of love.

C. Self, Ego, And Super-Ego

Montagu wrote "in spite of assertions to the contrary it seems indisputably clear that the infant is not born with an ego, with a "self" but that the infant acquires its "self" from other selves, long before it is aware of its own "self." The "self" is learned from other selves, and therefore the type of its own self depends largely, if not entirely, upon the kinds of selves to which the child has been exposed."[256] Moreover,

---

[256] Montagu, op. cit., pp.186 and 187.

he also added "...the infant is not born with an ego, it acquires an ego only as a result of the stimulation of other egos. What its own ego will become depends very largely upon the kind of egos which condition it. The fact is that the human infant is born an actively cooperating organism." [257] So many words have been written about CoDependency; yet, save Lancer's research and a few others, the vast majority of the discussion about the subject boils down, like Collard Greens cooking in a pot, to an elaboration of CoDependency stories. An in-depth analysis of the importance of mother or mother surrogate love still begs for attention.

As we have consistently shown thus far, CoDependency's roots are found in the failure of the mentioned caregivers to love their children. By not doing so, an affected infant does not learn what love is, and more importantly, he or she develops a Self that is similar to the parents' and other siblings' he or she is exposed to during childhood. If the parents are codependent, they expose their infants to their own Selves that are void of genuine love. Montagu added "that, indeed, is why children so often resemble their parents, and why the self of the child is a good clue to the covert self of the parent. The overt self worn by the parent may conceal the real covert self."[258] The overt self of the codependent parents is the alien impostor self of CoDependency.

The alien impostor self of CoDependency is an unrefined and uncultured ego. Rather than feelings and needs nurtured by the love of the mother or mother-surrogate, the infant develops–instead–an insatiable thirst for love. The child's ego emerges imbalanced presenting a disproportionate preoccupation with love for self. Since the infant is abandoned by the parents, he or she develops an unhealthy love for self, namely, the beginning of his or her alien impostor self of CoDependency. In dysfunctional families, this development is passed on from one generation to the next. Being abandoned by mother love or mother-surrogate love, Montagu added "the infant's ego, its self, develops...like the neurotic, was found to be constantly thinking

---

[257] Ibid., p. 193.
[258] Ibid., p. 187.

and acting in terms of his [or her] individualized self. He [or she] has established an image of himself [or herself] as an isolated unit of behavior with private values, wishes and motivations, and this same image dominates his [or her] social interrelations."[259]

When E and L got together in 1979, E's parents had already, during her childhood years, implanted, or imprinted, a neurotic, individualized, alien impostor self of CoDependency Addiction in her. In self-reflection, E was adamant about being an individual. L tried to explain, with no success, that socialism does not focus on the individual, but, rather, on the collective efforts working people make to produce their livelihoods during production. *E still insisted she was an individual!* This was L's biggest mistake he made in his lifetime, namely, to remain in a social relationship with E, who viewed herself as an individual. Everything E subsequently engaged in for the 40 years we were in a relationship together was based on individualism. L, in his desire to create another way for people to think about themselves other than being isolated "units of behavior with private values" was completely compromised by his remaining in a relationship with E, who could only see herself within the context of a narrow individual. All of L's research and study shows this thought is anti-revolutionary, antisocial, anti-change, counterproductive, and non-productive among others. Because L was deep into research and writing for at least 80% of the day during the early years of his relationship with E, this contradiction did not get resolved by him. E's alien impostor self of CoDependency used the right words during this time as a means of remaining addicted to L's feelings and needs, for the single purpose of her personal survival. Nothing more! Becoming asocialist with instincts for the masses were merely words used to maintain her CoDependency Addiction to L. The Lion Image and message shown in the Introduction of this book is a testament of this indisputable fact.

In the absence of mother love, or mother-surrogate love, an affected infant devolves into a preoccupation with private values mixed in with an evolving focus on individualism. The mother and father have failed

---

[259] Ibid., pp. 189 and 190.

to show their child how to love it Self characterized by high self-esteem, worthiness, deservedness, and security among other positive traits. Montagu wrote "deprivation leads to isolation and asocial behavior… and antisocial behavior…During the development of his [or her] ego and super-ego the child needs a firm hand…at the helm…otherwise his [or her] own steering mechanism remains unorganized."[260] As such, and left without a rudder to steer an infant into the development of an awareness that he or she's Self is not an alien impostor of CoDependency Addiction, but a powerhouse of love, the affected infant is set on a path down which the search for the love his or her mother or mother-surrogate did not give leaves the child chronically adrift in the world. *The steering mechanism is love.* Moreover, Montagu added "it is his [or her] mother who guides him [or her] when he [or she] is helpless and teaches him [or her] gradually how to meet the requirements of his [or her] environment, and thus helps construct his [or her] ego."[261]

The entire New Age Movement came into being purporting to offer answers to the American Public that will help them to calm the ego down. An ego, without a mother or mother surrogate's steering mechanism that demonstrates to her infant how to develop one's own, is left with a preoccupation with material things and instant gratification. Everything is an object, including people, to the child's ego because the authentic feelings and needs of the infant are repressed inside the Self. The New Age Gurus offer meditation as the answer to the unbridled ego, or a 10,000 headed monster as Don Juan, Yaqui Indian Shaman, calls it. As such, an infant does not learn what love is, and many affected children live tormented lives searching for love throughout adulthood. They suffer from a poverty of love. Montagu stated "it is the mother who gradually teaches the child its obligations to others, and thus builds up his [or her] super-ego. If the mother or her substitutes fail in this they produce a person who is likely to be crippled both in his [or her] ego and super-ego structure."[262] According to what E told L, her mother and father failed in helping her to develop her own healthy

---

[260] Ibid., pp. 212 and 213.
[261] Ibid., p. 213.
[262] Ibid., p. 213.

steering mechanism, namely her ego. Because of this gross failure, E and L's relationship ran aground and shipwrecked by early 2019, after 40 years being in it together. Montagu added "unless the child has been firmly grounded in the discipline of love and dependency, it is injured in its capacity to develop clear and definite judgments concerning people and things, and its ability to form such judgments as an adult is seriously handicapped."[263] E's dislike of judgment is manipulation of the failure of not having been loved by her mother and father. So, E joined the chorus of like-minded people who think it is wrong to develop clear and definite judgments about people and things. To hide her CoDependency Addiction, E twisted the normal course of judgment into it is bad or wrong to judge people and things.

In addition, what is seriously injured, along with a low functioning capacity by adulthood, is an emotionally traumatized and handicapped Self. Every action one takes is contaminated by an ego that is out of control in which its codependent host is constantly searching and seeking love desperately, like a drowning man or woman in the ocean. According to X, codependent "Americans are engaged in seeking, but not ever finding what they are in search of-love!"[264] The codependent person's search for love outside of oneself must inevitably end up in frustration and failure because no other person anywhere, albeit a counselor, lawyer, psychiatrist, psychologist, minister, Pope, family member, or other, cannot provide love to fulfill the Grand Canyon size hole inside of the Self of a codependent person! E tried to fill up this hole inside of her Self by attaching herself to L's feelings and needs, thereby thinking, however erroneously, that she could put a band aid on her emotionally injured and traumatized Self; and, L's love would be enough for her and him. E could not love L because she was living with a seriously handicapped Self of the type mentioned earlier. However, but to control L's thinking and belief that E could love from her own Self, she repeatedly told L the following: "I did not think I would ever find a man who could love me as deeply and hard as I loved him." Wow!

---

[263] Ibid., p. 213.

[264] X, op. cit., p. 17.

When L heard E say this, he felt good being told by E that he is giving her a lot of love. The opposite was true then and now!

E was not giving L any love originating from within her own injured and handicapped Self. She was using L's love to survive because similar to a person unable to breathe in sufficient oxygen, E's internal wounds were suffocating her and she needed love that L could never satisfy her need for. This was E's CoDependency at work very early in our relationship, but L did not have a clue about its existence, or how it would be destined to destroy everything that he would accumulate while in a relationship with E. By early 2019, this fact hit the target! And, all L can ask himself is "how on this Earth did he allow himself to get tangled up with a codependent person, who needs everything from another person without giving any emotional love and support in return? Amazing is an understatement.

X wrote codependent people "...see others *as prey, from whom [they] must take whatever [they] can*...In short, the Law Of The Ego is "Giving To Get." ACIM stated, "giving to get" is an inescapable law of the ego...you give only because you believe that you are somehow getting something better, and can therefore do without the thing you give."[265] The codependent views its Self as an object as well as other people. To them, there is no difference between an object and a person; the two are the same. Failure on the part of a mother or mother-surrogate to love one's infant establishes the ego as a unit of self-indulgence and getting to satisfy an endless stream of fantasy. Because there is an undeveloped conscience, the super-ego is non-existent, therefore, the codependent person lives an asocial existence, and everything that is social is interpreted as antisocial.

Many codependent people, like E, have seemingly outgoing, pleasant personalities, but just beneath the surface is an inordinate amount of fear, insecurity, anger, and aggressive tendencies. Unable to self-generate any feelings due to the fact the codependent's Self is shut down, X wrote the latter's "...ego thrives on external stimulation; it has no use for knowledge [or past history], save how it can be utilized to

---

[265] Ibid., p. 167.

further its [chameleon] image. {Their] ego also has a constant desire for excitement and sensationalism."[266] The greatest fear any codependent person lives with on a daily basis is the person whom he or she is addicted to will wake up one day and discover how one's feelings and needs have been used clandestinely to the advantage of a codependent person for survival, and to the disadvantage of the other as an exploited human being, who is seen only as an object for the satisfaction of the codependent's ego-desires. With the super-ego all but non-existent, the other person's fate is sealed, for as long as he or she is asleep to the destructive mental forces of CoDependency Addiction. However, when L was told by E the news that she is codependent, and has been suffering with the CoDependency disease since her birth, L, to the chagrin, or disapproval of E, woke up from his 40 years of sleep and slumber, and put an end to E's attachment to his feelings and needs as a means for her survival.

D. Reactionary Behavior

When it became clear to E that L would no longer allow her to manipulate and control his feelings and needs, E went into *massive damage control* of her codependent behavior. That is, she had a big decision to make, either *take responsibility* for the fact that she took direct advantage of L's feelings and needs for 40 years by *piggy backing* on them, or going into immediate denial that she did so manifested by engaging in several years of *reactionary behavior,* from 2015 to 2019 in particular. Reactionary behavior is caused by stress or emotional upset. E told L shortly after she had her stroke that *he was not ever suppose to find out she is codependent, and that she used him to navigate through life attached to L's feelings and needs* similar to the way a GPS System operates. An address is typed into the search engine, and the owner click "Get Direction," and the exact driving directions are provided to an intended destination precisely. E figured out L's life directions while she was attached to his feelings and needs; however, when L woke up, E became extremely

---

[266] Ibid., p. 205.

closed-minded and reactionary! Lancer wrote "codependents react. This means your actions are predominantly determined by outside influences. A few words in a text message can hit you like a cyclone and blow you off course from what you're doing, feelings, or thinking."[267]

In an attempt to manage the fall-out of her codependent behavior, E went into over-drive calling her friends and L's family members, informing them that L is being awfully "unkind to her and disrespectful." She poisoned the minds of her own children-both her son and daughter with misinformation suggesting L was abusing her; thus, creating the false impression she had been a perfect partner for 40 years. Interestingly, what alerted L to E's plan of sowing hateful ideas about him was 100% of E's friends, including those selected family members who would talk with her, abruptly discontinued communication with L. To survive, E went into reactionary overdrive. She needed people to talk for her to advance her reactionary motivations. Lancer added "rather than act, you react; rather than change, you adjust to your circumstances. You need another person or structure, such as an assignment, to take action, risk, create, or produce. You find it hard to motivate and sustain your efforts on your own."[268] To demonstrate just how desperate E was to cast L in negative light, she encouraged our own children to stop talking to L.

For example, in 2017, L assisted his daughter with the completion of her doctoral degree, and he provided her support during her actual dissertation defense. L's daughter stopped talking to him the day after she completed the requirements for this degree, owing to E's infiltration of her mind with untruths. E's son was supported by L, both financially and emotionally, throughout his undergraduate college years and during his early married life. L always supported E sending her son money for whatever his request was at the time. L purchased E's son a brand new Isuzu Truck when he attended the University as an undergraduate. Yet, as soon as L found out about his mother's CoDependency Addiction, the latter poisoned her son's mind with negative things about L's character. *Months passed, and not one of our children had enough guts or heart to reach*

---

[267] Lancer, op. cit., p. 57.

[268] Ibid., p. 54.

out to L and ask him, if the negative things shared with them by E were true? This silence is as heartbreaking as when L found out about E's CoDependency Addiction for the first time.

What is even more sickening about E's reactionary plan is the fact everyone who is slightly knowledgeable about CoDependency knows it is not the person that the codependent person is attached to, who needs to take responsibility for the devastating affects it has on the emotional well-being of the person a codependent is addicted to. Yet, through the use of reactionary tactics, devious as they are, E has worked constantly to paint herself as a *victim in the eyesight of her children, friends, and the larger community.* E refuses to take responsibility for her reactionary choices after she had a stroke, which exposed her CoDependency that she kept a secret from L for 40 years. How could E explain her decision to do this to anybody, including her own Self? Because it is impossible to explain her choice to any sane, sensible, and feeling person, E was, therefore, forced to classify herself a *victim of circumstances* over which she has no control; and, furthermore, of all the people whoever injured her Self, including her mother, father, and siblings, E chose to use L as her scapegoat, rather than admit the true part played by them, regarding the creation of the conditions in their dysfunctional household in which E's CoDependency originated.

That being so, L, ironically, is the only person on this Earth who brought E from the back woods of the nearly isolated village she grew up in to the steps of the Great Pyramid of Giza and Sphinx in Cairo, Egypt, Rift Valley in Kenya, Door of No Return in Elmina, Ghana, Bering Glacier, Alaska, Niagara Falls in New York, Maori Village in New Zealand, Red Square in Moscow in the Soviet Union, Hermitage in the Soviet Union, Catherine The Great Palace in the Soviet Union, Bolshoi Theater in the Soviet Union, Eifel Tower in Paris three times, including the Luve Museum, Montego Bay, Jamaica, Grand Canyon, Library of Congress, Enoch Pratt Library in Baltimore, MD, and to many more Wonders of the World not named here. E's mental disease, namely, CoDependency Addiction, blocked her ability to process the intrinsic value of the identified experiences. Because E's feelings and needs are shut up inside of her Self due to

CoDependency Addiction, these great world travels failed to enrich E's Spirit, and at best, all of them were processed by her as merely *objects of consumptions*, including her own Self as well as L. These cultural experiences grew out of L's feelings and needs to grow into a deeper awareness of the world community; E piggy backed on L's desire; yet, she could not feel the richness and meaning of any of the world travels L thought E mutually wanted and needed to experience because E brought, everywhere she went, the codependent baggage of a severely injured and wounded Self to all the places mentioned, which, in each case, *E could not feel the intangible, subtle, and intrinsic beauty of anyone of the places we traveled.* While traveling to these great places, E was clandestinely sheltering within her Self a ticking time bomb of CoDependency Addiction, which exploded openly in the form of high blood pressure and a stroke.

Thus, for E to save her Life and family, she would have to admit she did not disclose her ticking time bomb of CoDependency Addiction over the 40 years she was in a relationship with L, during which time, all of the mentioned world travels were experienced. Since E is still in extreme denial, she decided to take a reactionary path, hoping that she could convince her family members, friends, and the community that L is the singular reason her life has taken a sudden downward spiral into chaos, confusion, and self-destruction. Rather than admit her life has been secretly on this reactionary course since she was born into a dysfunctional family, E would prefer to die than admit the mistake she made, namely playing Russian Roulette with the Devil, hoping her CoDependency Addiction would never be discovered by L during his or her lifetime. Of all the creative activities L successfully engaged in through the 40 years of relationship shared with E, one situation is worthy of mentioning because it clearly demonstrates E's willingness to sabotage any positive action taken by L so she can stay in the public image E has woven, namely, one of perfection and flawlessness, which is overlain with her insatiable compassion for the little man or woman who has a challenge. E use to ask anyone who came by our house to visit this revealing question of self-perfection and narcissism: *"What is your challenge?"* L never heard E mention one time in 40 years that she has a challenge, and asked could L help her with understanding it in the area of her feelings and needs, which are shut down inside of her Self-never!

The situation that stands out in bold relief is L's daughter's refusal to communicate with L unless he goes to therapy with her (It was only after E had a stroke in 2015 that H started asking L to go to counseling). Does this dogmatic request sound like "Bullying?" H is totally confused by the subtle sabotage E engaged in during H's childhood, during which time, E subtly undermined anything L tried to build, regarding having a relationship with his daughter-H. For example, L has published six books, and never once has E told H in L's presence, how proud she is of L for writing those books. E never once told H she should be very proud of her father for being an accomplished researcher and writer. To date, H has not read one of the books her father has published, nor has any conversation about anything in anyone of the books ever been discussed by E, L and H. In addition, L attended the Million Man March in Washington, DC in 1995; while there, he had an opportunity to visit the home of Frederick Douglas. L bought several books written by Frederick Douglas related to the role of women in the Abolition Movement during the Nineteenth Century. When L returned home, he was excited to give the books to H in E's presence.

As always, E was not overtly supportive, and this subtle sabotage sent a signal to H that the books written by Frederick Douglas are not important. In 1995, L had absolutely no clue E was codependent, and during her childhood two generations earlier, E's mother and father sent the message to her, both verbally and non-verbally, that her feelings and needs are not important either. Thus, E role modeled that same emotional sabotage for our daughter-H. One day L believes H will search deeper and find out for her own self the real reason behind the broken down communication between H and L. E has been engaging in family sabotage for a very long time. Lancer informed the reader a codependent person need "…someone dependable to lean on and to provide structure that he or she is lacking. In many cases, when [the addicted to person]starts to improve. [the codependent person] unwittingly sabotages…[the addicted person's awakening and] recovery to avoid becoming the Underdog. That would threaten his or her entire personality structure of being self-sufficient, invulnerable, strong, and flawless. A crisis, illness, or financial reversal could cause their roles to flip."[269]

Moreover, H told L, her father, she will only talk with him if he goes to counseling with her. The counseling scheme is a tactic to get L in a counseling session so he will feel that he did something wrong to H. The plot conjured up by E and H is a fraudulent attempt to try to get L to take responsibility for the breakup of E and L's relationship. This ploy did not work because L told H the only way he would go to a counselor with her is she must first share with him specifically what he did to her that would warrant L to go to counseling with her. H, thus far, has not revealed any reason in this regard. The prefix "Co" in the word CoDependency means a codependent person attached oneself to another person's feelings and needs, thereby creating a one-sided relationship. If I am codependent, which L is not, he would be the first person sitting in a counselor's office seeking help. CoDependency Addiction, ultimately, destroys a relationship similar to the way termites eventually destroys wood.

How powerful is Lancer's insight; it hit the target, and explained what happened in E and L's relationship. E's CoDependency Disease broke out of her; and, it cracked wide open her shell of invulnerability the moment she had a stroke in July 2015! Up to that time, E's daily task was to control L's behavior; keep him down; make him feel unsteady; avoid helping him with any creative project as a way to send a subtle message to L that that project is not important to her. This is the same message E's parent's sent to her! So, after her stroke episode, E's true colors emerged, and they are unflattering!

A constant stream of anger, negative thinking, defensiveness, and denial occurs daily. E can no longer talk to L without judging him; yet, before her stroke, she was adamant judgment is not a productive thought and no one should engage in it. E is in constant judgment due to her fear of abandonment. L now knows who she is!! Moreover, things got really bad when L received a sizable inheritance from his mother's estate. The

---

[269] Ibid., p. 65.

entire ground shifted in a matter of seconds similar to an earthquake. E's denial tactics do not work anymore with L; and, hopefully, one of her friends, who may have a little love left in his or her heart for her, may choose to sit down with E one day and explain to her what he or she has observed in her behavior through the years.

In sum, codependents react because they are constantly fighting against abuse and neglect that they experienced during their childhoods. Interestingly, the battles they fight are not constructive based on a search for answers to why their mothers and fathers abused and neglected them. To the contrary, codependent people wage a constant struggle against the person they are addicted to, who are the focus of their CoDependency Addiction. Lancer wrote "in actuality, You're fighting battles that happened long ago in your childhood when you developed one of the many ways of reacting: Blamers (It's your fault.) Placaters ("Whatever you say.") Apologizers ("I'm sorry you feel that way.") Distracters (Acting irrelevant...") ...Withdrawers ("I don't want to talk about it.")...Attackers..."[270] These are a few of the reactionary behaviors L observed E use since her CoDependency Disease came to light after her stroke in July 2015. The two that stand out prominently among the many others are blamers and attackers. In a dysfunctional family, these negative behaviors are commonly used, and they are learned by an infant from his or her codependent mother, father, and siblings. According to Lancer, "attack and blame avoid self-examination."[271] Anytime L make an attempt to engage E in a self-examination discussion, she almost immediately became emotional, manifested by speaking in a loud voice tone, and withdrew before the conversation hardly got started. If anything was said by E, usually her remarks could be neatly classified as blame, attacks, and judgment.

In view of this common desperation going-on inside of codependent people, and in order to create a loving public persona, or image, albeit a very superficial one, the former consistently go out of their way to serve the external causes of other people; they do so in an attempt

---

[270] Ibid., p. 201.
[271] Ibid., p. 202.

to "get" other "objects" —people-to love and give them the attention they have been starved for all of their lives, beginning during the first moments and days after their birth, when their mothers and mother-surrogates rejected them by withholding their vital life-sustaining love. This rejection of love is a generational phenomenon.

Therefore, it is timely to address the great extent to which codependents extend themselves, *by always overdoing and over-compensating to serve other people, while their external search for love blocks the self-same people codependents serve from actually loving them due to their repressed Selves.* The Self can be referred to as a Honeybee Honeycomb, where Honeybees store the love-nectar-they receive from flowers on a blue sky, warm, sunny day. The nectar is an exchange made between the flower and the Honeybee only after the latter has completed its vitally important responsibility of pollinating the flower so it can produce its fruit or others.

CHAPTER FOURTEEN

Codependent People's Overdoing, Over-Compensating, And Over-Extension Of Themselves In Their Vain External Search For Mother, Father, Or Mother-Surrogate Love

Throughout the 40 years E and L were in a relationship, invariably E would complain about how much work she was always doing for L and our daughter-H. L usually brushed it off as a case of frustration after the workday was over. Seldom, if ever, did E say how happy she was, or how much she appreciated L's support for the things he did for her such as paying the bills, home every night, helping to prepare a meal, fold clothes, sweep the floor, mowing five acres of land, taking her to the beach once or twice a year, and taking E on international travel adventures such as the many identified earlier. L felt the more he tried to satisfy E, nothing he did could do so in a sustaining way. For a moment, E might seem satisfied, but very soon she would relapse into melancholy. For a very long time, L could not figure it out; he kept creating and producing but every time the result was the same-more melancholy in the end. L did not know, during all of the 40 years he and E were in a relationship, nothing he did could fill the hole in inside of her repressed injured, and emotionally wounded Self. The hole Is similar to radioactive atoms, which takes years, decades, and lifetimes before a radioactive atom's Gamma Ray's poisonous material cease to be harmful to human and other life-forms.

The CoDependency Disease works this way. An unloved infant grows up unfulfilled with mother, father, or mother-surrogate love. The codependent person's addiction to another person usually takes one of two forms: (1) He or she attach oneself to another person who is generally socially inadequate, and is looking for someone to be his or her mother or father and (2) He or she attach oneself to another person who is socially adequate, highly educated, and one who does not spend any time on who is in control in the relationship; rather, most of this person's time is spent engaged in creative pursuits. The common denominator in whatever choice the codependent person makes is he or she must always be in control. One of the ways this end is achieved, without the codependent person's control plan being discovered, is *self-sacrifice*.

A. Self-Sacrifice And Victimization

Victimization is a word a codependent person is very uncomfortable self-referring and admitting he or she is a victim of their CoDependency Addiction. If a man or woman, for example, allows another person to pick up a bat and beat them down with it without putting up any fight, then, what would we call the person who got beaten with the bat? Would we call him or her a champion; a winner; a martyr; a role model; or a leader? What would you call the beaten person? After thinking about your choices, it is likely you might call the beaten man or woman a *victim*. Webster's Ninth New Collegiate Dictionary defines a victim as follows: "One that is subjected to oppression, hardship, or mistreatment...one that is tricked or duped..."[272] E does not believe she is a victim of her own CoDependency Addiction. Since she has not acted on her feelings and needs during the 40 years she and L have been in a relationship, and because she was attached to L's feelings and needs, E does not know she is a victim because the

---

[272] Webster's Ninth New Collegiate Dictionary, op. cit., p. 1314.

latter must be aware of his or her feelings and needs to know whether one is a victim or not. How could E think she is a victim while attached to L's feelings and needs?

E does not think she is a victim because she is self-deceived. CoDependency Addiction is self-oppression, self-imposed hardship, self-mistreatment, self-tricked, and self-duped. Therefore, L told E he is not a victim; E is attached to L's feelings and needs; thus, similarly, E argues she is not a victim either. What is E, if she has repressed her own feelings and needs for 40 years? She is a victim of her own CoDependency Addiction, and she does know it! *Therefore, all of the external services provided to other people during the 40 years we were together, generated within E a victimization mentality, namely, self-imposed oppression, hardship, mistreatment, and self-deception-tricked and duped.* Attempting to function with her distorted ego, and as we already have seen, the latter always seeks to "get" something better in return for what is given to other people. E knows she is a victim of CoDependency Addiction because she fell head over heels when she discovered a book titles <u>A Course In Miracles</u>. The prevailing thesis of this work is the untamed ego. E instantly connected to ACIM because of her own ego imbalance caused by her CoDependency Addiction that she contracted during her *tumultuous* childhood.

B. Overdoing, Over-compensation, And Over-Extension of Self is Motivated By A Vain External Search For Mother, Father, or Mother-Surrogate Love

Although the codependent person's thinking is flawed, he or she, nevertheless, thinks, it is alright for him or her to engage in victimization consciousness, if, by doing so, one will find the unbestowed love of the mother or mother-surrogate, which was lost during an infant's childhood, through the present day feverish over-extension of the Self, overdoing of the Self, and over-compensation of the Self, by providing *tireless services* to other people. Lancer added codependent people "...do more than their share at work or in a relationship to earn acceptance, but they end up feeling unappreciated, used, or resentful."[273] This victim consciousness was role modeled for E by her mother, who shared her story with her later during her adult life.

According to the story witnessed by E as a young girl, which was later retold to her as an adult, her mother's sisters, who lived in Houston, TX, came back home regularly to visit their mother. In preparation for her mother's sister's visit, E told me her mother would clean the house; purchase the food; cook it; serve the food and drinks; and cleanup the dinner table and wash all of the dishes after her mother's sisters left. They returned to Houston, TX without contributing any money for the purchase of food or anything else. Afterwards, E observed her mother complain and feel resentful about how her sisters treated her. Having had this stressful experience, one would think E's mother would make a change and ask one of her sisters to pay for their next visit home. But, that did not happen according to E. Once again, E's mother laid-out everything as before, and she complained with deep resentment after her sisters returned to Houston, TX. From what E shared with me about this practice, it went on for years, and her mother never made a change, although she became increasingly resentful and angry. E's mother ignored her feelings and needs, and her behavior was role modeled for E and her other siblings.

Lancer wrote "codependents ignore their needs and depend upon others and frequently self-sacrifice to an unhealthy degree. They care for others in a way that leads to control, resentment, and conflict.... *Codependency itself limits our ability to have satisfactory intimate relationships.*"[274] One of E's patent statements to L, through the years, was "I did all of this for you for all these years and you do not appreciate what I have done." How victim consciousness is this statement? Resorting to the imbalanced tape loops in her mind, E, similar to the behavior her mother role modeled during her childhood related to her mother's sister's visits a generation earlier, she used such victimization remarks to project her inner pain inside of her wounded Self when her outward

---

[273] Lancer, op. cit., p. 9.
[274] Ibid., p. 15.

giving did not result in love and appreciation. Usually, L offered E the latter, but he could not satisfy E's need for unbestowed mother and father love during her childhood. For many years, L did not know E's victim consciousness was so deep-rooted in her early childhood years and later. Had I known this type of mother love was missing in E's life, L would not have agreed to get in a relationship with E because no man or woman could fill this Black Hole. The more love put into it, more love is needed next time and so forth. It is the Sisyphus Stone Affect! This fact raises an important question, That is, of all the external services provided by E to anyone, including intimacy, did her giving originate from a place of caregiving or caretaking?

C. Caregiving And Caretaking

Based on what we already know about the behavior of a codependent person(s), it is extremely important for them to sustain a public image demonstrating that in face of great challenges, others perceive codependent people as selfless givers of their time, attention, and love to others. Thanks to Darlene Lancer's Research on this subject, it is now an accepted fact that codependent people present themselves to the public as Mother Teresa Type caregivers; however, upon closer examination, the opposite is true beneath the surface.

Lancer wrote "mothers are wired to care for their children. Codependent *caretaking* is different from giving care to someone. In fact, with codependency, there may be more taking than giving when the needs of the giver take precedence. This is because caregiving comes from abundance, and caretaking emanates from need and deprivation."[275] In E's case, first, she shared with me that her mother and father did not give her any love and quality attention throughout all of the years of her childhood. Second, E consistently approached nearly every social situation I was privileged to be in her company with a disproportionate amount of insecurity and scarcity. And, third, except around her African-American Women Friends, E always placed her

---

[275] Ibid., p. 35.

Self in a lower position, especially on occasions when White Women were primarily involved. One example previously mentioned earlier is worth revisiting here.

That is, once a White Female Painter brought one of her painting to show at an evening dinner party; L was standing near E and the artist and heard E remark to her "I could never do that kind of creative work." L does not do canvas paintings; on the other hand, he does do woodcarving art. Rather than E reply with an admiration of the painters artwork, she went into victim consciousness instead of replying that she does this or that type of artwork. E bashed her own Self due to the fact her self-esteem is very low.

So, E may come off like she is "with it" on the surface; whereas just beneath the surface is an empty hole in her Self large enough to fit an endless number of compliments and well-wishes. Ironically, none of the compliments and love make any difference in her life since she feels she does not deserve them. Lancer stated codependents "...don't feel entitled to compliments, to be truly loved, or to set limits"[276] on their overdoing for others. This is because their caregiving is not what it seems on the surface, but it is, in reality, *caretaking masked as caregiving.* A person's caregiving emanates from an abundance of love received in one's childhood. On the other hand, caretaking originates from a codependent person's neediness and general deprivation. One of the attacks E has consistently poisoned the minds of her family members and friends with is L is not *KIND* to her.

E is constantly starved for *kindness.* The more masked caregivng she provides to others masked as caretaking, she sabotages other's kindness given to her in return for her overdoing because E always, beneath the surface, seeks to get more than she gives. Thus, her imagined kindness is not kindness at all but *unmasked getting.* Stated another way, E's kindness does not exist because all of her overdoing for other people comes from her low self-esteem. There is always a hidden agenda at work.

That being so, E, in her best dressed victim consciousness, repeatedly attacked L saying "All I ever wanted from you is kindness." Yet, having

---

[276] Ibid., p. 9.

repressed her feelings and needs inside of her injured and wounded Self, which is surrounded by dark clouds of low self-esteem, E failed to realize she must first give what she always wanted-kindness. The social cost of kindness is authentic feelings and needs given to L by E, who, in return, reciprocates by giving E his kindness wrapped-up in his expressed feelings and needs for her. E desires kindness from people but she is unable to feel L's kindness, or anyone else's, due to the fact her feelings and needs, as we have already established, are tightly sealed within her injured Self like gold is stored in a Fort Knox Vault. Interestingly, all of E's family members and friends have been repeatedly told many times that L is an unkind person; he has changed; he is mean spirited; uncaring; and insensitive among many other unflattering descriptions. Sadly, everyone, like a hungry fish, never questioned is there a hook enclosed inside the bait; and, without question, consumed the hook of false misinformation spread about L. This is root cause of divisiveness! Hopefully, this information will help someone rethink their thoughts, and look deeper to see what's going on? According to Lancer, "it's certainly natural and satisfying to be helpful and kind to others. However, codependent pleasing emanates from low self-esteem-more to get than give. Many codependents don't have a choice! They can't say no. As with care-giving, it's not so much the actions that determine codependency, but the pleaser's state of mind. The essential question is whether you are giving from a place of self-esteem, or from guilt, fear, or insecurity."[277]

Everything E ever gave L for 40 years was given from her state of mind of guilt, fear, and insecurity. This is why E used the manipulative tactic, namely, calling for each one of us to put ALL of our cards on the table, when we got together in Baltimore, MD in 1979. By coming off like she was pure and transparent, E self-deceived her Self and lied to L, for the purpose of controlling the conversation so she could keep hidden her massive pain and emotional trauma inside of her Self, which had been smoldering since her first birthday. Engaging in this behavior was not only premeditative but an act of treason against the social welfare

---

[277] Ibid., p. 36.

of humankind. E's fear destroys any kindness someone gives her. She is an object receiver of kindness; the giver, likewise, is perceived by E as an object giver of kindness. The sum of this equation is any kindness L gave E through the years was never received as a genuine feeling and need, and all she could ever do was complain in her best victim consciousness voice.

Moreover, after E had a stroke in July 2015, she has engaged in a negative campaign against L based on the platform that he does not show her any kindness, regarding the impacts it has on her. To understand the backwardness of this assertion, consider the following example.

If a man or woman murders another person, would you expect the mother, whose son or daughter or other relative is the victim of this crime, to show kindness toward the murderer? Is it normal behavior for the murderer to ask the mother to show him kindness? This is insanity thinking! What makes such disassociated from reality thinking insane, is rather than the murderer provide a motive for committing his crime against person, which would establish the historical cause for his criminal behavior is never established. From childhood to the moment he took another person's life, the murderer remarks "I am not concerned about my past; I just want to talk about the present. While talking about the present is definitely important, this is the same as talking about one tree in the forest without examining the history of the big picture of the forest itself. By examining the history of the big forest picture, an idea why one of its trees died of a certain disease can be determined.

Similarly, regarding E's contention that L does not show her any kindness related to the affects the stroke she had is having on her, the latter, similar to the above murder example, does not want to consider past history because the cause of her stroke can be discovered during her childhood years. E is totally against this *historical examination of her past;* yet, she has painted L an insensitive villain for not showing her kindness for the stroke she caused her own Self, which is rooted in her past history, beginning with the failure of her mother, father, and siblings to genuinely love her. E would prefer to die than face up to this historical fact.

D. Where Is The Love And Kindness in Codependent People's Caretaking And Overdoing For Others?

When E an L got together in Baltimore in 1979, both of us pledged to each other that we were, free of the other's coercion, embarking on a new way of thinking based on a *Socialist Philosophy*. That is, we were in complete agreement that cooperation was the mission of human beings rather than conflict, discord, secrecy, oppression, exploitation, and competition. However, after years of intense socio-economic and political research, during which time L wrote several books and articles, which could help the masses work out an understanding of the economic forces working against their working class interest, by the late 1990s, E swerved away from the purpose we mutually agreed to work on during our lifetime, and she moved full steam ahead in an area we got together to enlighten people about, namely, idealism, metaphysics, and the illusions and delusions interwoven in this one-sided philosophy. L recognized E's shift away from objective reality thinking, but he had just started a new job at a local university in LA, and hired as a junior professor on tenure track, much of his time was spent working hard to earn an income and continue to engage in socio-economic and political research. It is necessary to mention here E was a codependent person attached to L's feelings and needs so in perfect chameleon fashion, E never meant to engage in Socialist Work but, rather shadow L's feelings to keep her CoDependent Addiction a secret. Throughout the more than 36 years we were in a relationship, never once did E use Socialist ideas in her many WEG Sessions or others.

During this time, E worked in the public school system, which she complained about all of the time. In fact, she would work a few years and get out of the public school system altogether. Each time she left the public school system, E withdrew her retirement money out of it. At that time, we were not desperate for money because L had a good paying job at the university so E's retirement money was not needed to pay any bills. However, E withdrew her retirement money out of the Teacher Retirement System each time she left it. L did not think about the reasons E behaved this way. He was too busy teaching and doing his own social research. To this day, L does not know why E decided to waste her retirement fund, or not work to increase her retirement account. It is unreasonable for anyone to prematurely withdraw their retirement funds, knowing that once one reach retirement age, this money will be important. The only reason E mistakenly withdrew her retirement funds prematurely is she was Codependent, and as such, she did not see any difference between L's retirement funds and she not having any. E thought L's retirement fund was hers' since she was attached to his feelings and needs.

Thus, at the beginning of the 2000s, E dove into the deep end of her search for kindness and love that she missed as a child growing up in her dysfunctional family. E and a friend traveled to one of Iyanla Vanzant's Women Only Workshops during this time, and when E returned, her friend did not start a Women Empowerment Group, E did. She jumped into this work head over heels. L had a gut feeling something was going on inside of E that did not just start when she attended the Iyanla Vanzant Workshop. It felt like E had some bizarre interest suddenly in fantasy thinking, or metaphysics. What L did not know is E was moving rapidly backward toward her years of religious training, given the fact she attended a Catholic High School during the course of her middle and high school years. Although E professed that this experience did not have any residual effect on her thinking process, L's mistake was he did not challenge E on her beliefs, but allowed E the freedom to self-correct her thinking process, which never happened because, during that time of default back into idealism, E was actively hiding her feelings and needs, and although L and E by 2000 had been together 20 years already, E, during this time, had kept her feelings and needs closed up inside of her injured, wounded, and emotionally traumatized Self. L thought E was sharing her feelings and needs with him since 1979, but, in reality, E was living in L's feelings and needs *blind spot*. He did not see any of E's feelings and needs because they were not there to be seen or felt, or loved. What L thought were E's feelings and needs were actually his own. How tragic!

Returning to the early 2000s, E figured-out a way to seek love and attention from other women by initiating the formation of a Women only Empowerment Group. The use of the word empowerment tricked a lot of women to join the group, hoping E would say something to them that could erase their troubles. What these women did not know, and what many of them to the present day, still do not know is, E, from the very beginning had an ulterior motive going into this venture. For 20 long years, L sat up late into the early morning hour waiting for E to return home from one of her Women Empowerment Group (WEG) meetings. Initially, L was excited to listen to E share some of the highlights of the WEG Meeting. At the outset, E always told the story she did not say anything about what was bothering or troubling her because time ran out, and she did not have a *chance to share her feelings and needs with the women*. At first, L thought that is understandable; however, the same story was told by E after 10 years in the WEG, and a pattern of non-self-disclosure emerged. What is particularly interesting about this pattern of non-self-disclosure is the woman who suggested E join a CoDependency Therapy Group after she had a stroke, also attended the latter during earlier years of her life.

It is obvious, then, if E disclosed her repressed feelings and needs nearly two decades ago, there is a good chance she would have received a lot of help from the women in the WEG. Since she acted as the facilitator/teacher, E came off to the women in the group like *mother superior* to them. Thus, E sat up on the throne, and professed her life was in total order, freeing her time up to work with the women in the group toward solving their problems. In reality, E had more personal problems than many of the women in the WEG, but none of them knew she did throughout the 20 years or more of existence of the WEG. To a woman in the WEG, E was God; she used all of the deep philosophical questions L raised through the years about the social behavior of working class people to achieve her own self-serving, narrow ends. The Introduction of this book is worth reviewing again.

One of the phrases E frequently used through the years is "Never Leave Your Thoughts Unguarded." L believes the reason this idea touched a chord inside of E is at the self-same time she was imploring the WEG to follow this dictum, she was, at a subconscious level, "Guarding Her Own Thoughts" of CoDependency Addiction to L and others. E was in the WEG to *get* rather than give as we already have seen. Accordingly, Lancer wrote codependents "...feel anxious if others are unhappy with you, and you give their needs, feelings, and opinions precedence over your own. In fact, you silence…even to yourself, your own needs, feelings, thoughts, and values to become what you believe is expected or desired by someone else, especially in romantic relationships…"[278] E guarded and silenced her own thoughts so they would never become known to anyone–not even her closest so-called WEG friends. Although repression of one's thoughts, feelings, and needs produce increasing anxiety within the repressor, the codependent person, generally speaking, would prefer to die than allow anyone to learn about their shame, guilt, fear, rejection of love for them by parents, and anger. So, E guarded her thoughts to a fault. How could E love L, or anybody else, if her feelings and needs were locked down inside of her Self?

Thus, the WEG for E was an opportunity to "fit in, "get love," and "attention" without having to disclose anything about her wounded and emotionally injured Self! As it was, the WEG was conceived as an organization where each participant could share their pain and suffering within a safe environment. Similar to the Iyanla Vanzant Workshop E attended, E set up a WEG where she could feed on the pain and suffering of the women participants. During the Iyanla Vanzant Workshop, Iyanla Vanzant, at one point, had to call E out and tell her to sit down and stop going from one crying woman to another offering to console them like an Usher in a church. Rather than E doing some crying of her own, which she needed to do desperately, she walked around as if she did not have one problem in her own life that she needed to be concerned about resolving.

Lancer stated "you try to fit in, be perfect, be nice, look good, be responsible, do well, and take care of others, further hiding your wounds, your shame, and your pain. When you feel extremely insecure, you…mimic other's actions and feelings or pretend to feel and behave the way you assume another person wants"[279] or group. Thus, reckless shortsightedness and repression has meant the loss of valuable life force, and the destruction of E and L's relationship.

---

[278] Ibid., p. 43.

[279] Ibid., p. 43.

As already mentioned, one of the women in the WEG son was sentenced to life in prison without the possibility of parole. Because E's CoDependency Addiction was kept a secret by her from the WEG, E gave off an energy of invulnerability, and this minimalization of the seriousness of her codependent problem had a paralyzation affect on the women's attitudes toward taking concrete action to solve their personal problems. For example, nearly ten years ago when the woman's son was presenting some early signs of distress in his life, E spoke to her, and others, about metaphysical ideas such as "waiting in the right attitude," everybody is going to get to heaven," listen to your gut," and peace and love is an inside job," among many other slogans.

When enough time for the cake to bake passed, these machinations, chimericals, and illusions sentenced the woman's son to prison for life without parole, and it resulted in E having a stroke and a failed relationship. All of these tragic outcomes could easily have been avoided, if E would have chosen to role model her CoDependency Addiction to L, from the outset of the formation of the WEG, and disclose the pain and suffering she experienced in her childhood, in addition to the impact the latter has had on L and her ownself. It is alright for us to be redundant to reinforce a previously made point, namely, E set up the WEG to hide her feelings and needs behind the big Wizard of Oz Curtain. All of her overdoing, fixing, encouraging, and 2 to 5 hour telephone calls, with some WEG members, were not care-giving to the other person in distress; but, rather, every effort she made was to fit in the WEG so someone in this group would tell her "they appreciate her help," "they could not have done it without you," and the magical "I LOVE YOU." Being addicted to these remarks from women in the WEG, like an alcoholic is addicted to Jack Daniels, etc., E and L, over the past 20 years, sometimes drove two hours one-way so E could "fix" this or that woman's personal problem.

None of E's efforts were real, but narrowly designed to demonstrate she is worthy of love because who among you would do what E did to support a member of the WEG? Oddly enough, just like an alcoholic who needs another bottle soon as the one he or she is drinking from is empty; E needed another "fix it" situation, yet, the more someone told her thank you, or said I love you, the more her codependent addiction increased because, as we have already pointed-out, E's Self was repressed by her and she could not feel her own feelings and needs nor anyone else's. Lancer wrote "the reality is that so much of yourself is invested in others that you lose who you are-your feelings, needs, hobbies, and goals. Your thinking and actions revolve around getting…and reacting to someone else. In advance stages of the disease, codependents have become shells-their entire life having been squandered on someone else in the way a compulsive gambler or debtor squanders his or her life savings."[280]

E depended on L her entire life, and since she repressed her own feelings and needs, she squandered her life on C Farm. Lancer added "codependents joke that, at the moment of death, someone else's life flashes before them."[281] Year after year, L and E worked to build our lives together based on what L thought included both of our feelings and needs. However, as it was recently discovered, E participated in the construction process using L's feelings and needs and not her own. By 2019, E realized she did not put any of her own feelings and needs into the construction process of her own life or C Farm, and like most codependent people, she squandered her relationship with L and C Farm. C Farm is for sale, although L paid for it with a $50,000 check he received from the Federal Government in 2009.

Although this outcome is irreversible today due to gross dishonesty and impossibility to take responsibility for the mistakes made, E has expressed no human feelings about her losses such as crying, admission of errors, remorse, or others. She has a coldhearted veneer covering her soul similar to the way dark cumulus clouds hide the sun on a very cloudy day. This behavior is directly reflective of the strong grip E's CoDependency Addiction continues to have on her life, particularly the Pit Bull type grip this disease still has on her injured, wounded, and emotionally traumatized inner Self. All of this self-destruction emanates from her low self-esteem. Some of the major signs of the

---

[280] Ibid., p. 51.
[281] Ibid., p. 51.

CoDependency Addiction active in E's daily life, which has directly caused her to squander everything she has are listed below:

- "Excessive thinking, worrying, or talking about someone
- Valuing others' opinions over your own
- Difficulty making decisions on your own
- Often giving up plans, hobbies, or interests to be with someone
- Fear of being left or rejected
- Feeling unhappy, empty, or discontent being with yourself
- Fear of being alone
- Inability to go places or start projects on your own
- Adapting to others' tastes or point of view
- Following researching, or snooping on someone
- Feeling unhappy or trapped in a relationship you can't leave…
- Focusing your energy on someone else's problem or life…"[282]

L witnessed each one of the above behavioral characteristics in E's personality during the course of our 36 years in a relationship together. Actually, if I did not know better, L could easily think Lancer interviewed E, given the fact the aforementioned traits are so seamlessly a part of E's daily codependent thought process. One of the codependent signs L observed throughout their relationship is how tenacious and committed E was to thinking, worrying, and talking about someone else's problem to the complete exclusion of hardly any discussion about her own feelings and needs. She valued everybody else's opinion and devalued her own Self at the same time. L recognized this behavior but he enabled it because he did not know it was connected to E's desperation for the love she missed getting from her mother, father, and siblings as a child. All of the above behavioral characteristics flow through the eye of the needle of a search for love in someone else. The stimulant in the CoDependency Addiction is a *fear of rejection*, which was first experienced by E when her mother and father rejected giving her love at a crucial stage during childhood.

---

[282] Ibid., p. 52.

We will address fear of rejection and abandonment later. More need to be mentioned here about a codependent person's single-minded addiction to "fix" other people's problems and not their own.

Throughout the 20 or more years E facilitated the WEG, L thought her motivation for seemingly tireless giving to this or that woman in the group to help her solve a personal challenge was admirable, noble, and beyond reproach. The WEG-All-sang E's praises! After E's stroke, L woke up from his Rip Van Winkle type sleep, and discovered underlying her public motivation was a current of getting love because E does not believe she is lovable. L cannot place himself on higher ground because, similar to the members of the WEG, he was not given love by E unconditionally but E gave love to L as his caretaker to get love.

Lancer wrote "caretakers give love to get love. They give more in relationships…They don't feel worthy of love unless they're giving because they don't believe that they're lovable and enough as they are."[283] In a nutshell, E's drive to serve others revolved around her severely damaged core Self. That is, she was not able to be patient and trust others would love her because of who she is as a human being. E tempted the odds of fate, thinking if she gave love to others, then, they would have no choice but to give love to her. What E failed to realize, both then and now, is *giving love to get love to fill a void of unworthiness negates love.* Such an exchange is at best fake, and at its worst, mechanical. For L, the greatest tragedy in his relationship with L is none of the love he gave to E was received by her as a worthy person, who feels she is lovable, and, this feeling by itself, will attract genuine love to her in any circumstance. E read a book called the <u>Law of Attraction</u>. She became intoxicated with the book, singing its praises to anyone who was suffering with some personal problem, In a nutshell, I often heard E say, "If something is going-on hurtful in your life, you attracted the problem to yourself." This was nothing but metaphysical nonsense.

E used the Law of Attraction idea to manipulate others into believing they caused their own problem by attracting it to them; yet, underlying this public discourse, E surrounded her Self with the WEG so she could

---

[283] Ibid., p. 63.

work tirelessly everyday trying to fix the problems the women attracted to themselves. The irony is E brought the WEG together so she would have a group of women she could get love from by working extremely hard to fix their problems. Therefore, as a caretaker, E used the WEG as a smoke screen behind which she could comfortably hide her feelings and needs. As long as E remained preoccupied with fixing somebody's problem, no one would think to ask her "Do you have any personal problems?" Lancer added "caretaking allows you to hide the needs, feelings, and flaws you're ashamed of. You also compensate for not feeling lovable by giving, being needed, and becoming indispensable."[284] For 20 or more years, our telephone-Land Line-rang off the hook with women, and sometimes men callers, seeking E's help to solve a problem the caller supposedly attracted to him or herself. However, after E's stroke, there was a sharp decline in the number of caller. During this time, E packaged her Self as being a Perfectionist; the latter is not suppose to create a stroke only those of us who are less perfect.

Tina Turner, the world renown Soul Singer, made a hit song called "What Does Love Have To Do With It?" Somewhere in the song Tina Turner described love as a worn-out emotion! Although L had his suspicions from the beginning related to E's intention for starting the WEG, he couldn't bring his mind to believe the woman he is in relationship is a "Great Pretender." L was tricked, duped, and bamboozled! All of E's fixing did not have anything to do with her giving love to anybody, but more so with her unconscious expectation of getting love, from the WEG. Lancer wrote "because caretaking emanates from guilt, shame, and fear more than love, you give with expectations of having your own needs met-usually unconscious needs for love..."[285] Of course this is a hard pill to swallow, but it is true! L can hear E saying after she reads this paragraph saying something like "That is L's truth, or that is his perception." Because E's need for mother love is so deeply imprinted on her consciousness, she has searched for it throughout the 36 years L and E were in a relationship, and her search

---

[284] Ibid., p. 63.

[285] Ibid., p. 63.

was not limited to our relationship, but it spilled over, like Niagara Falls, into all other aspects of her social life, including the WEG among others.

Earlier, we mentioned CoDependency is an addiction. It is to the codependent person what Crown Royal is to an alcoholic. Lancer remarked "codependents can't stop trying to help. It's a personality style that's been learned and become habitual. You believe you know what's best for others and how to run their lives, even in situations in which in which you have no experience."[286] For example, one night, during the late 1980s, E an L were at her mother's house visiting. Several women, who had given birth to their children, were seated at a table talking about their own experiences related to childbirth. As an observer and listener to what the women were sharing about their childbirth experiences, L's attention was drawn to one of the women seated at the table who was speaking very authoritatively about child birth. That woman was E's oldest sister. What was strikingly obvious to me is E's oldest sister had never given birth to a child, although she spoke more about childbirth than any of the women seated at the table who had given birth to their children. L was moved to interject, from the sofa he was seated on near the table where the women were talking about childbirth, saying "The only person seated at the table talking the most about childbirth is the only one who has never given birth to a child of her own!" This person was E's oldest sister.

L was given a window to look through to see how CoDependency works, but, at that time, he had no clue what he was observing, nor did he realize E grew up in the same household, and, since we now know CoDependency is generational, she–too–was exposed to this disease. Through the years, L has observed E talking to people about a subject for which she had not had any direct experience like her oldest sister spoke authoritatively about childbirth without ever having given birth to a child of her own. This is a classic indicator of CoDependency Addiction because this behavior flows out of an emotionally traumatized Self, which manifests itself as low self-esteem among the many other characteristics we have discussed thus far. If L had known beforehand about CoDependency

---

[286] Ibid., p. 63.

Addiction when he observed E's oldest sister dominate the childbirth conversation, that would have been the ideal time to address the existence of CoDependency Addiction, rather than allow 36 years to pass before this disease destroyed E and L's relationship, along with all of the property we accumulated during this time period. Moreover, just like E's oldest sister dominated the childbirth conversation, E dominated the conversation in the WEG, which served her purpose of not having to address any of her injured and wounded feelings and needs. This is what her oldest sister did when she dominated the childbirth conversation; that is, she prevented any of the women who had actually experienced childbirth from asking E's oldest sister the simple question: Why did you choose to not have any children of your own? By controlling the childbirth conversation, this question could never be asked by anyone! And, the real reason E's oldest sister never had any children would never be disclosed by her. Lancer warns us codependent people fear any form of real self-examination, especially if a study of their past is involved in it.

All-in-all, codependent people engage in CoDependency Addiction Behaviors, which is focusing on another person's feelings and needs, or group of people, for their single-minded goal of setting up a "smoke-screen" which pushes farther in the distance their need to face their own pain. In addition, if for some reason, another friend, relative, or partner in a relationship, albeit accidental, ask a codependent person a question that threatens the exposure of their codependent secret, the latter, having already anticipated such a self-exposure pop-up is possible, default to a safety net, namely, usually blaming their partner in their relationship for all of one's personal troubles. Lancer wrote "focusing on others protects you from facing your pain and taking responsibility for your own happiness. It keeps you stuck pursuing the fruitless goal of trying to change others or seeking someone to make you happy, based on the false premise that your happiness lies in others. Blaming others or feeling superior helps you avoid self-examination..."[287]

Codependent people do not want their CoDependency Addiction to another person, or group such as the WEG, to be found out. They

---

[287] Ibid., p. 76.

will do anything to keep hidden their codependent secret. Recently, in a text message exchange L had with E's son, the latter told him that "I would have never thought in a MILLION years y'all relationship would be like this…" When L read the latter text from E's son, L feels the same way. What is difficult for E's son to face is both he and L were kept in the complete dark about his mother's CoDependency Addiction. Similarly, when it finally came to light after E's stroke in July 2015, and although E does not deny she is codependent, the problem comes down to one simple question: *Why did E keep secret her CoDependency Addiction to L, and go along with his feelings and needs to the complete exclusion of her own, and-simultaneously-participate in the development of a relationship with L, along with the accumulation of property called C Farm, all of which was developed without the input of any of E's feelings and needs ever being expressed? All of the decisions that had to be made, during the course of the 36 years L and E's relationship was in existence were made by L.* No doubt, this is one of the most painful questions anyone can pose to one's partner; L and E, have been in a relationship for 36 years; and, due to E's extreme fear of rejection and abandonment, *she behaved as if everything in our relationship was right in the world.* That CoDependency Addiction World can only be built on quicksand and a fantasy, and its longevity is proportional to how long the codependent person in a relationship can endure the pain and trauma suffered at birth and during one's childhood, as a result of the rejection of love and fear of abandonment imprinted in E's mind, which, undoubtedly, was caused by the non-existence of mother or mother-surrogate love, and a generational deficit of love in her dysfunctional family.

Moreover, the single most important task codependent people must execute daily, is to create a false perception of high self-esteem in order to hold at bay their worst nightmare, namely, fear of abandonment and rejection.

CHAPTER FIFTEEN

Fear Of Abandonment, Fear Of Rejection, And The Startled Affect

ecause of a deep-rooted emotional trauma, which is collectively known as the wounded and injured Self, codependent people are constantly in fear of abandonment and rejection, which can be traced back to the fear of abandonment and fear of rejection imprinted in the minds of the former caused by a mother or mother-surrogate's refusal to nurture and love their newborn babies. It is unimaginable how a newborn baby feels when he or she is in the dependent state, but his or her mother or mother surrogate does not consistently supply the former with her love. No doubt, this absence of mother love produces in the newborn a feeling of fear of abandonment and fear of rejection. The infant, only hours and days old quickly learn to develop an unnatural clinging to his or her mother or mother-surrogate because the infant's survival is at stake. Without mother love, the infant feels he or she will die so the only recourse one has is to tenaciously cling to the mother hoping soon his or hers' basic need for love will be suddenly satisfied. Because the infant's basic need for love is not satisfied during their childhood, he or she does not mature age appropriately, from the dependent state to interdependency.

Thus far, everything we have discussed related to the psychological troubles of a codependent person comes down to one thing: That is, finding someone who can satisfy the codependent person's insatiable need for mother and father love, which was withheld during childhood. Obviously, this is a recipe for disaster because no one externally can satisfy the internal feelings and needs *"missing"* inside another person. Lancer stated "if you're unable to meet your needs, you hope someone else will. Relationships add to your life but can't fix what's missing inside."[288] The emotional trauma suffered by a codependent person during their childhood is just too great a hurdle for another person to jump over to satisfy the codependent person's need for the mother love he or she missed! This is a mission impossible; yet, the untrained, unaware, uninformed, and uneducated person goes around judging the other person saying such rubbish as "no relationship can exist without love." Superficially this is true; what is missing is an understanding of the nature of the love that is missing; and, an understanding of who was supposed to give it to the codependent person at a crucial time in his or her life? "Where ignorance is bliss, it is folly to be truthful."

As Lancer pointed-out earlier, a relationship can add to one's life but it "can't fix what's missing inside." The uninformed and uneducated person, due to a lack of any detailed, historical information related to CoDependency, cannot see pass the obvious, and make the connection that exist between the absence of mother love and the cause of a person's CoDependency. This is the central reason the latter destroys relationships. Yes, it is true a relationship cannot exist without love, and may we inform you that a relationship a codependent person is in inevitably fails because both persons in the relationship must first bring love to it, from their childhoods so that each person will have this essential ingredient to share with each other in a relationship. If one person is sharing love and the other one does not due to the limitations caused by CoDependency, the codependent person, having been abandoned and rejected by his or her parents during childhood, eventually arrives at a point, which is characterized by the latter's complaints that the other person, who he or she is addicted to, no longer loves him or her, which usually leads to relationship failure.

---

[288] Ibid., p. 52.

Unfortunately, the uninformed and uneducated cannot grasp the fact that the codependent person does have any mother and father love required to help sustain the relationship. At best, the codependent, as we already have observed, works overtime daily attempting to hide, within the decaying relationship, his or her underlying self-hate, low self-esteem, fear of abandonment, fear of rejection, and a generalized, negative self-rejecting attitude, which is glossed over by a loving one.

A. Fear Of Abandonment And Fear Of Rejection

In the CoDependency World in which the codependent person lives every day, the maintenance of a public persona of perfection, by whatever means necessary, is high. Why? Lancer wrote "abandonment in early childhood produces shame, low self-esteem, and insecurity about whether you're loved and cared for and whether you can count on it in the future. Resulting *shame anxiety* creates apprehension about rejection and sometimes perceived rejection that may not be the reality."[289] Regardless, the *Twin Fears* produces such intense, chronic anxiety that the codependent person, who has already been abandoned and rejected by the parents, lives constantly at-risk of being abandoned and rejected once again by the person he or she is addicted to, given the fact no love is shared with the latter; and, he or she must, therefore, be kept in the dark about this deceptive scheme, or *survival anxiety* becomes, for the codependent person, an increasingly overt and tormented reality. As Lancer mentioned earlier, and due to the *Twin Sisters of Fear*, the codependent person does everything in his or her power to keep the other person in an emotional "blind spot" so that the latter carries on unwittingly, for as long as it is possible, engaged in the task of creating a life for both the codependent person and him or herself. E lived 36 years, albeit premeditative, within L's emotional blind spot. He could not phantom his partner for 36 years was lying to him, which simultaneously violated the sacred trust he placed in E. To E and codependent people as a whole, trust is merely an object of the

---

[289] Ibid., p. 52.

preposition or pronoun; the only thing that matters is the codependent person must clandestinely secure the goodwill of another person or group to insure one's survival, albeit it is a fragile one.

Towards this end, for example, when L was hired as a public schoolteacher in St. Martin Parish in the Spring 1982, he taught English at one of the high schools. It is customary for the principal to conduct an in-class evaluation of teachers at least twice per year. During the Spring 1982, the principal at the high school did not follow the customary evaluation policy by conducting an in-class teacher evaluation of L's work in the classroom. However, by the end of the Spring 1982 Term, L was called into the principal's office, and we he arrived, the principal asked him to sign a teacher evaluation, although the principal did not conduct one of his in-class teaching. In short, L refused to sign the prepared teacher evaluation form; to comply with school board evaluation policy, the principal forged L's name on the fraudulently prepared teacher evaluation form, and a copy was placed in his school mailbox in the Teachers Lounge.

This was a clear case of racism and a violation of L's human rights; he brought the fraudulent prepared teacher evaluation form home and showed it to E. L was fuming with displeasure and ready to seek immediate legal counsel toward filing a lawsuit against the St. Martin Parish School Board. When L asked E what she thought about his lawsuit idea aimed at seeking a solution to this blatant violation of his human rights, E urged him to drop the idea. Her rationale was if L files a lawsuit, we would no longer be able to work as schoolteachers in St. Martin Parish. At first hearing it, L rejected E's opinion; however, since she was so firm that L should drop his lawsuit idea, unfortunately, he did so. After 36 years, L finally realized why E strongly urged him to drop his lawsuit idea; it is because E could not take the risk of L winning his proposed lawsuit because the latter would directly threaten E's need for L to remain under her control, given the fact her long-term survival depended on L going to work and not asking any penetrating questions that might, in some small way, give him a clue of E's addiction to him, which she knew she must maintain, at all cost, for her selfish survival. If L filed the lawsuit mentioned earlier, he might have won a settlement of

$1 million or more? How can a codependent person control the person he or she is addicted to, given the wide range of options that would have opened up to L at such a young age-32 years old-had he followed through with his lawsuit idea?

With this amount of money, E was terrified of being abandoned and rejected by L the same way she was originally rejected by her parents due to their withholding of love from her during her childhood. Through the years we were together in a relationship, E never missed an opportunity to attempt to get L to feel he was abandoned by his mother the way she was abandoned by hers.'

B. Mother And Father Abandonment Of Their Children Within A Dysfunctional Family Household

E often asked L if he had any abandonment issues, given the fact L's mother did not raise him? For many years, his question was brought by E, and at some point, L began to take the hook since it is true L did not grow up in his mother's household. Because L did not know anything, at the time, abouit CoDependency, he started to gradually fall into E's trap of getting me to believe that I was abandoned and rejected by my mother. After drilling down deeper into CoDependency, L discovered that his early relationship with his mother is totally different from E's.

First, L's biological father made his transition at the very young age of 34 years. Second, his mother was only 25 years old when this most traumatizing event occurred in her life. Third, L's mother had two children when his father passed away-a 3 year old and a 8 months old. Fourth, L's mother was just starting out on her life journey when the father of her two boys died. Fifth, since she was now the sole breadwinner, and residing in Oakland, CA at the time, L's mother correctly assessed her situation, and decided to bring her two children to live with their grandmother on her large farm in LA. L's grandmother became his mother-surrogate, who nurtured him through this difficult time in his biological mother's life. Sixth, L received around the clock attention and love from his grandmother/mother-surrogate, in addition to the attention he received from his Aunts, throughout his childhood.

She cooked, washed, cleaned, addressed his health problems when necessary on a timely basis; she taught L how to be responsible by role modeling for him how to work, love himself and others, and, most impactful, L's grandmother/mother-surrogate instilled within L that he is a good person; and, she inspired him, at the tender age of 5 years old, that he could become a doctor in his chosen field of study. Lastly, L's grandmother/mother-surrogate brought L to visit his mother in Oakland, CA several times during his childhood via the then famous Santa Fe Luxury Train, which was in operation during the 1950s and early 1960s. When L put E's question about being abandoned and rejected by his mother to this test, his situation proved drastically different from what abandonment and rejection by a mother or mother-surrogate means within the context of CoDependency. There is no correlation between L's situation and E's. Absolutely none!

First, in E's case, she grew up in the same household with her mother, father, and other siblings. Second, E grew up in a very geographically isolated and impoverished household. Third, E grew up in a household in which several of her older siblings competed daily for the attention of their mother and father. Fourth, E never traveled outside of her immediate isolated village she grew up in during her childhood. Fifth, although E grew up very poor, she told L she thought her lack of travel was normal. Sixth, according to E, her mother and father never touched her, talked with her about positive things, or told her they loved during her entire childhood. Seventh, E felt weight of being unloved by her biological parents and siblings. Eighth, E grew up emotionally isolated, which caused her to shutdown her feelings and needs due to the pain she felt constantly caused by not being given demonstrative love by her parents and siblings. Ninth, E's parents never taught her how to work or be responsible for completing a task on a timely basis. Tenth, E witnessed her older siblings' abnormal competition among them, for their mother and father's love and attention.

Therefore, as we can see from these two contrasting childhoods, the striking difference is E felt abandoned and rejected by her parents even though she lived in the same household with them throughout her childhood. This is synonymous to an open wound on a person's arm, for example, which is never given medical attention; it never heals; and the wound stays painfully sore and life threatening. Moreover, although L was brought to live with his grandmother/mother-surrogate, he visited his mother throughout his childhood, and she came to visit him. In contrast, E's biological parents were in her eyesight daily, but she did not receive any love from them during her entire childhood. Without receiving love from her parents during her entire childhood, and as a growing child, E, according to CoDependency known facts, was abandoned and rejected by her mother and father. On the other hand, L was not abandoned and rejected by his mother; she loved him enough to place him in a home environment with his grandmother/mother-surrogate, who gave him love and attention, and taught him how to love other people through her example of providing food and other resources to people in the community who needed help. L's grandmother/mother-surrogate operated a large farm, and oftentimes more produce was harvested than could be consumed in house; the surplus was packaged up and one of my aunts would drive her to someone's home and give them food. Many times L was a witnessed to his grandmother/mother-surrogate sharing of love with other people, and this taught him the value of helping others. More importantly, some of the same food given to other people was cooked at home, and during mealtimes, L's grandmother/mother surrogate would sit with him, and his other siblings, and talk about how L felt about his life, work on the farm, education, and friends. This was an on-going nurturing experience throughout my entire childhood.

L's childhood experience was not without its challenges during his pre-and adolescent years. However, notwithstanding pimples, L grew up feeling worthy, optimistic, and good. L never felt isolated nor did he feel no one cared about his feelings and needs. His grandmother/mother-surrogate kissed him; held his hand walking across the street; and she saved money for me to attend college. However, when a child's mother or father do not touch him or her, or give them consistent love and attention, this negative behavior cause the affected host to shutdown, or repress, their feelings and needs within their injured and wounded self. As a consequence, the unloved child grows up feeling abandoned and rejected rather than good, hopeful, optimistic, and cooperative. The affected child, beginning at a very early age, becomes overwhelmed with *fears*.

According to Lancer, "fears of being left, rejected, or alone play a big role in dependent relationships...You won't have an inner life to sustain and nurture you, and being alone can feel empty...You can feel just as lonely in a relationship, and once attachment bonds take hold, dependency on the relationship turns into addiction."[290] Strikingly, since E claimed she is codependent, L discovered he has been engaged in a relationship characterized by addiction caused by E's *strong dependency* on it. An alcoholic is dependent on alcohol; a codependent person is dependent on a relationship in which the other person in it makes the former feel high similar to the alcohol in Jack Daniels, for example. The common denominator is addiction to a drug, and in the case of a codependent person, the drug is an attachment to the feelings and needs of the other person in the relationship for *survival*. Lancer accurately defined the codependent's addiction as follows: "Abandonment in early childhood produces shame, low self-esteem, and insecurity about whether you're loved and cared for and whether you can count on it in the future."[291] To survive, and get through life, similar to an alcoholic's dependency on alcohol to get through the day, a codependent person grossly depends on another person to get through the day and their life in general. Nothing is sacred! An alcoholic will sell his last pair of shoes to get money for another drink; a codependent person will, under the cover of a perfectionist public image, lie, self-deceive, manipulate, deny the truth, blame, self-sacrifice, and pretend to be who they're not, in an attempt to control another person. Similar to a vampire, the codependent person is addicted to his or her feelings and needs and, from day-to-day and year-to year, everything the codependent person does is to maintain control over another person so they can continue to suck the emotions out of the latter in the form of feelings and needs.

---

[290] Lancer, Ibid., p. 52.
[291] Ibid., p. 52.

In short, without blood, any living being will die. Any person will die without his or her active satisfaction of their own feelings and needs. Because the latter is repressed inside of the self of a codependent person, the latter knows he or she will die, if one is not attached to the feelings and needs of another person to get through the future. A mosquito dies under the hand of the person it bites risking its life for the possibility of getting some blood. The mosquito knows instinctively that it will die, if it does not risk death in an effort to extract blood from a person. Similarly, the codependent person risk death as long as he or she can keep his or her addiction to the feelings and needs of another person a secret. Usually, a crisis such as a catastrophic disease or financial shift shatters the codependent person's vampirism, which ends with the breakup of the relationship addiction. Fear of abandonment drives the codependent person's addiction to a relationship because the latter feels he or she is *unworthy of love and not good enough.* For the past 20 years or more, E often used the phrase not good enough in various conversations with people. It never dawned on me that she was actually referring to her own Self. By setting up the WEG, this organization gave her the cover she need to *vicariously talk about herself* without overtly sharing with others in the group that she needs help with feeling she is not good enough.

Because E was never told by her parents that they love her, E's fear of abandonment and rejection that she brought with her into her adult life was, no doubt, total and complete. Lancer stated "when shame and fear of abandonment are pervasive, you feel you're never enough and are unworthy of love. You hide your flaws, try to please and accommodate your partner, walk on eggshells, tolerate abuse, make yourself needed, and become a human pretzel-all to avoid being alone or rejected."[292] After E had her stroke, she clings doggedly to the point that she never knew beforehand that she was codependent. Yet, all of the CoDependency literature points to the fact that withholding mother and father love during one's childhood is the highest form of treason anyone can ever commit. That being

---

[292] Ibid., p. 53.

so, the one point that E cannot erase is this: If she came out of her childhood unloved by both of her biological parents, then, how could E not know she was conditioned to believe she is not good enough? When E facilitated her WEG, and whenever she mentioned the evils of the antisocial condition within the Self such as "not good enough," "unworthy of love," and "low self-esteem among others, isn't it clear that what E was teaching in the WEG was her own self-acknowledgement that she is codependent? What more evidence do we need to understand that unworthy of love, not good enough, and low self-esteem are composite cornerstones of the mental disease known as CoDependency?

In a nutshell, E knew, from the day she left home as an adult, and throughout the 36 years she and L were in a relationship, that she was codependent! She knew she was suffering emotionally with this mental disease, although she called it by another name, namely, NOT GOOD ENOUGH OR UNWORTHY OF LOVE. And, rather than admit this fact, days, months, and years have already been spent engaged in an argument about her not knowing these cornerstones of childhood deprivation are integral and indisputable components of CoDependency. This is synonymous with a blind man telling another man who can see that he cannot see. It is obvious the man with eyesight can see the blind man cannot see. And, it is obvious to E that she has known she feels not good enough and so forth, and, anyone who is authentically in touch with his or her feelings and needs can see a codependent person feels "not good enough" and "unworthy of love" without having to first know the latter are direct symptoms of CoDependency. Remember the codependent person does a phenomenal job employing *self-deception* in order to fool the public that he or she is *flawless and good enough*, when, in reality, the opposite is true. The great singer and songwriter, Smokey Robinson sung "if you look close enough, you can see the tracks of my tears running down my face." He called them the "Tears of a Clown when no one else is around." As long as codependent person is haunted by fear of abandonment and rejection, and as E so often told others to be mindful of the Law of Attraction, he or she attracts to oneself more abandonment and rejection.

For instance, Lancer wrote "losing a relationship is agony not only because it triggers an earlier abandonment, but also because you're losing part of yourself-the parts or functions, such as calming yourself, that are already missing"[293] which are mother and father love. It is never redundant to reiterate that the codependent person's addiction, that is, to another person in the relationship is *incapable of abandoning or rejecting the codependent person. In fact, the latter brings the secret of his or her early childhood abandonment and rejection, by the parents, which originated during the earliest years of an infant's life, and not during the codependent person's adult life in a relationship.* According to Lancer, the infant is abandoned and rejected at birth by the parents; this emotional trauma creates internal shame and insecurity in the infant; fear of abandonment emerges; and this thought creates abandonment in relationships throughout the codependent's lifetime.[294] Lancer called this process the Cycle of Abandonment. It is this very cycle that crushes a relationship and drains all of the marrow from its core structure.

C. Abandonment In A Relationship And Its Corrosive Effects On It: Either It's Survival Or A Dead-end

For many of our 36 years of pseudo or quasi-togetherness, E repeatedly took pride in making the comment that a person has to go all the way down a path until he or she reaches a dead end. At that point, there is glimmer of hope that a lesson is learned, or another path is taken. And, it-too-often ends in the same result. In our case, it is easy to utter eloquently sounding words void of practical meaning and pregnant with abstraction. E and L walked down their relationship path for 36 years, and to most observers, we were considered by many who knew something about us an ideal couple, namely, soul mates. L thought E was his soul mate and vis-à-vis. Or, were we something else hidden beneath a grand illusion of public perfection?

---

[293] Ibid. p.53.
[294] Ibid., p. 53.

Back in the mid-1980s, L and E lived in the village she grew up in for a brief period of time. Being a very small community, without any cultural outlets save the local nightclubs, it was an unspoken, but accepted fact, that the women in the village knowingly shared their male companiuons with other females in the community. E told me her oldest sister made this declaration to her many times while growing up in the community. Thus, when L moved to the village, where E grew up, and very soon after he arrived in town, one night another one of E's older sisters told L to his face that "don't think you are too good because like everyone else, you-too-will have intimate relationships with other women in the community. Initially shocked by the statement, L calmly laughed and responded saying "I have too much self-respect to lower myself to that level of abuse." E's sister replied, "just wait you'll see; you are just like everybody else." E's sister did not have the slightest idea who L is, but she automatically included me in the larger dysfunctionalism that apparently had been going-on, in the community where E grew up, for generations! As time passed, and given what E's sisters perceived L would do did not occur, L was told by her older sisters that the women in the community placed L in the category reserved for a Saint. After giving this Saint Question some deeper thought to determine if it had anything to do with CoDependency(?), L received a vision to review one of Charles Dickens most famous novels in which L discovered in it the pervasive, and conditioned underbelly thought that caused so many women to helplessly share their male companions with other women in the community.

Charles Dickens' famous novel titled **A TALE OF TWO CITIES: A STORY OF THE FRENCH REVOLUTION**, written, in 1859, more than a century ago, accurately captures E and L's path down the road to the dead end of our relationship. According to Charles Dickens (His work is quoted in some length to convey the workings of CoDependency in the mind that makes it its home), in Chapter "I. The Period, It was the best of times, it was the worst of times, it was the age of wisdom, it was the age of foolishness, it was the epoch of belief, it was the epoch of incredulity, it was the season of Light, it was the season of Darkness, it was the spring of hope, it was the winter of despair, we had everything before us, we had nothing before us, we were all going to Heaven, we were all going direct the other way-in short, the period was so far like the present period..." [295] Every line is prophetic; each one tells one dark story glazed over with a public persona suggesting to anyone who would be fooled by the shiny apple that it was the best of times; however, beneath this carefully waxed veneer, arranged with all of its colorful makeup and make believe, in reality, "it was the worst of times." Charles Dickens described E and L's path so perfectly saying "we had everything before us [in 1979], we had nothing before us, we were all going to Heaven, were all going direct the other way." L thought he and E were walking down our path toward Heaven was nothing but a mirage or a false Oasis in the Saharan Desert going direct the other way into chaos, darkness, confusion, secrecy, fraud, and untoward reality.

Moreover, on one hand, "it was the best of times," and on the other, it was the worst of times." The best of times refers to the Saint; the worst of times refer to CoDependency. During the 1980s and onward, L did not know E, his intimate companion and confidant, had grown up through the worst of times during her childhood, and her older sisters knew this was a fact, and that is exactly why L was suppose to take advantage of the CoDependency Disease, namely engaging in sexual intercourse with women who were desperate to attach themselves to another man's feelings and needs, if for only sex and their attention. Although L resisted falling into this wider contamination of CoDependency community-wide, he was, unwittingly, living and sleeping with a codependent person every day, namely E. Because E emerged out of her childhood into adult life extremely emotionally downtrodden with an awfully wounded and repressed self, she would do anything to materialize her wish to survive at the expense of another person, and become a monumental detriment to her own downfall, both physically and mentally.

Lancer wrote "this is what codependents do. You're invested in other people and think and talk about them. You try to figure out

---

[295] Dickens, Charles, <u>A Tale Of Two Cities</u>, http://www.planetbook.com/free-ebooks/a-tale-of-two-cities.pdf, p. 3.

their motives, what they need, what they could or should be doing, and solve their problems…your attention is laser focused on that person to the exclusion of all other sensory input. When someone asks you how you're feeling, you report on the other person."[296] Clint Eastwood was the lead actor in a movie called "Play Misty For Me." In the movie he played the role of a radio station disc jockey. Every night during his on-air shift, he received a call from an admiring woman asking him to play the same song-"Play Misty For Me." This request led Clint Eastwood to arrange a date with the woman, and before long, he realized the woman was addicted to him; he was her codependent addiction. Lancer added "this is obsession…Your thoughts repeat themselves in circles…They grip your mind in an inescapable preoccupation that takes possession of you. Obsessions are driven by fear and pain."[297] For 36 years, E was a constant presence in L's life. When someone saw L, they also likely saw E. L thought this was a manifestation of E's love for him and vis-à-vis. However, this was not love but an obsession E had with L in an attempt to try to forget about the deep-rooted pain she felt having been abandoned and rejected by her mother and father during her childhood. E did not love L, and she has never loved him; she was trying to get the love from L that her mother and father never gave her. No human being on this Earth, or anywhere for that matter, can give another person the love they were suppose to receive from their caregiver. This is more than a tall order; it is imposibility!

For as long as L can remember, nearly every question he asked E she invariably did not answer it, but she used the same question, and asked L for an answer. When L gave his answer, E measured her response accordingly. E could not answer the questions L asked her because she engaged in long-term repression of her own feelings and needs. Lancer wrote "when ignoring your needs and feelings, you assess what others need and feel to gauge your response…[this is] denial and further reinforce it because, when you're focused on someone else, you don't feel yourself"[298] This is such a powerful realization

---

[296] Ibid., p. 54.
[297] Ibid., p. 54.
[298] Ibid., p. 66.

because for 36 years, E has been attached to the feelings and needs of L, and, during this entire time, she was numb and did not feel her own self. Due to her severe childhood-induced fear of abandonment and rejection, E internalized her mother and father's abandonment of her and simultaneously abandoned her own feeling and needs, or Self–Who am I? This is the greatest question every human being must answer, and during the 36 years L lived with E, she fraudulently professed to others that they need to answer this question for themselves, which she never answered for her own self due to E's cover up of her emotionally wrenching childhood experience. The I Ching, Tarot Cards, Daily Quotations, meditation, labyrinth walks, retreats, and many unnamed spiritual consumption activities–singularly or together–did not have any power or influence toward helping E breakthrough the barrier of self-imposed denial and feel herself! Never once was the shoe on the other foot where somebody else used these interventions and E was the subject of learning. She was always trying to fix somebody else, which provided her the perfect cover under which to hold onto her life-threatening CoDependency secret.

So far, emphasis on fear of abandonment and rejection has received a majority of our attention. Through the years we were together, E often talked about fear as if it was real person. Throughout the 36 years we were in a relationship, any discussion of fear E and L had primarily remained a highly abstract philosophical exercise. The next section will bring the word fear out of the abstract and connect it to the substance out of which it originated in E's life.

D. Fear And What Is Actually Feared?

The <u>Webster's Ninth New Collegiate Dictionary</u> defined fear as "an unpleasant often strong emotion caused by anticipation or awareness of danger...anxious concern...reason for alarm."[299] Codependency is a skewed psychological thought, which causes a high degree of imbalance in the mental structure of a codependent person. This objective fact was

---

[299] Op.cit., p. 453.

never addressed by E. She talked about fear only in the abstract without connecting to its existence within herself. The key ingredient in the definition of fear is "anticipation or awareness of danger." This is the mother of anxiety; E's family doctor has prescribed her medication for anxiety, which is concrete evidence that fear is not an abstraction but a mental condition. What then could the anticipation or awareness of danger be?

Lancer wrote "...codependents...experience churning emotions. Predominant are anxiety and resentment. Their mood...swings from fear or anger to hopelessness and despair...over time codependents experience depression, which is a lack of feeling."[300] She added "when parents withhold love or blame and shame their children, the shame and fear ofabandonment become internalized."[301] Now we have shifted fear from the abstract, ethereal world to the real world inside of a codependent person. The definition of fear mentioned above indicates E constantly anticipated an awareness of danger. What was so terrifying?! Having internalized fear of abandonment and rejection, and having been abandoned by her parents at an early age, E lived her entire life anticipating when the shoe would drop again, and she would be abandoned by L the same way she was abandoned by her parents. Lancer stated "your mind can spin into obsessions contemplating dreaded outcomes. Instead of responding to reality, you...react to your skewed thoughts and sabotage your...relationships."[302] Unable to feel, and being numb and depressed most of t he time, E, throughout the 36 years we were together in a relationship, knew our relationship was constantly at risk due to her CoDependency, and she anticipated our relationship's end. How can a relationship be maintained without feelings and love? Can it be maintained by depression, which is the absence of feelings? E's son declared our relationship is over during the Christmas Holidays 2018, but he had absolutely no clue why he declared our relationship was over? Or, what caused its downfall? The main point here is no relationship can exist between two people if one of them, or both of

---

[300] Lancer, op. cit., p. 66.
[301] Ibid., p. 111.
[302] Ibid., p. 67.

them, does not express their feelings and needs constantly. For 36 years, E never expressed them, yet she complained to her son she desires love from L, which he gave E, but she cannot feel his love because she has repressed the love receptors within herself.

In short, E worried about relationship failure all of her adult life due to the relationship failure she experienced between herself and her parents. Instead growing into a loving person and sharing it with others, E sought to "get" the mother and father love she lost as a child. This condition not only produced sustained fear inside of her, it also turned E into a *narcissistic personality.*

E. Narcissism And The Preoccupation With Artificially Loving Oneself

The codependent personality embodies all of the attributes of the narcissism personality. Throughout our discussion of CoDependency Addiction thus far, one central thesis dominates everything we have said about the codependent personality, namely, an affected person's feelings and needs are repressed within the Self, and every action he or she takes is devoid of feelings. Because feelings regulate a person's conscience, one's superego holds the ego in a balanced relationship between oneself and other people. The superego acts the same way as gravity does in our Milky Way Galaxy; it holds all of the planets in a regulated orbit around the sun. Without gravity, disorder and chaos would prevail in space. Therefore, without mother or mother-surrogate love, an infant's learns, during the first months of life, to not ask for love, and in order to avoid further pain, he or she represses their feelings within their Self. Because the mother or mother-surrogate failed to love her infant/child, the latter does not evolve from the dependency state into an interdependent one, characterized by a healthy love for self and a willingness to share love with other people. Due to this arrested development, the infant devolves into an individualism state in which he or she becomes preoccupied with loving oneself independently rather than giving love in order to be loved by others in return. The affected child grows into adulthood with one's feeling and needs repressed within oneself, and, in order to make it through the world, albeit in a terrified manner, an artificial image is put on like a dress to cover up the body and feelings within the repressed Self.

In his book titled <u>Narcissism: Denial Of The True Self</u>, 1983, Dr. Alexander Lowen, M.D. wrote "narcissism describes...a psychological... condition. On the individual level, it denotes a personality disturbance characterized by an exaggerated investment in one's image at the expense of the self. Narcissists are more concerned with how they appear than what they feel."[303] Before proceeding any further with this discussion, one fact must not be overlooked, or a connection unmade, and that is, a narcissist and a codependent are two adjectives, which accurately describe a person who is a victim of CoDependency Addiction. Every attribute Dr. Lowen discussed in his book applies to a codependent person. For example, he added "acting without feeling, they tend to be seductive and manipulative, striving for power and control. They are egotists focused on their own interests but lacking the true values of self-namely, self-expression, self-possession, dignity, and integrity. Narcissists lack a sense of self derived from...feelings. Without a solid sense of self, they experience life as an empty and meaningless. It is a desolate state."[304] The common thread is lack of self-expression of feelings and needs. As we have continuously drilled down on the point codependents' go through life with their feelings and needs repressed inside of them, and they attach themselves to other people's feelings and needs, like a parasite, and, if they are to move forward, they must manipulate and control their other person-addiction to survive. Once a dog, for example, scratch a flea off of itself, that casted-off flea will die, if it cannot attach itself to another dog or other animal. Once the codependent-person-addiction chain is broken by the latter, the relationship abruptly comes to an end. Because the codependent person overvalues *image*, he or she, in the words of Dr. Lowens "...must be

---

[303] Lowen, Alexander, <u>Narcissism: Denial Of The True Self</u>, Macmillan Publishing Company, New York, 1983, p. ix.
[304] Ibid., p. ix.

regarded as narcissistic."[305] It is timely to give an example of one aspect of E's image.

Earlier, we spent some time discussing E's overdoing activities for other people; we gave the Women Empowerment Group (WEG) she facilitated for more than 20 years as an example. The whole effort had little, if anything to do with change, understanding, or spiritual growth! It was all centered around maintaining power and control over people. According to Dr. Lowen, and using his example of Erich's case, we will substitute E's name appropriately to demonstrate how she used the WEG to manipulate and control the women in the group to satisfy her own narrow, selfish plan of manipulation, control, and search for her mother and father's love withheld from E as an infant.

According to Dr. Lowen, "another aspect of narcissism that was evident in [E's] personality was [her] need to project an image. [She] presented [herself] as someone committed to "doing good for others," to use [her] words. But this image was a perversion of reality. What [she] called "doing good for others" represented an exercise of power over them which, despite [her] stated good intentions, verged on the diabolical... Such exploitativeness is common to all narcissistic personalities."[306] Many of the women, who went through this experience under the mesmorization of E's narcissistic personality, will likely be very shocked to learn how they were manipulated. L–too–was equally shocked, and even more so, given the fact he lived with E for 36 years before he realized how he was duped and bamboozled, controlled, manipulated, and exploited by her. We have discovered just how deep-rooted the pain of a codependent is whose depth goes beyond the deepest trench in the Pacific Ocean. This is insanity, which may be hard to digest but its true. Dr. Lowen added "...insanity describes the state of a person who is out of touch with reality. Since feelings are a basic reality of a human life, to be out of touch with one's feelings is a sign of insanity."[307] L is like a "deer in headlights," paralyzed by the fact he has been involved with E for 36 years, and during this time, she never once self-expressed her

---

[305] Ibid., p. ix.

[306] Ibid., p. 5.

[307] Ibid., p. 4.

feelings and needs to him. If Jimmy or Susan says "I feel Johnny cannot read because he lives in the ghetto;" this is not a self-expression of their feelings. When Jimmy or Susan says "I feel sad and hurt that Johnny cannot read" is now an internal self-expression of their feelings. There is clearly a difference; the former is merely an external expression of a non-feeling about Johnny, and it self-expresses absolutely nothing about how one feels inside about Johnny's reading condition. In this regard, Jimmy or Susan will do nothing to assist Johnny to change his reading condition beyond what is institutionally prescribed in this or that public school district's Teacher Handbook.

E's lack of self-expression of her feelings was on fukk disp;ay recently. On June 10, 2019 L repaired our hot water heat pump-Steibel Eltron-with the supervision of technical support from this company. For a week, we had no running hot water in our house. After following the repair instructions, the heat pump started working properly again.

With hot water flowing again in our house, E was unable to express her feelings of gratitude or appreciation to L for the work he did. This has been a pattern for 36 years in our relationship. Regardless of the accomplishment L made, because E's feelings and needs were repressed inside of her Self, and every achievement L made was *never* celebrated, or given proportionate attention.

As we see, there is a definite connection between a lack of self-expression of one's feelings and insanity. Earlier we mentioned the Self is Who We Are, and since human feelings are at the heart of it; tragically, as in the case of codependent people, who generally repress and deny their feelings, Dr. Lowen added "…the basic disturbance in the narcissistic personality is the denial of feeling. I would define the narcissist as a person whose behavior is not motivated by feeling."[308] This is, according to Dr. Lowen, an indicator of insanity. For example, three days after Christmas Day 2018, E, without having any prior discussion with L about withdrawing money out of their joint credit union account, clandestinely withdrew $3,000 from it, leaving only $100 in it that was required by the credit union to keep the account

---

[308] Ibid., p. 8.

active. Acting on an intuitive feeling, L drove to the credit union in Lafayette, LA to inquire what the balance in the joint account was in February 2019. The attendant told him E withdrew $3,000 from the joint account.

Thus, from December 28, 2018 to February 2019, E never mentioned one word about withdrawing the funds from our joint account; and, when L confronted her about her unilateral, devious action, she showed no feelings or remorse at all! E simply coldly responded saying "Yea, I withdrew the $3,000." Then, maintaining my calm, L asked E to give him his half of the $3,000, and she again coldly commented "I am not going to give you anything!" At the time, L felt this was insanity, and Dr. Lowen's research, which was published in 1983, reaffirmed L was a witness to insanity. E's robbery of our joint account was not motivated by feelings because as we have pointed out throughout our research, codependent people's decisions are not guided by their conscience, which is the center of the subconscious brain that helps a person to determine what is right and wrong before making a decision to act. What is the cause of the narcissistic disorder? Is it the failure of a mother, father, or mother-surrogate, to nurture and love their infant, as we have consistently pointed-out throughout our research?

The answer is a resounding yes! Dr. Lowen stated "unfortunately… Parents fail to provide sufficient nurturing and support on an emotional level…The lack of nurturing and recognition aggravates the distortion, but it is the distortion that produces the narcissistic disorder."[309] The lack of mother, father love, or mother surrogate love, creates a distortion in the development of an infant's ego, and this aggravation inhibits any healthy, normal social relations with other people. The ego becomes a "Jokers Wild" manifested by antisocial behavior, which is one of the fingers on the CoDependency Addiction Hand. Montagu had this to say about the narcissistic personality distortion. He wrote "'Narcissism,' is a pathological development resulting from inadequate love by others… When others do not love it the organism attempts to love itself." [310] The

---

[309] Ibid., p. 12.
[310] Montagu, Op. Cit., p. 184.

withholding of mother and father love, including mother-surrogate's, creates the narcissistic pathological distortion commonly associated with a codependent person's personality.

Moreover, a person, who was sufficiently nurtured and loved throughout his or her childhood, evolves into a realization that he or she is "…a *part* of a whole of which he always remains a part. It is the unhealthy person who regards himself [or herself] as the whole and everyone and everything else as the part." [311] For example, E saw herself as the Women Empowerment Group, and everybody else was a part of it. She never disclosed anything about herself because her image was one of *perfection*. In truth, E used her distorted egoistic thinking to avoid any self-disclosure related to her CoDependency Addiction to L. None of the women in the WEG ever challenged E about her non-self-disclosure because E's ego distortion used the other women's pain and suffering to make her externally feel her self-esteem was higher than everybody's else's. In other words, most of the women thought, albeit erroneously, that *E's life with L was the perfect kind of relationship they would like to create for themselves.* So, nothing changed as the years went by. Some years earlier, E and one of her close girlfriends attended an Iyanla Vanzant Women Empowerment Workshop; during the several days event, E constantly circulated around the room offering consoling assistance to various women, who were crying and searching for ways to heal their pains. E's "people pleasing behavior became so disturbing that Iyanla Vanzant had to ask E to sit down and stop it! Rather than E trying to work on her own internal, repressed pains and wounds, she tried to hide behind *people pleasing* so others would think she had already addressed them.

Since E's feelings and needs were repressed and inactive during her years of facilitation of the WEG, she could not emotionally become involved with the loved one, namely, the women in the WEG. All E ever did was talk externally about this or that woman's problem in the WEG. For example, when one of the women's son was recently sentenced to life in prison without the possibility of parole, E did not express any

---

[311] Montagu, Op. Cit., p. 173.

feelings about the death of the woman's son. L never saw her cry, nor did E ever express any hurt, pain, or deep disappointment related to the fate of the woman's son. This is the ego distortion manifested by E's use of her favorite camouflage phrase: "I have compassion." How can anyone say they have compassion for another person's plight when their own feelings and needs are repressed inside of their Self? Montagu wrote "to love, one must be emotionally involved with the loved one-unemotional love is not love, and this emotional involvement must be conveyed to the loved one. To love is to be, and to convey the feeling of being absorbed in another."[312] Surely, E presented herself as a loving person in the WEG; however, if the truth is told, it is likely she never showed any emotional involvement with any member in the WEG. Deepak Chopra once remarked and we paraphrase: Be aware of the person who cries out I have been enlightened; he or she has realized nothing!

A narcissist person is created by the withholding of mother, father, or mother-surrogate love from her infant. This maternal deprivation lay the foundation for a distortion of the infant's personality over time-during childhood and beyond-which leads to an imbalanced ego, and simultaneously to the erroneous belief one is an individual and independent of others. Montagu wrote "it is when human beings begin to think, erroneously, that they can be independent of one another, "social isolationists," that they begin to frustrate and hate each other, that they do violence to all that they are and create much psychological and social havoc."[313] This is the soil out of which capitalist thinking originates as a result, and in the form of an unloved child. Although this is a subject for another book, it is clear CoDependency, Narcissism, and Capitalism are fingers attached to the same hand. To break this destructive chain, infants must be loved from birth throughout their childhood so they can share love with other human beings. To the contrary, unloved children "begin to frustrate and hate each other' within a capitalist society where the vast majority of people make

---

[312] Ibid., p. 176.
[313] Ibid., p. 185.

decisions daily without consideration of their feelings. We mentioned earlier that E plundered E and L's joint credit union account without remorse, sorrow, or feelings related to how L will feel when he finds out his hard earned money was stolen behind his back. What caused E to raid our joint credit union account began the first day she was born when her biological parents failed to nurture and love her.

Montagu stated the matter as such: The super-ego is an outgrowth and modification of the ego. Its special function in relation to the ego is to rule it. It is essentially the same as conscience…The super-ego represents the integrated value system of the person…Quite obviously, then, failure to receive adequate gratification from external sources [such as the mother, father, or mother-surrogate] will maintain the person in his [or her] autoerotic and narcissistic activities."[314] E's pillage of our joint credit union account was one of her narcissistic activities; and, the stealing of the money from the joint credit union account occurred decades earlier when her mother and father failed to adequately love her. Moreover, between 2015 and 2018, E repeatedly told L he is always right, regardless of the subject being discussed. After grasping the depth of the devastation an absence of mother and father love have on the psychological well-being of a child, E's constant reminding L he is always right comes from her lack of conscience or "integrated value system." Montagu added "the development from selfish to altruistic behavior is arrested,"[315] which means E does not have a developed conscience, which is why she always tells L he is always right. If she had a developed conscience, sometimes E would acknowledge she is right and L would agree with her.

Therefore, without parental love, a child's feelings and needs are repressed by him or her; to develop a conscience, mother, father, or mother surrogate love is required; and, without a conscience, a value system that regulates right and wrong is non-existent, and, consequently, everything a codependent person does is based on a narcissistic, autoerotic and self-serving premise. What is the alternative

---

[314] Ibid., p. 261.
[315] Ibid., p. 261.

a codependent person substitutes for his or her arrested development of a conscience?

Emile Durkheim published his groundbreaking book titled <u>Suicide: A Study In Sociology</u> in 1951. More than twenty years before CoDependency Addiction was identified as a mental disease in the early 1970s, Durkheim documented how a codependent person compensate without a conscience. He wrote "once the social instinct is blunted, intelligence is the only guide left us and we have to reconstruct a conscience by its means. Dangerous as is the undertaking there can be no hesitation, for we have no choice."[316] If you are wondering what Durkheim means when he wrote "once the social instinct is blunted," the latter idea refers directly to the abandonment and rejection of a newborn infant by its mother, father, or mother-surrogate. With an arrested development of one's conscience, the regulator of right from wrong, the affected child, in many cases, turns to "intelligence, or the intellect," as the only "guide left us." Thus, intelligence, which is data and information filtered through one's conscience to determine right from wrong, is inappropriately and solely relied upon by a codependent person when one has to make minor or major decisions. This is very dangerous because intelligence is the data and information a computer operator, for example, inputs into his or her computer, for the purpose of analyzing it to make an appropriate, timely decision. The intelligence and the computer are incapable of making choices and decisions; they are made by someone with a conscience, who analyzes intelligence first! In the absence of analysis, which is a key function of human conscience, poor decisions will be made over and over, and by using intelligence over and over, without analyzing or processing it; and, at the same time, hoping to get a result without the use of one's conscience, in this human way, is called insanity. Another sign of a person whose conscience is arrested is pathological lying.

Melodie Beattie made an exhaustive list of characteristics of a codependent person. All of them describes a codependent person, ranging

---

[316] Durkheim, Emile, <u>Suicide: A Study In Sociology</u>, The Free Press: A Division of Macmillan, Inc., New York, 1951, p. 169.

from caretaking, low self-esteem, repression, obsession, controlling, denial, dependency, poor communication, weak boundaries, lack of trust, anger, sex problems, miscellaneous, and progressive. Every descriptor in every category listed is applicable to a codependent person, who does not use his or her conscience to conduct the affairs of daily life. A few of them are good examples, given the fact they relate to pathological lying. According to Melodie Beattie, they are: "believe lies, lie to themselves, lie to protect and cover up for people they love, lie to protect themselves and cover up, lie, and protect the problem."[317]

Without a conscience, the affected person, who is a victim of Codependency Addiction, can easily misguide another person because similar to E, he or she does not utilize a value system to socially interact with other people. E attached herself to L's feelings and needs; thus, *she never argued the rightness or wrongness of how she feels about any subject.* E simply joined the bandwagon to avoid "rocking the boat," and sacrificed herself over and over. This narcissistic behavior was designed purposely to fool L that E's feelings and needs about "right and wrong" was the same as his own. Those persons, who were loved by their caregivers are vulnerable to being *misguided by those persons who were not loved by them.* Montagu added "it is possible to misguide human beings, and human beings are constantly in danger of being so misguided."[318] When a codependent person attaches one's repressed self to another person, the latter feels the former is behaving according to *Free Will, and true to his or her own feelings and needs.* But the contrary is true.

The misguided codependent person, who functions with an arrested and cretin conscience development based on mother, father, and mother-surrogate love deprivation, which can only end in self-delusion and fantasies, along with misguiding, or lying, to the other person to survive. Exactly how long a codependent person addiction to another person lasts, and how long the latter is misguided, depends, to a large extent, on how long the codependent person's CoDependency Addiction to the other person is kept a secret.

---

[317] Beattie, Melodie, Codependent No More, Hazelden Publishing, 1986, pp. 45, 47, and 50.
[318] Ibid., p. 178.

At the core of a codependent person's addiction is an enormous amount of fear of abandonment and rejection, which is spiced in a gumbo with narcissism, low-self-esteem, denial, and purposelessness. If otherwise, there would be no need for a codependent person to attach him or herself to another person's feelings and needs, if he or she had a purpose for living of their own choosing and making. (!) Emile Durkheim wrote "…because of [our] psychological constitution, man [and woman] cannot live without attachment to some object which transcends and survives him [or her], and that the reason for this necessity is a need we must have not to perish entirely."[319] In this regard, the codependent person has not attached himself or herself to a self-generated purpose larger than oneself, which transcend and outlives the Self. Instead, the codependent person attaches oneself to the feelings, needs, and *purpose* of another person's life such as what E did throughout her 36 years of CoDependency Addiction to L. As the Ancient Probverb says "without a purpose, the people will perish." During the mid-1980s, so many people in American Society were struggling and searching desperately for a purpose in their lives that a popular sit-com was created to reflect their confusion called "Get A Life." Today, more American people than before, especially the Mellenials and I-Gens, are still wandering in the desert of materialism, erroneously investing disproportionate screen time in gossip, tweeting, overeating, and engaging in bodily fantasies among many others. These pursuits of life and liberty corrode, quickly turn to dust in a few years, leaving their worshippers without a purpose for living. A Rolex Watch is not transcendent! Emile Durkheim peered into the mind of a codependent person, and many others, revealing the torment one's lack of employing a transcendent purpose in their lives cause.

He wrote prophetically "life is said to be intolerable unless some reason for existing is involved, some purpose justifying life's trials. The individual alone is not a sufficient end for his activity. He [or she] is too little. He [or she] is not only hemmed in spatially; he [or she] is also strictly limited temporally. When, therefore, we have no object than

---

[319] Durkheim, op. cit., p. 210.

ourselves we cannot avoid the thought that our efforts will finally end in nothingness, since we ourselves disappear. But annihilation terrifies us. Under these conditions one would courage to live, that is, to act and struggle, since nothing will remain of our exertions. The state of egoism, in other words, is supposed to be contradictory to human nature and, consequently, too uncertain to have chances of permanence."[320] There is hardly a need to write more. Can a codependent person be vetted psychologically any better?

The most beautiful thing about Durkheim's wisdom on this very broad human subject is his aim to awaken us to the fact *individualism* is not a sufficient end-purpose. Can a codependent person's addiction be a sufficient end to his or her life activity? Durkheim, if we may say so, writes even more deeply and powerful adding "...the more the family and community become foreign to the individual, so much the more does he become a mystery to himself [or herself], unable to escape the exasperating and agonizing question: to what purpose?"[321] We ask this question to the codependent person: *What is the purpose of attaching yourself to another person's feelings and needs, allowing you to become a foreigner to your family and community and a puzzling mystery to yourself?* We could end this book here but we have some more ground to cover before we sleep. In the words of the transcendent Poet Laureate-Robert Frost:"The woods are lovely, dark, and deep, But I have promises to keep, And miles to go before I sleep, And miles to go before I sleep."[322] We have more work to do before we sleep.

For those human beings who struggle to achieve a transcendent purpose during their lifetime, many external forces conspire against them toward the successful completion of their purpose, one which lives on beyond the grave. Durkheim added "those are few whose memories are closely enough bound to the very history of humanity to be assured of living until its death."[323] Codependency Addiction

---

[320] Ibid., p. 210.

[321] Ibid., p. 212.

[322] Lathem, Edward Connery, editor, <u>The Poetry Of Robert Frost</u>, Holt, Rinehart, And Winston, Inc., New York, 1916, pp.224 and 225.

[323] Durkheim, op. cit., p. 211.

conspires against the codependent person, hemming him or her in spatially and temporally. The very power needed to fulfill one's purpose is found inside the Self; when the codependent denies the Self, it is the same as unplugging a light from an electrical socket resulting in darkness, terror, and fear. In E's case, she spent the majority of our 36 years together talking about what she called the "Fifth Dimension."

Everything was better in another unknown place in the universe than the concrete ground upon which she stands on the Earth in the *known* universe. L always thought this was such a bankrupt viewpoint, and a dogmatic attempt to prove real human life is senseless. What L has found out about E's Fifth Dimension belief is that it was her way of devaluing her personal need to have a purpose for life! Durkheim wrote "...metaphysical and religious systems spring up which by reducing these obscure sentiments to formulae, attempt to prove to men [and women] the senselessness of life and that it is self-deception to believe that it has purpose...He [or she] effects communion through sadness when he [or she] no longer has anything else with which to achieve it...Egoism is not merely a contributing factor in it; it is its generating cause."[324]

Having no purpose for his or her life, the codependent personality, in which egoism and narcissism are dominant features, *seeks to find one's purpose* externally by attaching oneself to another person's feelings, needs, and purpose. According to Durkheim, the codependent person "...readily find external objectives to which they become attached."[325] One other point that is worth mentioning about a codependent person in this regard is, according to Durkheim, his or her "...moral balance...is more easily disturbed...[and]...excessive individuation leads to suicide, insufficient individuation has the same effects."[326] In either case, we have demonstrated repeatedly that the absent of mother, father, or mother-surrogate love leads to this psychological condition within the codependent person. It should be pointed-out here that, generally speaking, codependent people are vulnerable to numerous

---

[324] Ibid., p. 214.
[325] Ibid., p. 215.
[326] Ibid., pp. 216 and 217.

health maladies such as strokes, cardiovascular diseases, respiratory disease, and cancers among others. Thus, their commission of suicide is not always sudden but plays out over many decades. In E's case, she was in a relationship with L for 36 years before she had a stroke. Lancer added "somehow you learn to live with constant fights, insecurity, even suicide attempts, and still try to work, raise children, and maintain an appearance of normalcy. This has become your *normal*; a life lived in terror is *NOT* normal."[327] The abnormality is the buried self within the codependent person, and this is the ultimate self-abandonment, self-rejection, and self-alienation.

F. Buried Repressed Self And Abandonment

For a person to be codependent, there is one prerequisite, namely, the Self must be buried and abandoned. Because codependent people are so wrapped up in other people's lives and affairs, Lancer wrote "… they can't identify their own…The feedback loop from body to brain is not well connected."[328] They're completely out of touch with reality! Imagine a lion in the jungle being unaware it is a lion? In the Wizard of Oz Musical, the lion buried it's Self, and forgot completely that it is a lion with the courage that make it the "King of the Jungle." Likewise, the codependent person is alienated from Self, and is powerless and purposeless. As such, Lancer added "you decide that it's easier not to rock the boat and don't realize the high price you pay. Each time you do this, you abandon yourself. Your Self retreats and your voice gets weaker, like a candle dying out…You've "de-pressed" all of your natural vitality. Before you can expect to find happiness in a relationship, you must first discover how to make yourself happy."[329] When E and L got together in a relationship in 1979, E self-deceived herself first and L second when she declared to L that "only he can make himself happy, and vis-à-vis for E." E made this declaration to throw L's attention away from E's

---

[327] Ibid., p. 67.
[328] Lancer, op. cit., p. 139.
[329] Ibid., pp.139 and 140.

pain caused by the fact her own Self was buried and abandoned by her years before we got together in a relationship in 1979. E's word sounded good but, as L reflects back over the years, he does not remember E ever having sustained time during which she consistently expressed her happiness about anything, including the birth our daughter! At best, she just uttered empty words without any substance. She used her intellect because her conscience was undeveloped, which inhibited her self-expression of her fellings and needs.

This was caused by the fact E had buried and abandoned herself years earlier during her childhood due to the fact her mother and father did not give her love; they essentially abandoned and rejected her. In short, L got involved with a person whose Self was buried and abandoned! To survive, she went along with everything L recommended, and his biggest mistake he ever made was to believe E was happy with his suggestions, although her own Self was buried and abandoned within her. How could E be happy with anything, given the fact she was alienated from her own Self? Incredible is an understatement!

In the end, are codependent people alive, if their Selves are buried and abandoned? No they are not! They are plugged into another person's feeling and needs, and their power source goes unutilized. Their lives are, generally speaking, wasted and sacrificed on the alter of CoDependency Addiction. To struggle through an ever demanding maze of trickery, and as a friend once remarked-"fuckery," codependent people do not have any boundaries that they respect, given their conscience is inactive and arrested in its development; they, therefore, have weak, or non-existent boundaries as a result.

CHAPTER SIXTEEN

Boundaries, Communication, Responsibility And Codependency Addiction

One of the most important ways anyone can demonstrate RESPECT for another person is to STAY IN ONE'S LANE, and reframe from crossing the human rights boundaries of another person. While this seems easy to comprehend, many Americans of all ages, especially the codependent population, violate the human rights boundaries (HRB) of others every day. Currently, with the increasing proliferation of social media platforms such as Facebook, Twitter, Snap Chats, and e-mails among others, bullying has emerged as forms of emotional and physical abuse among American Youth and Adults. The common denominator, which drives human rights boundary (HRB) violations, is low self-esteem. That is, where high self-esteem is evident, violations of a person's HRB is low or non-existent. On the other hand, where self-esteem is low, violations of the HRB of people are high.

According to Lancer, "boundaries are an expression of self-esteem. They define where you end and others begin. They set limits between you and others that allow you to embody your individual Self. As we have already discussed at length, if a person's conscience is deformed, or its development is arrested as a result of one's parent's failure to give love to their infant(s), then, he or she's conscience fails to develop; that is, one's superego does not develop normally, thereby predisposing the affected person to overemphasize his or her ego within an abnormal narcissistic personality structure. This is the soil that HRB violations best germinate, take root, and grows. Having a healthy conscience, Lancer wrote "awareness of boundaries both protects you from others and prevents you from violating other's boundaries. They are learned growing up, when parents protect and respect your boundaries and teach you not to invade those of others. If you were not taught, you won't recognize when you're being inappropriate, and if your parents invaded your boundaries, it feels natural when others do."[330] When the parents do not teach their infants and children to not invade the HRB of others, the latter feels it is alright to invade the HRB of another person because they learned it is alright to do so, given the fact their own parents invaded their HRB when they were children.

A. Material Boundaries

Therefore, it follows that a codependent person, by virtue of being attached to another person's feelings and needs, violates the HRB of the person or group and so forth, who is the focus of his or her CoDependecy Addiction. For 36 years, E violated L's HRB! During this time, *it was a pattern when L began talking with other people about a topic, regardless of what its nature, E would consistently enter into L's sentence midstream and begin talking as if she originated the point L was attempting to make.* Even though L asked E to cease interrupting him while he was talking, she could not stop violating his HRB. Though L did not know it at the time, E could not stop barging in on his comments about a topic because E thought it was natural for her to violate L's HRB because hers' were violated during her childhood, by her parents.

Recently, as it was mentioned earlier, E took $3,000 out of our joint saving account at a credit union located in Lafayette, LA. She never discussed this action with L; he found out when he went to the credit union to inquire about the balance in the account. Lancer explained E's codependent behavior as follows: "Taking…money or belongings

---

[330] Ibid., p. 46.

without permission or without returning them also shows a lack of respect for others' boundaries."[331] When L asked E about disrespecting his boundaries, given half of the $3,000 belonged to him, E acted self-righteous saying "Yes, I took the money, and I am not giving you any of it." The only thing that could cause E to behave in this way is the absence of a developed conscience; if she had one actively engaged, E would know the difference between *right and wrong*. Mental boundaries is another area in which E and L engaged in on-going arguments throughout the 36 years we were together.

Lancer wrote "mental boundaries apply to opinions and beliefs, and whether you can formulate and hold on to your own when challenged, without becoming rigid, or dogmatic..."[332] As a reminder, a codependent person's feelings and needs are repressed rigidly inside one Self, including his or her opinions and beliefs. So, E was out of touch with her reality and attached to L's opinions, beliefs, thoughts, visions, and purpose. Therefore, the only way for E to hide this fact about herself, she violated the mental boundaries of L; she used a long history of arguments to create a false and pretentious atmosphere that she was expressing her own opinions and beliefs when, in fact, hers' were repressed; so *E used an argument to cover up the fact that she was not expressing her own opinions and beliefs about any situation that surfaced.* The arguments progressed to the point our daughter refused to go anywhere with E and L because she became very fatigued being in the presence of her parents arguing all of the time. For many years, L was highly puzzled by the fact something simple he brought up like expressing his opinion and belief related to why Etoufee should not be cooked in a certain way, triggered a long drawn out argument. E used the Argument Card to give the impression, although she may have expressed her opinions and beliefs, L did not respect what she was saying, or considered it valid. Moreover, it never failed that during those times E and L engaged in sexual intercourse, we always got into an extended argument or discussion about some meaningless subject. The

---

[331] Ibid., p. 47.
[332] Ibid., p. 48.

purpose of this behavior was to avoid talking about intimate feelings and needs related to E's childhood challenges.

E "reacted" angrily because as Lancer noted "if growing up you were denied the right to think for yourself, make your own decisions, or have your ideas and opinions respected, then you may not know what you think or believe. When you do, you might become confused, lose hold of your opinion, or become very angry in an argument. This may be a reaction influenced by your past when parents dismissed, criticized, or silenced your views."[333] This is exactly and precisely what happened to E during the vulnerable years of her childhood. She told L that her parents and older siblings *never* listened to her, nor did they *ever* have real conversations with her related to how she felt about her life and other things. E also shared with L that no one ever taught her how to work or do anything, which caused her to withdraw her feelings and needs deeper and deeper within her injured, wounded, and enclosed Self. In addition to the mental boundaries violations, when a codependent person attaches oneself to another person's feelings and needs, by doing so, this is a violation of the latter's emotional boundaries.

B. Emotional Boundaries

For 36 years, E was attached to L's feelings and needs; she lost herself in them. In effect, E abandoned her Self and deceptively took refuge in L's. Lancer added "...emotional boundaries...separate your feelings from those of others. People with healthy emotional boundaries don't lose themselves in intimate relationships...Because each is separate... The integrity of each Self is maintained, so they can be close and remain whole...they don't...take things personally."[334] On the other hand, the opposite is true for a codependent person, and in E's case, being codependent, she relied heavily on the emotional feelings and needs of L. Lancer added "codependents don't have healthy emotional boundaries. If your feelings weren't respected as you were growing

[333] Ibid., p. 48.
[334] Ibid., p. 48.

up, you may be unable to sense differences between your feelings and those of someone else, or you may not know when your boundaries are disrespected."[335] To know the difference between one's feelings and another person's is dependent on both persons having healthy emotional boundaries. Because E is codependent, she crossed over the emotional boundary line and attached herself to L's feelings and needs, and, therefore, she cannot distinguish her feelings and needs from L's because hers' were repressed for 36 years. To compensate for this emotional boundaries violation, E initiated a campaign against L by attempting to blame him for the wounds and suffering she experienced during her childhood.

Since July 2015, and every year following her stroke, E intentionally told anyone who would listen, both friends and family members, that L is the cause of her codependent problem. E does not respect the fact L is separate from her, and he has his own feelings and needs, which differs from hers.' This is evidence of E crossing L's emotional boundaries! Lancer wrote "...if you blame, are abusive, or tell others what they should do, you're ignoring their separateness and crossing their boundaries. Doing this in order to make you feel better ignores your responsibility for your own feelings. You imply that someone else is responsible for how you feel, denying the separateness between you."[336]

Thus, for more than 36 years L was in a relationship with E, she disrespected him by dishonoring his separateness from her. Otherwise, E would not be codependent, if she honored my beingness and separateness from her. L felt the disrespect through the years because crossing "emotional boundaries are subtle and difficult to understand... Your boundaries are crossed when others assume what you're thinking, feeling, or what is right for you. Respecting others' boundaries honors their separateness."[337] One of the subtleties E used to hide crossing L's emotional boundaries and others is she frequently used the metaphysical phrase "All is One." Yes, we are all social creatures and human beings;

---

[335] Ibid., p. 49.
[336] Ibid., p. 49.
[337] Ibid., p. 49.

however, each of us has our own feelings and needs that make us Who We Are. For example, we all need a house to live in, but one person's feeling about what kind of house he or she desires to live in is quite different from someone else's viewpoint on the matter. So, this All Is One ignores human separateness, and it grossly disrespects the emotional boundaries of people in general.

Another easy way to grasp what is meant by crossing the boundaries of another person is *identity theft*. When someone subtly hacks into your personal identity, your boundaries have been violated. Codependent people behave similarly inasmuch as they covertly steal the feelings and needs of another person as their own without the person whose personal identity boundaries have been grossly violated. In order for their identity theft to continue to go unnoticed and unchallenged by the other person whose feelings and needs have been stolen, Dr. Henry Cloud and Dr. John Townsend added codependent people "… are chameleons…controllers are isolated…If they're honest, controllers rarely feel loved. Why? Because in their heart of hearts, they know that the only reason people spend time with them is because they are pulling the strings. If they stopped threatening or manipulating, they would be abandoned."[338]

As long as E was pulling the strings in our relationship and controlling everybody's behavior, her identity theft scheme remained active. But, the strings she was pulling broke when she had her stroke in 2015, and rather than take responsibility for her manipulation of L during the course of the 36 years they were together, E defaulted to blame and gross denial. A tactic many codependents use to get through the day being a chameleon is their use of poor communication. Before we proceed to this discussion, it is useful to give the last word to Drs. Cloud and Townsend related to how important boundaries are to every day healthy well-being. They wrote "boundaries define us. They define what is me and what is not me. A boundary shows me where I end and someone else begins, leading to a sense of ownership."[339]

---

[338] Cloud, Henry Dr. and Townsend, John Dr., <u>Boundaries</u>, Zondervan, 1992, p. 59.
[339] Ibid., p. 31.

Codependent people, generally speaking, are mostly unaware of this social rule because their conscience is shutdown, which causes them to cross boundaries recklessly, similar to a person driving a car weaving in-and-out of traffic endangering their lives and others.

C. Poor Communication And Boundaries Violations

Before we are born, while we are still in utero, the fetus is in communication with the rhythm and sounds of our mother's voice. By way of our umbilical cord connection with our mother, the latter transmits vibrations to her fetus, which can either be harmonious or discordant. Lancer wrote "you start learning communication before you're able to speak. Even in utero, you're learning the rhythm and sound of your mother's voice. Your parents were your role models..."[340] Unfortunately, many codependent people are conditioned by parents who are members of dysfunctional families. As a result, CoDependency Addiction is communicated to infants during their childhood. Consistent with what we have established thus far, Lancer added "fear, driven by shame, is the biggest obstacle to being direct in communication. Without assertiveness, problems in relationships never get squarely addressed or solved."[341] The mother and father, or mother-surrogate, transmits their CoDependency Addiction energy to their infant or child, and this role modeling has long lasting effects on social relations throughout life. Lancer made a list of poor communication habits generally presented by codependent people. To follow are several L observed during the many years of conversations he engaged in with E. They are:

- "Say "Yes" when you mean "No""
- "Hide what you think and feel or the fact that you don't know"
- "Edit what you say in order to avoid controversy or criticism"
- "Ask questions instead of making statements"
- "Talk about someone other than yourself"

---

[340] Lancer, op. cit., p. 56.
[341] Ibid., p. 56.

- "Don't tell people when you dislike what they say or do"
- "Don't ask for your needs or wants to be met"
- "Avoid frank conversations and serious problems"
- "Blame someone else for causing your feelings"

Together, these poor communication habits-ALL-fit neatly into the CoDependency Addiction Relationship E and L shared. This is the language used by many codependent people to keep their repressed Selves a secret. When E and L came together in a relationship in Baltimore, MD in 1979, one of the things we enjoyed was our emphasis on objectivity. That is, we primarily allowed the facts to determine the best approach to take in a situation, or direct us to make the most broadminded decision possible. However, through the years, L recognized E's movement toward metaphysics, which was a shift backwards into subjectivity. All of the above items in the above list of poor communication habits are a manifestation of subjective thinking. The communication lines between L and E became so incoherent that, from 2010 to 2019 in particular, E began to react to any viewpoints shared by L saying "That is your interpretation." In other words, our conversation devolved from the Level of Knowledge and Wisdom backwards into perception, which is the lowest point in the thought process, including perception, knowledge, and wisdom. As the years L an E were in a relationship wore on, it, undoubtedly, became more difficult for E to keep up her façade of objective thinking, especially now that L realizes, for the first time, E did not embrace objective thinking as her own mode of communication, but she attached herself to L's objective thought process as her own. In face of the latter, and without a foundation upon which her objective thinking was rooted such as revolutionary philosophy, the subjective thinking E presented, in recent years, was hidden beneath the surface, from the very beginning of our relationship in 1979.

Moreover, the car analogy is timely to show how this objective-subjective thinking ruined E and L's relationship. The two front tires and two rear tires on a car must all pull in the same direction. When CoDependency Addiction is present, the two front tires (Objective thinking) pull forward, and the rear tires (Subjective thinking) pull backward. Thus, the car cannot move forward except under the greatest strain. Eventually, the engine of the car is destroyed similar to E and L's relationship.

This communication default was not done mean spirited to harm L or anyone else. Being codependent, E was predisposed from her childhood to engage in subjective communication. When we got together in Baltimore, MD in 1979, L envisioned this new beginning would allow E to openly examine her internal injuries and negativity incurred during her childhood; deconstruct it; and reconstruct her communication based on a revolutionary philosophy. This is what L decided he needed to do to improve his thinking, and change it from subjective to objective. Although this sounds easy to do, it is not so simple, especially if one's childhood was emotionally dissatisfying and unfulfilling. Growing up in such a dysfunctional household produce many latent and deep-rooted fears, which are bound to resurface at some time or another in a person's life. Rather than building a purpose for living and acquiring a philosophy to carry it out into reality, a codependent person spends a disproportionate amount of his or her time expending valuable mental energy on trying to hold back the floodgate of feelings and needs repressed in their wounded and injured Self.

One day, as it was in the case of Land E, the dam breaks caused by a catastrophic event such as a stroke, and all of the dogmatic, putrefied, and hardened and decayed feelings exploded out onto to the table of our relationship. Usually, the explosion is so great that making some self-corrections and redirections are virtually impossible, given the fact denial, shame, guilt, absence of conscience, and more stand as major limitations to reviving the relationship. A good analogy is in the medical community, doctors often say if a disease is recognized at a very early stage, the chance of a patient's recovery is very good. However, if the disease is allowed to metastasize through stage 4, the prospect for relationship recovery is very slim to non-existent. Too much repressed damage occurred in L and E's relationship over 36 years, making it all but impossible to retrieve from the precipice.

After E's CoDependency Addiction came to light shortly after she had a stroke in 2015, she has clung tenaciously to the position that she did not know she was codependent caused by a difficult childhood. Given the fact by 2015, every bill E and L had was paid for free and clear, including house, land and cars. In addition, there was enough money available to enjoy life. When L found out about E's CoDependency Addiction, along with how it had impacted his life for 36 years, he was still prepared to work out the problem, and go forward in his relationship with E. However, what was unthinkable is L was not prepared for the *intense denial* he came up against when he asked E for an explanation related to how we lived so long in our relationship without CoDependency ever surfacing? Even though the breakup of our relationship would mean everything we worked for 36 years would be lost, E's *denial dial* would not move a nanometer, or by one hair, towards her taking responsibility for her CoDependency Addiction. This, by far, for L is the most difficult development related to the whole CoDependency issue. No matter what L tried to find a breakthrough, or remorse of any kind, the denial dial would not move; it remained frozen in place. But, when L read Lancer's research, he discovered the reason E's denial dial would not shift forward. Lancer added "awareness of your fears can help you risk being honest."[342]

When L pondered this profound statement, he discerned the answer to why E's denial dial would not move. That is, because of *hypnotic rhythm*, the belief in honesty, over the years, becomes compromised by personal fears; and, therefore, to admit the adverse impacts CoDependency Addiction had on our relationship was internalized by E as something she did that was "bad," thus, making it too painful to confront the potential loss of everything. Given many codependent people engage in *self-sacrificing behavior*, losing one's relationship is not a strong enough counterforce to move the denial dial toward responsibility, thereby saving L and E's relationship. The denial dial does not move toward any solutions because codependents intentionally shy away from talking about their addiction problems to another person because, according

[342] Ibid., p. 56.

to Lancer, it "...can feel as if you're in a life-threatening situation-that your only option is to blame, hide or shade the truth, or apologize and agree in order to please, appease, or control someone else's feelings. This *is defensive manipulation* because it's motivated by fear to avoid conflict. Codependents...manipulate...with criticism and guilt trips."[343]

As we see, hardly any positive communication can take place between the codependent person and the one he or she is in an addiction relationship because to talk about the CoDependency Addiction feels like the codependent person is in a life-threatening situation. They are because as we mentioned earlier, people without a purpose will perish; Emile Durkheim commented unless a person has a purpose for living larger than their physical reality, which is based on conspicuous consumption, those persons are prone to *egoistic suicide*. And furthermore. Since the codependent person's self-esteem is low, the latter uses manipulation tactics to evoke a negative reaction from the one who is the focus of the former's CoDependency Addiction. By doing so, Lancer wrote "manipulating focuses on someone else whose reaction becomes the measure of your self-esteem."[344] This behavior is similar to cognitive dissonance where another person, group, race or nation is demonized in order to justify treating them disrespectful, or responding subsequently to them with emotions ranging from anger to war.

In short, because love is absent in the lives of codependent people, the vast majority spend years engaging in broken communication due to the fact healthy communication is dependent upon the free exchange of one person's feelings and needs with another without any barriers such as repression of one's feelings and needs due to an emotionally traumatic childhood experience. For example, L made another attempt to see if E could breakthrough her repressed Self, and allow her true feelings to come out and share them with him. During an hour of talking, E sat in our rocking chair silently and said hardly anything. Once she felt threatened that her CoDependency Addiction is recognized by L as the *breakdown in our communication and the breakup of our relationship*, L was

---

[343] Ibid., p. 57.
[344] Ibid. p. 57.

shocked to see E go into another personality characterized by anger and a high level of emotional outbursts. This was E's manipulation tactic that had, for many years, triggered a negative reaction in L, which made E feel better about her self-esteem. L concluded that there is nothing that can be done to alter E's rigid determination manifested by her refusal to move pass her CoDependency Addiction, and accept responsibility for the horrific impacts it has had on our relationship for more than 36 years. Nothing can be done to salvage our relationship from the Pit Bull like bite E's CoDependency Addiction has on it. One of the insurmountable hurdles, which stands in the away of repairing our relationship, is codependent people, generally speaking, have major difficulty taking responsibility for their behavior.

D. Taking Responsibility

During the mid-1990s, L developed a polyp in his left nostril while working in a very stressful job at the Maximum Secure Care Prison for Juveniles, which was located in Baker, LA at the time. When he discovered this health issue, L's first response was to go immediately into damage control, and seek out an answer to how he created his adverse health condition. When L shared with E his polyp health condition, he did not once project any of his responsibility for creating the polyp in his left nostril on E. This health condition was created by L alone; E had nothing to do with creating a polyp in L's nostril, nor did he ever imply that she was responsible for the health problem L created in his own body. If L had accused E of creating the polyp in his left nostril, he cannot imagine how E would feel, notwithstanding her astonishment, that her partner of 36 years would be capable of shifting his responsibility for creating a polyp in his left nostril to her. No doubt, this would be devastating to E under the best of circumstances!

As the growing body of CoDependency Literature suggests, it is not unusual for codependent people to project their responsibilities, for their own codependent behavior, on another person, who is usually the primary focus of their CoDependency Addiction in their relationships. Once E no longer was able to keep a secret her CoDependency Addiction to L, and rather than accept her responsibility for her codependent behavior, she defaulted to her childhood role modeling, during which time, and sadly, she likely was blamed for many things caused by another one of her siblings, or even by her parents. Fortunately for L, he got out from in front of the Projection-Blame Steam Roller, and given his feverish observations and study of the subtle ways CoDependency Addiction manifest itself in the form of negative behavior, L was able to calmly listen to E's Projection-Blame Steam Roller, and having some advanced knowledge of the tendencies and personality traits of codependent people, L was able to diffuse most of the Projection-Blame Handgrenades thrown at him. For 36 years, L took responsibility for E's life; he figured it all out; and when something did not go right as expected, L covered up for E. For example, when our daughter was around 8 years old, one afternoon L was sitting at the dinner table and H walked from the Great Room to the kitchen, where L was seated. In a stressed voice H told me unedited that momma told me a few minutes ago that *"I get all of my bad habits from my daddy."* At first, L just laughed H's comment off as a child being a child. However, in serious reflection this is a real experience where E was conditioning our daughter to develop a hateful attitude toward her father. That is to say, as many positive things L did for his daughter, *E was, unbeknownst to L, sowing discord between himself and his daughter.* For seventeen consecutive years, L contributed disproportionately to summer vacations at the beaches located in Gulf Shores, AL and Pensacola, FL. L thought surely, by nurturing his daughter among other things like telling her your father loves you, certainly E, L, and H would be so in love with each other that we would be the envy of every person who knew something about us.

How significantly wrong was L-totally!! Lancer helped L get over this difficult hurdle of being, doing, and loving his family; yet, after H was assisted with getting her Doctoral Degree, she stopped communicating with L altogether. During March 2019, E spent the entire month in Tampa, FL with our grandchildren. During this 30 plus days of being away from home, L was holding down the home front, and he did not receive one telephone call from H to check on him to see if he was still alive! He did not receive one telephone call from E inquiring about how he was doing? These are examples of Codependency Addiction. Earlier, we mentioned children, who were not loved by their parents, or surrogate-mothers, are trapped in a great contradiction. On one hand, they hate their caregivers, and on the other, they tolerate them because they have no choice, and they fear if they challenged the abuse of their caregivers, the latter would abandon and reject them. Although this absence of love threatens to destroy E and L's relationship, the former believes, even though she is codependent, that L is responsible for the mentioned examples of breakdown in communication and breakup of our relationship.

For example, as recent as April 2019, E asked L "What are you willing to do to save our relationship?" Even though E is codependent, and given the fact the CoDependency Literature informs the reader that CoDependency Addiction is capable of destroying any relationship, E persists with her perception that L is responsible for the problems in our relationship. This is the same attitude expressed by H when she remarked "Momma told me I get all of my bad habits from you daddy." However, when L took a closer look at this antisocial behavior, he discovered it is a characteristic part of the CoDependency Addiction discussed thus far. Accordingly, Lancer wrote "codependents don't know how to meet their needs and believe that others can't take care of themselves. They attract…people and invade their boundaries by trying to control them, while not taking responsibility for their own… Many addict codependents are irresponsible when it comes to work, money, childcare, or personal safety, health, and hygiene."[345] This irresponsibility is upside down thinking and self-delusional based on the erroneous belief that the *effect is the cause and the cause is the effect.*

For example, does it make sense to believe that alcohol is the cause of an alcoholics' drinking problem? Or, that a firearm is the cause of a homicide? Or, rape is the cause of a male's physical abuse of a woman? Or, the teacher is the cause Johnny and Susan cannot read? These are examples of one-sided, subjective thinking. Similarly, many codependent people, who do not take responsibility for their

---

[345] Ibid. p, 61.

irresponsible behavior, believe the person they are addicted to, in their relationship(s), is responsible for their codependent behavior. Such deep-rooted denial and upside down thinking makes it nearly impossible for an affected codependent person to recover from their CoDependency Addiction to another person. Moreover, for example, this is the reason an alcoholic, who has stopped drinking alcohol, is always considered to be one drink away from relapsing back to his or her previous self-destructive pattern of heavy drinking. That is because the *effect (alcoholism)* is widely thought, by many professionals, to be the *cause of the addiction* itself, rather than drilling down into an alcoholic's past history to discover the buried cause inside of one Self.

The addiction, regardless if it is alcoholism, CoDependency, pedophilia, rape of children by Catholic Priests, abuse of women by men, or any antisocial behavior, has a common tap root in utero and, after birth, when an infant's basic need for love is not satisfied with the love of his or her biological parents or surrogate-mother. This is why an entire Chapter was dedicated to a thorough consideration of the significance of the overthrow of mother rights by the Patriarchal System, which, no doubt, secured a man's children would definitely inherit his or her father's wealth; yet, although the children inherits material possessions of all kinds, they are, simultaneously, placed at risk of experiencing maternal deprivation, along with the development of this or that addiction. It may be useful to re-read this information. Until the FEAR of abandonment, rejection and many others, which are rooted in a person's childhood, are identified, extinguished permanently, and abandoned, *recovery will always remain a descriptive series of stories that are spoken about;* and, unfortunately, permanent change will remain a fleeting illusion. The Sisyphus Stone Affect applies! The first change Sisyphus must make in order to get his stone up the hill, and secured there so it will not roll back down again, is he must take responsibility for his or her addiction; that is, he or she must go deep into their past childhood history, and excavate all the repressed layers of denial, shame, and guilt, in order to see clearly how one was emotionally traumatized by the loss of mother, father, or mother-surrogate love during a very vulnerable time.

Rather than meet this challenge head-on, Lancer wrote "codependents especially don't take responsibility for their feelings and emotional needs in relationships…you may be unaware of your feelings and needs but instead try to control and blame someone else in order to get your needs met."[346] The King of Popular Culture-Michael Jackson-remarked days before his death: "This Is It." Failure to take responsibility is the "This Is It" in CoDependency Addiction.

When a codependent person fails to take responsibility for his or her CoDependency Addiction, an attempt is made to shift, or project, all of the negative attributes of the disease on another person, hoping to relieve oneself of any responsibility. Lancer added "…you deny responsibility for your feelings and actions yet feel responsible for those of your partner. This externalizes control of your actions and feelings and puts your partner, who you expect should make you happy, in charge of your self-esteem. It relinquishes responsibility for your own life and happiness and relieves you of responsibility for your self-care, choices, and actions. You may try endlessly to control, advise, and manipulate someone whose feelings and opinions you believe are critical to your own well-being. The result is that you focus on, feel responsible for, and react to the feelings and needs of others."[347] When L left his family and son in Baltimore in 1979 to get in a relationship with E, she repeatedly stressed to me that L was not leave his family for her but this was a decision L wanted to make independent of any outside influence. This was a classic CoDependency Addiction tactic used by E to manipulate L into feeling she had nothing to do with this decision; yet, when E's CoDependency Addiction explode out into the open in our relationship 36 years later, E continually asked L what role did he play in the breakdown in our relationship? When E needed to manipulate L to think leaving his family for her was unique to him

---

[346] Ibid., p. 61.

[347] Ibid., p. 62. This quotation is intentionally included although it is longer than others. The entire quotations is included because it goes to the heart of CoDependency Addiction, and it clearly reveals the unspoken desires of the codependent person, namely, an on-going attempt is made to shift responsibility on the other person in a CoDependency Relationship.

only, L was suppose to believe this untruth because hidden beneath the surface, in the repressed chambers of E's heart, soul, and Self, CoDependency Addiction generated the script.

And, the hand that threw the rock was hidden; but, it was exposed by July 2015, when E had a stroke, and her hidden hand that casted the stone 36 years earlier became transparent. Did L cause the breakup of their relationship, or was it only a matter of time before the truth would come to light?

This is the truth! Because E's CoDependency Addiction had been kept repressed inside of her for 29 years before L divorced his family in 1979, she could claim on the surface innocence, but right beneath it lurked the sordid baggage of CoDependency Addiction that she brought with her to Baltimore, MD in 1979, namely E's need to get in a relationship with L so she could "relinquish responsibility for [her] own life and happiness to L…" When L divorced his family, E began to repeat the idea that "Each one of us is responsible for making our own self happy." This declaration also sounded true; however, knowing what L knows today about CoDependency Addiction, E used it to divert L's attention away from the fact that codependent people use other people's feelings and needs so it is not possible for them to create their own happiness using someone else's feelings and needs. By telling L he is responsible for his own happiness, this released E from any responsibility to make her own self happy because as a codependent person, she could not without going through years of intense therapy! More importantly, E could be in our relationship without sharing any happiness with L since he was bought into the idea that he had to make himself happy no matter what E did. Yet, unbeknownst to L, he had to make himself and E happy! L thought he could achieve this impossible goal; by feeling this way, E did not have to face the fact that she did not have any love to give L due to t he fact her own biological parents did not give her any consistent love and attention during her childhood.

To pull this tragedy comedy off, E used *manipulation and victimization* to get what she wanted. According to Lancer, "playing the victim is a way to manipulate with guilt. Some codependents manipulate with…intimidation, fear, and rage to get what they want…Addicts routinely deny, lie, and manipulate to protect their addiction."[348] E used a combination of these tactics, through the years, to get what she wanted, namely, to get L to create her life for her and make her happy! For 36 years, L did just that! This is the tragedy because L could never make E happy because she seldom smiled or experienced any sustained joy and happiness. It was not within her to do so based on the role modeling she grew up in the midst of. When E and L got together in Baltimore, MD in 1979, and if E would have shared honestly her childhood experience, our relationship would not have ended today. She could not engage in this level of self-disclosure because the risk was too great! *Either to die or live a lie!* E chose the latter path and it worked for her for 36 years!

What E failed to realize, as one of our mutual friends usually said, was she was filled with fear of abandonment and rejection when we got together in a relationship in Baltimore, MD; if E had been honest about her early childhood life, we could have easily dealt with the situation in 1979 because L started doing social research and E could have easily joined in and researched her early childhood years; this would have allowed her to destroy the demons in her mind and body that tormented her constantly throughout the 36 years we were together. That did not happen. L played the role of the Knight In Shining Armor or the *part of the enabler,* for 36 years.

Every time L felt like E was not giving him love, he made up an excuse in his mind saying to himself "things will change tomorrow." Tomorrow turned into another year, and another for 36 years of tomorrows. For example, one of the things that really hurt L's feelings is when E an L returned to Louisiana from Oakland, California during the mid-1980s, we quickly purchased five acres of farmland in LA. On a pretty Saturday morning (L can remember the day like it was today) E an L met G and MK at the property we were interested in purchasing, E, before she and L talked over our feelings about the property we were looking at before us, E, without any discussion with L, told MK and G we will buy the property immediately! Although L liked the property

---

[348] Ibid., p. 62.

he was looking at before him, he found it strange in his "gut" that E so quickly told MK and G "We" would buy the property? Though L had this feeling in his gut, he did not challenge E's quick decision to buy the property. He essentially *enabled* E's controlling behavior. What played out, from the very beginning of our C Farm Experience is E knew L was very fond of farming as a carryover from his childhood so she was attached to L's feelings and needs and made a unilateral decision to buy the land without ever realizing her decision was primarily based on L's feelings and needs while her own were secretly being repressed inside of her Self since her childhood. For 36 years, E never engaged in any self-directed farming; during this time, she never bought one seed; planted it; cared for the germinated vegetable plant; and harvested its produce. E quickly agreed to buy the farmland as a means of controlling L's behavior. L kept encouraging E to become actively involved in farm work, but the more L asked E to get involved, his request for 36 years fell on deaf ears.

Yet, L enabled E in her anti-farming behavior by allowing her to ignore growing food, and by taking responsibility for E's role in the farming process. Lancer wrote *"enabling* refers to caretaking that removes the natural consequences of someone's irresponsible behavior. It also includes handling responsibilities for someone that he or she can *and should* be handling."[349] This is the great mistake L made throughout the 36 years he was in a relationship with E. He enabled her to continue repressing her dark secrets from her childhood. Just as the old Pennzoil Commercial said back in the day "You can pay me now or pay me later." L enabled E to engage in private self-destructive behavior. Lancer added "today enabling is more widely applied to behavior that enables anyone to continue acting in a self-destructive manner."[350] Although L did not challenge E's CoDependency Addiction to him during the 36 years we were in a relationship together, L's inaction could not free E from her responsibility to share her feelings and needs with L, rather than repress them, for a shortsighted end.

---

[349] Ibid., p. 65.
[350] Ibid., p. 65.

For example, E discovered a book called <u>A Courses In Miracles</u>, 1975 in 1996 (ACIM). She read it passionately, and spoke about its content regularly with L. In fact, E was so excited about ACIM that she read the book three times. L became interested in what was so interesting about the book that he asked E to buy a copy for him to read. L read the book in 1997, and he referenced it in one of his own books called <u>Triumph Of The Spirit</u>, 2000. ACIM is primarily about the ego. L's contribution to the literature is as follows: All of the foregoing information discussed in this research related to CoDependency Addiction stands the *ego question* on its head. ACIM addresses the ego problem in isolation from how it *originates in the mind* of a human being. As we have observed thus far, the ego is an essential part of the psychological structure of human beings; however, it has been made very clear so far that if the mother, father or surrogate-mother do not *consistently satisfy* an infant's basic need for love, affection, and attention during his or her childhood, the latter will fail to learn one's Self is the embodiment of love; and, having helped the infant/child learn "Who he or she Is," the caregiver(s) also contributes simultaneously to the infant/child's development of a Super-Ego Structure, which creates the potential, for the latter, to be love and loved by other human beings. ACIM stated "love wishes to be known, completely understood and shared. It has no secrets; nothing that it would keep apart and hide. It walks in sunlight, open-eyed and calm, in smiling welcome and in sincerity so simple and so obvious it cannot be misunderstood."[351] Without mother, father, or mother-surrogate love, this love is unavailable inside of a codependent person to share with another human being!

This book turned the ego question back up on its feet by demonstrating the ego is a valuable part of the human psyche, and it only becomes deformed, if an infant/child's caregivers do not consistently give the latter love during childhood. ACIM only address the ego as a mysterious phenomenon without any connection made to its healthy or unhealthy development.

---

[351]   <u>A Course In Miracles</u>, Foundation For Inner Peace, 1975, p. 436.

This is why L believes E became fascinated with ACIM's treatment of the human ego as an arbitrary occurrence without a definite source of malfunction. As such, ACIM did not encourage E to deal with the connection between her CoDependency Addiction formation and absence of parental love during her childhood. In short, it was safe for her to read ACIM in the *abstract*. When taken out of the abstract realm, many of the points ACIM makes about the ego question becomes applicable in their proper context. For instance, ACIM states the following: *"I **am** responsible for what I see, I choose the feelings I experience, and I decide upon the goal I would achieve. And everything that seems to happen to me I ask for, and receive as I have asked."*[352] In short, ACIM, one of E's favorite books instructs the codependent person that he or she is responsible for their CoDependency Addiction, and not the person who is the focus of it. The key word in this passage is *responsible*; and, as we see, the possessive pronoun **I** is used eight times (!), which indicates, by far, if a codependent person is in direct contact with his or her feelings and needs, *only* then will he or she take responsibility for the behavior, or effects, they create. Otherwise, denial, manipulation, lying, deception, and projections among many others are resorted to by the codependent person as a means to delay taking responsibility for one's CoDependency Addiction.

For 36 years, E talked about all of the sacrifices she made for L, H, and other people (WEG). We already discussed the codependent person's use of the sacrifice tactic as a diversion, from taking responsibility for one's behavior. ACIM added "sacrifice is attack, not love."[353] Wow! ACIM added "...fear demands the sacrifice of love..."[354] We also discussed the twin towers of fear-fear of abandonment and fear of rejection. Both of these fears interchangeably work together to produce sacrifice, which is *doing everything all of one's life for others is an attack on one Self and others, and such a projection is driven by the negative energy of the twin towers of fear itself, whose primary source is an absence of caregivers' love.* This was the first sacrifice experienced by and affected infant/child, who carries out this

---

[352]   A Course In Miracles, Foundation For Inner Peace, 1975, p. 448.
[353] Ibid., p. 325.
[354] Ibid., p. 607.

same sacrifice of love in their intimate relationships, and in other walks of life. Sacrifice was a cornerstone of E and L's relationship (!) as we have previously established. Without mother, father, or mother-surrogate love, the opposite is fear and love is sacrificed. The self-esteem of codependent people is low, and taking responsibility for their behavior is *unpredictable* at best.

Lancer added "taking responsibility for your feelings and actions is key to building self-esteem; otherwise, you'll continue to feel like a victim and be dependent upon others' feelings and behavior over which you have no control. This is a losing formula. If you go from one relationship to another looking for someone to make you happy or fulfill you…you forfeit the opportunity to grow into your wholeness and strength. Instead, your codependency grows. Until you accept responsibility for yourself, you cannot change your life…"[355] As long as E was attached to L's feelings and needs, how could she take responsibility for her own feelings and needs due to the fact she was simultaneously repressing them? Right up to the breakup of our relationship, E refused to accept responsibility for her CoDependency Addiction that destroyed our relationship just like drugs and alcohol addictions are *effects of a common cause.* Since the codependent person does not have a life to take responsibility for, he or she attempts to project their social inadequacies onto their addiction. For April 2019, E and L's Att Cell Phone Bill was $119; E's portion of the bill was $86 and L's $33. When L questioned E about her disproportionate share of the charges, she refused to accept responsibility for her overuse of her cell phone, which is causing us to pay a much higher monthly bill. Instead of examining her portion of the bill to determine its accuracy, E simply commented "We have always paid the Att Bill, regardless of the cost. This is projection. ACIM added "the mind…can deceive itself…It can project its guilt, but it will not lose it through projection."[356]

We have mentioned previously that one of the characteristics of a codependent person is his or feverish and constant search for love

[355] Lancer, op. cit., p. 160.
[356] _____ACIM, op. cit., p. 385.

externally, or outside of one Self. Projection is one example of the distorted search for love. ACIM accurately warns the codependent person to "seek not outside yourself. For it will fail...Heaven cannot be found where it is not...For all your pain comes simply from a futile search for what you want...You will fail...it is given you know the truth, and not seek for outside of yourself."[357] The truth is the failure of mother, father, or mother-surrogate to give love to their infant forms the mold which gives shape to an aimless search for love outside of one Self. ACIM adds the codependent person "...wanders aimlessly about, in search of something that he cannot find, believing that he [or she] is what he [or she] is not."[358] The aimless search of the codependent is for mother, father, or mother-surrogate love; it cannot be found in his or her co-addiction to another person! And, by erroneously thinking this love can be found externally, the codependent person becomes their addiction; hence, he or she becomes "what he or she is not." When L asked E Who she Is, invariably she denies she is not L's feelings and needs, but her Self. This led L to believe that E does not know the depth of the mental disease she is afflicted with.

For the codependent people who heed the call to cease and detach themselves from another person's feelings and needs, which is motivated secretly by an external search for mother, father, and mother-surrogate love, and although the number who doggedly persist in this codependent pattern far exceed the few who break free of it, the consequence of not detaching from another person's feelings and needs, ultimately and unfortunately, leads to many catastrophic health problems.

---

[357] Ibid., p. 617.
[358] Ibid., p. 617.

CHAPTER SEVENTEEN

Codependency Addiction And Its Many Related Health Consequences

At the heart of the creation of physical diseases of various kinds by the codependent person is the great stress they buildup in their physical bodies as a result of the repression of their feelings and needs within the Self. It is challenging for the codependent person to keep it a secret that they have a CoDependency Addiction to another person in a relationship. Every day one wonders will their secret be discovered today? When? This thought preoccupies their mind all the time, which erodes their joy, peace, happiness, and love. Instead, resentment buildup like air in a balloon, and similar to what Aretha Franklin sung in her hit song "Chain Of Fools," "And one day the chain is gonna break, but until then, I am gonna take all I can take until it break." One day the balloon is going to burst, and that is the day a catastrophic illness usually occurs; E's resentment and anger manifested in her creation of a stroke in July 2015. Lancer stated "some codependents use resentment to camouflage anger that's underneath."[359] E made it a habit of attempting to project her repressed anger on L for repressing her feelings and needs. She would invariably ask L "Are you angry." Or "Why are you so angry?" L's response to E's questions was simply: "I am not angry."

---

[359] Lancer, op. cit., p. 78.

In truth, resentment is self-anger; the codependent person resents one's own Self for not expressing his or her feelings and needs. Consciously, the latter tries to project their anger onto the person who is the focus of their CoDependency Addiction. **What makes the repression of one's feelings and needs so dangerous and life-threatening is, from the moment a caregiver withholds his or her love from an infant or child, the latter locks their feelings, impulses, and needs inside of their subconscious, and overtime, they forget they have done so. Thus, the codependent person uses repression to try to keep at bay their emotional trauma suffered during their childhood.** When E's stroke released her repressed feelings and needs into her conscious mind, which were locked in her subconscious mind since birth, she *repetitively told L that she did not know she was codependent; therefore, she further added she should not be held responsible for her CoDependency Addiction.* Although E alleges she does not remember, for example, how she felt about not being loved, or given any quality attention by her biological parents during her childhood, she, nevertheless, couldn't remove the worrisome, negative impulses that this parental behavior caused.

The <u>Webster's Ninth New Collegiate Dictionary</u> defines repression as follows: "a process by which unacceptable desires or impulses are excluded from consciousness and left to operate in the unconscious."[360] The most revealing revelation this definition uncovers about CoDependency Addiction is, although a codependent person's hurt, wounds, injuries, terrors, and pain were intentionally excluded by a codependent person, from his or her consciousness, the former unacceptable pain, nevertheless, continued to operate in their unconscious mind. Though repressed, the emotional trauma in the unconscious directly influences a codependent person's conscious behavior. Every conscious action E took, during the 36 years we were in a relationship, was directly influenced by the feelings and needs she repressed in her unconscious mind.

---

[360] Op. cit., p. 1000.

Therefore, it is impossible for a codependent person to claim he or she did not know they were codependent because in the same manner subliminal advertisements work, the subconscious messages in them continually influence the decisions made by the affected person every day. This is a process called Post-Hypnotic Suggestion.

Having established a defense against a codependent person saying "I did not know I was codependent," to follow are a few psychological problems repression cause.

A. Depression And CoDependency Addiction

Montagu wrote "…children deprived of mother-love show various degrees of depression…"[361] During their adult life, many enter into it having never advanced out of their initial dependency state into interdependent living. In order to cope, and as we have already seen, most codependents resort to a denial of their repressed feelings and needs. Lancer added "despite being in denial, codependents still experience churning emotions. Predominantly are anxiety and resentment. Their mood also swings from fear or anger to hopelessness and despair…over time codependents experience depression, which is a lack of feeling."[362] Lancer made a list of common behaviors presented by codependent people, which includes, but not limited to "a chronic sense of inferiority and shame…Having a series of unsuccessful relationships…Loneliness, Never getting your needs met, Loss of faith in the possibility of change for a better future."[363] Moreover, she also mentioned "depression can result from "de-pressing" or holding down feelings, especially anger… The excitement of romance, sex…melodramatic relationships, a bust schedule, and the tasks of being a caretaker provide sufficient stimulation and distraction from the depression that's just beneath the surface. A peaceful relationship or calm environment would soon be "boring"

---

[361] Montagu, op. cit., p. 209.
[362] Lancer, op. cit., p. 66.
[363] Ibid., p. 69.

without the adrenalin that drama and stress create to mask underlying depression."[364] Dr. David Perlmutter (MD), author of the popular book titled Grain Brain, 2013, wrote "the World Health Organization has estimated that by the year 2020, depression will become the second largest cause of suffering-next only to heart disease…Drugs like Prozac, Paxil, Zoloft, and countless others are by far the most common treatments for depression in the United States…Big Pharma companies…make a lot of money in this department-to the tune of nearly 15 billion dollars a year…"[365]

One of the main factors underlying the consumption of antidepressants is, regarding codependent people in particular, is their repression of their feelings and needs over time. In our case, E repressed hers' for 36 years while we were in a relationship. What is adverse to their personal well-being and health is the act of repression creates simultaneous production of rising levels of stress in their mind and body. Stress builds up in the mind and body, and it directly affects one's adrenalin gland. The latter is located atop each kidney and secrets a steroid hormone into the bloodstream when stress triggers a need for more energy to respond to the Fight of Flight Syndrome. Because a codependent person keeps pouring more stress into his or her mind-body system, and in response to repression-producing stress, more adrenalin is released into the bloodstream, and this leads to an imbalance in one's metabolic functions. One reaction to their perceived need for more energy, in view of the fact depression drains the mind-body of energy, which gives rise to prolonged or chronic fatigue, is the consumption of a diet-intake of refined sugar and carbohydrates.

Currently, "the United States Department of Agriculture (USDA) reports that the average American consumes between 150 to 170 pounds of sugar in one year…the average American consumes 17 teaspoons (71.14 grams) every day."[366] Thus far, our health equation includes repression, increasing stress, depression, and a high sugar and

---

[364] Ibid., p. 69.
[365] Perlmutter, David and Loberg, Kristin, Grain Brain, Little, Brown and Company, New York, 2013, pp. 160 and 161.
[366] _____http://www.google.com.

carbohydrate diet. Driven by stress, the average American, which includes many codependent people among the population, the high per capita consumption of sugar intake over stimulates the Adrenal Gland, and in its attempt to balance the high level of sugar/glucose in the human bloodstream, the Adrenal Gland releases Cortisol in the bloodstream in an effort to correct an imbalance in metabolic function. With the consumption of a high-carb diet, Dr. Perlmutter stated sugar "… speeds up the glycation process…Sugars in particular are rapid stimulators of glycation, as they easily attach themselves to protein in the body…"[367] Glycation refers to sugar molecules becoming bonded with protein, and "…they tend to attach themselves to other similarly damaged proteins and form cross-linkages that further inhibit their ability to function…But perhaps far more important is that once a protein is glycated, it becomes the source of a dramatic increase in the production of free radicals."[368]

Once the glycation process goes on for many years undiagnosed, it "…leads to the destruction of tissues, damaging fat, other proteins, and even DNA. But when it's excessive, many problems arise. High levels of glycation have been associated with not only cognitive decline, but also kidney disease, diabetes, vascular disease…and…the actual process of aging itself."[369] The central player in the formation of these diseases and others is free radicals. Dr. Perlmutter further added "when proteins are glycated, the amount of free radicals formed is increased fiftyfold; this leads to loss of cellular function and eventually cell death."[370]

In short, repression and depression contributes to the Adrenal Gland secretion of high levels of adrenalin in the bloodstream, which attempts to naturally remove excessive sugar and carbohydrates in it. However, because stress continues to increase due to the denial of codependent people in particular, the latter place more sugars and carbohydrates in their bloodstream, and once the amount of sugars exceed what the Adrenalin Gland can remove, the glycation process creates an

---

[367] Perlmutter, op. cit., p. 114.
[368] Ibid., p. 114.
[369] Ibid., p. 114.
[370] Ibid., p. 115.

overabundance of free radicals. The Adrenal Gland secretes cortisol into the bloodstream toward bringing the metabolic function back into balance. However, more sugar and carbohydrates produce the secretion of more cortisol by the Adrenal Gland, and eventually useful cortisol is changed into free radicals.

For clarification, "cortisol is a steroid hormone that is produced by the adrenal gland which sits on top of each kidney. When released into the bloodstream, **cortisol**…help…your body respond to stress and danger"[371] Moreover, "cortisol…help control blood sugar levels, regulate metabolism, help reduce inflammation, and assist with memory formulation. It has a controlling effect on salt and water balance that helps control blood pressure. All these functions make **cortiso**l a crucial hormone to protect overall health and well-being."[372] Similarly, when too much sugar goes into our bloodstream, our Pancreas tries to rebalance our blood-sugar ratio by secreting Insulin to remove the sugar, or over-supply of glucose. When too much glucose floods our bloodstream, overtime, an affected person's Pancreas stops functioning properly, and the result is development of diabetes disease. Too much sugar in the our bloodstream produces cortisol secretion like Insulin; however, cortisol changes into Free Radicals, which lay the foundation for a codependent person to create various diseases in his or her body and mind. We cannot emphasize enough that stress caused by the lack of mother love, father love, or mother-surrogate love causes stress to increasingly become a part of the everyday life of a codependent person. E repressed her feelings and needs for 36 years, which gave the buildup of stress in her mind and body more than a good opportunity to transform itself into various types of diseases. Another troublesome health problem many codependent people face daily is anxiety.

---

[371] _____http://www.google.com
[372] Ibid.

B. Anxiety And CoDependency Addiction

Though we have mentioned that the repression of their feelings and needs by codependent people generate unhealthy amounts of stress in their mind and bodies over time, most continue to hide their true feelings at the expense of making themselves ill. Lancer wrote "it's common for people to hide their feelings...Many codependents do this in personal relationships far too much."[373] Needless to say, by doing so, codependent people produce and live with high levels of stress in their mind and bodies, given the fact it takes energy, and more and more of it, to continue to *fool, trick, deceive, dupe, and bamboozled their addiction-partner into believing they are being honest and authentic when they're not.* Thus, anxiety is caused by fear of the future. The codependent person constantly worries if today or tomorrow is the day when his or her addiction-partner discovers how the codependent person has been abusing them by, on one hand, repressing their feelings and needs and on the other, attaching themselves to the feelings and needs of their addiction-partner. Lancer added "fear...breed anxiety, and anxiety can create fear... On a daily basis, codependents live with yet more fear-the fear of being themselves, of being alone, of showing their feelings, of others' reactions, especially anger, and of taking risks."[374]

In addition to mounting fears and stress, and because codependents are numb to their feeling and needs, their anxiety level remains unusually elevated. Lancer stated "anxiety is apprehension about a future threat...Interspersed with rationalizations and fantasies about how you'd like things to be, you project your hopes and fears into the future-even when there's no evidence that they will occur."[375] As we already mentioned, the "mystery future threat" is centered around "Who is going to take responsibility for me, thinks the codependent person?" During March 2019, E was given a prescription by her family doctor for anxiety. Because she is not self-generating her own future

---

[373] Lancer, op. cit., p. 208.
[374] Ibid., p. 67.
[375] Ibid., p. 67.

with a clearly defined vision and purpose, E is deep in the anxiety quagmire. And, while the quicksand has no tangible bottom, she continues to deny her feelings and needs; more stress is created in her mind and body as a result; and, she, therefore, is at-risk of creating more illnesses and diseases in her life.

Accompanying depression is despair. On many occasions E shared with L that she was an "invisible child who withdrew into her private world" during her childhood. On one occasion, E told me her family all rode to church one Sunday when she was in elementary school, and after church, her parents and older siblings got into the car and drove home. It was only when her parents and siblings got back to their house did they realize they had left E at church. According to Montagu, "the child is withdrawn and apathetic, makes no demands on the environment, and is in a state of deep mourning."[376] Because E was, according to her, an invisible child in her household, and since what is invisible is not seen, it makes sense her parents and older siblings did not miss her during their drive home from church. That being so, L cannot imagine how E must have felt being left behind at church by her family members and not strangers. However, E was an invisible stranger to them, and she was estranged from her own Self. That is to say, she was alienated from her own Self, including her feelings and needs.

If despair is prolonged over the course of a codependent person's childhood, and into one's adult life, the latter will, no doubt, suffer with negative feelings of hopelessness, pessimism, helplessness, low self-esteem, low self-worth, not good enough, undeservedness, and scarcity among others. Montagu added "the feeling of helplessness, of hopelessness, and the depression and depressive states accompanying such feelings, may in most cases be traced back to failure of expected satisfactions especially in the oral phase of development. Unable to satisfy its own nutritional needs, "to get affection, to be loved, to be taken care of, to get 'supplies'" results in a profound feeling of

---

[376] Montagu, op. cit., p. 214.

helplessness."[377] Moreover, if the infants basic needs are not met, he or she becomes regularly frustrated, which transforms into anxiety and anger. E has suffered with chronic anxiety and anger throughout the 36 years we were in a relationship, and because these negative feelings do not feel good under any circumstance(s), she constantly asked L are you angry? Or, why are you so angry?" L's response was "I am not angry." The strangest thing about E's attempted projection of her anger on L, is the fact her words did not match how L felt. If E could get L to feel he was angry, then, she could make up a fantasy in her mind, by deceiving her Self that she is peaceful; L is not peaceful; she has high self-esteem; L has low self-esteem. Thus, L is the problem, and although E is codependent and L is not; however, and nevertheless, E's life would be harmonious if L was not angry. This is classic denial of the truth.

As this mental condition plays itself out over the years, Montagu wrote "if frustration is continued…the anger will be replaced by feelings of exhaustion, of helplessness and depression. Whenever we meet with a failure to function as an adequate human being we may be certain that the cause or causes are to be looked for in the love relationship of the person during the first six years of his [or her] life."[378] Throughout this research, we have carefully and deliberately included a preponderance of evidence that consistently affirms the fact that if mother, father, or mother-surrogate is unavailable to an infant during the first six years of life and beyond, the affected infant, child, and adult, will fail to develop a conscience and consciousness of Self in relation to another person. Friendship development suffers greatly, and it is nearly non-existent save for a few relations with another person(s) that remain primarily artificial in scope, mundane, and generally trivial. Montagu added "for our purposes we place great emphasis on the importance of love in the socialization of the person because it is through the means of love that the infant first develops a consciousness of himself [or herself] in relation to another person-the

---

[377] Ibid., p. 259.
[378] Ibid., pp.259 and 260.

fundamental social relationship. By being loved the child learns to love…with gratification directed towards another object-the mother-and this is the beginning of the process of actively learning to love and cooperate with others."[379]

Whenever an infant does not receive the love he or she needs from their caregivers, the infant grows through childhood, and enters into adult life without a conscience or consciousness of Self, which is the cause a codependent person is unable to self-love and share that love with other people. The fundamental social relationship formation skills are non-existent, which places thousands of unsuspecting people at risk of becoming the focus of the addiction of a person suffering with the pains, wounds, and emotional trauma caused by a non-loving relationship with their mother, father, or mother-surrogate. L became involved with a codependent person, namely E, who did not learn the social skills required to form a loving social relationship, and after 36 long years, everything he worked for in his relationship with E was merely a mirage without any social foundation regulated by a conscience and conscious, or by the subconscious and conscious mind respectively. Given the deep breakdown in the balance between these two components of the mind, a codependent person's mental imbalance is caused by growing up in a dysfunctional family.

C. Startled Reflex, Decision-Making And CoDependency Addiction

Throughout my 36 years of being in a relationship with E, L recognized, on numerous occasions, that E audibly gasped, oftentimes loudly, in a panicked voice when he entered a room unannounced in our home. L first observed E's "startled reflex" (SR) to him as early as 1979. When L first observed it, he thought it was humorous, and jokingly laughed it off. Anybody can be startled but the cause underlying E's startled reflex has its roots in the dysfunctional family she grew up in during her childhood. Lancer wrote "abuse is common in dysfunctional

---

[379] Ibid., p. 260.

families and may take the form of neglect or physical, sexual, emotional, or spiritual abuse. Abuse violates your boundaries and seriously damages your self-esteem…Abuse is usually random and unpredictable, adding to an atmosphere of anxiety or even terror…Abusers commonly deny their abusive behavior and blame it on their victims. Victims also deny and minimize abuse they experience because they feel ashamed, even though they're not at fault."[380]

Herein lies the kernel of the seed that led to the breakup of E and L's relationship after 36 years. Although E was the recipient of some intense abuse of the various types mentioned above, and though she was a victim of abuse in the dysfunctional family in which she grew up in, *E has repeatedly denied and minimized her abusive childhood experience due to shame. Consequently, no healing could take place, given the fact E's denial crowded out possibilities for healing and change.*

Returning to E's "startled reflex" (SR), rather than dark welcomed as an essential part of the 24 hours day, in a dysfunctional family household, where chaos reigns most of the time, insecurity is a learned behavior, and fear produces a manifestation of the SR. Safety is always a question in the mind of the affected infant. Lancer wrote "as a child, you never have a sense of safety and consistency that you need in order to thrive. You don't invite friends over to avoid being embarrassed by your addict-parent. Your needs get ignored, and you learn not to ask rather than be disappointed."[381] Every day the family dynamics change, and the one consistency in it is more drama occurs, which creates added stress and fear to an already debilitating energy in the household. The symptoms of emotional trauma-oftentimes-do not show up until later in a child's adult life. One of the delayed symptoms E manifested, according to Lancer, is: "Being easily frightened and startled," and "Feeling depersonalized; a loss of Self or cut off from your body and environment-like you're going through the motions." [382]

---

[380] Lancer, op. cit., p. 114.
[381] Ibid., p. 117.
[382] Ibid., p. 136.

As a result of E's repression of her feelings and needs, that is, her true, authentic Self, she lived her entire 36 years in a relationship with L "cut off from [her] body and environment." She is alienated from her Self, or from Who she truly is *still*, due to the fact her repression means she separated her Self from her mind and body. Being alienated from her body and body from her mind, Montagu recognized "proper mothering of the infant is vitally important factor in bringing about a viable nervous integration of the organism, in conserving energy for mental growth…[and]socially approved emotional and later intellectual development."[383] Montagu added "in children who have been inadequately mothered…[alienation of mind and body] …persist for an abnormally long period of time."[384] This includes the SR L recognized in E's behavior; it has persisted for more than 36 years! And, as recently as April 24, 2019, L entered the study in his home, and E verbally said, "You startled me!" It will take more than going to a few CoDependency Meetings to excavate E's long standing repressed and buried Self." Moreover, given the long history of study L and E engaged in, and since 36 years of study and knowledge accumulation has done nothing to break through E's denial, it is likely she could have been physically abused by her father, or other during her childhood. If so, it is understandable why E is willing to sell her home, reather than admit to the truth of her past.

All-in-all, fear of the dark is common among codependent people because of the early experience they had as infants growing up in dysfunctional families. For example, fear of the dark and insecurity begins very early in an infant's life shortly after birth. Montagu stated "infantile anxiety typically "occurs when the child is left alone *in a dark room* (usually the bedroom at bed-time)." [385] Animal studies have confirmed that those animals that were gentled and given sustained attention were not easily frightened. However, those that were not cared for as such by their caregivers were easily frightened. According to Montagu, "…the exact opposite was the case with the ungentled

---

[383] Montagu, op. cit., p. 257.
[384] Ibid, p. 257.
[385] Ibid., p. 165.

rats, the rats which with reference to their relations with human beings had received no attention from them whatever, except that incident to feeding and cage-cleaning. These animals were frightened and bewildered, anxious and tense in the presence of human beings. This constitutes a very interesting confirmation on lower animals of conditions which we know to exist among children brought up under not dissimilar circumstances."[386] E told L that her *mother and father did not touch her*; tell her that they loved her; or gave her any quality attention beyond feeding and cleaning her clothes during her entire childhood. Similar to the ungentled rats, which were very easily frightened, E, likewise today, demonstrate the same symptom of being afraid of the dark and very easily startled.

Moreover, another appendage to the dysfunctional family tree is the affected infant eventually enters into adulthood with a repressed Self causing a generalized condition of a lack of confidence and poor self-trust in one's feelings and intuition. This leads to an impaired ability to make decisions. Also, due to an absence of mother, father or mother-surrogate love, during the first six years of a child's life, the development of a conscience, in which resides the power of a person to make decisions between what is right and wrong, is seriously and substantially distorted and flawed. According to Lancer, "if you grew up in a family where your feelings and perceptions were denied, you learned that you couldn't trust your internal cues-your observations, impressions, and feelings. As a result, your ability to trust your feelings and make decisions became impaired. By looking to others for answers, you give up living your own life."[387]

During E an L's 36 years relationship, nearly 98 percent of all decisions were made by L! Surely, you must be thinking this statement is farfetched and overstating the truth. I agree with you if I were looking from the outside at E and L's relationship. However, L was a witness on the inside of it, and while he was led to believe E was an equal partner in our decision-making process, to the contrary, E did

---

[386] Ibid., p. 254.
[387] Lancer, op. cit., p. 151.

not offer any of her feelings and needs during our deliberations about a particular matter; she generally shadowed L's feelings and needs, which misled him to make a grave error, namely, L thought E was self-expressing her feelings and needs but she was actually mimicking L's. It was difficult for L to figure-out the feelings and needs being expressed by E were not hers' because *she replied most of the time that she felt the same way about the topic* under discussion. For example, after E had her stroke in July 2015, it became only very clear to him thereafter that nearly everything outside of our home and inside of it was decided by L, ranging from the type of trees to plant; type of vegetables to plant in the garden; whether to add a screen porch to our house; what color paint to buy for the walls inside of our house; what type of decorations should be placed on the walls; when should we add a new addition to our house; and what type of furniture should we purchase. These are just a few examples of all the decisions made by L; E did not make any decisions *at all* beyond the mundane things like what type of cereal to buy or what will be prepared for dinner. Even in this case, L still had to step in make the decisions. While E's decision-making was paralyzed, L enabled her non-decision-making by rationalizing, if E went along with his feelings and needs, then, hers' must be the same as L's since she did not express any opposition ever! This is CoDependency Addiction at its very best!

Of everything we have discussed thus far, and although *Denial and Blame* are major cornerstones of CoDependency Addiction, the one factor that *levels the sanity playing field is personal health*. No matter how much a codependent person tries to blame their problems on their addiction-person in a relationship, the former's health challenges always give away their CoDependency Addiction. Their active repression of Self causes an increased buildup of stress in their mind-body system, and eventually an illness or disease will inevitably manifest itself.

D. CoDependency Addiction And The Manifestation Of Illness And Disease

Codependent relationships "...pose health risks from chronic stress."[388] Repression of one's feelings and needs overtime create Free Radicals in the codependent person's mind and body, and they attack cellular tissues, which produces inflammation and, ultimately, illness and disease. Throughout E and L's 36 years relationship, he noticed a pattern of illnesses associated with E's mind-body system. On some level, L thought this was odd because we were only 29 years old when we got together. Who would be challenged by a pattern of illness at such a young age, if something deeper and unspoken wasn't going-on in the subconscious mind of E? Rather than confront E about her health challenges, L explained them away by rationalizing in his mind that it is not unusual for human being to get ill frequently. L was 46 years old before he had a headache; when he was 21 years old, he got a high altitude headache when he moved to Boulder, Colorado to attend Graduate School in August 1972. Afterwards, L was free of any illness until his late 40s. Lancer wrote "as the [CoDependency] disease progresses, anger and conflict are more common, and self-esteem and self-care further decline. Hopelessness, emptiness, and depression prevail. The chronic stress of codependency manifests in new symptoms, such as stress-related health problems..."[389]

As we have already seen, by the time E and L had been together in their codependent relationship, particularly by the time we were in our 50s, we argued almost constantly about nearly anything, regardless of how trivial or mundane. We argued when L made it possible for E and H to travel to Cairo, Egypt to visit the Great Pyramid of Giza and the Sphinx. What could have been so wrong between us that while visiting these most sacred places, and walking on the grounds where all of the great Kings and Queens of Egypt once stood in Egyptian History? What was wrong is E was suffering with chronic stress caused

---

[388] Ibid., p. 15.
[389] Ibid., p. 22.

by her Codependency Addiction to L. She felt the pain of her neglected childhood sitting on one of the giant marble stones used to build the Great Pyramid of Giza. Chronic stress had turned E's world upside down long before L ever met her, and before she laid her eyes on the Sphinx, and observed its missing nose, which was shot off by Napoleon's Army more than a century earlier.

Moreover, Lancer added "despite being in denial, codependents still experience churning emotions. Predominant are anxiety and resentment. Their mood also swings from fear or anger to hopelessness and despair."[390] At the core of the chronic stress buildup in a codependent person is his or her loss of someone dear to them, namely, their mother, father, or mother-surrogate. Such abandonment and rejection cannot be emphasized enough. Lancer stated "when you lose someone or something dear, it's natural to have feelings about it. When you experienced losses growing up in a dysfunctional family, emotions go unexpressed...and their energy gets stored in your body. Not discharging emotion...lead to depression and chronic emotional and physical symptoms."[391] When a codependent person repress or ignore their feelings and needs, doing so sets the table for poor decision-making and health problems, both of which are driven by chronic stress. That being so, Lancer wrote "the danger lies in ignoring feelings, which...lead to poor decision and health problems."[392] Since codependent people, in many cases, have repressed their feelings and needs, similar to a prison in which they feel danger but cannot escape, the resulting end game is they become frozen in a state of chronic anxiety. As it is so often for many codependents, Lancer wrote "when you can neither fight or flee when in danger, you freeze in a state of constant anxiety...a life lived in terror is *NOT* normal."[393]

Therefore, underlying a myriad of health problems of codependent people is chronic stress, and beneath it is their repressed feelings and

---

[390] Ibid., p. 66.
[391] Ibid., p. 129.
[392] Ibid., p. 146.
[393] Ibid., p. 172.

needs, and denial, blame, projection, and failure to take responsibility for one's behavior are used to cap, or trap, chronic stress within one's Self. Regardless of how hard codependent people try to keep a cap on their repressed feelings and needs, they are not successful similar to the buildup of chronic stress in the Earth's Crust, which eventually result in an earthquake, or like a dormant volcano such Mt. St. Helens, which suddenly exploded, and released energy powerful enough to kill people instantly more than a mile away from the blast site. Below is a chronological outline of a series of health challenges that affected E's personal well-being-both mentally and physically. These health problems were observed by L, beginning in 1979 and continuing to 2019. In order to grasped a deeper understanding of exactly what each health problem means, regarding the energy package, or thought that E and L used to create them in our mind-body system, we used a book written by Louise Hay titled <u>You Can Heal Your Life</u>, Hay House, Inc., Carlsbad, CA, 1999.

L did not purchase this book; it was added to our home library by E, who used it to monitor the extent to which her CoDependency Addiction to L was taking a debilitating toll on her health. It should be made clear here that the energy package, or thoughts, presented by Louise Hay is her translation of it into words that are directly related to E's Codependency Addiction. Table 1.2 includes a chronological list of E's heath problems during the 36 years we spent in a relationship.

Table 1.2
Health Problems And Their CoDependency Causes

BEFORE 1979	ILLNESS	CODEPENDENCY CAUSE
,,	Thyroid	Humiliation. "I never get to do what I want to do. When is it going to be my turn?"
1979 TO PRESENT	**SAME**	**SAME**
,,	Headaches	Invalidating the self. Self-Criticism. Fear.
,,	Nose Bleeds	A need for recognition. Feeling unrecognized and unnoticed. Crying for love.
,,	Bruises	Self-Punishment
,,	Chills	Mental Contraction, pulling away and in. Desire to retreat. "Leave me alone."
,,	Gall Bladder	Anxiety. Holding on to old ideas. Fear of letting go. Be pissed off.
,,	Fibroid Tumors	Denial of Self. Rejecting femininity. Rejection of the feminine principle.
,,	Snoring	Stubborn refusal to let go of old patterns.
,,	Fatigue	Resistance, boredom. Lack of love for what one does.
,,	Blood Pressure	Long-Standing emotional problem not solved.
,,	Stroke	Giving up. Resistance. "Rather die than change." "Rejection of life."
,,	Heart	Long-Standing emotional problems. Lack of joy. Hardening of the heart. Belief in strain and stress.
,,	Hips	Fear of going forward in major decisions. Nothing to move forward to.
,,	Arthritis	Feeling unloved. Criticism, resentment.
,,	Respiratory Ailment (COPD)	Fear of taking in life fully.
,,	Bronchitis	Inflamed Family environment. Argument and yelling. Sometimes silent.

Source: Hay, Louise L., You Can Heal Your Life, Hay House, Inc., Carlsbad, CA, 1999, pp. 218, 197, 207, 184, 186, 182, 193, 215, 193, 182, 216, 197, 198, 180, 184, and 212.

The above illnesses that challenged E's health, during our 36 years relationship, are far from being arbitrary or random occurrences. Each illness was created by E in response to the chronic stress she allowed to buildup in her mind–body system due to her own, intentional repression of her feelings and needs since birth. What is even more interesting is the fact the majority of the CoDependency Literature consulted demonstrates that the causes, or energy thought packages used by E to create each one of her illnesses overtime, are common and recognizable thought patterns of codependent people in general. When E an L got together in Baltimore, MD in 1979, she invariably would have dark and blue color marks show up on her skin surface without regard to their location. Sometimes the dark and blue color marks, which one would get after a forceful impact to their body part, would randomly show up on her arms, legs, back, or stomach. L was ignorant about what those dark and blue marks represented, and about their source. When E an L moved from Baltimore, MD in 1982, we stayed several months in her mother's house; L noticed the same dark and blue marks showed up on E's mother's visible body parts. Was this a random coincidence, or was the dark and blue marks the effect of the same cause? Now that L has learned so much more today about CoDependency Addiction and its characteristics, the preponderance of information leads to one single common denominator, namely, dysfunctional families reproduce themselves, from one generation to the next.

According to Lancer's research, "it's a fact that stress is a major contributor to ill health and chronic illness. Years of stressful relationships and emotions wear down the body's immune and nervous systems and its ability to repair and replenish itself. The chronic stress of codependency...result in health problems, including heart diseases, digestive and sleep disorders, headaches, muscle tension and pain, obesity, ulcers, temporomandibular joint disorder (TMJD), and chronic fatigue syndrome...other physical symptoms, such as sexual disorders, cystitis, allergies, sciatica, tinnitus, and eating disorders... [are] also ...manifestations of repressed emotions."[394] In short, "the

---

[394] Ibid., p. 70.

apple does not fall far from the tree", as the saying is commonly spoken among wise men and women. L also has had a number of health challenges during his 36 years in a relationship with E. Table 1.3 show L's health challenges, which are, relatively speaking, fewer in number.

Table 1.3

Health Problems Caused by Institutionalized Stress

1993 TO 1996 (PRISON WORK)	ILLNESS	ENVIRONMENTAL CAUSE
"1993 To 1996	Nodule in Left Nostril	Resentment and Frustration and hurt ego over career.
"2007 To 2009	Hernia	Ruptured relationships. Strain. Burdens. Incorrect creative expression.
"	Knee Swelling	Stubborn ego. Won't give in.

Source: Hay, Louise L., You Can Heal Your Life, Hay House, Inc., Carlsbad, CA, pp. 207, 198, and 202.

The chronic stress L internalized in his mind-body system came from environmental demands of his work within the institutions where he worked, from 1993 to 2009. When L served as the Executive Director of the Model Continuum Rehabilitative Care Program, which he and seven other staff member implemented inside the maximum secure care prison for juveniles in Baton Rouge, LA, he encountered an enormous amount of resistance, from the warden, regarding provision of rehabilitation assistance to juvenile inmates. This work took a toll on L's emotional stability by 1996. This is when he observed a nodule in his left nostril. The hernia problem was caused by the strain and burden L felt in his relationship with E. According to Louise Hay, L was in the wrong relationship, a codependent one with E, but he did not know why the harder he tried to create opportunities for joy and happiness, E rarely, if ever, responded with sustained love and joy. This was a huge elephant in the room, but L could not, at the time, see E's Codependecy Addiction. That is, he did not know he was in a relationship with a codependent person, and the relationship was, nevertheless, a strain, burden, and incorrect creative expression. This caused chronic stress to build inside of L until he tore a hole in his stomach wall, which is the definition of a hernia.

Yet, after all of the illnesses shown above, E continues to be in denial about the psychological and physical impacts her CoDependency Addiction to L has had on her, L, and their relationship. As we mentioned earlier, the latter caused a massive breakdown in communication between E and L, and the breakup of their 36 year old relationship. L is very happy the CoDependency Addiction relationship with E is over! At best, it is life-draining and threatening! Lancer wrote "codependents have anger...They don't see a way out and yet still love the one they blame for their woes or feel guilty to leave...it's codependency that is the root of their anger."[395] And, it is the cause of E's mental and physical illnesses. The last topic we will address in this book pertains to what L calls the *Christmas Massacre* that occurred in the living room of his home three days after Christmas 2018.

---

[395] Ibid., p. 68.

CHAPTER EIGHTEEN

Codependency Addiction-Inspired Christmas 2018 Massacre

On Friday, December 28, 2018, a perfect CoDependency Addiction Storm (CAS) occurred in the living room of E and L's home. L call the CAS a Christmas Massacre because L had no prior warning of what was about to happen to him. An avalanche of emotional violence was about to erupt like an earthquake without any prior warning. Another appropriate word to describe what L went through is an *ambush*. A trap was set for him by the woman he had been in a relationship for 36 years! L did not expect E was capable of setting up an ambush against him to win over the emotional support of her family members, for the purpose of erroneously trying to convince them that he is the cause of her CoDependency Addiction and the breakup of our relationship. As we have already seen, this denial, lack of taking responsibility for one's behavior, and projection are-ALL-a part of this mental disease.

Friday, December 28, 2018 began uneventful. E's son and wife had gone to visit one of his college professors in Baton Rouge, LA, and they were expected to return home that evening. E mentioned to L, in passing, that our daughter-H-planned to visit Friday evening also. Nothing was usual about our daughter coming by to visit during the Christmas Holidays. E's niece was living with us so she could save some money to obtain her own place of residence. E and L's granddaughter was sitting in the kitchen but close enough to hear any conversation that would take place. Our two younger grandchildren were told by their parents to stay in the Great Room and watch television. Nothing seemed threatening to L about the people in the house.

E's grandchildren, her son and wife, E's niece, and our daughter were at home on Friday, December 28, 2018. The safest place in the world L thought he could be a few days after Christmas Day 2018 was in his own home in the presence of people he love and thought loved him.

L spent much of the day writing this book. My intent was not to engage the identified family members but continue to write some more on my project and and maybe watch some college football to relax and unwind. Around 7: 30 PM, L was working in his office when E entered and informed him that her son and his wife had returned home. Initially, my plan was not to leave my office and go to the living room where everyone was gathered. But, L changed his mind and told himself maybe I should go talk with everybody for awhile, then return to my study and shutdown my work for the evening. What a big surprise L was in store for; what transpired over the next two hours was absolutely horrible and disgusting.

When L arrived in the living room, the scene was set; E was sitting in the center of the room in a rocking chair similar to the way the sun controls all of the other planets moving around it using gravity; her son was sitting on the sofa; our daughter was sitting at the dinner table and so was E's niece. Our granddaughter was sitting on a bar stool in the entrance way, which leads from the kitchen into the living room. L took a seat at the dinner table because he did not intend to stay in this gathering long. As soon as L sat down at the dinner table, all of the blame from everybody, save our granddaughter, was immediately directed at him. He did not pick up on what was happening during the first 20 minutes; however, in my "gut" L felt something *pre-planned was happening,* and he was, regardless of the injury, the cause of it. Projection and blame was as thick in the living room as a dense foggy night covering the Atchafalaya Basin.

Before L go further into the unfolding drama of the Christmas Massacre, several points need to be made at the outset.

- First, L did not believe E would engage in such unbecoming, bullying, and unkind behavior in the presence of her own children and family.
- Second, L did not believe his daughter would sit in the presence of unfounded judgment(s) of her father, and actively participate in the Christmas Massacre.
- Third, L did not believe everyone in the living room, all of whom, at one time or another, he had helped, both financially and emotionally, would participate in such a vicious display of unfounded characterizations and attacks.

But, as the old saying goes "you live and learn," and, on this Friday Night, a few days after Christmas 2018, L learned more about the people he thought loved him, and vis-à-vis, than he had about them during the many years being in their presence. *One of the most important thing L learned on this night is how each person in the living room holds such a deep disregard for history, analysis, balance in a discussion, and truth, which surface-there from-and is independent of anyone's biases, but is based on historical fact, analysis, feelings, and justice.* The longer the Christmas Massacre went on, L felt deep on the inside of himself, that surely, someone in the living room will try, if unsuccessful, to make a connection between cause and effect, and move away from emotionalism, mysticism, and fantasy. This did not happen; what happened is discussed, to the best of my recollection, below.

Sitting in her rocking chair in the middle of the living room, E began the Christmas Massacre with an opening victimization statement. The following is what she opened the latter with to set the tone for everyone to measure their supporting remarks. Keep in mind L is paraphrasing what E shared with her gathered family members. She remarked,

- "L never touch me.
- L is unkind to me.
- L never takes me anywhere with him.
- L does not share his money with me.
- E poured all of her money in paying bills."

It should be clear by now that E and L were in a relationship for 36 years. So, the huge elephant in the room, which no one saw sitting on the dinner table is of all the fellows in the world, L loved and provided for E's every need for 36 years without a single complaint and unconditionally. As we pointed-out earlier, L made it possible for E to travel all over the world, traveling to exotic places that most people only dream about traveling to in their lifetimes! L wrote a grant, and he received an award of $62,000 cash in the mail (The IRS took $12,000 off the top for taxes and L received a check for $50,000.). Every cents of this money was used to pay off every bill E and L had, and on Friday, December 28, 2018, E and L owed no one a dime other than the variable bills we pay for utilities and food every month. Yet, one of the assertions in E's victimization statement is she poured all of her money in paying bills.

It should be pointed-out here that while E made these allegations against L, she had, earlier in the day-12/28/18-gone to the Meritus Credit Union located in Lafayette Parish and took $3,000 out of our joint savings account. Yet, E set self-righteously in her rocking chair, and unmoved consciously by her thievery action, telling her family members listening to her monologue how abusive L was being toward her. How can anyone, beginning with E herself, love her with this kind of deep-rooted anger and disregard for what is *right and wrong*?

Once the victimization statement was made by E, the roof came off of the house in an explosion of unfounded attacks in the form of blame and projection.

When L tried to offer a response to E's victimization statement claims, each person in the living room summarily spoke in one voice that "We are not talking about the past; the important thing is what are you going to do today moving forward?" L's response was again, we must first understand what happened that brought E and L to this point in our relationship, where he does not touch E or take her anywhere and so forth. *No one wanted to address any history going back to E's troubled childhood, and how it caused her to behave as an adult.* Every time L tried to get the conversation to consider this historical reality, he was confronted with more emotionalism. The conversation continued to be stuck in the *muck of denial based on unfounded judgments.* L was grossly attacked by everyone saying "You are too analytical, and you do not express any feelings about the situation."

Then, after doing some reflection, L woke up and realized that history is a hated subject among many codependent people, and it is an area of critical thinking most people are unaware of, or know its value as a tool toward reaching an independent solution to any problem, regardless of level. We are sure the American Higher Education System plays a significant role in this historical-analytical disconnect. For example, at most colleges and universities today, many Arts and Humanities Programs have been either outright dropped from the curriculum as a major, or drastically retrenched financially.

Rather than take advantage of history and the analytical powers of those present at the Christmas Massacre, the entire conversation, and we use this term carefully, centered primarily around control, projection, and judgment. Lancer stated "if your motive is to control, manipulate, or fix someone, your words reflect...codependent attitudes, but when your motive is to express your Self, your words convey that the focus is on you, not the other person, whose reaction becomes less important."[396] Lancer added "...blaming, and complaining are reactions that focus on the other person and aren't boundaries."[397]

As it was, the entire Christmas Massacre focused attention mainly on L–the other person, and no attention was directed toward E, who claims to be codependent. The only way the opposite could happen is if the family members present could use history to analyze E's childhood to sort out fact from fiction, and then clearly see she was emotionally traumatized during her childhood, which has led to the breakup of her relationship with L. What would E do then, if her family members could use historical analysis to achieve this end? The risk is too great because the lingering and smoldering question is "What will my family members choose to do if they learn E has lived a "double life," namely, one for the public of perfection and saintliness and two, the other being

---

[396] Ibid., p. 211.

[397] Ibid., p. 221.

someone who actively repressed her feelings and needs for 36 years. To be able to see between these two different worlds one being a fantasy and the other repressed reality, the family members, who took part in the Christmas Massacre, would have to be aware of historical analysis, and use it to sharply question E's childhood experience.

According to Christopher Lasch's book titled <u>The Culture Of Narcissism: American Life in An Age of Diminishing Expectations</u>, 1979, stated "having trivialized the past by equating it with outmoded styles of consumption, discarded fashions and attitudes, people today resent anyone who draws on the past in serious discussions of contemporary conditions or attempts to use the past as a standard by which to judge the present."[398] During the Christmas Massacre, every time L brought up history as a means toward deepening understanding of the CoDependency Addiction problem E is challenged with, every family member present offered a counter argument attempting to ex-communicate L's use of historical analysis to dig deeper into the mentioned disease.

The *reactionary response of Republicans* to the recent move by the Democratic Majority in the United States House of Representatives to Impeach President Donald Trump, and in view of the fact nearly 100% of the Republican members of this political body and the United States Senate, primarily support President Donald Trump's criminal behavior, although all of the information demonstrates that he committed "High Crimes and Misdemeanors, during a conversation he had with the President of the Ukraine on July 25, 2019. This is the same subjective and anti-historical thought process I witnessed during the Christmas Massacre 2018. Everyone present was quick to support E's claims without considering any of the facts-NONE. It is this type of thinking that presently is the foundation of the oppression of working class people in America and all over t he world. L lived in the midst of this mindset for nearly 40 years!

---

[398] Lasch, Christopher, <u>The Culture of Narcissism: American Life in An Age of Diminishing Expectations</u>, Warner Books, 1979, p. 24.

For example, just like every Republican criticizes any democratic person, who is searching for the truth related to President Donald Trump's behavior based on facts and history, L was repeatedly criticized most vociferously by E's son without offering one fact to justify any statement he made pertaining to the matter. At best, he has a low-functioning understanding of the CoDependency Addiction Disease! If he knows anything about it, he has never mentioned one single word to L about the subject. I welcome any discussion he would like to have with me about CoDependency Addiction anytime. That being so, it is a safe bet to place that what he knows about his mother's Codependency Addiction problem is what she has told him only. Since E had a stroke in July 2015, E's son has not called me once to ask me what do L feel is going-on, which threatens to cause a breakup of his mother's 36 years relationship with L.

However, during the Christmas Massacre, E's son was the most outspoken and emotional of everyone present! If he would have only called upon E and L's relationship history, he would have discovered that in 1979, his mother, at the inception of our relationship, placed three critical expectations on the table that she told L could not be "ever be violated" during our relationship. They are:

- We have to be able to sleep at night.
- We must make love.
- We must know our children.

When L thought about these relationship standards, he immediately agreed with all of them without a need for any additions. Yet, after 36 years living true to them, E sat in a rocking chair and told everyone present at the Christmas Massacre that "L never touch me." If history was used by anyone present, wouldn't it be a fair question to ask E "When did L stop touching you?" Instead of asking this or any other questions, each family member present resented L's use of history as a tool for understanding how and when did E become codependent, and how did the CoDependency Addiction Disease impact her personal life, and the man's, namely, L, who she has been in a relationship for

317

36 years. Lasch added "…loving memories constitute an indispensable psychological resource in maturity, and that those who cannot fall back on the memory of loving relations in the past suffer terrible torments as a result…I see the past as a political and psychological treasury from which we draw the reserves…in the form of "lessons"…that we need to cope with the future."[399] The Christmas 2018 Massacre proved that past history to those present, based on their presenting a-historical attitudes, is meaningless to them; and therefore, no lessons can be learned from history required to guide forward movement. Unfortunately, history was thrown out by them and totally ignored; subjective wishes reigned supreme!

Every family member present, including E, was far from searching for "lessons" that could help us understand E's Codependency Addiction, and possibly save our relationship. Everyone took the one-sided viewpoint that the "past is over and there is nothing to gain from a consideration of it; the most importance thing to them is "What do we do in the present going forward?" Cause was thrown out completely! If this sounds scary to you, then you are not alone like Michael Jackson once sung.

After any consideration of E's childhood was beaten down and trashed, E's son leaped up off of the sofa where he sat and made a *Godly Declaration*, namely, "the relationship E an L have been in for 36 years is over." Where E's son got the authority to make this pronouncement, and if there is a God, only God knows! To make matters even more humorous, and similar to a Greek Chorus back in the days of Greek Antiquity, E's son started to cry repeatedly saying "This relationship is over." Nobody present challenged his unilateral declaration! However, everyone started to cry, and L felt E was relieved since her plan seems to have worked. That is, blaming L for her CoDependency Addiction was accepted by her family members, and she was spared of the task of having to break the news to them that our relationship is over. E used this same approach for more than twenty years to cover up her hidden, repressed loneliness and wounded feelings she experienced during her childhood.

---

[399] Ibid., pp. 24 and 25.

After several hours of blaming L for E's CoDependency Addiction, which is impossible to do, and when all the tears were shed, an *eerie silence* fell across the atmosphere in the living room. It reminded me of what our ancestors faced constantly during the 500 years of existence of the American Slavery Institution. Although the slave master caused untold and unconscionable hardship, the African Slaves, in many instances, blamed themselves for their un-heavenly plight on Earth. Because an African Mother or Father did not get a chance to nurture and love their offsprings, they devolved into a history of CoDependency, which has flowed through the generations right up to the present day. Yet, E's family members chose to shed tears like our African Ancestors did centuries earlier. The only difference between the tears shed by our African Ancestors and those shed by E's family members, is the former knew who caused their hardship and social destruction, while many codependent people use denial today in an attempt to hide the cause of their CoDependency Addiction, which is the same in both cases, and that is, an absence of mother, father, or mother-surrogate love.

To all of the family members who participated in the Christmas Massacre 2018, L challenge each one of you to look deeper into the CoDependency Addiction Mental Disease, and maybe, one day you may be fortunate enough to understand exactly what it is; its origin; and if left untreated in a false cloak of denials, blame, projections, and non-acceptance of responsibility, you will also learn how the disease destroys life.

In closing, we refer to one of E's favorite books known as ACIM. In it the following is written: "Sacrifice is attack, not love...Fear demands the sacrifice of love."[400]

A brief conclusion is found in the next Chapter, which will lay down the key points underlying the formation and life of E's CoDependency Addiction Disease, which L lived with intimately, on a daily basis, for 36 years.

---

[400] _____ACIM, op. cit., pp. 325 and 607.

CHAPTER NINETEEN

Conclusion

A t this point in our closing discussion related to the CoDependency Addiction, one master question surfaced out of the chaotic realities of a dysfunctional family which produces it. How do human beings create meaning in their lives? This is the greatest question we all must answer during the course of our journey on Earth. It is not found in theoretical mysticism, requiring one to seek answers to real life problems inside of an intellectual discourse separated from the natural world. Regarding the cause of CoDependency Addiction, its root is connected to the umbilical cord like relationship that exists between mother, father, or mother-surrogate and infant.

Montagu added "in short, the physiological dependency of the fetus and the newborn becomes...a socially organized dependency, a social dependency in which the interacting person finds the meaning of his [or her] life in his [or her] relations with other persons and their thoughts and activities."[401] Social dependency acts similar to the blood exchange between mother and infant in utero; at birth, the umbilical dependency relationship between mother and infant is *love*. The first other person a newborn infant "finds the meaning of his [or her] life" is the mother, father, or mother surrogate. At the moment of birth, Montagu wrote "babies are born good

---

[401] Montagu, op. cit., pp. 180 and 181.

and desirous of continuing to be good."[402] With a steady, and uninterrupted supply of love from a baby's mother, father, or mother-surrogate, love sets him or her upon a course of healthy and balanced physical and mental development, for the rest of his or her life, evolving through the dependency state during childhood into the interdependent state during adulthood. The importance of love cannot be over-emphasized!

Moreover, Montagu adds "external defenses can never make up for the lack of internal controls. What needs to be done is to develop internal controls in human beings so that they can withstand external pressures and maintain internal equilibrium. This can never be achieved by doing violence to their nature. It can only be done by strengthening those basic needs with which all human beings are born-not by frustrating them."[403] As we already have seen, an absence of mother, father, or mother-surrogate love directly does violence to an infant's nature, which greatly inhibits him or her from living and functioning in optimum health and happiness. When the supreme value of love is missing, the infant's development in the dependency state is greatly frustrated, and he or she is predisposed to the formation of a Codependency Addiction, where external defenses take the place of internal controls. Without exception, Codependency Addiction is formed when an infant's mother, father, or mother-surrogate love fails to teach him or her how to love one's *Self*, which shuts down their ability to, later in life, love other people as an adult. Rather, other people are used, their feelings and needs in particular, because the unloved infant was not taught how to love other people; to survive their nightmare, *they engage in giving only to get something better in a desperate external search for mother, father, or mother-surrogate love.*

At the core of the matter of the CoDependency Addiction is absence of mother, father, and mother-surrogate love. Imagine a triangle where the latter sits at its Apex A; at intersect B sits infant learns to love Self and Ego is managed by Super-Ego; and at intersect C infant shares learned love of Self with another person. As we have discussed throughout this book, when mother, father, and mother-surrogate love is denied an infant at birth,

---

[402] Ibid., p. 198.
[403] Ibid., pp. 306 and 307.

and during the critical weeks, months, and first six years thereafter, he or she experiences a breakdown in the aforementioned Triangle of Mother, Father, Mother-Surrogate-Infant Development. When this Triangular Relationship is unbroken, and remains functional, it is an immunity against CoDependency Addiction formation later in a child's adult life. However, on the other hand, a sustained, denial of the mentioned love will inevitably create CoDependency Addiction Disease in a codependent person during his or her adult life. This fact cannot be over-emphasized, regarding the cause of this mental disease, and how it leads to the generational recreation of it through time. Consider the Triangular Relationship of Caregivers and Infant shown in Table 1.4 below.

Table 1.4
Triangular Relationship of Caregiver and Infant

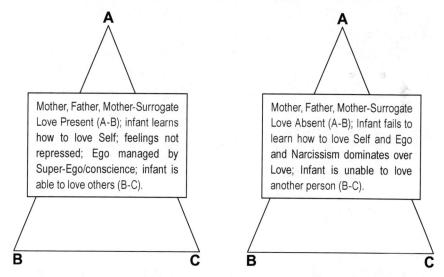

A

Mother, Father, Mother-Surrogate Love Present (A-B); infant learns how to love Self; feelings not repressed; Ego managed by Super-Ego/conscience; infant is able to love others (B-C).

B   C

A

Mother, Father, Mother-Surrogate Love Absent (A-B); Infant fails to learn how to love Self and Ego and Narcissism dominates over Love; Infant is unable to love another person (B-C).

B   C

CoDependency Addiction arises out of the Triangular Relationship of Caregiver and Infant dysfunctional family development where mother, father, or mother-surrogate love is absent. As we mentioned earlier, human beings are not atomistic, isolated individuals; we are social creatures whose essence is love. Montagu wrote "every human being is born a creature that evaluates all experiences in terms of the desire to be loved and the desire to love...To realize the good life in the person and behavior of each human being, our evidence indicates that each human being must be adequately loved, that is to say, he [or she] must have his [or her] needs adequately satisfied for being loved and loving others."[404] No matter which way we flip this coin, and no matter which way it falls, whether it is flipped one time or a thousand consecutively, nothing changes the fact an infant must be loved by his or her mother, father, or mother-surrogate so the loved one can give love to another person. This is human nature, and nature itself. Regardless of the life form, the same love dynamic exists, from one cell life forms to the multiple billion cell human being. The "good life" referred to by Montagu merely means, if a person is free of CoDependency Addiction Disease, he or she learns to love one Self from the mother, father, or mother-surrogate love given, and, with this knowledge and wisdom, a person realizes the good life by first loving one Self, and then he or she is able to offer the learned and experienced love to other human beings. This is what the Good Life personifies and mean.

The "Good Life" begins with the mother, father, or mother-surrogate love toward the creation of a human being who is a work of art. Montagu added "a human being should be a work of art…Knowing what is to be done, how else can one better achieve what is to be realized than with the tenderness and loving care of a mother?"[405] father, or mother-surrogate? From the Savagery Period through the Upper Stage of the Barbarism Period, mother right prevailed, and human beings were born cooperative; they were born in a communistic society; they were loved; they loved others in their families and commune-ity; and they developed into works of art based on mother right, and the love they give freely and consciously to their babies during this time.

When Civilization arose, roughly some 3,000 years ago, mother right was overthrown by father right, and a Patriarchal System grew up in the Monogamy Family. One of its noticeable mental diseases today is CoDependency Addiction. Disrobed, and in its most naked form, if you remove the prefix "Co," we are left with the root word "Dependency."

---

[404] Ibid. pp. 307 and 308.
[405] Ibid., p. 305.

Every human baby born since the beginning of the Savagery Period a million years ago, was born into the dependency state. Only mother, father, or mother-surrogate love can deliver him or her out of it into the interdependent state characterized by human beings sharing "learned" mother, father, or mother-surrogate love with each other.

Therefore, to achieve this "One Love" purpose, "...the first half dozen years of the child's life are so critically important for its development...Human beings must be satisfied in their need for love. The direction of human development lies in and through the course of love; all else is secondary to this. The primacy of love is unchallengeable-and unchallengeably clear as the first requirement of human development...there can be little doubt that the parents, and in particular the mother, constitute the most important [caregiver] in the life of the person."[406] To add more evidence to support this unalterable fact, let us consider Victor Hugo's book, a timeless classic and masterpiece titled Les Miserables, 1862.

Both of Victor Hugo's main characters in his novel, namely, Jean Valjean and Inspector Javert, met up with each other in their lives when Jean Valjean, a convicted prisoner, escaped from prison, who was sentenced to spend the rest of his life incarcerated in a French Prison for stealing a loaf of bread. Inspector Javert, head of law enforcement in Paris, France at the time of Jean Valjean's escape, vowed to apprehend him, and bring Jean Valjean to justice. Inspector Javert spent the better part of his work life tracking down Jean Valjean. Inspector Javert's obsession was equivalent to the CoDependency Addiction of millions of codependent Americans today. Inspector Javert's CoDependency Addiction was Jean Valjean; codependent people's- today-usually is the partner they share a relationship, regardless of race and sex. The basis for our assertion that Inspector Javert was codependent is explained below.

Throughout Victor Hugo's character development of Jean Valjean, the latter's character was portrayed throughout his novel as being a very sensitive, giving, compassionate, and loving human being. To the contrary, Inspector Javert's character development portrayed him

---

[406] Ibid, pp. 299, 298, and 300.

as a no non-sense disciplinarian, cold-hearted, strict believer in the conservative interpretation of man and woman as being "evil," who must be brought to justice at all cost. And, man and woman only deserve the harsh punishment(s) prescribed by the Law. Although Victor Hugo wrote an unmatched character development of these two men since his novel was first published in 1862, scant attention, if any, has been given to the early childhood development of them, which, as we have demonstrated throughout this book, *mother, father, or mother-surrogate love, or the absence thereof, is the primary determinant of the direction of social development of an infant, during his or her childhood and adult life.*

That being so, Jean Valjean, in order to consistently give love in every situation he faced during his lifetime, for example, purchasing the freedom of Cosette and rearing her as his daughter, or freeing Inspector Javert when he had ample opportunity to murder him, would have had a mother and father, who gave him their abiding love from his birth, and throughout his childhood. It was Jean Valjean's deep belief in the "Good" of human beings that allowed him to "free" Inspector Javert when he had an opportunity to murder him. On the other hand, Inspector Javert's desperate search to apprehend Jean Valjean was conditioned by his mother and father's infrequent giving him their love during the early stages of his development during his childhood. Even though Inspector Javert eventually received a college education, he remained self-accusing, insecure, and fearful of life, regarding his questionable self-worth as a human being.

Moreover, due to the infrequent love he received from his biological parents, this created a condition within his Self, which allowed his ego to gain undue sway over his moral compass, given the fact sporadic parental love weakened Inspector Javert's super-ego, allowing his ego and narcissism to dominate his decision-making capacity, and, what is more, caused him to develop a weakened belief in the "Goodness" of human beings.

All-in-All, in the end, Victor Hugo brought Inspector Javert to a face-to-face self-realization that everything he believed about the unworthiness of human beings was wrong! This epiphany was caused by the fact Jean Valjean, who Inspector Javert believed will certainly murder him with the chance he had to do so, but the former did not! Being allowed to go free, Inspector Javert could not reconcile how he had arrived at such a grand contradiction within him Self? Because Inspector Javert could not connect the infrequent love he received from his mother and father during his childhood with his ego-driven and narcissisictic belief that man and woman are evil beings by nature, although Jean Valjean had proven to him his beliefs were false, Inspector Javert was left emotionally naked, and as he perceived his plight in that moment of "life and death" decision, he laid down his Inspector's Hat and Sword of Honor besides the railing overlooking the river, and leaped off of the bridge into it, committing suicide.

Inspector Javert did not have enough mother, father, or mother-surrogate love inside of him Self to keep him from jumping into the river. To the contrary, Jean Valjean was reunited with his daughter Cosette and her husband, and even Cosette could not hold Jean Valjean's prison life against him due to the love her father gave her during a vulnerable time in her early life; and, because he was the recipient of sufficient mother, father, or mother-surrogate love, he lived out the last years of his life with them, and he died in peace.

After sharing this beautiful dichotomy of character development of Jean Valjean and Inspector Javert, L asked E which character did she most identify with, and in expected denial form, E quickly answered, "Jean Valjean!" Although, as it has been pointed-out time and again throughout this book, E, by her own admission, repeatedly told L that her mother and father did not give her any love or attention during her childhood. Obviously, this situation set E on a CoDependency Addiction course for the rest of her adult life, similar to Inspector Javert's external search for the love he missed receiving from his own mother, father, or mother-surrogate, by spending his whole work life attempting to capture Jean Valjean, and the artificial love, from his co-workers, he would have received by doing so.

It is worthwhile to give credit and recognition to Earth Wind, & Fire, one of the greatest Rhythm and Blues Bands of the Twentieth Century, for its contribution to American and world understanding of CoDependency Addiction. On June 8, 2019, L was riding in his friend

Edward Lenoir's truck on the way back to his house, after eating breakfast at the Waffle House in Covington, LA. During the ride back to Edward's house, a WYLD DJ played one of Earth, Wind & Fire's songs on the radio. As L listened to the song, it was one of the group's biggest hits known as *After the Love Has Gone,* which was released in 1979. That year, Earth, Wind & Fire received a Grammy Award for their hit song, and this is the same year E and L got together in a relationship. L had heard *After the Love Has Gone* many times through the years, but, interestingly, not one time in 40 years did he ever make a connection between the message conveyed in the song and CoDependency Addiction.

L always thought this message applied to other people and not to him or E. The song was sung for other people, who started out loving each other, and then, a hidden secret surfaced, and where love was once thought to be omnipresent all the time; and, without any prior warning, it suddenly vanished without a trace into thin air? The lyrics to *After the Love Has Gone* are shown below.

"After the Love Has Gone
Earth, Wind & Fire

For a while, to love was all we could do
We were young and we knew, and our eyes were alive
Deep inside we knew our love was true
For a while we paid no mind to the past
We knew love would last
Every night somethin' right
Would invite us to begin the dance
Somethin' happened along the way

Songwriters: David Foster / Jay Graydon / William B. Champlin
After the Love Has Gone lyrics © EMI Music Publishing, Sony/ATV Music Publishing LLC, Universal Music Publishing Group"[407]

---

[407] https://www.google.com/search?source=hp&ei=Zzz8XNnXC47wtAXrjKzoA Q&q=what+are+the+lyrics+of+earth%2C+wind%2C+and+fire%27s+song-Afte r+the+love+is+gone%3F&oq=what+are+the+lyrics+of+earth%2C+wind%2C+ and+fire%27s+song-After+the+love+is+gone%3F&gs_l=psy-ab.12...16823.58732.

When I heard the above lyrics while riding back to Edward's House, L woke up and realized it is CoDependency Addiction that this song's lyrics so perfectly describe.

For example, the first stanza admits E and L were young, alive, and in love L thought. Then, as if the songwriters asked L, "Did we talk about our past childhoods to insure nothing would happen to change how right we felt love was between us'? Nothing was shared, by E, related to the emotional traumas and wounds she experienced during her childhood. L thought everything was alright! E and L's relationship was erected on a solid foundation. Toward the end of the first stanza, Earth, Wind & Fire sung "Somethin' happened along the way."

As we have already mentioned many times before, on July 25, 2015, E had a stroke, and unexpectedly everything L thought E and himself used to form a relationship, namely, love, was untrue; to the contrary, what happened that demonstrated the relationship was never established based on love was an untimely outpouring of E's Codependency Addiction to L, which was in existence by 1979 and before L ever knew E existed. CoDependency Addiction happened along the way.

Then, as if Earth, Wind & Fire read my thoughts, in their second stanza, the latter asked a prophetic question: "And oh, after the love has gone How could you lead me on...What used to be right is wrong Can love that's lost be found?" After July 2015, L realized how deception, manipulation, and control were used by E to lead L on. The love L thought existed between himself and E *never* existed; and, therefore, how "Can love that's lost be found?" if it never existed? *If there is no knowledge of a known needle that existed before it was lost in a haystack, then, what good would it do for the seeker to keep looking in it for something that never existed?!*

There is one thing, among many other troubling issues related to CoDependency Addiction, and that is, it destroys all of the love a child needs to give to another child, for example, when both of them become adults. Both of these adults can look for love forever without finding

.61218...6.0..0.184.7310.51j30.......0.....1..gws-wiz.....0..0i131j0j0i131i70i251j0i10j0i22i
30j0i22i10i30j33i22i29i30j33i299j33i160j33i10.jku7qpCSFMI

329

it because it was withheld by their mother, father, or mother-surrogate during their childhoods. Earth, Wind & Fire's After the Love Has Gone song implies love departed long ago, during one's childhood, which is the "Somethin' happened along the way…"

The greatest barrier, which stands taller than Mt. Everest, between a codependent person and his or her healing is denial and fear of taking responsibility for the effects the host's CoDependency Addiction has had on one Self, and on the person who is the focus of it.

Afterword

The single most important result that surfaced from the foregoing consideration of CoDependency Addiction is its cause is found in the intimate relationship that exist between mother, father, or mother-surrogate and one's newborn infant. At birth, the latter is born into a natural, or normal, state of *dependency*. Every human being ever born began the journey of life in a dependent state. Regardless of the number of therapy meeting someone attends on a weekly basis or other schedule, the prospect for recovery from CoDependency Addiction is very slim, if there is no historical examination of an affected person's childhood. This analysis is paramount and trump all other lesser one-sided, anemic attempts made to recover from this very debilitating psychological disease. In fact, by bypassing such an historical examination of the mother and infant relationship in particular, hope for recovery is intentionally flat-lined, and at best, will ultimately end in gross disappointment.

During the first six years of an infant's life, and while the infant is directly dependent on his or her mother, it is the weighty responsibility of the mother to love and nurture one's child through a dependency upon the mother into a new phase of early childhood development called *interdependency*. In far too many cases, this nurturing and love, which the infant most desperately needs to grow normally, is not forthcoming,; and, as a result of failure, a child suffers through one's childhood unaware of one Self being love. Therefore, to survive this grave emotional trauma, the child enters into adult life guided by his or her ego and a narcissistic personality rather than having mother-inspired and awakened love within to give to another human being. This love, when reciprocally shared between two adults results in the establishment of cooperative social relations between them.

Unfortunately, without mother, father, or mother-surrogate love, CoDependency Addiction is created in the psychological structure of the affected person's mind and body. I lived in an unloving relationship with a person, who failed to grow out of the dependency state she was born in, which caused her to search for her mother and father love during the entire duration of the 36 years we were in a private, dysfunctional relationship. The only person who knew this was a fetter on our relationship was E, who consciously may not have known she was suffering secretly with a CoDependency Addiction, but, subconsciously, she was aware, from the day we started our relationship, that she emerged from her childhood feeling like an emotionally injured and *love-starved* person, who was secretly in search of her mother and father's love everyday during the 36 years we were in a relationship. How E navigated this task has already been well addressed throughout this book. However, it is worth revisiting the following information.

CoDependency Addiction is a serious psychological imbalance in the psychic structure of a codependent person. During the past 40 years, beginning in 1979 in particular (This malady was well-formed during the first six years of E's life), I have shared a relationship with a codependent person of which I was personally clueless about. During this period, I was completely unaware that E was suffering with a CoDependent Addiction. If asked, she would respond saying, "She was also unaware she was suffering with this mental illness." It would be the farthest thing from the truth for me to say that there were no warning signs along the way. There were many which I ignored due to my belief in revolutionary philosophy, and my unbending belief that an oppressed working class person, through an application of this philosophy, can inevitably defeat their oppressor, both within and without. *So, E was always given the benefit of the doubt!* My biggest mistake was I felt if E was given more time, she would realize, at a deep feeling level inside of her, that something was bothering her that had its roots in her childhood. I was wrong for thinking this way! The Law of Inertia states an object will continue on its path, for an eternity, if some outside force does not cause it to shift into another one. I did not act as that outside force; there was no shift from E's internal repression of her CoDependency Addiction, and, unfortunately, she remained on a non-disclosure course in our relationship for 36 years.

I was rudely awakened in 2015 to the truth. Similar to Malcolm X, when his consciousness awareness was expanded by going to Africa and the Middle East to learn more about the Islamic Faith, I woke up from my 36 years of being an *enabler* in E's web of CoDependency Addiction. While asleep to this reality, I participated in creating a life during which I helped raise a family; acquired and paid for a residence located on a five acres farm; and travelled all over the world. Like Malcolm X when his eyes became opened to the truth upon his return to America from Africa, I was more than shocked; I felt like I had been struck by lightning when I learned that all of the labor I expended to build this life was actually, in reality, built atop E's repressed CoDependency Addiction, a secret she kept hidden from me for more than 36 years.

E's stroke knocked her off of her non-disclosure of her CoDependency Addiction in July 2015. The formerly closed-minded floodgates, namely, denial, projections, arguments, blame, deception, and others, that she used to protect her childhood traumas inside of her repressed Self were revealed to me by her for the first time after living together for more than three decades; and, upon my discovery of them, I went into a free-fall without knowing where I would come to land, or if I would survive the CoDependency Addiction Information Explosion that flowed out of E's subconscious mind. Similar to the water that flowed across the broken levees into New Orleans East after Hurricane Katrina left the "Big Easy" battered by wind, rain, and storm surge, I felt emotionally battered by realizing that for 36 years, I lived in the grasp of CoDependency Addiction as a *first class enabler.* My first instinct was to try to reason with E, but the more I tried to delve deeper into how everything happened, the more she defaulted to massive denial, projection, and judgments.

E had become so codependent, or addicted to me over the 36 years or more we were in a relationship, that she could not see her Self *at all*, and she could see no reason, therefore, to *take responsibility* for creating her CoDependency Addiction; but, instead, she *blamed* me for her CoDependency Addiction because my feelings and needs were the *only ones she knew*, since her own had been repressed inside of herself for more than 36 years.

That being so, even though E spends at least 95% of her time every week going to CoDependency Meetings, it is highly probable that her CoDependency Addiction has become what Nathaniel Hill calls a hypnotic rhythm, and similar to mortar mix, the many years of repressed secrecy about it have turned it into unchangeable concrete. For E's sake, I sincerely hope one day she will free her Self of the chokehold CoDependency Addiction has on her life now.

Before closing, I would like to offer the reader one last metaphor, which I believe will provide a deeper understanding of CoDependency Addiction. It is called Crossing The Desert.

Two people, a man and woman are crossing the Sahara Desert; and, the woman is codependent of which the man knows absolutely nothing about. The two travelers have one container in which they keep their water supply. Water is a precious life-sustaining resource on their trek across the Saharan Desert. The man is quite efficient finding an Oasis from which their water container is refilled. Sometimes, it takes as long as one month to find a new Oasis, and there is no guarantee that it will have water in it. Thus, water held in their container is vital, and every drop of it must be used conservatively.

As the man and woman trekked across the hot, scorching Saharan Desert, mile after mile in the beaming sunlight, the codependent woman secretly engaged in tearing a small hole in the water container. As they trekked deeper into the Saharan Desert, water slowly seeped out of their water container. After two weeks of water seeping slowly out of the water container, the man discovers that their water supply is very low. Upon examination of how so much water escaped from their water container, he discovered the small hole the woman tore in the water container. When the man asked the woman did she tear the small hole in the water container, she denied she tore the hole in it. Worse, the woman blamed the man for tearing the hole in the water container!

Because of the woman's CoDependency Addiction, she felt so hopeless and powerless, along with a feeling of unworthiness mixed in it, that the woman was *willing to risk both of them dying in the Saharan Desert, rather than admit she has a CoDependency Addiction with a tap root stretching back to her childhood relationship with her mother and father.*

This metaphor is not a call out of the woman because males are certainly codependent also. The woman in this metaphor refers to the one in the relationship I lived in for more than 36 years. CoDependency Addiction tore a hole in my relationship. It cannot be stated thoroughly enough, or redundantly, that the absence of mother, father, or mother-surrogate love is horrifying in the life of a codependent person, who experienced this abandonment and rejection during one's childhood.

Dr. Alexander Lowen stated "people who have lived through experiences of horror in their childhood have an unreal quality in their personalities...That experience lies buried-a time bomb whose explosion might produce insanity."[408] In a vain attempt to survive and delay the inevitability of such an explosion, E engaged in a massive denial of her feelings and needs for 36 years, by denying her inner feelings and needs in her core Self. Dr. Lowen added "denying one's feelings is crazy because it is denial of the self...One lives in a world divorced from feeling."[409] As it was, E divorced herself from her feelings and needs, and by doing so, she simultaneously separated herself from her authentic personal reality in our relationship, and after existing 36 years in a buried state of insanity, the mentioned "time bomb" exploded in the form of a stroke. This was an attempt to *exit her created world of insanity without having to account for-or take responsibility for-its creation.* Through the eyes of insanity, everyone living in a sane world is the cause of everyone's problem who live in

---

[408] Lowen, op. cit., pp. 137 and 138.
[409] Ibid., pp. 144 and 137.

an insane world; the latter cannot see their world as an insane world, and the people who live in a sane world are viewed as being the cause of their problems. For many years, E constantly devalued the Earth we-All-live on; she repeatedly stated to anyone who would listen that the Earth is a "Third Dimension;" a place wrought with "dualities;" one in which the "ego" is totally out of control like a mad animal in the jungle; and, in order to escape this Earth, or more accurately her CoDependency Addiction World, E directed her listeners' attention away from reality to a non-reality place that she made up called the "Fifth Dimension." If one of E's listeners were asked to explain where this Fifth Dimension World is, I bet my life he or she would not have a clue where it is.

Again, this was E's make believe world into which she escaped for 36 years so she would not have to deal concretely and objectively with the truth about what happened to her as a child, or figure out what to do to heal her Self. I now see what Billie Holiday meant when she sung in Strange Fruit, "Them that got shall get," and God bless the child that got its own." Marvin Gaye sung in his hit song Let's Get It On, "There is nothing wrong with you giving yourself to me, if the love is true." These pearls of wisdom spoke to our inner Self, and offered us an opportunity to let go of emotional traumas so we can grow into the vision for which we were put on this Earth to carryout. CoDependency Addiction is certainly strong enough to prevent anyone from achieving this great purpose.

According to Maurice White, founder of the Earth, Wind & Fire Band, the single most destructive force that stands between anyone achieving their life purpose is attachment. CoDependency Addiction is as much an attachment to another person's feelings and needs as an alcoholic's to alcohol. He stated in his memoir titled My Life With Earth, Wind & Fire, 2016 "...that to cling to anything is to suffer..."[410] The suffering lies in an external motivation, which directly cancels any possibility of self-generation from within. I lived with a partner,

[410] White, Maurice, with Powell, Herb, My Life With Earth, Wind & Fire, Amistad 30, An Imprint of HarperCollinsPublishers, 2016, p. 74.

who suffered through years of distress and unspoken heartbreak due to her attachment to my feelings and needs and simultaneous repression of her own. Maurice White added "...human attachment dies very hard"[411] due to repression. To survive another day, week, month, or year, a codependent person resorts to the subtle use of control learned during their childhood growing up in a dysfunctional family. Similar to termites eating away solid oak wood, and I have witnessed them kill a mature Oak Tree, a codependent person's trust is compromised and weakened by it. Maurice White wrote "the great paradox of the spiritual life is that the more I control-the less I have to trust. I've controlled the things I could-my space in my home, my business affairs-and I've even tried to control some relationships."[412]

Of all the information discussed in this book about CoDependency Addiction, this point ranks in the top five of them. An infants relationship with his or her mother, father, or mother-surrogate ranks Number One and control is second. The marrow in the bones of CoDependency Addiction is control because the emotional account of a codependent person is bankrupt. His or her total focus is an external search for mother, father, or mother-surrogate love.

Interestingly, and although my codependent partner claims she has a Codependency Addiction to me, she, nevertheless, does not believe anything I have discussed here, or anywhere in this book, is true. Unfortunately, everything true is overridden by *denial*. Maurice White's assessment of denial is powerful. He stated "...denial is the little extra edge that makes the difference between greatness and mediocrity."[413] One other recent development with my codependent partner of 36 years is E believes the C Farm we both worked hard for in our lives solely belongs to her.

When we bought the farm in 1986-87, the finances used to purchase it was taken directly from money L earned while working at the City of Oakland, CA. L brought $40,000 in cash with him when we returned to Louisiana in 1986. Every penny of this money was invested in land

---

[411] Ibid., p. 351.
[412] Ibid., p. 354.
[413] Ibid., p. 148.

acquisition. From 1983 to 1986, E did not have a full-time job while we lived in Oakland, CA. She occasionally did substitute teaching. In short, E contributed no money toward the purchase of the C Farm Property. She knows this is an undeniable fact.

Having gone through a recent tumultuous divorce in 1979, L's ex-wife was obviously unhappy about the turn of events, and when L fell behind paying his child support payments, his ex-wife contacted the Department of Social Services in Baton Rouge, LA. This department contacted L and informed him that action would taken to place a lien on E and L's C Farm, if the child support arrears were not paid up-to-date. Afraid to lose our farm, L temporarily put the farm in E's name to shield it from being taken by the Department of Services. Over the succeeding years, and after L paid out his child support obligations in full, he and E did not take the C Farm Property out of her name as the Owner of Record at the St. Martin Parish Courthouse. By July 2015, E had a stroke, and everything changed for the worse.

E fantasized that the C Farm Property belonged to her *only*! Although her financial contributions to its purchase were far less than L's because E has a BS Degree in Secondary Education, and schoolteacher salaries are far less than someone who has a PhD Degree. L has a doctoral degree, and for every $1 E contributed toward the purchase of the C Farm Property, L contributed $10 over a 33 year period. Table 1.5 below shows the chronological path of financial contributions made by L toward the purchase of the property.

Table 1.5
L's Financial Contributions Toward The Purchase
Of C Farm Located In LA, 1986 To 2019

DATE	PROPERTY ACTION	AMOUNT OF CONTRIBUTIONS MADE
(1.) October 9, 1986	Purchase Tract-2: 2.0 acres from Gail and Mike Melancon	$15,000
(1A.) Mortgage taken out on: October 30, 2001	First National Bank of St. Martin, Brentwood Crossing, LA	$12, 688
(2.) July 6, 1987	Purchase Tract 3: 3.08 acres from Gail and Mike Melancon	$30,808
(2A.) Mortgage taken out on: July 9, 1987	Citizen National Bank	$30,802
(3.) Mortgage taken out on: September 23, 2011	Lafayette Parish Credit Union lien on (1) and (2)	$53,260
(4.) Mortgage taken out on: October 2010	Lafayette Parish Credit Union to add an Office-Bedroom Suite to home	$20,000
(5.) September 13, 2013	Black Farmers Class Action Award Received from USDA used to pay off ALL LIENS against C Farm Property shown above	$50,000
(6.) General Maintenance	Thirty-Six Years	$50,000
	TOTAL CONTRIBUTION	$219,068
NOTE: L has a Ph.D. Degree.	For every $1 E (BS Degree in Secondary Education) contributed to the above; L contributed $10.	Conclusion: L contributed 90% of the indicated money to purchase and maintain the C Farm, from 1986 to 2019, or 33 years.
Source: Court Records		

Over a 33 year period, L contributed $219, 068 toward the purchase, yet E, due largely to her stroke and CoDependency Addiction, has rationalized the C Property belongs to her only. Because E grew up in a highly dysfunctional family, she failed to get nurtured, from a dependency state to a higher form known as interdependency, which establishes a child, who, on one hand, recognizes one Self as being love, and on the other, as one who is capable of giving self-love to another human being. Because E grew up in a codependent household, Raymond D. Adams wrote in his article "The Development Of Personality" that "perversions, arrests, or regressions of this process are thought to be the source of psychopathic and neurotic behavior. This hormic, or motivational, aspect of behavior and the dependence of it on the formation of sexual bonds between infant and mother, family members, and others is confirmed by studies of monkeys by Harlow. The baby monkey, if deprived of the warmth of social contact with other animals of its kind, grows up to be totally inadequate as a sexual partner, parent, or member of monkey society."[414] As we have already seen, E was severely deprived of love as an infant, child, and teenager, and the CoDependency Addiction this social condition produced in her personality structure, has caused her pain and suffering right up to the present time. As a codependent personality, E's wishes are misrepresented by her as truths.

Although E knows she does not own the C Farm alone, she has come up with a fantasy to rationalize in her intellectual mind that she does. John Powell wrote the following: "We find some reason for our action that justifies it…Very often there are two reasons for everything we do: the alleged good reason and the real reason. Rationalizations not only results in self-deceit but eventually corrupts all sense of integrity (wholeness)…Rationalization is the bridge that makes my wishes the facts. It is the use of intelligence to deny the truth; it makes us dishonest with ourselves. And if we cannot be honest with ourselves, we certainly cannot be honest with anyone else. Rationalization consequently

---

[414] Wintrobe, Maxwell M., torn, George W., Adams, Raymond D, et. al. (Editors), Harrison Principles Of Internal Medicine, A Blankiston Publication, McGraw-Hill Book Company, New York, 1958, p. 36.

sabotages all human authenticity. It disintegrates and fragments the personality."[415] John Powell's insight shows that E's personality has fragmented into various ones, and among them, one personality type uses rationalization to invent a truth out of a wish. Thus, E's wish she is the sole owner of the C Farm Property is merely a rationalization of reality. Moreover, for E's Wish she owns the C Property independent of L's half share in it to seem real to her, or believable, all of the people E considers her friends must also believe she owns the C Property alone.

This fantasy bubble appears to be real only because E has cultivated in her co-called friends a cult-like obedience to her highly questionable spiritual thoughts over the years. Some attention was given to this closed-minded development earlier. Everyone knows E could not afford the lifestyle she was allowed to live during the 36 years she and L were in a relationship. None of E's friends, to my knowledge, have ever travelled to Cairo, Egypt to visit the Great Pyramid of Giza or the Sphinx, for example. Everyone knows L purchased the C Property, and likewise knows he provided the money for E to travel to the Bering Glacier in Alaska, and many other places worldwide. Yet, E has told many of her friends C Farm belongs to her never mentioning once the fact that L suggested hiding the property from bill collectors by placing it in E's name. L never signed any papers toward this end, although E contacted a notary public; had a cash sale document written up; and she signed my name on it. L has two copies of this document on which his signature appears different from the way he normally signs his name. And, on one of the documents, there are two witnesses' signatures, and on the second one, only one witness signature appears. What does this tell us?

As it has been pointed-out over and over during the course of the discussion in this book, codependent people, and E in particular, by having been psychologically conditioned by CoDependency Addiction from birth, was recently-August 2019-influenced by her ego to conjure up this plan to try to steal L's half share of the C Farm. Having been a witness to many emotional attacks through the years, E's attempt to

---

[415] Powell, John, <u>Why Am I Afraid To Tell You Who I Am?</u>, RCL, Allen, Texas, 1969, p. 98.

steal L's half share of the C Farm is consistent with the CoDependency Addiction personality, which is shaped by fear, scarcity, anxiety, anger, hopelessness, powerlessness, and generalized fraud. Not one of E's friends ever called L to find out what is the other side of this fraudulent situation, and worse, including his own children!?

Therefore, those Americans who desire to change, by making a conscious commitment to move beyond *denial*, can do so by seriously applying the information in this book to their own lives to find out where their therapeutic work must start, if they ever expect to have any chance of living a *CoDependency Addiction Free life!*

Before closing, the last section in this book is called the Appendices. There are Five, namely Temporary Restraining Order A (TRO), Temporary Restraining Order B (TRO), and Temporary Restraining Order C (TRO), Pleadings Filed Cost Now Due, D, and Text Message Exchanges between E and L, from January 1, 2019 to December 31, 2019-E. To understand these TROs, they must be understood within the definition of what we have said about CoDependency Addiction thus far. That is, when L finally, after 36 years, removed himself from the clutches of E's codependent addiction attachments, she, psychologically realized, for the first time, that she does not truly know who L is as a human being with his own authentic feelings, emotions, visions, creativity, and life in general. During the time L was untangling himself from E's CoDependency Web of Addiction, on several occasion E mentioned to L that "she does not know who L is anymore." In short, L was suddenly consciously viewed by E as who he was in her life for 36 years, and that is, namely, a stranger. This realization frightened E tremendously! It shocked L also.

Thus, when E no longer had L's feelings and emotions to prey on for her day-to-day survival, this change left her lonely and fearful of herself. Her anxiety was exacerbated when she was hit in the "gut" with the fact that she was sleeping in a bed with a man whose feelings and identity she never knew! What would L do about this massive manipulation, inclusive of property and family matters? Unable to realize all L desired is his exit from the relationship, along with a fair and equitable distribution of any accumulated property, E could not think about this high level thought, given the years of her manipulation that suddenly burst into plain day like a revolutionary explosion! Unable to wrap her mind around the situation, and although L never harmed anyone during the 36 years E observed his daily behavior, including her, and given what the television answer to every challenge is to find a solution in some form of violence, she ran to the 16th Judicial District Court and, acting in her best *"victim personality,"* claimed and pled to this court that L is a monster and predator, who intends to visit personal harm on her. Nothing can be farther from the truth! Actually, E attempted repeatedly to project all of her childhood wounds and traumas, usually known to most as demons on L(!) as the various attached TROs prove.

Specifically, the TRO shown in Appendix A clearly indicates E's intent to damage my character and reputation in the Southwest Louisiana Area. Upon closer examination, on Page 2 of 6-Part D "Findings: Domestic Abuse or Dating Violence THE COURT FINDS THAT THE ALLEGATIONS PRESENTED CONSTITUTE AN IMMEDIATE AND PRESENT DANGER TO THE PHYSICAL SAFETY OF THE PROTECTED PERSON(S). Moreover, on Page 4 of 6, "THE DEFENDANT IS ORDERED TO show cause on the below hearing date why s/he should not be ordered to pay the following…necessitated by the domestic abuse, dating violence, stalking, or sexual assault." Without any *evidence,* the court finds the allegations credible! Ironically, on Page 2 of 7 of the Petition For protection From Abuse, and on Page 2 of 7, Paragraph 8, every box listed under "Defendant abused protected person(s) in the following manner…" only one is checked for other-"Mental and Verbal." How could the court find L liable for domestic abuse, given all of its categories of such behavior are unchecked? What is E, the protected person, being protected from? How can E prove to the court L engaged in Mental and verbal abuse? Did she present the court with a tape recording of L mentally and verbally abusing her? E does not have a tape recording that verifies that L mentally and verbally abused her.

However, L does have evidence that unequivocally demonstrates that he did not commit such grotesque and barbaric acts(!) while he and E lived together. In fact none of E's friends ever heard me use profanity directed at her person; nor, did any of E's children ever witness me engaging in such violent behavior. Yet, the 16th Judicial District Court is certain I engaged in this type of behavior toward E. The evidence L has, which categorically refutes all of E's claims to the court that L *mentally and verbally* abused her, is located in Appendix E, namely, Text Message Exchanges Between L and E, From January 1, 2019 to December 31, 2019.

I challenge anyone to read the text message exchanges during this period, which is inclusive of the time when each of the E inspired TROs were served against L, from November 2019 to March 11, 2020. The TROs remain in effect until June 18, 2021! As we see, every Text Message Exchange L and E engaged in, from January 1, 2019 to December 31, 2019, does not show any evidence of verbal of mental abuse directed toward E. More will be mentioned about them later.

Unfortunately, and in spite of this fact, L has had to endure sustained damage to his reputation and character. CoDependency Addiction is a very powerful mental disease; it splits the human psyche into several personalities-public and private. The TROs were initiated by E's public persona. In an effort to save face in her community, and being unwilling to take responsibility for her CoDepedency Addiction, in all of its manifestations, L was the closest person to her who could be made an outcast in an attempt to vindicate and extricate herself from the disease, by making it appear the sole problem she has faced all of her life, since birth, was caused by L.

Before proceeding, L was forced to pay court cost to the 16th Judicial District Court, despite the fact, as we already know, there was no evidence presented to this court by E that would warrant L being asked *to pay all court cost.* (See Appendix D-Pleadings Filed Cost Now Due)

Where is the justice to be found, can someone tell me? How many more years must a cannonball be fired before innocent people are free?

In view of all of this codependent drama, L's only desire, since E told him she is codependent, is to free himself from the clutches of E's CoDependency Addiction Web. I just wanted out so I could begin the great healing task of finding a positive and productive way to move forward with my life, especially after being unconsciously entrapped in a powerful CoDependency Addiction Web.

A worm encases itself completely inside of its natural cocoon with the expectation, as decreed by Nature, during the correct season and moment, it will transform itself into a beautiful butterfly; exit its cocoon; and take flight into a totally new life experience. To the contrary, being unwittingly caught up in an invisible CoDependency Addiction Web is a *choice* of life or death. Freedom depends on the enabler's courage to "wake up and live," although, in L's case, he remained asleep for 36 years, while a CoDependency Addiction Web was subtly being woven around him daily. And, once he realized his predicament, and due to the significant emotional shock it caused in his nervous system, L called upon all of the power within himself to unravel the CoDependency Addiction Web his codependent partner had been weaving around him for 36 years. Rather than resign himself to this emotionally troublesome fate, he chose to free himself and take flight into a life free of the baggage of *imposed* CoDependency Addiction limitations in all its unflattering forms. Death was in close pursuit of L like a hundred Bloodhound Dogs on the trail of an escaped prisoner, who was bound and chained for 36 years, for an offense he unwittingly enabled but did not commit. It was either flight to *freedom,* or accept the responsibility for the creation of a codependent reality created by his codependent partner's thought. Similar to the message captured in the Queen of Soul's hit record called "Chain Of Fools" in which Aretha Franklin sung she would go on being a link in her partner's Chain of Fools until one day the linked broke. (Paraphrase is mine).

Moreover, far from being portrayed as a heartless, violent, and abusive animal with no redeeming human values, consider the Text Message Exchanges between L and E during 2019 shown in Appendix E.

Many of the texts span the period when E, both wrongly and falsely, flung herself upon the alter of the 16th Judicial District Court in St. Martinville, LA, and complained to the latter, like a child would after being stung by a Bumblebee that her partner-L, who provided her a dream life the type many of her friends likely will not experience in this lifetime, and uttered the untruths that she was "mentally and verbally abused" by L. In contradiction to this unfounded claim, every text message exchange E and L had with each other, during 2019, not one-NONE-reveal she was fearful of L, or her personal well-being was being threatened, directly or indirectly, by L, or that L had engaged in a pattern of abuse toward her during 2019. The fact is: In every Text Message L received from E during this time, they-All-consistently reveal E's expressed LOVE for L in some way. While E expressed her love for L in text messages during 2019, she **simultaneously unleashed her "Dark Night of the Soul" against L in the form of the baseless TROs** contained in the Appendix. One can feel the betrayal of truth blowing in the winds of family dysfunctionalism and human degradation and deprivation since childhood. Without a powerful intervention such as the one highly recommended in this work, the CoDependency Addiction thought will continue on its course for another 36 years, or for centuries to come, affecting the lives of millions more people, if it is not arrested, analyzed, deconstructed, and permanently abandoned. Lastly, the TRO contained in Appendix B with the heading: Information For Service Of process, several questions are ask: (1) "Does the Defendant have a history of violence toward others (Other than victim)? [The court checked]: NO; Have a history of using/abusing drugs or alcohol? [The court checked] NO; Carry a weapon? [The court checked]: NO. By the 16th Judicial District Court admission, it did not find L to be a violent and abusive person.

The Lesson is learned...

During his acceptance speech, after winning the Best Actor Award, Joaquin Phoenix delivered a profound speech in which he stated: When his brother Rivers Phoenix was 17 years old, he wrote, "Run to the rescue with love, and peace will follow."

Peace be unto All who have the audacity to still feel and believe that life is not a Third or Fifth Dimension or other Fantasy, but merely a canvas on which anyone can reflect the beauty of their real life in one form or another such as the sun reflects its beauty on the face of the moon on a full moon night against the backdrop of darkness and the rhythmic sounds of the nightlife-crickets, frogs, owls, and more...

APPENDIX A

Temporary Restraining Order:
November 19, 2019 to December 4, 2019

NOV. 20. 2019 9:26AM   SMPCOC   NO. 489   P. 7

CITATION & RULE TO SHOW CAUSE
PROTECTIVE ORDERS

Received:
2-1-19
1:30 PM
EST

	E'		Case: 0838
Versus			Division:
			16ᵗʰ Judicial District Court
			Parish of St. Martin
L)			State of Louisiana

TO: L.

9009 ERIMIKE COURT

RANDALLS TOWN, MD 21133

You are hereby cited to comply with the demand contained in the Petition and Temporary Restraining Order, a certified copy of which accompanies this citation. File your answer or other pleading to said petition in the office of the Clerk of the 16th Judicial District Court at 415 St. Martin Street, St. Martinville in said Parish on or before DECEMBER 4, 2019.

By virtue of an order, issued in the above numbered and entitled matter, out of the Honorable 16th Judicial District Court, bearing date, the 19TH day of NOVEMBER, 2019;
You are hereby ordered to show cause, if any you have, in open Court, at 415 S. Main St., St. Martinville, Louisiana, at 8:30 A.M. on the 4TH day of DECEMBER, 2019, before Judge CURTIS SIGUR. Before going to the Court room, you are to report to Hearing Officer Maggie Simar.

WHY Temporary Restraining Order and other relief requested should not be made Protective Orders.

In accordance with the allegations and prayer for the issuance of this rule, a true and correct attested copy whereof accompanies this rule and is served herewith.

Witness the Honorable 16th Judicial District Court, at St. Martinville, St. Martin Parish,

Louisiana, NOVEMBER 19, 2019.

Becky P. Patin
Clerk, 16th Judicial Court
St. Martin Parish, Louisiana

Toni L. Theriot

By: TONI L. THERIOT
Deputy Clerk of Court
Parish of St. Martin

[RETURN]

11/20/2019   10:45AM (GMT-05:00)

NOV. 20. 2019 9:27AM   SMPCOC   NO. 420   P. 4

```
................ FOR LPOR USE ONLY ....
LPOR _____
Date Entered: _____
Initials:_____  Verified by:_____
```

LOUISIANA UNIFORM ABUSE PREVENTION ORDER

Docket No. [   ]

Order of Protection

☒ Temporary Restraining Order

☐ Protective Order/Preliminary or Permanent Injunction

☐ Modified Protective Order/Preliminary or Permanent Injunction

Court: ___16th JDC__   Div.: _____

City/Parish   State

ST MARTIN   Louisiana

Filed: _____   Clerk: _____

PETITIONER

E.

First   Middle/Maiden   Last

PETITIONER IDENTIFIERS

| 01/11/51 | BL | X |
| Date of birth | Race | Sex: F Sex: M |

Protected person is: ☒ Petitioner ☐ other(s) List other(s) name & date of birth:

V.

DEFENDANT NAME AND ADDRESS

L.

First   Middle   Last

Name of minor defendant's parent or guardian

Defendant's Alias

9009 ERIMIKE COURT

No. & Street

Apt. No. RANDALLS TOWN   MD 21133

City   State   Zip Code

DEFENDANT IDENTIFIERS

SEX	RACE	DOB	HT	WT
M	BL	07/25/50	6'2"	180
EYES	HAIR	SOCIAL SECURITY #		
BR	BR			
DRIVER'S LICENSE #		STATE	EXP DATE	

THE COURT HEREBY FINDS:

That it has jurisdiction over the parties and subject matter, and the defendant has been or will be provided with reasonable notice and opportunity to be heard. Additional findings of this court are as set forth on the following pages.

THE COURT HEREBY ORDERS:

That the above named defendant be restrained from committing further acts of abuse or threats of abuse, stalking or sexual assault. Additional terms of this order are as set forth on the following pages.

This order shall be effective through 11:59 PM on [12-4-19] (month/day/year)

This order shall be enforced, even without registration, by the courts of any state, the District of Columbia, any U.S. Territory, and may be enforced by Tribal Lands (18 U.S.C. Section 2265).

WARNINGS TO DEFENDANT:

Crossing state, territorial, or tribal boundaries to violate this order may result in federal imprisonment (18 U.S.C. Section 2262).

Federal law provides penalties for possessing, transporting, shipping, or receiving any firearm or ammunition (18 U.S.C. Section 922(g)(8)). See further notice on page 5 of this Order.

ONLY THE COURT CAN CHANGE THIS ORDER.

Page 1 of 6   LPOR 1
                               v.11

11/20/2019 10:45AM (GMT-05:00)

NOV. 20. 2019 9:28AM   SMPCOC   NO. 480   P. 5

Docket No.: 868

LOUISIANA UNIFORM ABUSE PREVENTION ORDER

TEMPORARY RESTRAINING ORDER
Pursuant to:

☒ La. R.S. 46:2131 et seq. (Domestic Abuse)	☐ La. R.S. 46:2171 et seq. (Non-intimate stalking)	46:2171 and 46:2181 valid for relationships in Box C below ONLY
☐ La. R.S. 46:2151 (Dating Violence)	☐ La. R.S. 46:2181 et seq. (Non-intimate sexual assault)	
	☐ La. Ch. C. Article 1564 et seq. (Children's Code Domestic Abuse)	

PETITIONER B _____ Protected person is: ☒ Petitioner ☐ other(s)

V.

DEFENDANT L _____

The protected person(s) is related to the defendant as: *(check all that apply)*

A	☐ 1. current or former spouse ☒ 2. current or former intimate cohabitant ☐ 3. child, stepchild, or foster child ☐ 4. child of defendant's current or former intimate partner ☐ 5. protected person and defendant have a child(ren) in common	B	☐ 1. current or former dating partner ☐ 2. parent, stepparent, or foster parent ☐ 3. grandparent ☐ 4. grandchild
		C	Select ONLY if statute 46:2171 or 46:2181 is marked above ☐ 1. stranger/no relationship ☐ 2. acquaintance/co-worker/neighbor or other:

D	☒	FINDING: Domestic Abuse or Dating Violence THE COURT FINDS THAT THE ALLEGATIONS PRESENTED CONSTITUTE AN IMMEDIATE AND PRESENT DANGER TO THE PHYSICAL SAFETY OF THE PROTECTED PERSON(S).
	☐	FINDING: Stalking THE COURT FINDS THAT THE ALLEGATIONS PRESENTED CONSTITUTE AN IMMEDIATE AND PRESENT DANGER OF STALKING.
	☐	FINDING: Sexual Assault THE COURT FINDS THAT THE ALLEGATIONS PRESENTED CONSTITUTE A SEXUAL ASSAULT.

THUS THE COURT ISSUES THE FOLLOWING ORDERS, WITHOUT A HEARING:

IT IS ORDERED THAT THE DEFENDANT BE SERVED WITH A COPY OF THIS ORDER.

DOMESTIC ABUSE, DATING VIOLENCE, STALKING OR SEXUAL ASSAULT ONLY ORDERS CHECKED AND INITIALED BY A JUDGE SHALL APPLY

☒ 1. THE DEFENDANT IS ORDERED NOT TO abuse, harass, assault, stalk, follow, track, monitor, or threaten the protected person(s) in any manner whatsoever. This prohibition includes the use, attempted use, or threatened use of physical force that would reasonably be expected to cause bodily injury.

☒ 2. THE DEFENDANT IS ORDERED NOT TO contact the protected person(s) personally, through a third party, or via public posting, by any means, including written, telephone, or electronic (text, email, messaging, or social media) communication without the express written permission of this court.
Exceptions (if any): _____
NO CIRCUMSTANCES

☒ 3. THE DEFENDANT IS ORDERED NOT TO go within ____ 200 FT ____ (distance) of the protected person(s), without the express written permission of this court.
Exceptions (if any): _____
NO CIRCUMSTANCES

11/20/2019 10:45AM (GMT-05:00)

Docket No.: _____ 888

4. THE DEFENDANT IS ORDERED NOT TO go within one hundred (100) yards of the residence, apartment complex, or multiple family dwelling of the protected person(s).

2730 MAIN HIGHWAY BREAUX BRIDGE LA 70517
No. & Street   Apt. No.   City   State   Zip Code

☐ **5.** THE DEFENDANT IS ORDERED TO STAY AWAY from protected person(s)' place of employment/school and not to interfere in any manner with such employment/school.

Employment/School   Address   City   State   Zip Code

Employment/School   Address   City   State   Zip Code

☐ **6.** THE DEFENDANT IS ORDERED NOT TO damage any belongings or property of the protected person(s) and not to shut off any utilities, telephone service, or mail delivery to the protected person(s) or in any way interfere with the living conditions of the protected person(s).

☐ **7.** THE COURT GRANTS THE PETITIONER or protected person(s) the use of the residence located at:

No. & Street   Apt. No.   City   State   Zip Code

to the exclusion of defendant by evicting defendant. The Court orders the defendant to surrender any keys to that residence to the petitioner.

_____ (Sheriff's office) is ordered to evict the defendant.

☒ **8.** THE COURT GRANTS THE PETITIONER or protected person(s) the use and possession of the following property (including pets) and/or the return of protected person(s) property.

2002 FORD F250 TRUCK, 4 DOOR, NAVY BLUE AND GRAY AND ALL KEYS TO 2002 FORD F250 TRUCK, 4 DOOR, NAVY BLUE AND GRAY.

☒ **9.** THE COURT ORDERS a representative of ST. MARTIN PARISH _____ (Sheriff's office) to accompany petitioner to obtain property listed in Order No. 8 above.

☐ **10.** THE COURT PROHIBITS EITHER PARTY from transferring, encumbering, or otherwise disposing of property jointly owned or leased, except in the normal course of business or that which is necessary for the support of the petitioner and/or the minor child(ren).

☐ **11.** THE COURT WILL ALLOW _____ to return to the residence at a date and time to be agreed upon by petitioner and law enforcement agency to recover his/her personal clothing and necessities, provided that s/he is accompanied by a law enforcement officer to ensure the protection and safety of the parties. NO FORCED ENTRY ALLOWED.

☐ **12.** THE COURT ORDERS a representative of _____ (Sheriff's office)

to accompany _____ to the residence located

at _____ to recover her/his personal clothing and necessities.

DOMESTIC ABUSE, DATING VIOLENCE ONLY
ONLY ORDERS CHECKED AND INITIALED BY A JUDGE SHALL APPLY

☐ **13.** THE COURT GRANTS TEMPORARY CUSTODY of the following child(ren) or alleged incompetent to the petitioner: *(name, date of birth, and relationship to petitioner)*

11/20/2019   10:45AM (GMT-05:00)

NOV. 20. 2019 9:29AM   SMPCOC   NO. 480   P. 7

Docket No.: _____ 888

____ ☐14.   THE COURT ORDERS a representative of _____ (Sheriff's office) to accompany petitioner to where the minor child(ren) or alleged incompetent mentioned in paragraph above is/are currently, and to affect petitioner obtaining physical custody of said child(ren) or alleged incompetent.

____ ☐15.   THE DEFENDANT IS ORDERED NOT TO interfere with the physical custody of the minor child(ren) or alleged incompetent.

____ ☐16.   THE DEFENDANT IS ORDERED TO show cause on the below hearing date why s/he should not be evicted from the solely owned residence or household and the petitioner granted possession.

____ ☐17.   THE DEFENDANT IS ORDERED TO show cause on the below hearing date why s/he should not be ordered to pay child support and/or spousal support (alimony) pursuant to Louisiana Law. The court further orders the defendant to produce at the hearing: most recent income tax returns AND pay stubs or an employer statement documenting gross income to date for the CURRENT year. If the defendant is self-employed, income and expense statements shall be produced.

> **STALKING, SEXUAL ASSAULT ONLY**
> ONLY ORDERS CHECKED AND INITIALED BY A JUDGE SHALL APPLY

____ ☐18.   THE DEFENDANT IS ORDERED NOT TO contact family members or acquaintances of the protected person(s).

> **DOMESTIC ABUSE, DATING VIOLENCE, STALKING OR SEXUAL ASSAULT**
> ONLY ORDERS CHECKED AND INITIALED BY A JUDGE SHALL APPLY

____ ☒19.   THE DEFENDANT IS ORDERED TO show cause on the below hearing date why s/he should not be ordered to pay the following:

    ☒ all court costs   ☒ attorney fees

    ☒ evaluation fees   ☒ expert witness fees

    ☒ cost of medical and/or psychological care for the petitioner, the minor child(ren), alleged incompetent, and/or other protected person(s) necessitated by the domestic abuse, dating violence, stalking or sexual assault.

____ ☐20.   THE DEFENDANT IS ORDERED TO show cause on the below hearing date why s/he should not be ordered to seek professional counseling, complete a court-monitored domestic abuse intervention program, submit to a medical evaluation and/or submit to a mental health evaluation.

____ ☒21.   Other:

    THE COURT ORDERS the defendant to show cause why he should not enroll in and successfully complete the Batterer's Intervention Program.

NOV. 20. 2019 9:29AM   SMPCDC   NO. 480   P. 8

Docket No. 888

☑ IT IS FURTHER ORDERED THAT DEFENDANT show cause on __12/4/19__ (month/day/year)
at __8:30__ o'clock __A__. M. in Courtroom No. ____ of the __16ᵗʰ J.D.__ Court, located
at __415 S. Main St.__ in __St. Martinville__, La., why the
above Temporary Restraining Order and other relief requested should not be made Protective Orders.

Date of Order	Time of Order	Order effective through 11:59 PM on	SIGNATURE OF JUDGE
11/19/19	11:48 ☑AM ☐PM	12-4-19	☑ Order issued ex parte ___ Order issued after notice and opportunity for hearing given to defendant. Anthony Thibodeaux PRINT OR STAMP JUDGE'S NAME

(handwritten left margin: uly 31, 2019 ↓ Dec 1, 2019 never saw ↓ oct. 12, 2019 () LH)

NOTICE: C.C.P. Article 3603.1 - Any person against whom such an order is issued shall be entitled to a court-appointed attorney if the applicant has likewise been afforded a court-appointed attorney.

NOTICE TO DEFENDANT - VIOLATION OF ORDER:

PURSUANT TO LA. R.S. 14:79, A PERSON WHO VIOLATES THIS ORDER MAY BE ARRESTED, JAILED, AND PROSECUTED.

PURSUANT TO LA. R.S. 13:4611 AND LA. CH. C, ARTICLE 1571, A PERSON WHO VIOLATES THIS ORDER MAY BE PUNISHED FOR CONTEMPT OF COURT BY A FINE OF NOT MORE THAN $1,000 OR BY CONFINEMENT IN JAIL FOR AS LONG AS 6 MONTHS, OR BOTH, AND MAY BE FURTHER PUNISHED UNDER CRIMINAL LAWS OF THE STATE OF LOUISIANA. THIS ORDER SHALL BE ENFORCED BY ALL LAW ENFORCEMENT OFFICERS AND COURTS OF THE STATE OF LOUISIANA.

NOTICE TO DEFENDANT – FIREARMS POSSESSION (Domestic abuse or dating violence ONLY):

AS A RESULT OF THIS ORDER, IT MAY BE UNLAWFUL FOR YOU TO POSSESS, RECEIVE, SHIP, TRANSPORT OR PURCHASE A FIREARM, INCLUDING A RIFLE, PISTOL, OR REVOLVER, OR AMMUNITION, FOR THE DURATION OF THIS ORDER PURSUANT TO STATE AND/OR FEDERAL LAWS. See below.

If you have any questions whether these laws make it illegal for you to possess or purchase a firearm or ammunition, consult an attorney.

Federal law: 18 U.S.C. 922 (g)(8) prohibits a defendant from purchasing, possessing, shipping, transporting, or receiving firearms or ammunition* for the duration of this order if the following conditions apply:
- Protected person(s) relationship to defendant is checked in Box A on page 2 of this order AND
- Notice and opportunity for a hearing provided AND
- EITHER Judicial finding of credible threat, OR Certain behaviors are prohibited (item 1 on page 3 of this order is initialed)

*Under 18 U.S.C. 921 the term "firearm" means (A) any weapon (including a starter gun) which will or is designed to or may readily be converted to expel a projectile by the action of an explosive; (B) the frame or receiver of any such weapon; (C) any firearm muffler or firearm silencer; or (D) any destructive device. Such term does not include an antique firearm. The term "ammunition" means ammunition or cartridge cases, primers, bullets, or propellant powder designed for use in any firearm.

RECEIVED AND FILED

2019 NOV 19 PM 3:43
DEPUTY CLERK OF COURT
ST MARTIN...

A TRUE COPY
ATTEST _____

11/20/2019 10:45AM (GMT-05:00)

NOV. 20. 2019 9:30AM   SMPCOC   NO. 480   P. 9

Docket No.: 888

NOTICE TO DEFENDANT – FIREARM TRANSFER AND SUSPENSION OF CONCEALED HANDGUN PERMIT
(Domestic abuse or dating violence ONLY)

IF A PROTECTIVE ORDER IS ISSUED AGAINST YOU, YOU MAY BE REQUIRED TO TRANSFER ANY AND
ALL FIREARMS OWNED OR POSSESSED BY YOU AND SURRENDER YOUR CONCEALED HANDGUN
PERMIT. AS YOU MAY ALSO BE REQUIRED TO STATE UNDER OATH THE NUMBER OF FIREARMS YOU
POSSESS, THE SERIAL NUMBER AND LOCATION OF EACH AND COMPLETE A FIREARMS
INFORMATION FORM VERIFYING SUCH, BRING THIS INFORMATION TO THE HEARING.

Louisiana law, C.Cr.P. Art. 1000 requires the transfer of all firearms owned or possessed and the suspension of a
concealed handgun permit:
- When a person is subject to a permanent injunction or a protective order pursuant to a court-approved consent
agreement or pursuant to the provisions of R.S. 9:361 et seq., R.S. 9:372, R.S. 46:2136, 2151, or 2173, Children's
Code Article 1570, Code of Civil Procedure Article 3607.1, or C.Cr.P. Articles 30, 320, or 871.1.
OR
- When a person is subject to a Uniform Abuse Prevention Order that includes terms prohibiting possession of a
firearm or carrying a concealed weapon.

FULL FAITH AND CREDIT pursuant to 18 U.S.C. § 2265

The issuing court certifies that it has jurisdiction over the parties and the subject matter under the laws of the State of
Louisiana; that the defendant was given reasonable notice and an opportunity to be heard sufficient to protect the defendant's
right to due process before this order was issued; or if the order was issued ex parte, the court ordered that the defendant be
given reasonable notice and an opportunity to be heard within the time required by the laws of the State of Louisiana, and in
any event, within a reasonable time after the order was issued, sufficient to protect the defendant's due process rights.

THIS ORDER SHALL BE PRESUMED VALID AND ENFORCEABLE IN ALL 50 STATES, THE DISTRICT OF COLUMBIA,
TRIBAL LANDS, U.S. TERRITORIES, AND COMMONWEALTHS.

SIGNATURE OF JUDGE

PRINT OR STAMP JUDGE'S NAME

NOTICE TO LAW ENFORCEMENT

Pursuant to La. R.S. 14:79, the crime of violation of protective orders – you shall use every reasonable means,
including but not limited to immediate arrest of the violator, to enforce this order. Further, you shall at a
minimum issue a summons to the person in violation.

Pursuant to La. R.S. 46:2140(A), if you have reason to believe that a family or household member or dating
partner has been abused AND the abusing party is in violation of this order, you SHALL immediately arrest the
abusing party.

If the expiration date of this order falls on or within five (5) days of the conclusion of a declared state of
emergency, this order/injunction shall be enforced throughout that time period.

☐ DEFENDANT WAS SERVED AT CLOSE OF HEARING.
   Date_____ Clerk_____

☐ FAXED or ELECTRONICALLY TRANSMITTED TO LOUISIANA PROTECTIVE ORDER REGISTRY
   Date_____ Clerk_____ RECEIVED AND FILED

Copies to: 1) Court file 2) Petitioner/protected person(s) 3) Defendant 4) Local law enforcement officials of the parish where the
          protected person(s) resides 5) Louisiana Protective Order Registry.

2019 NOV 19 PM 3:43

DEPUTY CLERK OF
OF MORRIS

A TRUE COPY
ATTEST_____

Page 6 of 6

11/20/2019 10:45AM (GMT-05:00)

NOV. 20. 2019 9:30AM   SMPCOC   NO. 480   P. 10

E̶   16th JDC _____ COURT
PETITIONER   PARISH/CITY OF ___ST MARTIN___

         V.   STATE OF LOUISIANA

L̶   DIVISION: _____ NUMBER: _____
DEFENDANT   FILED: _____ CLERK: _____
Parent/Guardian name if defendant is a minor

PETITION FOR PROTECTION FROM ABUSE
Pursuant to La. R.S. 46:2131 et seq. or La. R.S. 46:2151

This petition is: ☒ Initial Petition ☐ Supplemental and Amending Petition

The petition of ___B̶_____, born 01/11/51
                  your name   month/day/year

a resident of the State of Louisiana, respectfully represents:

Paragraph 1

Petitioner files this petition on behalf of:

a. __v__ Petitioner, and/or

b. ____ Minor child(ren) as follows: (Name, Date of Birth, Relationship to Petitioner)

c. ____ Alleged Incompetent as follows: (Name, Date of Birth, Relationship to Petitioner)

Paragraph 2

a. ____ Petitioner requests that his/her address, or that of the minor child(ren) or alleged incompetent, remain confidential to the court and files the address pursuant to La. R.S. 46:2134(B). *(Ask clerk of court for the Confidential Address Form.)*

OR

b. __X__ Petitioner's current address:
273 Kansas Drive
No. & Street   Apt. No.
Brentwood Crossing, LA   71862
City   State   Zip Code

c. ____ The minor child's or alleged incompetent's current address:
No. & Street   Apt. No.
City   State   Zip Code

Paragraph 3

F̶_____, defendant, resides in ___BALTIMORE___ Parish at
Abuser's Name

9009 ERIMIKE COURT RANDALLS TOWN   MD 21133
No. & Street   Apt. No.   City   State   Zip Code

                                           LPOR B
                                             v.11
Page 1 of 7

11/20/2019 10:45AM (GMT-05:00)

NOV. 20, 2019 9:10AM SMPCCJC   NO. 480   P 11

Paragraph 4

This Court is the proper venue for this action because:

___ The marital domicile is located in _____ Parish.

___ The household is located in _____ Parish.

___ The defendant resides or is domiciled in _____ Parish.

_X_ The abuse occurred in ___ST MARTIN___ Parish.

_X_ The protected person(s) resides or is domiciled in ___ST MARTIN___ Parish.
(Do not fill this out if address is to remain confidential.)

Paragraph 5

The protected person(s) is related to the defendant as: (check all that apply)

___ Current or former spouse   ___ Current or former dating partner

_X_ Current or former intimate cohabitant   ___ Parent, stepparent, or foster parent

___ Child, stepchild, or foster child   ___ Grandparent

___ Child of defendant's current or former intimate partner ___ Grandchild

Paragraph 6

___ A suit for divorce between the parties is not pending.

___ A suit for divorce between the parties is pending (fill out page 7 of this form, "Addendum")
NOTE: If you were NOT the petitioner in the divorce suit, use form LPOR B-R entitled "Petition for Protection
From Abuse, (Filed by the Defendant in the Pending Action as Petitioner-in-reconvention)" instead of this
one.

___ There is a suit for custody pending involving children named in this petition (fill out page 7 of this form, "Addendum").

___ There is a custody order in effect involving children named in this petition (fill out page 7 of this form, "Addendum", or
attach a copy of the order if available).

Paragraph 7

___ The protected person(s) and defendant have child(ren) in common.

Paragraph 8

a. Defendant abused protected person(s) in the following manner:

___ Slapped protected person(s)   ___ Threatened protected person(s) with bodily harm

___ Punched protected person(s)   ___ Threatened protected person(s)' life

___ Choked protected person(s)   ___ Threatened protected person(s) with a weapon

___ Shoved protected person(s)   ___ Sexually abused protected person(s)

___ Kicked protected person(s)   ___ Abused petitioner's child(ren) or alleged incompetent

___ Stabbed protected person(s)   _M_ Other: ENTAL AND VERBAL

b. The facts and circumstances of this abuse are as follows:

The most recent incident of abuse which caused petitioner to file this petition happened on or about

___/___/___ (month/day/year), at which time the defendant did:

I am filing a protective order against L____ because I am afraid of him. I left my home for four months. because I was afraid and intimidated. He sent ugly text messages to me while I was away. When I was around him he would be very aggressive. [See my Text Message to ____

Amy Filed complaints.

Page 2 of 7   LPOR B
                                               v.11
                 11/20/2019 10:45AM (GMT-05:00)

verbally
When I finally found out he was gone he had remodeled
the house stripping all valuables leaving the house in unliveable
conditions.
Although I am back in my home I have a friend
living with me because of fear of his return
and what he would do.

_____

_____

Past Incidents: _____

_____

_____

_____

_____

_____

_____

_____

Paragraph 9

Because of the immediate and present danger of abuse, petitioner requests that an *ex parte* Temporary Restraining Order
be issued immediately without bond:

X a. prohibiting defendant from abusing, harassing, assaulting, stalking, following, tracking, monitoring, or threatening
the protected person(s) in any manner whatsoever. This prohibition includes the use, attempted use, or
threatened use of physical force that would reasonably be expected to cause bodily injury.

X b. prohibiting the defendant from contacting the protected person(s) personally, through a third party, or via public
posting, by any means, including written, telephone, or electronic (text, email, messaging, or social media)
communication without the express written permission of this court.

X c. prohibiting defendant from going within one hundred (100) yards of the residence, apartment complex, or
multiple family dwelling of the protected person(s) located at:

2731 KANSAS Drive   Brentwood Crossing, LA   71862
No. & Street Apt. No.   City   State   Zip Code

_____ d. ordering the defendant to stay away from the protected person(s)' place of employment/school and not to
interfere in any manner with such employment/school located at:

Employment/School	Address	City	State	Zip Code

Employment/School	Address	City	State	Zip Code

_____ e. ordering the defendant not to damage any belongings of the protected person(s), not to shut off any utilities,
telephone service, or mail delivery to the protected person(s), or in any way interfere with the living conditions of
the protected person(s).

LFOR B
v.11

356

NOV. 20. 2019 9:31AM   SMPCOC   NO. 480   P. 13

___ f. granting the petitioner or protected person(s) the use of the residence located at:

No. & Street Apt. No.	City	,	State	Zip Code

to the exclusion of defendant by evicting defendant and ordering the defendant to surrender any keys to that
residence to the petitioner, and ordering _____ (Sheriff's office) to evict the
defendant.
Said residence is:
___ jointly owned by defendant and petitioner or protected person(s).
___ jointly leased by defendant and petitioner or protected person(s).
___ solely leased by defendant who has a duty to support petitioner or protected person(s).
    (NOTE: If solely owned by defendant AND petitioner is awarded custody of child(ren) of the parties, check
    appropriate item in Paragraph 10.
___ solely owned or leased by petitioner or protected person(s).

Presently occupied by _____

X g. granting petitioner or protected person(s) possession of the following property (including pets) solely owned or
leased by petitioner or protected person(s) (state location of each item by street address and who is
presently in possession).

2002 FORD F250 TRUCK, 4 DOOR, NAVY BLUE AND GRAY AND ALL KEYS TO 2002
FORD F250 TRUCK, 4 DOOR, NAVY BLUE AND GRAY.

granting petitioner or protected person(s) the exclusive use and possession of the following property (including
pets) jointly owned or leased by petitioner or protected person(s) (state location of each item by street
address and who is presently in possession).

_____
_____
_____
_____
_____

for the following reasons: _____
_____
_____

And ordering ___ ST MARTIN PARSIH _____ (Sheriff's office) to accompany petitioner to where the
above listed property is located to allow petitioner to take possession of the property.

___ h. prohibiting either party from transferring, encumbering, or otherwise disposing of property jointly owned or
leased, except in the normal course of business or necessary for the support of the petitioner and/or the minor
child(ren) or alleged incompetent.

___ i. allowing _____ to return to the residence at a date and time to be agreed
upon by petitioner and law enforcement agency, to recover his/her personal clothing and necessities, only if s/he
is accompanied by a law enforcement officer to ensure the protection and safety of the parties. NO FORCED
ENTRY ALLOWED.

___ j. ordering a representative of _____ (Sheriff's office) to
accompany _____ to the family residence to recover her/his personal clothing
and necessities.

Page 4 of 7   LPOR B
                                                         v.11

                                    11/20/2019   10:45AM (GMT-05:00)

NOV. 20. 2019 9:32AM   SMPCUC   NO. 480   P. 14

_____ k. · awarding the temporary custody of the minor child(ren) or alleged incompetent,

_____

_____

to petitioner; the minor child(ren) or alleged incompetent is currently in the physical custody of_____

_____

_____ l. ordering a representative of _____ (Sheriff's office) to accompany petitioner to
where the minor child(ren) or alleged incompetent mentioned above is/are currently and to effect petitioner
obtaining physical custody of said child(ren) or alleged incompetent.

_____ m. prohibiting defendant from interfering with the custody of the minor child(ren) or alleged incompetent.

Paragraph 10

Petitioner desires that a rule issue herein ordering defendant to show cause why the orders requested in Paragraph 9 should
not be made into protective orders, and why defendant should not also be ordered:

_____ to pay petitioner a reasonable amount of child support in accordance with Louisiana Law.

_____ to pay petitioner a reasonable amount of spousal support (alimony).

__X__ to seek professional counseling or complete a court-monitored domestic abuse intervention program.

_____ to submit to a medical evaluation and/or a mental health evaluation

__X__ to pay costs of court in this matter.

__X__ to pay attorney fees.

__X__ to pay evaluation fees.

__X__ to pay expert witness fees.

__X__ to pay cost of medical and/or psychological care for the petitioner, minor child(ren), and/or alleged incompetent,
necessitated by the domestic abuse or dating violence.

_____ to vacate the residence or household, thereby granting petitioner possession thereof.

__X__ other: THE COURT ORDERS the defendant to show cause why he should not enroll in and successfully complete the
Batterer's Intervention Program.

PRAYER

WHEREFORE, petitioner prays that service and citation issue herein, and that: (check all that apply)

__X__ ex parte orders requested in Paragraph 9 be granted.

__X__ a rule issue to show cause why protective orders as requested in Paragraph 10 should not be granted.

__X__ defendant be cast with costs.

__X__ defendant be advised of penalties for violating Abuse Prevention Orders.

__X__ all other equitable relief as the court deems proper and necessary.

Respectfully submitted by

PETITIONER, IN PROPER PERSON

PLEASE SERVE DEFENDANT: _____

personally at his/her home or place of employment at the following address:

9009 ERIMIKE COURT

RANDALLS TOWN   MD 21133

OR

Page 5 of 7

LPOR B
v.11

11/20/2019 10:45AM (GMT-05:00)   :

NOV. 20. 2019   9:32AM   SMPCOC   NO. 480   P. 15

AFFIDAVIT/VERIFICATION

STATE OF LOUISIANA
PARISH OF ___ST. MARTIN___

BEFORE ME, the undersigned Notary Public, duly commissioned and qualified in and for the state and parish aforesaid, personally came and appeared _____ E _____,
Petitioner in the foregoing Petition for Protection from Abuse, who, after being duly sworn by me, did depose and say that s/he has read the allegations contained therein and declared them to be true and correct to the best of her/his knowledge, information, and belief.

Petitioner further said that s/he believes that the defendant poses a threat to petitioner's safety and/or to the child(ren) or to others for whom petitioner has requested relief.

Petitioner further said that s/he is aware that any false statement made under oath contained in the foregoing petition and this affidavit shall constitute perjury and shall be punishable by a fine of not more than one thousand dollars ($1,000.00), or by imprisonment, with or without hard labor, for not more than five (5) years, or both.

PETITIONER

SWORN TO AND SUBSCRIBED before me, Notary Public, on: NOV 16, 2019 (month/day/year),
at _____, Louisiana.

NOTARY PUBLIC 7 0 0 6 2

RECEIVED AND FILED
2019 NOV 19 AM 3: 43
DEPUTY CLERK
ST MARTIN PH.

Page 6 of 7

A TRUE COPY
ATTEST
LPOR B
v.11

11/20/2019 10:45AM (GMT-05:00)

NOV. 20. 2019 9:32AM   SMPCDC   NO. 480   P. 16

INFORMATION FOR SERVICE OF PROCESS
PROVIDED BY PETITIONER/PETITIONER-IN-RECONVENTION

PLEASE PROVIDE AS MUCH INFORMATION AS POSSIBLE. THIS INFORMATION WILL HELP LAW ENFORCEMENT LOCATE DEFENDANT (or DEFENDANT-IN-RECONVENTION) TO SERVE A COPY OF THE PETITION AND TEMPORARY RESTRAINING ORDER (IF ISSUED). THE FOLLOWING INFORMATION IS NEEDED ON THE DEFENDANT (or DEFENDANT-IN-RECONVENTION).

NAME __L__

Name of minor defendant's (or defendant-in-reconvention's) parent or guardian: _____

OTHER NAMES USED _____

DATE OF BIRTH _07/25/50_ (month/day/year)   SOCIAL SECURITY # _____

DRIVERS LICENSE # _____   STATE _____ EXP. DATE _____

HOME ADDRESS _9009 ERIMIKE COURT_
No. & Street   Apt. No.
RANDALLS TOWN _MD_ _____ TEL. NO. _____
City   State   Zip Code

WORK ADDRESS _____
Name of employer
No. & Street   Apt. No.
                                    DEPARTMENT _____
City   State   Zip Code
TEL. NO. _____   WORK DAYS/HOURS _____

PHYSICAL DESCRIPTION: ☒ MALE ☐ FEMALE   RACE _BL_
EYE COLOR _BR_   HAIR COLOR _BR_   HEIGHT _6'2"_   WEIGHT _180_
DISTINGUISHING FEATURES (scars, tattoos, facial hair, etc.) _____

MOTOR VEHICLE:
LICENSE PLATE # _____ YEAR _02_ MAKE _FORD F250_ COLOR _BLUE/G_

DOES THE DEFENDANT (or DEFENDANT-IN-RECONVENTION):
HAVE A HISTORY OF VIOLENCE TOWARDS OTHERS (OTHER THAN VICTIM)? ☐YES ☒NO
HAVE A HISTORY OF USING/ABUSING DRUGS OR ALCOHOL? ☐ YES ☒NO
CARRY A WEAPON? ☐YES ☒NO
IF YES, WHAT KIND OF WEAPON? _____

OTHER PLACES AND TIMES S/HE MAY BE FOUND: (Friends, relatives, bars, hangouts) _____

☐ DEFENDANT/DEFENDANT-IN-RECONVENTION CURRENTLY INCARCERATED
Where: _____
☐ DEFENDANT/DEFENDANT-IN-RECONVENTION CURRENTLY ON PROBATION/PAROLE
Probation or parole officer/department: _____

ANY OTHER INFORMATION WHICH MAY BE HELPFUL: _____

_____ Date   Petitioner's / Petitioner-in-Reconvention's Signature

LPOR H
v.11

11/20/2019 10:45AM (GMT-05:00)

APPENDIX B

Temporary Restraining Order: December 4, 2019 to December 18, 2019

DEC. 4. 2019 1:41PM   SMPCOC   NO 552   P 2

CITATION & RULE TO SHOW CAUSE
PROTECTIVE ORDERS

K.

Versus

L.

Case: D8X8
Division:
16th Judicial District Court
Parish of St. Martin
State of Louisiana

TO: L.

9009 ERIMIKE COURT

RANDALLS TOWN, MD 21133

You are hereby cited to comply with the demand contained in the Petition and Temporary Restraining Order, a certified copy of which accompanies this citation. File your answer or other pleading to said petition in the office of the Clerk of the 16th Judicial District Court at 415 St. Martin Street, St. Martinville in said Parish on or before DECEMBER 18, 2019.

By virtue of an order, issued in the above numbered and entitled matter, out of the Honorable 16th Judicial District Court, bearing date, the 4TH day of DECEMBER, 2019;

You are hereby ordered to show cause, if any you have, in open Court, at 415 S. Main St., St. Martinville, Louisiana, at 8:30 A.M. on the 18TH day of DECEMBER, 2019, before Judge LEWIS H. PITMAN, JR. *Before going to the Court room, you are to report to Hearing Officer Maggie Simar.*

WHY Temporary Restraining Order and other relief requested should not be made Protective Orders.

In accordance with the allegations and prayer for the issuance of this rule, a true and correct attested copy whereof accompanies this rule and is served herewith.

Witness the Honorable 16th Judicial District Court, at St. Martinville, St. Martin Parish, Louisiana, DECEMBER 4, 2019.

Becky P. Patin
Clerk, 16th Judicial Court
St. Martin Parish, Louisiana

Kristie Prejean

By:
Deputy Clerk of Court
Parish of St. Martin

[ORIGINAL]

12/04/2019   2:54PM (GMT-05:00)

DEC. 4. 2019 1:34PM   SMPCOC   NO. 551   P. 1.

BECKY P. PATIN
CLERK OF COURT
415 ST. MARTIN ST.
ST. MARTIN PARISH

PH. #(337) 394-2210 (Ext. 1224)

CIVIL DEPT. FAX #(337) 394-2240

TO: _Central Records- Baltimore County Sheriff Dept._

FROM: _Kristie Drejean_

OF PAGES INCLUDING

COVER SHEET __14__

As per your office this could be faxed for
service on L

Vffutt

12/04/2019 2:52PM (GMT-05:00)

DEC. 4. 2019 1:34PM   SMPCOC   NO 591   P. 1

```
------FOR LPOR USE ONLY-----
PNO# _____
Data Entered: _____
Initials: _____  Verified by: _____
```

LOUISIANA UNIFORM ABUSE PREVENTION ORDER

Order of Protection	Docket No. 88 81
☑ Temporary Restraining Order	Court: 16th HC Div.:
☐ Protective Order/Preliminary or Permanent Injunction	City/Parish State
☐ Modified Protective Order/Preliminary or Permanent Injunction	St Martin Louisiana
	Filed: _____ Clerk: _____

PETITIONER _____   **PETITIONER IDENTIFIERS**
First   Middle/Maiden   Last   Date of birth 1-11-51   Race BL   Sex: F ☑ Sex: M ☐

Protected person is: ☐ Petitioner ☐ other(s) List other(s) name & date of birth: _____

V.

DEFENDANT NAME AND ADDRESS:

DEFENDANT IDENTIFIERS				
SEX	RACE	DOB	HT	WT
		7/25/50		
EYES	HAIR	SOCIAL SECURITY #		
DRIVER'S LICENSE #		STATE	EXP DATE	

First   Middle   Last

Name of minor defendant's parent or guardian

Defendant's Alias: _____

No. & Street   9009 eri mike Court

City   Randalls Town MD 21133   State Zip Code

THE COURT HEREBY FINDS:
That it has jurisdiction over the parties and subject matter, and the defendant has been or will be provided with reasonable notice and opportunity to be heard. Additional findings of this court are as set forth on the following pages.

THE COURT HEREBY ORDERS:
That the above named defendant be restrained from committing further acts of abuse or threats of abuse, stalking or sexual assault. Additional terms of this order are as set forth on the following pages.

This order shall be effective through 11:59 PM on   12-18-19   (month/day/year)

This order shall be enforced, even without registration, by the courts of any state, the District of Columbia, any U.S. Territory, and may be enforced by Tribal Lands (18 U.S.C. Section 2265).

WARNINGS TO DEFENDANT:

Crossing state, territorial, or tribal boundaries to violate this order may result in federal imprisonment (18 U.S.C. Section 2262).

Federal law provides penalties for possessing, transporting, shipping, or receiving any firearm or ammunition (18 U.S.C. Section 922(g)(8)). See further notice on page 5 of this Order.

ONLY THE COURT CAN CHANGE THIS ORDER.

Page 1 of 6   LPOR 1
                                               v.11

12/04/2019   2:52PM (GMT-05:00)

DEC. 4. 2019 1:35PM   &MPCOC   NO. 251   P. 3

Docket No. __88.8__

LOUISIANA UNIFORM ABUSE PREVENTION ORDER

TEMPORARY RESTRAINING ORDER
Pursuant to:

☐ La. R.S. 46:2131 et seq. (Domestic Abuse)	☐ La. R.S. 46:2171 et seq. (Non-intimate stalking)	46:2171 and 46:2181 valid for relationships in Box C below ONLY
☐ La. R.S. 46:2151 (Dating Violence)	☐ La. R.S. 46:2181 et seq. (Non-intimate sexual assault)	

☐ La. Ch. C. Article 1564 et seq. (Children's Code Domestic Abuse)

PETITIONER _C_____ Protected person is: ☑ Petitioner ☐ other(s)

V.

DEFENDANT _____

The protected person(s) is related to the defendant as: (check all that apply)

A
☐ 1. current or former spouse
☑ 2. current or former intimate cohabitant
☑ 3. child, stepchild, or foster child
☐ 4. child of defendant's current or former intimate partner
☐ 5. protected person and defendant have a child(ren) in common

B
☐ 1. current or former dating partner
☐ 2. parent, stepparent, or foster parent
☐ 3. grandparent
☐ 4. grandchild

C Select ONLY if statute 46:2171 or 46:2181 is marked above
☐ 1. stranger/no relationship
☐ 2. acquaintance/co-worker/neighbor or other:

D
☑ FINDING: Domestic Abuse or Dating Violence
THE COURT FINDS THAT THE ALLEGATIONS PRESENTED CONSTITUTE AN IMMEDIATE AND PRESENT DANGER TO THE PHYSICAL SAFETY OF THE PROTECTED PERSON(S).

☐ FINDING: Stalking
THE COURT FINDS THAT THE ALLEGATIONS PRESENTED CONSTITUTE AN IMMEDIATE AND PRESENT DANGER OF STALKING.

☐ FINDING: Sexual Assault
THE COURT FINDS THAT THE ALLEGATIONS PRESENTED CONSTITUTE A SEXUAL ASSAULT.

THUS THE COURT ISSUES THE FOLLOWING ORDERS, WITHOUT A HEARING:

IT IS ORDERED THAT THE DEFENDANT BE SERVED WITH A COPY OF THIS ORDER.

DOMESTIC ABUSE, DATING VIOLENCE, STALKING OR SEXUAL ASSAULT
ONLY ORDERS CHECKED AND INITIALED BY A JUDGE SHALL APPLY

☑ 1. THE DEFENDANT IS ORDERED NOT TO abuse, harass, assault, stalk, follow, track, monitor, or threaten the protected person(s) in any manner whatsoever. This prohibition includes the use, attempted use, or threatened use of physical force that would reasonably be expected to cause bodily injury.

☑ 2. THE DEFENDANT IS ORDERED NOT TO contact the protected person(s) personally, through a third party, or via public posting, by any means, including written, telephone, or electronic (text, email, messaging, or social media) communication without the express written permission of this court.
Exceptions (if any):

☑ 3. THE DEFENDANT IS ORDERED NOT TO go within _200 ft_ (distance) of the protected person(s), without the express written permission of this court.
Exceptions (if any):

Page 2 of 6   LPOR 1 v.11

12/04/2019 2:52PM (GMT-05:00)

DEC. 4, 2019 1:35PM   SMPCOC   NO. 551   P. 4

Docket No.: 888

4. THE DEFENDANT IS ORDERED NOT TO go within one hundred (100) yards of the residence, apartment complex, or multiple family dwelling of the protected person(s),

273 Kansas Drive   Brentwoodcrossing, LA
No. & Street   State   Zip Code
                                                                           71862

☐5. THE DEFENDANT IS ORDERED TO STAY AWAY from protected person(s)' place of employment/school and not to interfere in any manner with such employment/school.

Employment/School	Address	City	State	Zip Code
Employment/School	Address	City	State	Zip Code

☐6. THE DEFENDANT IS ORDERED NOT TO damage any belongings or property of the protected person(s) and not to shut off any utilities, telephone service, or mail delivery to the protected person(s) or in any way interfere with the living conditions of the protected person(s).

☐7. THE COURT GRANTS THE PETITIONER or protected person(s) the use of the residence located at:

No. & Street   Apt. No.   City   State   Zip Code

to the exclusion of defendant by evicting defendant. The Court orders the defendant to surrender any keys to that residence to the petitioner.

_____ (Sheriff's office) is ordered to evict the defendant.

☐8. THE COURT GRANTS THE PETITIONER or protected person(s) the use and possession of the following property (including pets) and/or the return of protected person(s) property:

☐9. THE COURT ORDERS a representative of _____ (Sheriff's office) to accompany petitioner to obtain property listed in Order No. 8 above.

☐10. THE COURT PROHIBITS EITHER PARTY from transferring, encumbering, or otherwise disposing of property jointly owned or leased, except in the normal course of business or that which is necessary for the support of the petitioner and/or the minor child(ren).

☐11. THE COURT WILL ALLOW _____ to return to the residence at a date and time to be agreed upon by petitioner and law enforcement agency to recover his/her personal clothing and necessities, provided that s/he is accompanied by a law enforcement officer to ensure the protection and safety of the parties. NO FORCED ENTRY ALLOWED.

☐12. THE COURT ORDERS a representative of _____ (Sheriff's office) to accompany _____ to the residence located at _____ to recover her/his personal clothing and necessities.

DOMESTIC ABUSE, DATING VIOLENCE ONLY
ONLY ORDERS CHECKED AND INITIALED BY A JUDGE SHALL APPLY

☐13. THE COURT GRANTS TEMPORARY CUSTODY of the following child(ren) or alleged incompetent to the petitioner: (name, date of birth, and relationship to petitioner)

Page 3 of 6   LPOR 1
                                               v.11

12/04/2019 2:52PM (GMT-05:00)

Docket No.: _____ 888. _____

___ ☐14.   THE COURT ORDERS a representative of _____ (Sheriff's office)
to accompany petitioner to where the minor child(ren) or alleged incompetent mentioned in paragraph above
is/are currently, and to effect petitioner obtaining physical custody of said child(ren) or alleged incompetent.

___ ☐15.   THE DEFENDANT IS ORDERED NOT TO interfere with the physical custody of the minor child(ren) or alleged
incompetent.

___ ☐16.   THE DEFENDANT IS ORDERED TO show cause on the below hearing date why s/he should not be evicted
from the solely owned residence or household and the petitioner granted possession.

___ ☐17.   THE DEFENDANT IS ORDERED TO show cause on the below hearing date why s/he should not be ordered to
pay child support and/or spousal support (alimony) pursuant to Louisiana Law. The court further orders the
defendant to produce at the hearing: most recent income tax returns AND pay stubs or an employer
statement documenting gross income to date for the CURRENT year. If the defendant is self-employed,
income and expense statements shall be produced.

| STALKING, SEXUAL ASSAULT ONLY |
| ONLY ORDERS CHECKED AND INITIALED BY A JUDGE SHALL APPLY |

___ ☐18.   THE DEFENDANT IS ORDERED NOT TO contact family members or acquaintances of the protected
person(s).

| DOMESTIC ABUSE, DATING VIOLENCE, STALKING OR SEXUAL ASSAULT |
| ONLY ORDERS CHECKED AND INITIALED BY A JUDGE SHALL APPLY |

___ ☐19.   THE DEFENDANT IS ORDERED TO show cause on the below hearing date why s/he should not be ordered to
pay the following:

☐ all court costs   ☐ attorney fees

☐ evaluation fees   ☐ expert witness fees

☐ cost of medical and/or psychological care for the petitioner, the minor child(ren), alleged incompetent, and/or
other protected person(s) necessitated by the domestic abuse, dating violence, stalking or sexual assault.

___ ☐20.   THE DEFENDANT IS ORDERED TO show cause on the below hearing date why s/he should not be ordered to
seek professional counseling, complete a court-monitored domestic abuse intervention program, submit to a
medical evaluation and/or submit to a mental health evaluation.

___ ☐21.   Other:

DEC. 4. 2019 1:36PM   SMPCOC .   NO. 551   P. 6

Docket No.: 888

IT IS FURTHER ORDERED THAT DEFENDANT show cause on ___12-18-19___ (month/day/year)
at ___ o'clock ___ in Courtroom No. ___ of the ___16th JDC___ Court, located at
in ___St Martinville___ La., why the
above Temporary Restraining Order and other relief requested should not be made Protective Orders.

Date of Order	Time of Order	Order effective through 11:59 PM on	SIGNATURE OF JUDGE
12-4-19 month/day/year	9:50 ☑AM ☐PM	12-18-19 month/day/year	☐ Order issued ex parte ☑ Order issued after notice and opportunity for hearing given to defendant PRINT OR STAMP JUDGE'S NAME

NOTICE: C.C.P. Article 3603.1 - Any person against whom such an order is issued shall be entitled to a court-appointed attorney if the applicant has likewise been afforded a court-appointed attorney.

NOTICE TO DEFENDANT - VIOLATION OF ORDER:

PURSUANT TO LA. R.S. 14:79, A PERSON WHO VIOLATES THIS ORDER MAY BE ARRESTED, JAILED, AND PROSECUTED.

PURSUANT TO LA. R.S. 13:4611 AND LA. CH. C. ARTICLE 1571, A PERSON WHO VIOLATES THIS ORDER MAY BE PUNISHED FOR CONTEMPT OF COURT BY A FINE OF NOT MORE THAN $1,000 OR BY CONFINEMENT IN JAIL FOR AS LONG AS 6 MONTHS, OR BOTH, AND MAY BE FURTHER PUNISHED UNDER CRIMINAL LAWS OF THE STATE OF LOUISIANA. THIS ORDER SHALL BE ENFORCED BY ALL LAW ENFORCEMENT OFFICERS AND COURTS OF THE STATE OF LOUISIANA.

NOTICE TO DEFENDANT – FIREARMS POSSESSION (Domestic abuse or dating violence ONLY):

AS A RESULT OF THIS ORDER, IT MAY BE UNLAWFUL FOR YOU TO POSSESS, RECEIVE, SHIP, TRANSPORT OR PURCHASE A FIREARM, INCLUDING A RIFLE, PISTOL, OR REVOLVER, OR AMMUNITION, FOR THE DURATION OF THIS ORDER PURSUANT TO STATE AND/OR FEDERAL LAWS. See below.

If you have any questions whether these laws make it illegal for you to possess or purchase a firearm or ammunition, consult an attorney.

Federal law, 18 U.S.C. 922 (g)(8) prohibits a defendant from purchasing, possessing, shipping, transporting, or receiving firearms or ammunition* for the duration of this order if the following conditions apply:
- Protected person(s) relationship to defendant is checked in Box A on page 2 of this order AND
- Notice and opportunity for a hearing provided AND
- EITHER Judicial finding of credible threat, OR Certain behaviors are prohibited (Item 1 on page 2 of this order is initialed)

*Under 18 U.S.C. 921 the term "firearm" means (A) any weapon (including a starter gun) which will or is designed to or may readily be converted to expel a projectile by the action of an explosive; (B) the frame or receiver of any such weapon; (C) any firearm muffler or firearm silencer; or (D) any destructive device. Such term does not include an antique firearm. The term "ammunition" means ammunition or cartridge cases, primers, bullets, or propellant powder designed for use in any firearm.

RECEIVED AND FILED

Docket No.: *888*

NOTICE TO DEFENDANT – FIREARM TRANSFER AND SUSPENSION OF CONCEALED HANDGUN PERMIT
(Domestic abuse or dating violence ONLY)

IF A PROTECTIVE ORDER IS ISSUED AGAINST YOU, YOU MAY BE REQUIRED TO TRANSFER ANY AND ALL FIREARMS OWNED OR POSSESSED BY YOU AND SURRENDER YOUR CONCEALED HANDGUN PERMIT. AS YOU MAY ALSO BE REQUIRED TO STATE UNDER OATH THE NUMBER OF FIREARMS YOU POSSESS, THE SERIAL NUMBER AND LOCATION OF EACH AND COMPLETE A FIREARMS INFORMATION FORM VERIFYING SUCH, BRING THIS INFORMATION TO THE HEARING.

Louisiana law, C.Cr.P. Art. 1000 requires the transfer of all firearms owned or possessed and the suspension of a concealed handgun permit:
- When a person is subject to a permanent injunction or a protective order pursuant to a court-approved consent agreement or pursuant to the provisions of R.S. 9:361 et seq., R.S. 9:372, R.S. 46:2136, 2151, or 2173, Children's Code Article 1570, Code of Civil Procedure Article 3607.1, or C.Cr.P. Articles 30, 320, or 871.1.

OR
- When a person is subject to a Uniform Abuse Prevention Order that includes terms prohibiting possession of a firearm or carrying a concealed weapon.

FULL FAITH AND CREDIT pursuant to 18 U.S.C. § 2265

The issuing court certifies that it has jurisdiction over the parties and the subject matter under the laws of the State of Louisiana; that the defendant was given reasonable notice and an opportunity to be heard sufficient to protect the defendant's right to due process before this order was issued; or if the order was issued ex parte, the court ordered that the defendant be given reasonable notice and an opportunity to be heard within the time required by the laws of the State of Louisiana, and in any event, within a reasonable time after the order was issued, sufficient to protect the defendant's due process rights.

THIS ORDER SHALL BE PRESUMED VALID AND ENFORCEABLE IN ALL 50 STATES, THE DISTRICT OF COLUMBIA, TRIBAL LANDS, U.S. TERRITORIES, AND COMMONWEALTHS.

SIGNATURE OF JUDGE

PRINT OR STAMP JUDGE'S NAME

NOTICE TO LAW ENFORCEMENT

Pursuant to La. R.S. 14:79, the crime of violation of protective orders – you shall use every reasonable means, including but not limited to immediate arrest of the violator, to enforce this order. Further, you shall at a minimum issue a summons to the person in violation.

Pursuant to La. R.S. 46:2140(A), if you have reason to believe that a family or household member or dating partner has been abused AND the abusing party is in violation of this order, you SHALL immediately arrest the abusing party.

If the expiration date of this order falls on or within five (5) days of the conclusion of a declared state of emergency, this order/injunction shall be enforced throughout that time period.

☐ DEFENDANT WAS SERVED AT CLOSE OF HEARING.
Date _____ Clerk _____

☐ FAXED or ELECTRONICALLY TRANSMITTED TO LOUISIANA PROTECTIVE ORDER REGISTRY
Date _____ Clerk _____

Copies to: 1) Court file 2) Petitioner/protected person(s) 3) Defendant 4) Chief Law Enforcement Agency in the district where the protected person(s) resides 5) Louisiana Protective Order Registry.

A TRUE COPY

ATTEST _____
DEPUTY CLERK OF COURT

Page 6 of 6

DEC 04 2019   LPOR 1
DEPUTY CLERK OF COURT
12/04/2019 2:52PM (GMT-05:00)

NOV. 20. 2019 9:30AM   SMPCOC   NO. 480   P. 10

E'	16th JDC _____ COURT
PETITIONER	PARISH/CITY OF ____ ST MARTIN
V.	STATE OF LOUISIANA
L	DIVISION: _____ NUMBER: _____
DEFENDANT	FILED: _____ CLERK: _____

Parent/Guardian name if defendant is a minor

PETITION FOR PROTECTION FROM ABUSE
Pursuant to La. R.S. 46:2131 et seq. or La. R.S. 46:2151

This petition is: ☒ Initial Petition ☐ Supplemental and Amending Petition

The petition of ____ E _____, born __01/11/51__
                        your name   month/day/year

a resident of the State of Louisiana, respectfully represents:

Paragraph 1

Petitioner files this petition on behalf of:

a. __Y__ Petitioner, and/or

b. ____ Minor child(ren) as follows: (Name, Date of Birth, Relationship to Petitioner)

c. ____ Alleged incompetent as follows: (Name, Date of Birth, Relationship to Petitioner)

Paragraph 2

a. ____ Petitioner requests that his/her address, or that of the minor child(ren) or alleged incompetent, remain
confidential to the court and files the address pursuant to La. R.S. 46:2134(B).
(Ask clerk of court for the Confidential Address Form.)

OR

b. __X__ Petitioner's current address:

__273 Kansas Drive__
No. & Street   Apt. No.

__Brentwood Crossing, LA__   __71862__
City   State   Zip Code

c. ____ The minor child's or alleged incompetent's current address:

_____
No. & Street   Apt. No.

_____
City   State   Zip Code

Paragraph 3

L _____, defendant, resides in ___ BALTIMORE ___ Parish at
  Abuser's Name

__9069 ERIMIKE COURT RANDALLS TOWN__   __MD 21133__
No. & Street   Apt. No.   City   State   Zip Code

                                                            LPOR B
                                                            r.11
Page 1 of 7

Paragraph 4

This Court is the proper venue for this action because:

____ The marital domicile is located in _____, Parish.

____ The household is located in _____, Parish.

____ The defendant resides or is domiciled in _____, Parish.

_X_ The abuse occurred in __ST MARTIN__ Parish.

_X_ The protected person(s) resides or is domiciled in __ST MARTIN__ Parish.
(Do not fill this out if address is to remain confidential.)

Paragraph 5

The protected person(s) is related to the defendant as: (check all that apply)

____ Current or former spouse

_X_ Current or former intimate cohabitant

____ Child, stepchild, or foster child

____ Child of defendant's current or former intimate partner

____ Current or former dating partner

____ Parent, stepparent, or foster parent

____ Grandparent

____ Grandchild

Paragraph 6

____ A suit for divorce between the parties is not pending.

____ A suit for divorce between the parties is pending (fill out page 7 of this form, "Addendum")
NOTE: If you were NOT the petitioner in the divorce suit, use form LPOR B-R entitled "Petition for Protection From Abuse, (Filed by the Defendant in the Pending Action as Petitioner-in-reconvention)" instead of this one.

____ There is a suit for custody pending involving children named in this petition (fill out page 7 of this form, "Addendum").

____ There is a custody order in effect involving children named in this petition (fill out page 7 of this form, "Addendum", or attach a copy of the order if available).

Paragraph 7

____ The protected person(s) and defendant have child(ren) in common.

Paragraph 8

a. Defendant abused protected person(s) in the following manner:

____ Slapped protected person(s)

____ Punched protected person(s)

____ Choked protected person(s)

____ Shoved protected person(s)

____ Kicked protected person(s)

____ Stalked protected person(s)

____ Threatened protected person(s) with bodily harm

____ Threatened protected person(s)' life

____ Threatened protected person(s) with a weapon

____ Sexually abused protected person(s)

____ Abused petitioner's child(ren) or alleged incompetent

_M_ Other: __ENTAL AND VERBAL__

b. The facts and circumstances of this abuse are as follows:

The most recent incident of abuse which caused petitioner to file this petition happened on or about

__11__ (month/day/year), at which time the defendant did:

I am filing a protective order against L_____, because I am afraid of him. I left my home for four months. because I was afraid and intimidated. He sent ugly text messages to me while I was away.
When I was around him he would be very aggressive

LPOR B
v.11

Page 2 of 7

NOV. 20 2019 9:31AM DMPCOC   NO. 480   P. 12

verbally
...When I finally found out he was gone he had ransacked
the house selling all valuables, leaving the house in unlivable
conditions.
Although I am back in my home I have a fear
living with me because of fear of his return
and what he would do.

Past Incidents: _____

Paragraph 9

Because of the immediate and present danger of abuse, petitioner requests that an *ex parte* Temporary Restraining Order
be issued immediately without bond:

X a. prohibiting defendant from abusing, harassing, assaulting, stalking, following, tracking, monitoring, or threatening
the protected person(s) in any manner whatsoever. This prohibition includes the use, attempted use, or
threatened use of physical force that would reasonably be expected to cause bodily injury.

X b. prohibiting the defendant from contacting the protected person(s) personally, through a third party, or via public
posting, by any means, including written, telephone, or electronic (text, email, messaging, or social media)
communication without the express written permission of this court.

X c. prohibiting defendant from going within one hundred (100) yards of the residence, apartment complex, or
multiple family dwelling of the protected person(s) located at:

2731 KANSAS DRIVE   BRENTWOOD CROSSING, LA 71862
No. & Street   Apt. No.   City   State   Zip Code

___ d. ordering the defendant to stay away from the protected person(s)' place of employment/school and not to
interfere in any manner with such employment/school located at:

Employment/School	Address	City	State	Zip Code
Employment/School	Address	City	State	Zip Code

___ e. ordering the defendant not to damage any belongings of the protected person(s), to not shut off any utilities,
telephone service, or mail delivery to the protected person(s), or in any way interfere with the living conditions of
the protected person(s).

Page 3 of 7

LFOR B
v.11

11/20/2019 10:45AM (GMT-05:00)

_____ f.   granting the petitioner or protected person(s) the use of the residence located at

| No. & Street   Apt No | City | State | Zip Code |

to the exclusion of defendant by evicting defendant and ordering the defendant to surrender any keys to that residence to the petitioner, and ordering _____ (Sheriff's office) to evict the defendant.
Said residence is:
_____ jointly owned by defendant and petitioner or protected person(s).
_____ jointly leased by defendant and petitioner or protected person(s)
_____ solely leased by defendant who has a duty to support petitioner or protected person(s)
(NOTE: If solely owned by defendant AND petitioner is awarded custody of child(ren) of the parties, check appropriate item in Paragraph 10.
_____ solely owned or leased by petitioner or protected person(s).

Presently occupied by _____

__X__ g.   granting petitioner or protected person(s) possession of the following property (including pets) solely owned or leased by petitioner or protected person(s) (state location of each item by street address and who is presently in possession).

2002 FORD F250 TRUCK, 4 DOOR, NAVY BLUE AND GRAY AND ALL KEYS TO 2002 FORD F250 TRUCK, 4 DOOR, NAVY BLUE AND GRAY.

granting petitioner or protected person(s) the exclusive use and possession of the following property (including pets) jointly owned or leased by petitioner or protected person(s) (state location of each item by street address and who is presently in possession).

_____
_____
_____
_____
_____

for the following reasons: _____
_____

And ordering __ST MARTIN PARSIH_____ (Sheriff's office) to accompany petitioner to where the above listed property is located to allow petitioner to take possession of the property.

_____ h.   prohibiting either party from transferring, encumbering, or otherwise disposing of property jointly owned or leased, except in the normal course of business or necessary for the support of the petitioner and/or the minor child(ren) or alleged incompetent.

_____ i.   allowing _____ to return to the residence at a date and time to be agreed upon by petitioner and law enforcement agency, to recover his/her personal clothing and necessities, only if s/he is accompanied by a law enforcement officer to ensure the protection and safety of the parties. NO FORCED ENTRY ALLOWED.

_____ j.   ordering a representative of _____ (Sheriff's office) to accompany _____ to the family residence to recover her/his personal clothing and necessities.

DEC. 4. 2019 1:39PM   SMPCOC   NO. 551   P. 17

k.   awarding the temporary custody of the minor child(ren) or alleged incompetent,

_____

to petitioner; the minor child(ren) or alleged incompetent is currently in the physical custody of _____

_____

l.   ordering a representative of _____ (Sheriff's office) to accompany petitioner to
where the minor child(ren) or alleged incompetent mentioned above is/are currently and to effect petitioner
obtaining physical custody of said child(ren) or alleged incompetent.

m.   prohibiting defendant from interfering with the custody of the minor child(ren) or alleged incompetent.

Paragraph 10

Petitioner desires that a rule issue herein ordering defendant to show cause why the orders requested in Paragraph 9 should
not be made into protective orders, and why defendant should not also be ordered:

____   to pay petitioner a reasonable amount of child support in accordance with Louisiana Law.
____   to pay petitioner a reasonable amount of spousal support (alimony).
_X_   to seek professional counseling or complete a court-monitored domestic abuse intervention program.
____   to submit to a medical evaluation and/or a mental health evaluation
_X_   to pay costs of court in this matter.
_X_   to pay attorney fees.
_X_   to pay evaluation fees.
_X_   to pay expert witness fees.
_X_   to pay cost of medical and/or psychological care for the petitioner, minor child(ren), and/or alleged incompetent,
necessitated by the domestic abuse or dating violence.
____   to vacate the residence or household, thereby granting petitioner possession thereof.
_X_   other: . THE COURT ORDERS the defendant to show cause why he should not enroll in and successfully complete the
Batterer's Intervention Program.

PRAYER

WHEREFORE, petitioner prays that service and citation issue herein, and that: *(check all that apply)*

_X_   ex parte orders requested in Paragraph 9 be granted.
_X_   a rule issue to show cause why protective orders as requested in Paragraph 10 should not be granted.
_X_   defendant be cast with costs.
_X_   defendant be advised of penalties for violating Abuse Prevention Orders.
_X_   all other equitable relief as the court deems proper and necessary.

Respectfully submitted by,

_____
PETITIONER, IN PROPER PERSON

PLEASE SERVE DEFENDANT: _____ L.

personally at his/her home or place of employment at the following address:

9009 ERIMIKE COURT

RANDALLS TOWN   MD 21133

OR

A TRUE COPY

ATTEST _____   Page 5 of 7   LPOR B
DEPUTY CLERK OF COURT   v.11

12/04/2019 2:52PM (GMT-05:00)

INFORMATION FOR SERVICE OF PROCESS
PROVIDED BY PETITIONER/PETITIONER-IN-RECONVENTION

PLEASE PROVIDE AS MUCH INFORMATION AS POSSIBLE. THIS INFORMATION WILL HELP LAW ENFORCEMENT LOCATE DEFENDANT (or DEFENDANT-IN-RECONVENTION) TO SERVE A COPY OF THE PETITION AND TEMPORARY RESTRAINING ORDER (IF ISSUED). THE FOLLOWING INFORMATION IS NEEDED ON THE DEFENDANT (or DEFENDANT-IN-RECONVENTION).

NAME __L__

Name of minor defendant's (or defendant-in-reconvention's) parent or guardian: ____

OTHER NAMES USED ____

DATE OF BIRTH __07/25/50__ (month/day/year)   SOCIAL SECURITY # ____

DRIVERS LICENSE # ____   STATE ____   EXP. DATE ____

HOME ADDRESS __9009 ERIMIKE COURT__
No. & Street   Apt. No.
__RANDALLS TOWN   MD__   TEL. NO. ____
City   State   Zip Code

WORK ADDRESS ____
Name of employer
No. & Street   Apt. No.
                                          DEPARTMENT ____
City   State   Zip Code
TEL NO. ____   WORK DAYS/HOURS ____

PHYSICAL DESCRIPTION: ☒ MALE ☐ FEMALE   RACE __BL__

EYE COLOR __BR__   HAIR COLOR __BR__   HEIGHT __6'2"__   WEIGHT __180__

DISTINGUISHING FEATURES (scars, tattoos, facial hair, etc.) ____

MOTOR VEHICLE:
LICENSE PLATE # ____   YEAR __02__   MAKE __FORD F250__   COLOR __BLUE/G__

DOES THE DEFENDANT (or DEFENDANT-IN-RECONVENTION):

HAVE A HISTORY OF VIOLENCE TOWARDS OTHERS (OTHER THAN VICTIM)?   ☐ YES ☒ NO

HAVE A HISTORY OF USING/ABUSING DRUGS OR ALCOHOL?   ☐ YES ☒ NO

CARRY A WEAPON?   ☐ YES ☒ NO

IF YES, WHAT KIND OF WEAPON? ____

OTHER PLACES AND TIMES S/HE MAY BE FOUND: (Friends, relatives, bars, hangouts) ____

☐ DEFENDANT/DEFENDANT-IN-RECONVENTION CURRENTLY INCARCERATED
Where: ____
☐ DEFENDANT/DEFENDANT-IN-RECONVENTION CURRENTLY ON PROBATION/PAROLE
Probation or parole officer/department: ____

ANY OTHER INFORMATION WHICH MAY BE HELPFUL: ____

____
Date   Petitioner's / Petitioner-in-Reconvention's Signature

LPOR H
v.11

12/04/2019 2:52PM (GMT-05:00)

APPENDIX C

Temporary Restraining Order: March 11, 2020 to June 18, 2021

DEC. 18. 2019 2:15PM SMPCOC NO. 641 P. 3

REVIEW HEARING

B

Versus

L

Case: 0882
Division:
16ᵗʰ Judicial District Court
St. Martin Parish
St. Martinville, Louisiana

TO:
L
9009 ERIMIKE COURT
RANDALLS TOWN, MD 21133

You are hereby summoned to appear in the 16ᵗʰ Judicial District Court for the Parish of St. Martin at 415 South Main Street, St. Martinville, Louisiana 70582 at 9:00 A.M. on March 11, 2020 for a Review Hearing for Court Cost in the above captioned case before the Honorable SUZANNE DEMAHY.

Failure to appear at the specified time and place will result in penalty of the Law

In evidence whereof, witness my hand officially, at St. Martinville, St. Martin Parish, this day of DECEMBER 18, 2019.

BECKY P. PATIN
Clerk of the 16ᵗʰ Judicial District Court for
St. Martin Parish, Louisiana

BY: Jordan Cruize

Deputy Clerk of Court

SEE ATTACHED PROTECTIVE ORDER

PROPER ATTIRE REQUIRED: NO SHORTS, MUSCLE SHIRTS, OR SANDALS, ETC.
NO HANDBAGS, ELECTRONIC DEVICES, OR TOBACCO ALLOWED IN THE COURTHOUSE

SHERIFF'S SERVICE LOG

DATE SERVICE ATTEMPTED: _____ TIME SERVICE ATTEMPTED: _____ AM/PM
DATE SERVICE ATTEMPTED: _____ TIME SERVICE ATTEMPTED: _____ AM/PM
DATE SERVED: _____ TIME SERVED: _____

TYPE SERVICE:
_PERSONAL _DOMICILIARY_____
ADDRESS OF ATTEMPTED SERVICE/EXECUTION: _____

REASON FOR NON-SERVICE:
_MOVED, (NEW ADDRESS) _____
_POST OFFICE HAS NO ADDRESS   _NOT KNOWN AT THIS ADDRESS
_MOVED, ADDRESS UNKNOWN   _DISTRICT ATTORNEY RECALLED
_UNABLE TO LOCATE   _ADDRESS NOT IN OUR PARISH
_RECEIVED TOO LATE FOR SERVICE   _IN THE ARMED FORCES
_NOT SERVED IN TIME FOR COURT   _HOSPITALIZED/DECEASED
_DATE/PAST COURT DATE   _HOLD-REQUEST OF_____
_COMMENTS: _____

_____
DEPUTY SHERIFF

Original
12/18/2019 3:31PM (GMT-05:00)

DEC. 18 2019 2:16PM   SMPCOC   NO 641   P. 4

----FOR LPOR USE ONLY----
PNO#
Date Entered:
Initials:_____ Verified by:_____

LOUISIANA UNIFORM ABUSE PREVENTION ORDER

Order of Protection	Docket No. 888
☐ Temporary Restraining Order	Court 16th Judicial District Div:
☒ Protective Order/Preliminary or Permanent Injunction	City/Parish St. Martin/St. Martinville State Louisiana
☐ Modified Protective Order/Preliminary or Permanent Injunction	Filed:_____ Clerk:_____

PETITIONER	PETITIONER IDENTIFIERS
E'	01/11/51 · B · X ·

First   Middle/Maiden   Last   Date of birth   Race   Sex: F   Sex: M
Protected person is: ☐ Petitioner ☐ other(s)   List other(s) name & date of birth:

V.

DEFENDANT NAME AND ADDRESS	DEFENDANT IDENTIFIERS

			SEX	RACE	DOB	HT	WT
L'			M	B	07/25/50	6'2"	180

First   Middle   Last

EYES	HAIR	SOCIAL SECURITY #
Br	Br	

Name of minor defendant's parent or guardian

Defendant's Alias:_____

9009 Brimike Court

No. & Street

DRIVER'S LICENSE #	STATE	EXP DATE

Apt No.   Randalls Town   MD 2113
City   State   Zip Code

THE COURT HEREBY FINDS:
That it has jurisdiction over the parties and subject matter, and the defendant has been or will be provided with reasonable notice and opportunity to be heard. Additional findings of this court are as set forth on the following pages.

THE COURT HEREBY ORDERS:
That the above named defendant be restrained from committing further acts of abuse or threats of abuse, stalking or sexual assault. Additional terms of this order are as set forth on the following pages.

This order shall be effective through 11:59 PM on   6-18-21   (month/day/year)

NOTE: Some provisions of this order MAY NOT EXPIRE. See paragraphs 1-5.

This order shall be enforced, even without registration, by the courts of any state, the District of Columbia, any U.S. Territory, and may be enforced by Tribal Lands (18 U.S.C. Section 2265).

WARNINGS TO DEFENDANT:

Crossing state, territorial, or tribal boundaries to violate this order may result in federal imprisonment (18 U.S.C. Section 2262).

Federal law provides penalties for possessing, transporting, shipping, or receiving any firearm or ammunition (18 U.S.C. Section 922(g)(8)). See further notice on pages 6-7 of this Order.

ONLY THE COURT CAN CHANGE THIS ORDER.

Page 1 of 8   LPOR 3
                                               v.11

12/18/2019   3:31PM (GMT-05:00)

DEC 18, 2019 2:16PM   SMPCOC   NO 641   P. 5

Docket No. 88£

LOUISIANA UNIFORM ABUSE PREVENTION ORDER

PROTECTIVE ORDER
Pursuant to:

☒ La. R.S. 46:2131 et seq. (Domestic Abuse)	☐ La. R.S. 46:2171 et seq. (Non-intimate stalking)	46:2171 and 46:2181 valid for relationships in Box C below ONLY
☐ La. R.S. 46:2151 (Dating Violence)	☐ La. R.S. 46:2181 et seq. (Non-intimate sexual assault)	
	☐ La. Ch. C. Article 1564 et seq. (Children's Code Domestic Abuse)	

☐ Court Approved Consent Agreement

PETITIONER E   Protected person is: ☐ Petitioner ☐ other(s)

V.

DEFENDANT L

The protected person(s) is related to the defendant as: *(check all that apply)*

A
☐ 1. current or former spouse
☒ 2. current or former intimate cohabitant
☐ 3. child, stepchild, or foster child
☐ 4. child of defendant's current or former intimate partner
☐ 5. protected person and defendant have a child(ren) in common

B
☐ 1. current or former dating partner
☐ 2. parent, stepparent, or foster parent
☐ 3. grandparent
☐ 4. grandchild

C
Select ONLY if statute 46:2171 or 46:2181 is marked above
☐ 1. stranger/no relationship
☐ 2. acquaintance/co-worker/neighbor or other:

D THIS ORDER WAS ISSUED AFTER ACTUAL NOTICE AND AN OPPORTUNITY TO PARTICIPATE IN A HEARING WAS PROVIDED TO THE DEFENDANT. THUS THE COURT ISSUES THE FOLLOWING ORDERS:

ONLY ORDERS CHECKED AND INITIALED BY A JUDGE SHALL APPLY

E ☐ THE COURT FINDS THAT THE DEFENDANT REPRESENTS A CREDIBLE THREAT TO THE PHYSICAL SAFETY OF A FAMILY MEMBER, HOUSEHOLD MEMBER, OR DATING PARTNER. THEREFORE, PURSUANT TO R.S. 46:2136.3, THE DEFENDANT IS PROHIBITED FROM POSSESSING A FIREARM FOR THE DURATION OF THIS ORDER.

F ☐ THE DEFENDANT IS HEREBY ORDERED TO TRANSFER TO THE SHERIFF ANY AND ALL FIREARMS OWNED OR POSSESSED WITHIN FORTY-EIGHT (48) HOURS, EXCLUSIVE OF LEGAL HOLIDAYS; ANY CONCEALED HANDGUN PERMIT IS HEREBY SUSPENDED, PURSUANT TO LA. C.CR.P. ARTICLE 1000 ET SEQ. See further notice on page 7 of this Order.

IT IS ORDERED THAT THE DEFENDANT BE SERVED WITH A COPY OF THIS ORDER.

DOMESTIC ABUSE, DATING VIOLENCE, STALKING OR SEXUAL ASSAULT
ONLY ORDERS CHECKED AND INITIALED BY A JUDGE SHALL APPLY

1. THE DEFENDANT IS ORDERED NOT TO abuse, harass, assault, stalk, follow, track, monitor, or threaten the protected person(s) in any manner whatsoever. This prohibition includes the use, attempted use, or threatened use of physical force that would reasonably be expected to cause bodily injury.

☐ Does not expire

2. THE DEFENDANT IS ORDERED NOT TO contact the protected person(s) personally, through a third party, or via public posting, by any means, including written, telephone, or electronic (text, email, messaging, or social media) communication without the express written permission of this court.
Exceptions (if any):

☐ Does not expire

Page 2 of 8   LPOR 3
v.11

12/18/2019 3:31PM (GMT-05:00)

DEC 18. 2019 2:17PM   SMPCOC   NO. 641   P. 6

Docket No. ___888___

☒ 3. THE DEFENDANT IS ORDERED NOT TO go within ___100 yards___ _____ (distance) of the protected
       person(s), without the express written permission of this court.
       Exceptions (if any): _____
       _____

       ☐ Does not expire

☒ 4. THE DEFENDANT IS ORDERED NOT TO go within one hundred (100) yards of the residence, apartment
       complex, or multiple family dwelling of the protected person(s).

       2730 Main Highway, Breaux Bridge, LA 70517
       No. & Street   Apt. No.   City   State   Zip Code
       ☐ Does not expire

___ ☐ 5. THE DEFENDANT IS ORDERED TO STAY AWAY from protected person(s)' place of employment/school and
       not to interfere in any manner with such employment/school.

       Employment/School   Address   City   State   Zip Code

       Employment/School   Address   City   State   Zip Code
       ☐ Does not expire

___ ☐ 6. THE DEFENDANT IS ORDERED NOT TO damage any belongings or property of the protected person(s) and
       not to shut off any utilities, telephone service, or mail delivery to the protected person(s) or in any way interfere
       with the living conditions of the protected person(s).

___ ☐ 7. THE COURT GRANTS THE PETITIONER or protected person(s) the use of the residence located at:

       No. & Street   Apt. No.   City   State   Zip Code

       to the exclusion of defendant by evicting defendant. The Court orders the defendant to surrender any keys to
       that residence to the petitioner.

       _____ (Sheriff's office) is ordered to evict the defendant.

___ ☐ 8. THE COURT GRANTS THE PETITIONER or protected person(s) the use and possession of the following
       property (including pets) and/or the return of protected person(s) property:

       _____
       _____
       _____
       _____
       _____

___ ☐ 9. THE COURT ORDERS a representative of _____ (Sheriff's office)
       to accompany petitioner to obtain property listed in Order No. 8 above.

___ ☐ 10. THE COURT PROHIBITS EITHER PARTY from transferring, encumbering, or otherwise disposing of property
       jointly owned or leased, except in the normal course of business or that which is necessary for the support of
       the petitioner and/or the minor child(ren).

___ ☐ 11. THE COURT WILL ALLOW _____ to return to the residence at a date and
       time to be agreed upon by petitioner and law enforcement agency to recover his/her personal clothing and
       necessities, provided that s/he is accompanied by a law enforcement officer to ensure the protection and safety
       of the parties. NO FORCED ENTRY ALLOWED.

___ ☐ 12. THE COURT ORDERS a representative of _____ (Sheriff's office)
       to accompany _____ to the residence located
       at _____ to recover her/his personal clothing and necessities.

                          Page 3 of 8   LPOR 3
                                                               v.11

                          12/18/2019 3:31PM (GMT-05:00)

Docket No. __888__

13. THE DEFENDANT IS ORDERED TO pay:
☐ all court costs, payable to _St. Martin Parish Clerk of Court_

_____ no later than __03/11/20__ _(date)_

☐ attorney fees, payable to _____
in amt. of $_____ no later than __/ /__ _(date)_

☐ evaluation fees, payable to _____
in amt. of $_____ no later than __/ /__ _(date)_

☐ expert witness fees, payable to _____
in amt. of $_____ no later than __/ /__ _(date)_

☐ cost of medical and/or psychological care for the petitioner, the minor child(ren), and/or alleged
incompetent, necessitated by the domestic abuse, dating violence, stalking or sexual assault: _____

14. THE DEFENDANT IS ORDERED TO seek professional counseling and/or complete a court-monitored domestic
abuse intervention program.

☐ 15. THE DEFENDANT IS ORDERED TO submit to a:
☐ medical evaluation, no later than __/ /__ _(date)_

AND/OR

☐ mental health evaluation, no later than __/ /__ _(date)_

DOMESTIC ABUSE, DATING VIOLENCE ONLY
ONLY ORDERS CHECKED AND INITIALED BY A JUDGE SHALL APPLY

☐ 16. THE COURT GRANTS TEMPORARY CUSTODY of the following child(ren) or alleged incompetent to the
petitioner: _(name, date of birth, and relationship to petitioner)_

☐ 17. THE COURT ORDERS a representative of _____ (Sheriff's office)
to accompany petitioner to where the minor child(ren) or alleged incompetent mentioned in paragraph above
is/are currently, and to effect petitioner obtaining physical custody of said child(ren) or alleged incompetent.

☐ 18. THE COURT GRANTS THE DEFENDANT
☐ unsupervised ☐ supervised visitation with minor child(ren) or alleged incompetent as follows:

The supervising person shall be: _____

(NOTICE: La. R.S. 9:362(6) - The supervising person shall not be any relative, friend, therapist, or associate of
the parent perpetrating family violence.)

DEC. 18. 2019 2:18PM   SMPCOC   NO. 641   P. 8

Docket No. 888 _____

Supervised visitation between the defendant and the child(ren) shall occur in the immediate presence of the supervising person under conditions which shall prevent any physical abuse, threat, intimidation, abduction, or humiliation of either the petitioner or the child(ren).

Exchange of child(ren) or alleged incompetent is to be effected as follows:

_____
_____
_____
_____

____ ☐19. THE DEFENDANT IS PROHIBITED FROM removing the child(ren) from the jurisdiction of the court except for good cause shown and with the prior approval of the court.

____ ☐20. THE DEFENDANT IS ORDERED NOT TO interfere with the physical custody of the minor child(ren) or alleged incompetent.

____ ☐21. THE DEFENDANT IS ORDERED TO pay support for:
☐the petitioner at the rate of $_____ per ☐ week ☐ month ☐other: _____
beginning _____ (date)
_____
_____

☐the child(ren) at the rate of $_____ per ☐ week ☐ month ☐other: _____
beginning _____ (date), ☐ made payable directly to the petitioner
_____
_____

☐other: _____

☐Payment by mail to: OR   ☐ By direct deposit to:

No. & Street   Apt. No.   City   State   Zip Code   Name of bank

---

STALKING, SEXUAL ASSAULT ONLY
ONLY ORDERS CHECKED AND INITIALED BY A JUDGE SHALL APPLY

____ ☐22. THE DEFENDANT IS ORDERED NOT TO contact family members or acquaintances of the protected person(s).

DOMESTIC ABUSE, DATING VIOLENCE, STALKING OR SEXUAL ASSAULT
ONLY ORDERS CHECKED AND INITIALED BY A JUDGE SHALL APPLY

____ ☐23. Other:

12/18/2019 3:31PM (GMT-05:00)

APPENDIX D

Pleadings Filed Cost Now Due December 18, 2019

PLEADINGS FILED COST NOW DUE

E.	Case: 0888
Versus	Division:
	16th Judicial District Court
L.	Parish of St. Martin
	State of Louisiana
	Tax ID # 726001272

App. D

18TH day of DECEMBER, 2019

TO:
L
L

9009 ERIMIKE COURT RANDALLS TOWN
BALITMORE, ME 21133

THE JUDGE HAS CAST YOU WITH COURT COST IN THIS MATTER IN THE AMOUNT OF $604.50

This statement **MUST** be returned with your payment in order that we may process your pleadings.

Chrissie Segura

Deputy Clerk of Court
St. Martin Parish
P.O. Box 308
St. Martinville, LA. 70582

[FILE]

✓

December 12, 2019

Office of the Clerk

Attn: Becky P. Patin, Deputy Clerk of Court

16ᵗʰ Judicial District Court

Parish of St. Martin

415 South Main Street

St. Martinville, LA

RE: Case: 088

Dear Mrs. Becky P. Patin,

This letter is in response to the Citation & Rule To Show Cause-Protective Orders that I received on December 12, 2019 at approximately 9 AM EST related to the Protective Order E⋯⋯ has filed against me. This is my answer and pleading to the Protective Order, which expires on December 18, 2019. This case is assigned to Judge Lewis H. Pitman, Jr.'s Court. Please forward a copy of this letter to Judge Pitman and Mrs. Maggie Simar, Family Court Hearing Officer.

Accordingly, every complaint filed in the above Case is false. E⋯⋯ has saved on her cell phone every Text Message Exchange we had, from January 1, 2019 to August 5, 2019, and when I analyzed them, not one indicates ANY EVIDENCE that proves the allegations made by E⋯⋯ in the Protective Order are true and sustainable (I have every Text Message we exchanged saved on my cell phone). In fact, on Page 2 of 6, I have never been an immediate and present danger to the physical safety of E⋯⋯ today, or during the 36 years we were in a relationship. E⋯⋯ abandoned me in July 2019, and I have not been in her physical presence since that time to date. From July 1, 2019 to date, I have not seen her. I have not stalked her or tried to call her in any way. I am just trying to live my life and do my work. I only wish E⋯⋯ well.

During the time this Protective Order has been effect, I was not in direct or indirect contact with E⋯⋯ and more importantly, I moved to Baltimore, MD to live with my family at

least a month before the December 4, 2019 Protective Order was filed against me by E
                    That is, during the period E   , alleged I offended her, I was living in
another state. I did not abandon E   she refused to reply to any outreach I made to
determine if she was alright. She is using her abandonment of me as a tactic to make the
representatives of the court feel the reason for her disappearance is she was afraid of me. I am a
peaceful, law-abiding citizen.

Moreover, on Page 2 of 7, E   alleges she was abused by me in St. Martin Parish.
In this Protective Order, E.   did not list one fact-based mental and verbal abuse I
acted out against her. There is not one "Ugly Text Message" I sent to E·   . I
recommend you examine her text messages we exchanged, from January 1, 2019 to August 5,
2019; you will not discover one that I sent to her that is abusive. On Page 3 of 7, E
            reveals the true reason underlying her Protective Order.

That is, she does not want me to return to the Ce ʸ   Property that I worked for 36 years to build
and pay for. A Protective Order will force me to stay away from the C   Property, thus
allowing her to rob me of my 50% interest in the property. During the early 1990s, I simulated a
sale of the C   "roperty to E.   . to shield it from being auctioned by the
Louisiana Department of Social Services; the latter was threatening to put the C   . Property
up for auction because I had fallen behind in paying my child support. Because I loved E
            and trusted her, she put the property in her name, and she signed my name on the
Bill of Sale also. In addition, I put my Ford Truck in her name for the same reason. However,
now, E.   claims this property belongs to her only. It should also be pointed out
that I bought E·   . a 2016 Ford Escape and paid cash for it. Both of our names are
on the purchase application. I am not trying to rob E.   of her means of
transportation as she allegedly is trying to rob me of mine on Page 4 of 7 of this Protective
Order. I pray the St. Martin Parish 16th Judicial Court does not allow her to do so.

On Page 5 of 7, I am of sane mind and body; I have not abused anyone; I do not have a grievance
against E.   or anyone; I am retired and I cannot afford to pay the cost of
psychological care for E   for the primary reason one, I have not harmed her in
any way, and two, E   had a stroke in July 2015, and she was diagnosed with
Dementia. Her short-term memory was significantly impacted, which is why she is trying to get
the court to favor her for a health condition I had nothing to do with creating. E
poor childhood, which was void of mother and father love, and as a result of her repressing her
deep-rooted pain and wombs during the 36 years we were in a relationship, in July 2015, she
could no longer do so and her hidden stress resulted in a stroke and Dementia. I only have
Medicare as a means to pay for my healthcare. I cannot pay for anyone else's.

As I have already made known, I am facing a pending surgery. At the earliest, my surgery is
being scheduled for January 17, 2020. Thus, I am being prepared for surgery now leading up to

this date. In addition, it is a financial hardship for me to travel to St. Martinville, LA by December 19, 2019.

Lastly, I simply pray to the St. Martin Parish 16th Judicial District Court to look beyond the surface emotions of E   and, by studying the Text Messages she claimed I mentally and verbally abused her with, could objectively conclude: (1) I am not a present and immediate danger to E   and (2) that I have NEVER EVER done her any harm, and I never intend to do so. She is the mother of my daughter! Any interaction with E   related to my claim of a 50% interest in my Cecilia Property will be pursued through legal channels, and I will have no contact, either physically or verbally, with E: per this existing Protective Order and years to come.

If E   needs money to take care of her health matters, I am willing to agree to sell the Cecilia Property so she can obtain her 50% interest in it to do so.   I pray an equitable solution is found, and I am not an obstacle to this end.

Respectfully,

E

APPENDIX E

Text Message Exchanges Between L and E: From January 1, 2019 to December 31, 2019

E   **TEXT MESSAGE EXCHANGES**

WITH   **L**

JANUARY 1, 2019 TO DECEMBER 31, 2019

The purpose of this document is threefold: (1) To provide text message evidence that establishes the fact that no evidence of emotional of physical violence was directed toward E   by   L   during 2019 (2) To offer some insight into E   's thought process by emphasizing the transition in her thinking, from no longer understanding   L   to her total abandonment of him by July 2019 and (3) To demonstrate that the purpose of the three Temporary Restraining Orders issued by the 16th Judicial District Court, at the request of E   ., had nothing to do with a threat to her personal well-being and safety; but, to the contrary, they were timely designed by her to create an atmosphere in which she could engage in a defamation of   L   s' Character so she could secure sole ownership of his 50% share of ownership in the Cecilia Farm Property Estate.

Moreover, the three Temporary Restraining Orders are a direct defamation of   L   s' Character, and they simultaneously restrict, forbid, alienate, separate, and cutoff all connections   L   could pursue to advance his employment, family relations, and good name in the Southwest Louisiana community. The following historical analysis of the text message exchanges systematically shows that no violence of any kind was directed to E   by   L   through a use of her own words in various text messages shown below.

     I.   E   Text Message Exchanges with   L   : January-March 31, 2019

         A. E   Text Message: "H   ordered an Uber to bring me home. I will shower and return. I believe this is her [V   , E   .'s sister] last day." Jan 1, 2019, 11: 58 AM

         B.   L   Reply: I am feeding Metu and Calypso. In 15 minutes I am on my way to Hospice where you are. Any change in the situation now?" Jan 1, 2019 5:14 PM

         C.   L   Text Message: "Good morning E   . Has there been any new change with Velma? What is the situation now?" Jan 3, 2019, 9:51 AM

         D. E   Text Message Reply: "She had a very restful night. Don't know if they increased her medication or what but her night was much better. The weather for today is challenging but when Poe arrives I will try to make it home. If all goes well. **Enjoy your morning.** I am feeling a little tired." Jan 3, 2019, 9:51 AM

E.   L   Text Message: "Hello E   . When you get home this evening, feed Metu and Calypso. I am leaving home now and will return after the Dallas Cowboys Football Game. **Thank you. My thoughts are with you and family."** Jan 5, 2019, 2:19 PM

F.   E   Text: "Meeting with priest went well. Will explain details at home…Funeral Saturday. Viewing 9 to 11. Mass at 11. Burial in Breaux Bridge. Repast in Parks **Headed to my sponsor. Enjoy your day."** Jan 8, 2019, 1:33 PM

G.   E   Text: "At the dealership. Your friend is working with me. Don't drive home until you check with me. If the battery is OK he will let me know and check something else. Your friend is helping and he very nice…In Harold Fils office trying to see if I can get a loaner. Got a loaner thanks to Harold. Going to cracker barrel to get food. They will call me about the car. **Let me know your plan."** Jan 14, 2019, 7: 39 AM

H.   L   Reply Text: "Where are you? Did you get a call about you're your car from the dealership?" Jan 14, 2019, 3:02 pm

I.   E   Text: "At CODA meeting is 12 to 1. If you need before then let me know." Jan 21, 2019, 12: 46 PM

J.   L   Text Reply: "John just called me. The truck is ready to be picked up now." Jan 21, 2019, 2:23 PM

K.   L   Text: "I made it safely to Edward's House. Good weather and no problems. **Take care of yourself and everything."** Jan 22, 2019, 11: 46 AM

L.   E   Text Reply: "Enjoy yourself!! Weather is deteriorating here. Getting lunch then meeting with my sponsor. **Thanks for the contact. Much love Iz."** Jan 22, 2019 , 12:58 PM

M.   L   Reply: Good morning E   . Edward and I are on the road now. Six hours drive ahead. Not bad. Be sure to keep your eye on the weather temperature. Let the water drip in the bedroom bathroom, if the temp falls to 33 or less. **Keep you posted on our movement."** Jan 23, 2019, 8:37 AM

N.   E   Text Reply: "Boy we have a winter day on our hands. I received your text just as I was posting. No sun! Grey day windy. My plans are to stay close to home but I need groceries? Will go to Beaux Bridge CODA if it is not raining. Looking

forward to a most relaxed day. **Sending the Angels to guide you and Ed** .
Have a wonderful trip. Much love Iz" Jan 23, 2019, 8:37 AM

O.   L   Text Reply: Good evening E   We made it to Little Rock, ARK safely around 3:30 PM. We drove in rain for a while but not heavy. It is 33 degrees here now. We are checked in to our room at the Marriott where the Farmers Conference is being held. I am in the room resting up from the long drive. **How was your day?** Jan 23, 2019, 6:20 PM

P. E   Text Reply: "Strong day. CODA meeting then groceries then returned home to eat and relax…No nap today. **All is well…Get your rest and enjoy your time.**" Jan 23, 2019, 6:20 PM

Q. E   Text: "So regardless of what the weather report says I must drip the water in the bathroom both sinks." Jan 23, 2019, 6:20 PM

R.   L   . Reply: "If the temperature is below 33 degrees tonight. Then, yes let the cold water faucets drip in both of the bathroom sinks in the bedroom." Jan 23, 2019, 6:20 PM

S. E   Text Reply: "Hopefully you had a good day. All is well on this end. The weather was sunny and chilly. Normal exercise and CODA day for me. **Enjoying the solitude and meditation time. Take care of yourself. Give my regards to Ed** ." Jan 24, 2019, 7:12 PM

T. E   Text: "**Enjoy the conference and yourself!!!** Jan 26, 2019, 2:46 PM

U.   L   Text Reply: "Good morning E   We left Little Rock at 7:30 AM. Expect to be at Ed   s House around 2 PM. I will drive home today by 5 PM." Jan 27, 2019, 10: 27 AM

V. E   Text Reply: "I will probably be in Parks when you arrive. **Drive safely and give my regards to Ed**   ." Jan 27, 2019, 10: 27 AM

January 2019 Summary: The month came to an end without any emotional violence or physical violence committed by   L   against E Cooperation and a spirit of love prevailed.

FEBRUARY 2019

W. E   Text: "Just left CODA. Do you have idea for lunch. Can go to Walmart." Feb 6, 2019, 12: 57 PM

X. E   Text: "Forgot about my meeting at hospice at 2:00. Did not go to Walmart." Feb 6, 2019, 2:04 PM

Y. Text: "At Walmart if you need something let me know." Feb 6, 2019, 4:43 PM

Z. L. Reply: "Tuna, apples, small bananas from Africa, milk (40 calories)." Feb 6, 2019, 4:43 PM

AA. E Text: "My class starts at 10. If the police cannot help I need to know in enough time to get to you and be back here for my class. Pop a lock will be there by 8:10." Feb 13, 2019, 7:39 AM

BB. L Reply: "I am on my way home now. Hope you had a good day so far." Feb 14, 2019, 3:11 PM

CC. .L Text: "I am just leaving my last faculty meeting at Southern University. On my way home now." Feb 18, 2019, 4:41 PM

DD. E Text Reply: **"Be safe"** Feb 18, 2019, 4:41 PM

EE. E Text: "H asked me to stay with LUNA tonight and tomorrow. She is in New Orleans. Enjoy your evening." Feb 22, 2019, 3:08 PM

FF. L Text Reply: "Did you prepare any dinner? I am just ending my work in the School of Agriculture today. Where is Brent going to be tonight?" Feb 22, 2019, 3:08 PM

GG. E Text: " No I did not prepare anything. Brent will be at the camp." Feb 22, 2019, 3:08 PM

HH. L Text Reply: "Feed Metu and Calypso before you leave to go to H House. I am sorry you did not prepare any dinner. Is there a reason you did not do so?" Feb 22, 2019, 3:08 PM

E: Text Reply: "I have already left." Feb 22, 2019, 3:08 PM

L .eply: " Did you answer the questions I asked?"Feb 22, 2019, 3:08 PM

KK. E Text: "Tina's apartment is lovely. We organized her closet. Got the bed in and together, then watched a movie THE WIFE. Most enjoyable. I am at Harmony's entertaining Luna. Have a great evening Feb 23, 2019, 7:18 PM

LL. L Text: "Good morning. On your way home, stop at Wal-mart and buy Calypso some cat food. It is completely out. What is your plan this morning?" Feb 24, 2019, 9:03 AM

MM.E: Text Reply: "Just getting up. Meditation, little cleaning up, breakfast, then I should be on my way home. May go to the Walmart on this end." Feb 24, 2019, 9:03 AM

NN. E: Text: "At the Walmart in Lafayette do we need anything besides catfood?"

OO. L: Text Reply: "Yes. Get a box of milk, honey Bunches of Oats Cereal with almonds, and maybe some chicken pieces to stew for dinner. We have potato salad already made. Get bananas and apples also." Feb 24, 2019, 11:10 AM

L: Text: "Did you feed Metu this morning. He acts like he did not eat yet?" Feb 28, 2019, 11:51 AM

QQ. E: Text Reply: "   No!! I was not home this morning" Feb 28, 2019, 11:51 AM

RR. L: Text Reply: "Where are you?" Feb 28, 2019, 11:51 AM

E: Text Reply: "On my way to Cecilia. Forgot CODA meeting today is Thursday." Feb 28, 2019, 11:51 AM

TT. L: Text Reply: "Where are you? Feb 28, 2019, 7:31 PM

UU. L: Text: "   Apparently you have decided to leave for Tampa. The conscience goes where everyone alive goes. My hope is you find peace on your journey." Feb 28, 2019, 8:33 PM

VV. NOTE: At this point, E   has freely chosen to stay in Lafayette, LA; she is not residing at 2730 Main Highway, Breaux Bridge, LA 70517 at this time, which is the address for the Cecilia Farm Estate. E   abandoned   L   in February 2019!

WW.E: Text: "Intense!!! J   S   's son got Life without parole?? I am at H   's house. U   is not going to work so we may leave earlier. L: I love you and I have loved you since the day I met you. I will continue to love you. I no longer understand you and you deserve someone who does. May the Force be with you always L" Feb 28, 2019, 9:56 PM

MARCH 2019

XX.   L: Text: "Have you left for Tampa yet? I am sorry S   's son-J   -received the sentence he did. I know some people who work at Angola.

They might be able to look out for him in some minor ways, if e is incarcerated there. How is Sharon doing when you spoke to her?" March 1, 4:18 PM.

YY. E: Text Reply: "Have not left yet. Tired. Sharon is holding up…The leaving time is still 7…All is well. Need to eat before getting on the road!! Enjoy your down time and remember you are lovedMar 1, 4:18 PM

ZZ.   ∴   Text: "Are you still at H   's House? I thought you were on the road. We could have had lunch today…"Mar 1, 4:18 PM

AAAE: . Text Reply: "Intense drive!! The weather was very challenging…I know we have made the correct decision to recreate ourselves. I love you and always will but our time has passed. Let's do what we know is right. I only want to bring love to the planet and I feel that you do also. Much love Iz .." Mar 3, 11:58 PM

BBB.   L.   Text Reply: "The song sounds familiar. What you say about me you told me for years the same thing about s.   [Former husband of E   's]: That you always will love him but the relationship is over…" Mar 3, 1:09 PM

CCCE   Text: "…Imagining living my life without you is big, hard, and deep but I have no choice but to move forward learning to honor, respect, and love myself. I feel you can understand this. The money issue is big because I didn't know this was your attitude about money??? When money is on the table it's another ballgame??? I feel we had to live that experience. I am OK with that. We will all get to heaven in our own way and our own terms. **Nothing you do or say will stop me from loving you.**" Mar 5, 12:21 PM

DDD L.   . Text Reply: "It is not about money. It's about dishonesty. You cannot think of one incident where I spent money that was EARNED by us. If the problem is about money, I would have left the relationship long time ago. For me, it has always been about truth.   The truth is when you came to Baltimore in 1979, you did not have any money at all. I gave you the money to pay   .B: for what you owed him on your Chrysler [$500]; I basically supported you financially in Baltimore. You did some teaching[substitute] but we would not e able to live on that. I supported you financially in Oakland, California. For the years we stayed in Oakland, CA, you did not have a full-time job. You did some substitute teaching but that is all. So, do not throw the money card on the table. If our relationship was based on money, it would have ended before it started. Check your facts. I am working now for Southern University. This work has nothing to do with work before my retirement. Yet, you have chosen not to work but criticize me for working and not behaving like I use to when I put my check on the table and walked around for years with no money in my pocket at all. So don't get self-righteous with me about money. I worked out the Black Farmers Lawsuit and received $100,000 for my work. N   [your brother-in-law got $50,000 of that but nobody criticized him asking him for some of the money he got for doing nothing. Yet, my mother's Estate gave me an inheritance and you closed out[stole $3,000 of my earned money] the [Lafayette Parish] Credit Union account. If you had challenged N.   , I could slightly understand. But you did not. Even though R   . died[your sister and N   .'s wife], your family still was entitled to some of the $50,000. Nobody asked for a dime!! It is a lack of honesty that has ended our relationship. Not another woman or man, but a failure to acknowledge the truth. I know what role I played in building C   and before. Can you acknowledge it is the question?" Mar 5, 12:21 PM

EEEE.   _ Text Reply: "**You are Right. Much love to you and success on your journey. I will always love you for the life we have shared.**" Mar 5, 12:21 PM

FFF.   . L   _ Text Reply: " Good evening. I have not heard from you. How are things going? Update. Your Medicare Bill came in the mail today; I will pay it tomorrow by check." Mar 11, 9:06 PM

GGGE.   Text Reply; "Got on T   WIFI did not know my wifi was turned off...All is well here[Tampa, FL]...**Much love Iz**" Mar 11, 9:06 PM

NOTE: E   **abandoned** _ **L**   , **and by the beginning of March 2019, she was living in Tampa, FL;**   **L** **traveled to Baltimore, MD to participate in the recording of a new Jazz CD with his son-L**   **II. This business activity was pre-discussed with E**   **in early January 2019.**

HHHE.   Text Reply: "Have not heard from you. How are things going? How is D   .?...H   said she did not see Kaliso when she went to feed her? Hope a ll is well. I suspect Metu is with K   ...Enjoy your time." Mar 16, 9:40 AM

DILIL   . Text Reply: "Wrightway Recording Studio. Two days of 4 hours of recording. Great success. I did my recording in one take!" Mar 21, 12:13 PM

JJJ. E   . Text Reply: "So excited for both of You!!!Enjoy. Z   's birthday was Wednesday 13. Continue to have a good time." Mar 21, 12:13 PM

KKK   L.   Text: "Good morning E   When do you return to Cecilia? How is it going?" Mar 30, 10:22 AM

LLL.   L   · Text: "How did you miss purchasing your return ticket, given the time you had in advance.?" Mar 30, 11:41 AM

MMM: Text Reply: "Sorry about delay. Saturday for a family of 5??? All is well…These will be my final days until return. **All is well Much love Iz**" Mar 30, 8:26 PM

NOTE: From January 1, 2019 to March 31, 2019, the majority of

E   's time was spent in Tampa, FL. None of the

text message exchanges between us show no sign of aggression in

any form. E   's text messages and replies do not show

any fear of her personal well-being.

APRIL 1, 2109 TO JUNE 31, 2019 TEXT MESSAGE EXCHANGES

A. E   Text: "Return date is Sunday not Saturday??? Those prices keep changing!!!Will text itiniary…Enjoy your day. I really miss Metu. Kind of surprised?? **Much love Iz**" Apr 2, 12: 43 PM

B. E: Text: "Lots of changes because of weather?? My flight now leaves Houston at 11:30 maybe?? Left beautiful weather in Florida. Enjoy your time . **All is well with me.**" Apr 7, 11:19 AM

C. E   Text: **[Verbatim copy of an airline carrier announcement]** "Mother Nature is really impacting our operations today, so your continued patience is greatly appreciated. We're doing our best to get you on your way. Your estimated departure time is 01:00 PM, arriving in Lafayette at 02:04 PM. I really don't believe we will be clear by 1:00???" Apr 7, 1:58 PM

D. E   Text: **[Verbatim copy of an airline carrier announcement]** "Your 220pm United flight to Lafayette is delayed because an earlier delay impacted your plane's arrival. We value your time and we're sorry for the inconvenience. UA4131 now departs Houston at 445pm and arrives at 549pm" Apr 7, 7:45 PM

E. E   Text: "Landed!!! H: is picking me up…" Apr 7, 7:45 PM

392

NOTE: L attended the French Quarters Festival in New Orleans, LA in early April 2019, and E attended the Festival Internationale in Lafayette, LA at the end of April 2019. Most of E 's time was spent at her daughter's house or a friend. By early May 2019, E abandoned L again.

F. L Text: "I made it to Edward's House at 12 Noon. Drive was alright but heavy traffic." Apr 11, 2:30 PM

G. E Text Reply: "Long chat with T about her visit with her brother. Did make my yoga class and CODA class. Home now eating spaghetti…Enjoy your friend. Why do you think there was heavy traffic?' Apr 11, 2:30 PM

H. L Text: "Good morning. Hope you doing well. Threatening rain here. Be sure to secure Metu when the weather turns stormy. Also, can you cover the small cucumber plants if the rain is expected to be very hard? Headed to New Orleans with the young boys." Apr 13, 9:07 AM

I. L Text: "We just got back to E 's House. Heavy rain now. I am tired. Hope the power come back on soon." Apr 13, 10: 13 PM

J. E Text Reply: "The power just returned!!!!" Apr 13, 10:13PM

K. L Text Reply: Great! I am getting in the bed. return tomorrow morning." Apr 13, 10:13 PM

L. L Text: "On my way home now. Driving. Nice weather." Apr 14, 9:14 AM

M. E Text Reply: On the road to Baton Rouge. All is well. Surgery is at 1:00. Lovely weather. **Enjoy your day.**" Apr 15, 9:15 AM

N. L Text: "How did H 's Oral Surgery go today?" Apr, 15, 10:03 PM

O. E Text Reply: "intense day!!! Still moving. All is well. Success taking medication Will text more later. Tired shower, sleep. Talk tomorrow." Apr, 10:03 PM

P. L Text: "Hello E Have not heard from you. Wassup? Are you staying at harmony another night?" Apr, 17, 2:34 PM

Q. E Text: "Dinner is just about ready. If you plan to eat with me let me know. Otherwise I will take a bath and eat. Enjoy your time. I will be going back to the festival so do not change any plans on account of me." Apr, 27, 1:25 PM

R. . L: Text Reply: "yes. I will eat dinner with you. I will be home in the next hour or less." Apr 27, 1:25 PM

S. E: Text Reply: "Got it. Thanks for telling me. **Listening to Zydeco music guest I forgot Just be yourself you are loved.**" Apr 27, 1:25 PM

E   ABANDONED   L   AGAIN IN
MAY 2019

T. E   Text: I have lived with you for the last forty years and I do not have another forty years. It pains me greatly that our final act is as it is. When we got together this ending was not conceivable to me but here we are. Let's make this as pain free as possible especially for our daughter. I will always love you for the man I knew in your prime. **I spent the night at Lynette and will be flying back to Tampa soon. This is all to much for me emotionally. We will make the sale as soon as possible.**" Apr, May 5, 5:17 PM

E.   'S SCHEME TO LIVE HER LIFE O. F OF
L.   AS A CODEPENDENT PERSON HAD NOW BEEN
REVEALED SO SHE DECIDED TO ABANDON . L   AGAIN SO
THAT SHE COULD SET IN OPERATION HER PLAN TO ATTEMPT TO
ROB HIM OF HIS 50% SHARE IN THE CECILIA FARM ESTATE.

U. . L: · Text Reply: "So why are you choosing to stay away from Cecilia? Is this another one of your attempts to paint yourself as a victim? **Stay away and then say I am causing you emotional stress. I have done you no harm since the day I first met you. I am sorry you are trying to blame me for your problems. The source is in you and it cannot be projected. It's on your hook; you put the bait on it, and now you want to say I put the bait on your hook. Your Spirit and I Ching know differently. Read your own cards. What do they tell you?**" May 5, 9:55 PM

V. E   Text: "**All is well.** L   is fed and flippy. Big empty house. Ned to adjust. Will eat some leftovers in the refrigerator .forgot my stuff is not in this refrigerator. Will read and watch TV." May 23, 8:50 PM

W.   L   Reply: "**Enjoy the alone time and think about you.**" May 23, 8:50 PM

X. E   Text Reply: "Thanks L.   that is excellent advice. **Much love Iz**" May 23, 8:50 PM

Y. E: Text: "Have some delicious corn for boiling and lovely avocado. See you after my CODA class. **Enjoy your morning.**" May 27, 10:40 AM

Z. ⌐ .L.   Text: "I made it to Edwards safely. He has been cleaning chickens since I arrived at 11:30 AM. I will dress out my chickens Saturday morning." Jun 7, 3:13 PM

AA. E   Text Reply: "**Hopefully you are having great success with the chickens. All is well on this end.**" Jun 8, 2:45 PM

BB. L   Text Reply: "Finished the chickens successfully. On my way home now." Jun 8, 2:45 PM

CC. E   L   Text: "**Let me know when you are headed home. Cooking fish.**" Jun 12, 1:46 PM

DD.   L   Reply: I am on my way home now. Just leaving Southern University." Jun 12, 1:46 PM

EE. E   Text: "I am spending the night at C   's." Jun 29, 10: 23 PM

E   AND   L   TEXT MESSAGE EXCHANGES-JULY 1, 2019 TO SEPTEMBER 31, 2019

It was during this time period that E   discovered in the St. Martin Parish Clerk of Court Record that our jointly owned C i Farm Estate is in her name as the **OWNER OF RECORD.** The estate was placed in her name via a **SIMULATED SALE SO THAT IT COULD BE HIDDEN FROM THE LOUISIANA DEPARTMENT OF SOCIAL SERVICES.** The latter was threatening to seize the Estate because I had fallen behind in payment of my child support-$10,000. My son's mother wanted the unpaid child support and the **FORCED SALE OF THE C¹   FARM ESTATE WAS A VIABLE AN INEVITABLE OPTION. SO, E   AND   L** **MUTUALLY AGREED TO HAVE A NOTARIZED STATEMENT DRAWN UP TO SAVE OUR C¹   FARM ESTATE FROM SALE AT AUCTION IN 1991.**

FF. E   Text: "Ferrell gas is calling about payments?? The bill is on the counter." Jul 1, 4:41 PM

GG.   L.   Text Reply:"Why have you chosen not to pay the bill? It has been sitting there for several months? I [will] write the bill and send it out Tuesday morning." Jul 1, 4:41 PM

HH.   E   Text Reply: "I do not have money to pay this bill. All I have is the small 500 check I get to pay every bill I have. Medicare bill was 406 I had to borrow money tot pay this." Jul 1, 4:41 PM

NOTE: Because of E **'s psychological wounds experienced during her childhood, which led to a mental illness called CoDependency Addiction, she failed to realize she would need a retirement at the end of her work life. E** **was blinded to this fact due to her CoDependency Addiction to L THIS LEFT HER DESPERATE FOR MONEY WHEN SHE RETIRED IN 2013 FROM THE LAFAYETTE PARISH PUBLIC SCHOOL SYSTEM.**

This fact, no doubt, laid the foundation in her mind to rob   L   of his 50% share of the value of the C   Farm Estate. Later Texts exchanged with   L bear out her intention to do so.

II E   Text: **"Hopefully you had a great 4th. I know you are getting excited for your trip. Don't forget you have to give me a time to bring you to the airport.** Also don't forget to make arrangements for Metu. **Enjoy."** Jul 5, 12: 46 PM

NOTE: E. **, by this time, had not been living at home with L   at the C   Farm Estate.**

J. How do you know what kind of 4th I had? Where were you? After 40 years, don't you think these questions are strange? This is not the kind of 4th I imagined. My flight leaves out of Lafayette at 8:15 AM, Sunday, July 14, 2019. I need to be at the airport by 6 AM. So, you need to pick me up at home at 5 AM. How does this sounds to you. " Jul 5, 1:57 PM

K. E   Text Reply: **"Will do."** Jul 5, 1:57 PM

L.   HAS NOT SEEN E. SINCE LATE JUNE 2019. I WOULD NOT SEE HER AGAIN IN 2019 AND THEREAFTER. THIS FACT RAISES THIS QUESTION: WHY DID E.   HAVE THREE TEMPORARY RESTRAINING ORDERS ISSUED AGAINST ME WHEN SHE ABANDONED ME IN JUNE 2019?

very happy!! All my desire everyone involved is happiness. I simply want to be treated fairly financially. We all have to live and I only desire what is rightfully mine. May God bless you and D   and M   ." Jul 24, 7:43 AM

M.   L: Text: "Good morning. D.   [my son] played a jazz gig last night in DC. He did an outstanding job. His jazz is approaching the John Coltrane Style...I agree with you about being treated fairly financially. That is my intent. WE both deserve to be treated this way, and I am committed to see this happen...The C(farm will go on the market when I return[from Baltimore, MD]. The land and house will be equally divided. How much should we set the selling price for?" Jul 24, 7:43 AM.

N. E.   Text Reply: "Thank you for your calm reply. I have prayed for a fair resolution we both deserve that. D   is extraordinarily talented and I know it makes you feel good to be with him now. Going to C(. this morning the appraisal papers are there and will get back to you. Give my regards to M   ertain she is in the mix and D   is a product of her determination. Enjoy both of them." Jul 24, 7:43 AM

O.   L.   Text Reply: "I am here to visit with my son. Try to let that thought of truth resonate in you. I have no other goal here but working through the 40 years I was not in contact with my son. Can you understand this fact?" Jul 24, 10:09 AM

Text Reply: "Yes. And this is a noble idea and opportunity. God bless." Jul 24, 10:09 AM

L.   RETURNED FROM BALTIMORE, MD ON JULY 31, 2019 AND E.   WAS NOT AT HOME-C.   FARM. SHE HAD ABANDONED THE C.   FARM AND   L.

P.   L.   Text: "Can you give me a call now? I just got back home. It is an emergency!" Jul 31, 2:38 PM

L.   Text: "Hello E.   Why aren't you answering your phone when I call? When I got home today at Noon, I found some household items missing. I need to know if you know anything about the situation because I am about to call the police Department and file a complaint. Please give me a call because I plan to call the police in the next fifteen minutes. I also need to talk with you about putting the C(Property on the market for sale. Give me a call." Jul 31, 5:05 PM

E: Text Message Reply: "Ok." Jul 31, 5:05 PM

"Can you come home tonight so we can talk?" Jul 31, 5:05 PM

E: Text: "I have decided not to sell the house. As you know, I put my entire retirement into it and all I get is 500$ a month. The property is the only thing I have, and I do not have any other place to live. Don't list the property." Jul 31, 7:34 PM

Q. E   . Text: "Buy you out??? I have owned this property for almost 30 years. I have no reason to buy you out." Aug 1, 11;34 AM

. L: Text: "We have owned this property. Next week, the property will go on the market for sale…When do you plan to return to Cecilia?" Aug 1, 11:34 AM

E.   Text Reply: "L   u are wrong this is my house. I have owned it in my name since 1991. I forbid you to list my property for sale." Aug 1, 11:34 AM

E.   MOVES TOWARD CREATING A NEGATIVE ATTACK ON L.   , CHARACTER AS A MEANS OF HIDING HER PLAN TO CEASE COMMUNICATING WITH HIM BY LATER HAVING THE 16TH JUDICIAL DISTICT COURT, ST. MARTIN PARISH SERVE THREE TEMPORARY RESTRAINING ORDERS AGAINST HIM.

L.   .L· ˉext: Hello E: Increasingly, I have witnessed your use of judgment when we talk to each other. My personal goal is to avoid using any judgmental words to refer to you. This is beneath my dignity and integrity. If I stumble an use a judgmental expression aimed at you, please bring it to my attention so I can correct myself. Today, when you were here you referred to me as being vicious. The only thing I feel is vicious is in the coming days we will sell our home because of information you withheld related to CoDependency through the years. There was a time when the opportunity existed to resolve this issue. Because of fear of abandonment and rejection, your CoDependency was kept a secret but it manifested itself in various subtle ways through the years. Not sharing pain, wounds, and childhood emotional traumas is vicious. It is equally vicious for parents to abuse and neglect their infant babies during a vulnerable time in their early lives. This is vicious too! It is the origin of it! I encourage you to reread your CoDependency Books so you can see this is **a vicious situation to be placed in by parents; it caused you to repress your feelings and needs and then try to compensate for the DEEP LOSS by attaching yourself to my feelings and sacrifice your own…this is why we are forced to sell our home! I encourage you to help prepare Cecilia Farm to be sold. We have talked enough."** Jul 7, 9:39 PM

M. E Text: Are you at the airport?? Did your flight get out? Was electric power restored before you left? **Praying all goes well**. Enjoy. Please answer this text. Give my regards to Deano." Jul 14, 9:43 AM

N.   L. Text Reply: "My flight at 8:15 AM was cancelled; I rebooked to depart at 2:17 PM. The electrical power in on; it did not go out last night. **There are two cucumbers in the refrigerator and two tomatoes in the study if you want them.**" Jul 14, 9:43

O. E: Text Reply: **"Enjoy!! You deserve it."** Jul 14, 4:39 PM

P. E: Text: "Two bills which I can't afford to pay. The Visa bill which is $200 and Escape 547.75. This is more than my monthly check. What am I supposed to do?? Jul 23, 8:05 PM

U never called because you were weaving a devious plan.

Q. L Reply: "Ask H and T for help. I paid the bills for everybody for 40 years. I even went through a Hurricane Barry-and nobody called to see if I was alright. I plan to put the C. Farm on the Market to sale when I get back home on July 31, 2019." Jul 23, 8:05 PM

E: Text Reply: "L you are wrong this is my house. I have owned it in my name since 1991. I forbid you to list my property for sale." Aug 1, 11:34 AM

L. Text Reply: "Both of our names are on this property. I will list it for sale. What is the matter with you? We both own this property and I have a deed to prove it. We bought the land with the money I earned while working in Oakland, CA I paid for this land with the Black Farmers money I was awarded in 2009..." Aug 1, 11:34 PM

WHILE I WAS AWAY VISITING MY SON IN BALTIMORE IN JULY 2019, E REMOVED SOME OF MY PERSONAL BELONGING FROM THE C. FARM HOUSE. SHE STOLED THEM.

R. Text: "I hope the behavior you are presenting is not "Who You Are?" I have done you absolutely no harm all of the years we were together; yet behind my back you treat me like I have been unhelpful to you...while I was away in Baltimore, you never called because you were weaving a devious plan. You intended to rob me of my woodcarvings, which is why you removed them from the wall. You lied about cleaning up! What changed your mind? Why didn't you just steal them?...You took these items: My shell Necklace from Africa, my Onyx Indian Picture of Quannah, My LSU Graduation picture I took with my daughter was stolen from the shelf in the study, My Musician Figurines from the Hutch, My Kubota Tractor Owners Manual. I am sure you plundered more than what is on the list, but remember, your cherished Course In Miracles says a person's thought does not ever leave their source. So, you can scream from the highest mountaintop, that you are a spiritual person, but you have to live with the truth of what you did while I was gone, and what you did to literally destroy your own life over the last 36 years. Your son had it right: This relationship is over. So let us stop fooling ourselves and do what it takes to dissolve it rather than engage in meaningless blame and denial..." Aug 1, 10:26 PM

S. E. Text: "L you want me to put my property up for sale soon as possible. I don't have to do this. However, we do need to go our separate ways so I am willing to work with you as long as I do not feel bullied by you. If you want me to work with you, you must listen carefully to what I am saying to you. **I will not meet with you in person. I mean I will not meet with you in person!!! Do not ask again."** Aug 5, 8:33 PM

E   Text: Just to be clear, please understand you do not enter any agreement concerning any property with my name on it. This is very important." Aug 6, 9:45 PM

T.   .L: Text Reply: "I do not know why you refuse to talk with me? Can you give me a call?" Aug 12, 7:24 PM

The August 5, 2019 Text message I received from E.   is last communication I received from her, in any form, during August, September, October, November, December, 2019 through January 2010. It is clear all communications ceased when the subject of the sale of the Cecilia Farm Estate became a question raised by me. Moreover, in order to prevent me from continuing to obtain my 50% share in this mentioned property, E   used the 16 th Judicial District Court to which she claimed she was harmed by me and felt threaten for her personal safety and well-being.

The above chronology of Text message exchanges between E   : and . .L: learly demonstrate the opposite. From January 1, 2019 to August 12, 2019, not one text message I sent to her was of a threatening nature, which would warrant E   to file three Temporary Restraining Orders (TRO) against me. Interestingly, each one was issued to me in Randallstown, MD, which is roughly 1,200 miles away from the Cecilia Farm Estate, which I own a 50% share. The TRO were used to establish a barrier to communication related to my need to talk to E   about the sale of the Cecilia Farm Estate. Yet, E signed an Affidavit/ Verification on Nov. 18, 2019, Which says L abused her. Perjured herself
In addition, the TROs severely damaged my character and reputation. Through false allegations, and the personal humiliation associated with each unfounded statement made about me in them, I have experienced a Defamation of my Character as a result, from November 2019 to date.

SSSS

Bibliography

PREFACE

[1.] Lancer, Darlene, <u>Codependency For Dummies</u>, 2nd Edition, For Dummies, A Wiley Brand, 2015, p. 1.

CHAPTER ONE: Introduction

[2.] Montagu, M.F. Ashley, <u>The Direction of Human Development: Biological and Social Bases</u>, Harper & Brothers Publishers, New York, 1955, p. 306.

[3.] Ibid., pp. 290, 291 and 310.

[4.] Ibid., pp. 292 and 293.

[5.] Ibid., p. 298.

[6.] _____ https://www.google.com/search?rlz=1C2BLWB_enUS568 US568&source=hp&ei=e6LZXPDVEImT0PEPmOOVgAg&q=how +many+known+codependents+are+in+the+United+States%3F&oq =how+many+known+codependents+are+in+the+United+States%3F&gs_ l=psy-ab.12..33i160.4397.49311..52833...21.0..0.212.8305.23j53j1......0....1.. gws-wiz.....0..0j0i131j0i10j0i22i30j33i22i29i30j0i13j0i13i10j33i10j33i299. Cz04BnYeqN8

[7.] These are reflections I remember from many conversations E and I had since July 2015. Before this date, we never spoke about CoDependency Addiction in our house. It was being repressed in E's subconscious, while we spoke about the typical daily world maters of politics, people issues, and others.

[8.] Payne, Lisa L., Olver, Kim, and Deborah Roth, "The 10 most Common Reasons People Get Divorce," By YourTango Contributors, September 16, 2016, pp. 1 and 2. Based on a poll taken of over 100 YourTango experts, "...communication problems came out on top as the **number** one **reason** marriages fail," www. Google.com.

CHAPTER TWO: Origin And Development Of CoDependency And The Part Played By Family Dysfunctionalism

[9.] Montagu, M.F. Ashley, <u>The Direction of Human Development: Biological and Social Bases</u>, Harper & Brothers Publishers, new York, 1955, p. 171.

[10.] Ibid., p. 171.

[11.] Ibid., pp. 171 and 172.

[12.] Ibid., p. 172.

[13.] Cornforth, Maurice, <u>Historical Materialism</u>, International Publishers, New York, 1954, P. 16.

[14.] Ibid., p. 69.

[15.] Marx, Karl, <u>Economic and Philosophic Manuscripts of 1844</u>, Progress Publishers, Moscow, 1959, p. 64.

[16.] Ibid., pp.67 and 68.

[17.] Ibid., pp. 68 and 69.

[18.] Marx Engels, <u>German Ideology</u>, Progress Publishers, Moscow, 1964, p. 37.

[19.] Zeitlin, Irving M., <u>Marxism: A Re-Examination</u>, D. Van Nostrand Company, New York, 1967, p. 63.

[20.] Marx Engels, Op. Cit., p. 42.

CHAPTER THREE: Mother Right

[21.] Engels, Frederick, <u>Origin Of The Family, Private Property And The State,</u> Pathfinder Press, New York, 1972, p. 39.

[22.] Reed, Evelyn, Introduction, Ibid., p. 9.

[23.] Ibid., p. 39.

[24.] Ibid., pp. 39 and 40.

[25.] Ibid., p. 40.

[26.] Ibid., p. 40.

[27.] Ibid., p. 41.

[28.] Reed, Evelyn, Introduction, Op. Cit., p. 9.

29. Ibid., p. 41.

30. Ibid., p. 42.

31. Engels, Frederick, Lenin, V. I., Marx, Karl, and Stalin, Joseph, The Woman Question, International Publishers, New York, 1951, P. 9.

32. Engels. Op. Cit., p. 65.

33. Ibid., p. 43.

34. Ibid., p. 45. See Lewis Morgan, Ancient Society, 1877.

35. Ibid., pp. 60 and 61.

36. Ibid., p. 61.

37. Ibid., p. 61.

38. Ibid., p. 65.

39. Engels, The Woman Question, Op. Cit., p. 12.

40. Engels, Op. Cit., p. 66.

41. Ibid., p. 66.

42, Ibid., p. 67.

43. Ibid., p. 67.

44. Ibid., p. 67.

45. ibid., p. 67.

46. Engels, The Woman Question, Op. Cit., p. 16.

47. Marx, Karl and Engels, Frederick, The German Ideology, Progress Publishers, Moscow, 1964, p. 38.

48. Engels, The Woman Question, Op. Cit., p. 11. "At this stage one man lives with one woman, yet in such manner that polygamy and occasional infidelity remain men's privileges, even though the former is seldom practiced for economic reasons; at the same time, the strictest fidelity is demanded of the woman during the period of cohabitation, adultery on her part being cruelly punished. The marriage tie can, however, be easily dissolved by either side, and the children belong solely to the mother, as previously."

49. Engels, Op. Cit., p. 68.

50. Ibid., pp. 71 and 72.

51. Ibid., p. 72.

52. Ibid, p. 72.

53. Ibid., p. 68.

54. Amen Nefer Un Ra, <u>Metu Neter: The Great Oracle of Tehuti And The Egyptian System of Spiritual Cultivation.</u>, vol. 1, Khamit Media Trans Visions, Inc, Brooklyn, New York, 1990, p. 94.

55. Ibid., p. 125.

56. Marx, Karl, <u>Economic and Philosophic Manuscripts of 1844</u>, Progress Publishers, Moscow, 1959, p. 63.

57. Ibid., p. 64.

58. Ibid., pp. 65 and 66.

59. Ibid., p. 68.

60. Ibid., p. 68.

61. Ibid., p. 66.

62. Ibid., p. 63.

63. Ibid., p. 64.

64. Ibid., p. 66.

65. _____ "Willie Lynch Letter: The Making of a Slave," <u>Final Call</u>, August 23, 2005, p. 22.

66. Heningburg, Keith, Professor, "THE DEATH OF THE WILLIE LYNCH SPEECH," https://www.scc.losrios.edu/ethicsstudies/williw-lynch/, Sacramento City College.

67. Ibid.

68. _____ "Full text of "willie lynch letter, 1712," https//archive.org/stream/WillieLynchLetter1712/the_willie_lynch_letter_the_making_of_a_slave_1712_djvu.txt, p. 1.

69. Ibid., p. 1.

70. Ibid., p. 1.

71. Ibid., p. 1.

72. Ibid., p. 1.

73. Ibid., p. 1.

74. Ibid., p. 2.

75. Ibid., p. 2.

76. Ibid., p. 2.

CHAPTER FOUR: CoDependency, Alienation, And The Lost Self: Perfectionism, Public Persona, And Fraud

[77.] Lancer, Op. Cit., p. 7.

[78.] Beattie, Melody, Codependent No More: How to stop Controlling Others and Start Caring for Yourself, Hazelden Publishing, 1986, p. 34.

[79.] Montagu, M.F. Ashley, The Direction of Human Development: Biological and Social Bases, Harper & Brothers Publishers, New York, 1955, p. 305.

[80.] Lancer, Op. Cit., p. 31.

[81.] Ibid., p. 32.

[82.] Lancer, p. 8.

[83.] Mish, Frederich C., Webster's Ninth New Collegiate Dictionary, Merriam-Webster Inc., Publishers, Springfield, Massachusetts, U>S.A., 1984, p. 490.

[84.] Lancer, Op. Cit., p. 32.

[85.] Ibid., p. 32.

CHAPTER FIVE: Mother, Infant, And CoDependency: Origins And Development From Birth Through Adulthood

[86.] Ibid., p. 33.

[87.] Montagu, Op. Cit., p. 161.

[88.] Ibid., p. 161.

[89.] Ibid., p. 162.

[90.] Ibid., p. 170.

[91.] Ibid., p. 176.

[92.] Ibid., p. 201.

[93.] Cornforth, Maurice, Historical Materialism, International Publishers, New York, 1954, p. 35.

[94.] Montagu, Op. cit., p. 176.

[95.] Ibid., p. 201.

[96.] Ibid., pp. 200 and 245.

[97.] Ibid., p. 257.

[98.] Ibid., pp. 249 and 260.

99. Ibid., p. 290.

100. Ibid. p. 231.

101. Ibid., p. 161.

102. Ibid., p. 168.

103. Ibid., p. 168.

104. Ibid., p. 182.

105. Ibid., pp. 162 and 163.

106. Lancer, Op. Cit., p. 35.

107. Montagu, Op. Cit., p. 244.

108. Ibid., p. 244.

109. Ibid., p. 182.

110. Bowlby, John, <u>Maternal Care &Mental Health</u>, Jason Aronson Inc., Northvale, New Jersey, 1995, p. 89.

111. Montagu, op. cit., pp. 181 and 182.

112. Ibid., p. 168.

113. Ibid., p. 200.

114. Ibid., p. 262.

115. Bowlby, op.cit., p. 11.

116. Lancer, op. cit., p. 7.

117. Montagu, op. cit., p. 148.

118. Ibid., p. 247.

119. Ibid., p. 247.

120. Ibid., p. 247.

121. Ibid., p. 247.

122. Ibid., p. 184

123. Ibid., p. 199.

124. Ibid., pp. 169 and 243.

125. Ibid., p. 247.

126. Ibid., p. 212.

127. Bowlby, op. cit., p. 59.

[128.] Ibid., p. 67.

[129.] Ibid., p. 91.

[130.] Guevarra, Che, **CHE GUEVARRA READER: writings on politics & revolution,** Duetschmann, David, and Ariet, Maria del Carmen, Second, Expanded Edition (Editors), Ocean, 2003, p. 117.

[118.] Ibid., p. 91.

[119.] Montagu, op. cit., p. 199.

[120.] Ibid., p. 297.

[121.] Ibid., p. 247.

[122.] Ibid., p. 188.

[123.] Ibid., p. 189.

[124.] Bowlby, op.cit., p. 26.

[125.] Ibid., p. 13.

[126.] Ibid., p. 46.

[127.] Montagu, op. cit., p. 238.

[128.] Ibid., p. 238.

[129.] Ibid., p. 238.

[130.] Guevarra, Che, <u>Che.Guevarra Reader: writings on politics & revolution,</u> Duetschmann, David and Ariet, Maria del Carmen, Second, Expanded Edition (Editors), Ocean 2003, p. 117.

[131.] Ibid., p. 91.

[132.] Montagu, op. cit., p. 199.

CHAPTER SIX: Affects Of Maternal Deprivation On The Normal Development Of The Child During The Childhood Years And Into Adulthood

[133.] Ibid., p. 297.

[134.] Ibid., 247.

[135.] Ibid., p. 188.

[136.] Ibid., p. 189.

[137.] Bowlby, op. cit., p. 26.

[138.] Ibid., p. 13.

[139.] Ibid., p. 46.

[140.] Montagu, op. cit., p. 238.

[141.] Ibid., p. 238.

[142.] Ibid., p. 238.

[143.] Ibid., p. 256.

[144.] Bowlby, op.cit., p. 54.

[145.] Montagu, op. cit., pp. 258 and 259.

[146.] Lancer, op. cit., p. 50.

[147.] Ibid., p. 51.

[148.] Ibid., p. 52.

[149.] Montagu, op. cit., p. 213.

CHAPTER SEVEN: CoDependency, Characteristics Of A CoDependent Person, And Psychopathology Behavior

[150.] _____ RealisticRecovery, 27 CoDependency Characterisitcs (Person Addiction), realisticrecovery.wordpress.com/2009/05/20/27-characteristics

[151.] _____ http://fullspectrumrecovery.com/wp-content/uploads/2013/06/characteristics-of-Codepency.pdf

[152.] Bowlby, op.cit., p.31.

[153.] Ibid., p. 33.

[154.] Mish, Frederick C., et al, Webster's Ninth New Collegiate Dictionary, Merriam-Webster Inc., Publishers, Springfield, Massachusetts, U. S. A., 1984, p. 278.

[155.] Hare, Robert, "This Charming Psychopath," http://www.psychologyToday.com/US/articles/199401/charmingpsychopath, January 1, 1994, p. 2.

[156.] Ibid., p. 4.

[157.] Ibid., p. 4.

[158.] Ibid., p. 4.

[159.] Hare, Ibid., p. 4.

[160.] Bowlby, op. cit., p. 31.

[161.] Ibid., pp. 34 and 35.

162. Ibid., pp. 38 and 39.

CHAPTER EIGHT: Psychological Impacts Of Codependency On The Psychic Structure Of Infants During Their Early Childhood Development And Into Adulthood

163. Lancer, op. cit., p. 204.

164. Ibid., p. 99.

165. Ibid., p. 100.

166. Ibid., p. 101.

167. Ibid, p.106.

168. Ibid., p. 106.

169. Ibid., p. 106.

CHAPTER NINE: A Worthy Jail-keeper Of The Repressed CoDependency Addiction Oppressor Of The Self Within

170. Ibid., p. 66.

171. Ibid., p. 66.

172. Ibid., p. 66.

173. Montagu, op. cit., p. 215.

174. Ibid., p. 216.

175. Lancer, op. cit., p. 71.

176. Ibid., p. 71.

177. Ibid., p. 72.

178. Ibid., p. 115.

179. Ibid., p. 129.

180. Bowlby, op. cit., pp. 49 and 50.

CHAPTER TEN: Shame And Guilt: Secrets Held On The Otherside Of The Wizard Of Oz Curtain

181. Lancer, op. cit., p. 8.

182. Ibid., p. 11.

183. Ibid., p. 40.

184. Ibid., p. 127.

185. Ibid., p. 40.

186. Ibid., p. 40.

187. Ibid., p. 159.

188. Ibid., p. 111.

189. Ibid., p. 45.

190. Lancer, Ibid., p. 107.

CHAPTER ELEVEN: CoDependents' Greatest Secret: Repression Of The Self By Their Learned CoDependency Trauma(s) During Childhood

191. Montagu, op. cit., p. 288.

192. Ibid., p. 289.

193. Ibid., p. 289.

194. Ibid., p. 289.

195. Ibid., p. 289.

196. Lancer, op. cit., p. 31.

197. Ibid., p. 31.

198. Ibid., p. 44.

199. Ibid., p. 31.

200. Ibid., p. 77.

201. Ibid., p. 79.

202. Ibid., p. 111.

203. Ibid., p. 122

CHAPTER TWELVE: By-Products Of The CoDependent Person's Lost And Repressed Self: Feelings And Needs, And Creativity Aborted Replaced By-Self-Hate, Blame, Conflict, And Control

204. Ibid., p. 32.

205. Ibid., p. 66.

[206.] Ibid., p. 77.

[207.] Ibid., p. 77.

[208.] Ibid., p. 79.

[209.] Ibid., p. 101.

[210.] Ibid., p. 101.

[211.] Ibid., p. 40.

[212.] Ibid., p. 11.

[213.] Montague, op. cit., p. 225.

[214.] Lancer, op. cit., p. 128.

[215.] Ibid., p. 20.

[216.] Ibid., p. 218.

[217.] Ibid., p. 111.

[218.] Ibid. pp. 200 and 202.

[219.] Ibid., p. 22.

[220.] Ibid., p. 45.

[221.] Ibid., p. 114.

[222.] Ibid., p. 159.

[223.] Webster's Ninth New Collegiate Dictionary. Op. cit., p. 285.

[224.] Lancer, op. cit., p. 15.

[225.] Ibid., p. 37.

[226.] Ibid., p. 61.

[227.] Ibid., p. 102.

[228.] Ibid., p. 102.

[229.] Ibid., p. 191.

[230.] Ibid., p. 211.

CHAPTER THIRTEEN: Self-Esteem, Ego, Super-Ego, And CoDependency Addiction

[231.] Ibid., p. 25.

[232.] Ibid., p. 31.

233. Darling, Lynn, "Is There A Cure For LONELINESS?, <u>AARP</u>, Volume 63, Number 18, December 2019/January 2020, p. 51.

234. Ibid., p. 51.

235. Ibid., p. 51.

236., Ibid., p. 51.

237. Ibid., pp. 51 and 52.

238. Healy, Melissa, "US life expectancy declining," <u>The Baltimore Sun</u>, Thursday, December 26, 2019, p. 2.

239. Darling, Lynn, op. cit., p. 53.

240. Ibid., p. 53.

241. Ibid., p. 54.

242., Ibid., p. 54.

243. Ibid., p. 54.

244. Ibid, p. 54.

245. Ibid., p. 55.

246. Ibid., p. 55.

247. Ibid., p. 54.

248. Ibid., p. 2.

249. Healy, op. cit., p. 2.

250. Ibid., p. 2.

251. Ibid., p. 2.

252. Ibid. p. 2.

253. Ibid., p. 2.

254. Ibid., p. 2.

255. Marteaux X, Ph.D. <u>Triumph Of The Spirit</u>, Writer's Showcase presented by Writer's Digest, New York, 2000, p. 33.

256. Montagu, op. cit., pp.186 and 187.

257. Ibid., p. 193.

258. Ibid., p. 187.

259. Ibid., pp. 189 and 190.

[260.] Ibid., pp. 212 and 213.

[261.] Ibid., p. 213.

[262.] Ibid., p. 213.

[263.] Ibid., p. 213.

[264.] Lyles, op. cit., p. 17.

[265.] Ibid., p. 167.

[266.] Ibid., p. 205.

[267.] Lancer, op. cit., p. 57.

[268.] Ibid., p. 54.

[269.] Ibid., p. 65.

[270.] Ibid., p. 201.

[271.] Ibid., p. 202.

CHAPTER FOURTEEN: Codependent People's Overdoing, Over-Compensating, And Over-Extension Of Themselves In Their Vain External Search For Mother, Father, or Mother-Surrogate Love

[272.] Webster's Ninth New Collegiate Dictionary, op. cit., p. 1314.

[273.] Lancer, op. cit., p. 9.

[274.] Ibid., p. 15.

[275.] Ibid., p. 35.

[276.] Ibid., p. 9.

[277.] Ibid., p. 36.

[278.] Ibid., p. 43.

279.Ibid., p. 43.

[280.] Ibid., p. 51.

[281.] Ibid., p. 51.

[282.] Ibid., p. 52.

[283.] Ibid., p. 63.

[284.] Ibid., p. 63.

[285.] Ibid., p. 63.

[286.] Ibid., p. 63.

[287.] Ibid., p. 76.

CHAPTER FIFTEEN: Fear Of Abandonment, Fear Of Rejection, And The Startled Affect

[288.] Ibid., p. 52.

[289.] Ibid., p. 52.

[290.] Lancer, Ibid., p. 52.

[291.] Ibid., p. 52.

[292.] Ibid., p. 53.

[293.] Ibid. p.53.

[294.] Ibid., p. 53.

[295.] Dickens, Charles, <u>A Tale Of Two Cities</u>, http://www.planetbook.com/free-ebooks/a-tale-of-two-cities.pdf, p. 3.

[296.] Ibid., p. 54.

[297.] Ibid., p. 54.

[298.] Ibid., p. 66.

[299.] Op.cit., p. 453.

[300.] Lancer, op. cit., p. 66.

[301.] Ibid., p. 111.

[302.] Ibid., p. 67.

[303.] Lowen, Alexander, <u>Narcissism: Denial Of The True Self</u>, Macmillan Publishing Company, New York, 1983, p. ix.

[304.] Ibid., p. ix.

[305.] Ibid., p. ix.

[306.] Ibid., p. 5.

[307.] Ibid., p. 4.

[308.] Ibid., p. 8.

[309.] Ibid., p. 12.

[310.] Montagu, Op. Cit., p. 184.

311. Montagu, Op. Cit., p. 173.

312. Ibid., p. 176.

313. Ibid., p. 185.

314. Ibid., p. 261.

315. Ibid., p. 261.

316. Durkheim, Emile, Suicide: A Study In Sociology, The Free Press: A Division of macmillan, Inc., New York, 1951, p. 169.

317. Beattie, Melodie, Codependent No More, Hazelden Publishing, 1986, pp. 45, 47, and 50.

318. Ibid., p. 178.

319. Durkheim, op. cit., p. 210.

320. Ibid., p. 210.

321. Ibid., p. 212.

322. Lathem, Edward Connery, editor, The Poetry Of Robert Frost, Holt, Rinehart, And Winston, Inc., New York, 1916, pp.224 and 225.

323. Durkheim, op. cit., p. 211.

324. Ibid., p. 214.

325. Ibid., p. 215.

326. Ibid., pp. 216 and 217.

327. Ibid., p. 67.

328. Lancer, op. cit., p. 139.

329. Ibid., pp.139 and 140.

CHAPTER SIXTEEN: Boundaries, Communication, Responsibility, And CoDependency Addiction

330. Ibid., p. 46.

331. Ibid., p. 47.

332. Ibid., p. 48.

333. Ibid., p. 48.

334. Ibid., p. 48.

335. Ibid., p. 49.

336. Ibid., p. 49.

337. Ibid., p. 49.

338. Cloud, Henry Dr. and Townsend, John Dr., <u>Boundaries</u>, Zondervan, 1992, p. 59.

339. Ibid., p. 31.

340. Lancer, op. cit., p. 56.

341. Ibid., p. 56.

342. Ibid., p. 56.

343. Ibid., p. 57.

344. Ibid. p. 57.

345. Ibid. p, 61.

346. Ibid., p. 61.

347. Ibid., p. 62. This quotation is intentionally included although it is longer than others. The entire quotations is included because it goes to the heart of CoDependency Addiction, and it clearly reveals the unspoken desires of the codependent person, namely, an on-going attempt is made to shift responsibility on the other person in a CoDependency Relationship.

348. Ibid., p. 62.

349. Ibid., p. 65.

350. Ibid., p. 65.

351. _____ A Course In Miracles, Foundation For Inner Peace, 1975, p. 436.

352. _____ A Course In Miracles, Foundation For Inner Peace, 1975, p. 448.

353. Ibid., p. 325.

354. Ibid., p. 607.

355. Lancer, op. cit., p. 160.

356. _____ ACIM, op. cit., p. 385.

357. Ibid., p. 617.

358. Ibid., p. 617

CHAPTER SEVENTEEN: CoDependency Addiction And Its many Related Health Consequences

359. Lancer, op. cit., p. 78.

360. Op. cit., p. 1000.

361. Montagu, op. cit., p. 209.

362. Lancer, op. cit., p. 66.

363. Ibid., p. 69.

364. Ibid., p. 69.

365. Perlmutter, David and Loberg, Kristin, Grain Brain, Little, Brown and Company, New York, 2013, pp. 160 and 161.

366. _____ http://www.google.com.

367. Perlmutter, op. cit., p. 114.

368. Ibid., p. 114.

369. Ibid., p. 114.

370. Ibid., p. 115.

371. _____ http://www.google.com

372. Ibid.

373. Lancer, op. cit., p. 208.

374. Ibid., p. 67.

375. Ibid., p. 67.

376. Montagu, op. cit., p. 214.

377. Ibid., p. 259.

378. Ibid., pp.259 and 260.

379. Ibid., p. 260.

380. Lancer, op. cit., p. 114.

381. Ibid., p. 117.

382. Ibid., p. 136.

383. Montagu, op. cit., p. 257.

384. Ibid, p. 257.

385. Ibid., p. 165.

386. Ibid., p. 254.

387. Lancer, op. cit., p. 151.

388. Ibid., p. 15.

389. Ibid., p. 22.

390. Ibid., p. 66.

391. Ibid., p. 129.

392. Ibid., p. 146.

393. Ibid., p. 172.

394. Ibid., p. 70.

395. Ibid., p. 68.

CHAPTER EIGHTTEEN: CoDependency Addiction-Inspired Christmas 2018 Massacre

396. Ibid., p. 211.

397. Ibid., p. 221.

398. Lasch, Christopher, The Culture of Narcissism: American Life in An Age of Diminishing Expectations, Warner Books, 1979, p. 24.

399. Ibid., pp. 24 and 25.

400. _____ ACIM, op. cit., pp. 325 and 607.

CHAPTER NINETEEN: Conclusion

401. Montagu, op. cit., pp. 180 and 181.

402. Ibid., p. 198.

403. Ibid., pp. 306 and 307.

404. Ibid. pp. 307 and 308.

405. Ibid., p. 305.

406. Ibid, pp. 299, 298, and 300.

407. https://www.google.com/search?source=hp&ei=Zzz8XNnXC47wtAXrjKzoAQ&q=what+are+the+lyrics+of+earth%2C+wind%2C+and+fire%27s+song-After+the+love+is+gone%3F&oq=what+are+the+lyrics+of+earth%2C+wind%2C+and+fire%27s+song-After+the+love+is+gone%3F&gs_l=psy-ab.12...16823.58732..61218...6.0..0.184.7310.51j30......0....1..gws-wiz.....0..0i131j0j0i131i70i251j0i10j0i22i30j0i22i10i30j33i22i29i30j33i299j33i160j33i10.jku7qpCSFMI

AFTERWORD

[408.] Lowen, op. cit., pp. 137 and 138.

[409.] Ibid., pp. 144 and 137.

[410.] White, Maurice, with Powell, Herb, My Life With Earth, Wind & Fire, Amistad 30, An Imprint of HarperCollinsPublishers, 2016, p. 74.

[411.] Ibid., p. 351.

[412.] Ibid., p. 354.

[413.] Ibid., p. 148.

[414.] Wintrobe, Maxwell M., torn, George W., Adams, Raymond D, et. al. (Editors), Harrison Principles Of Internal Medicine, A Blankiston Publication, McGraw-Hill Book Company, New York, 1958, p. 36.

[415.] Powell, John, Why Am I Afraid To Tell You Who I Am?, RCL, Allen, Texas, 1969, p. 98.

Printed in the United States
By Bookmasters